THE CAMBRIDGE COMP/
BRITISH FICTION: 198

CW00923388

From 1980 to the present huge transformations
British cultural life. The election of Margaret Tha
neoliberal era in politics and economics that dramatically reshaped the British
landscape. Alongside this political shift, we have seen transformations to the
public sphere caused by the arrival of the internet and of social media, and
changes in the global balance of power brought about by 9/11, the emergence
of China and India as superpowers, and latterly the British vote to leave the
European Union. British fiction of the period is intimately interwoven with these
historical shifts. This collection brings together some of the most penetrating
critics of the contemporary, to explore the role that the British novel has had in
shaping the cultural landscape of our time, at a moment, in the wake of the EU
referendum of 2016, when the question of what it means to be British has
become newly urgent.

Peter Boxall is Professor of English Literature at the University of Sussex. He is
the author of many books on the novel, including *Don DeLillo: The Possibility
of Fiction* (2006), *Since Beckett* (2009), *Twenty-First-Century Fiction* (2013)
and *The Value of the Novel* (2015). He is editor of the bestselling *1001 Books*,
co-editor, with Byran Cheyette, of volume 7 of *The Oxford History of the Novel*,
and with Peter Nicholls of *Thinking Poetry*. He is also editor, since 2009, of the
UK journal *Textual Practice*. His most recent book, *The Prosthetic Imagination:
A History of the Novel as Artificial Life*, is forthcoming with Cambridge
University Press.

A complete list of books in the series is at the back of this book

THE CAMBRIDGE
COMPANION TO

BRITISH FICTION:
1980–2018

THE CAMBRIDGE
COMPANION TO

BRITISH FICTION:
1980–2018

EDITED BY
PETER BOXALL
University of Sussex

CAMBRIDGE
UNIVERSITY PRESS

CAMBRIDGE
UNIVERSITY PRESS

University Printing House, Cambridge CB2 8BS, United Kingdom

One Liberty Plaza, 20th Floor, New York, NY 10006, USA

477 Williamstown Road, Port Melbourne, VIC 3207, Australia

314–321, 3rd Floor, Plot 3, Splendor Forum, Jasola District Centre,
New Delhi – 110025, India

79 Anson Road, #06–04/06, Singapore 079906

Cambridge University Press is part of the University of Cambridge.

It furthers the University's mission by disseminating knowledge in the pursuit of
education, learning, and research at the highest international levels of excellence.

www.cambridge.org
Information on this title: www.cambridge.org/9781108483414
DOI: 10.1017/9781108649865

First published 2019

Printed and bound in Great Britain by Clays Ltd, Elcograf S.p.A.

A catalogue record for this publication is available from the British Library.

Library of Congress Cataloging-in-Publication Data
NAMES: Boxall, Peter, editor.
TITLE: The Cambridge companion to British fiction : 1980–2018 / edited by Peter Boxall.
DESCRIPTION: Cambridge, United Kingdom ; New York, NY : Cambridge University
Press, 2019. | Includes bibliographical references and index.
IDENTIFIERS: LCCN 2018056585 | ISBN 9781108483414 (alk. paper)
SUBJECTS: LCSH: English fiction – 20th century – History and criticism. | English fiction –
21st century – History and criticism.
CLASSIFICATION: LCC PR881 .C347 2019 | DDC 823/.91409–dc23
LC record available at https://lccn.loc.gov/2018056585

ISBN 978-1-108-48341-4 Hardback
ISBN 978-1-108-70492-2 Paperback

In memory of my mother, Judy Neil. 1940–2018.

CONTENTS

CONTENTS

CONTRIBUTORS

PETER BOXALL is Professor of English at the University of Sussex. His books include *Don DeLillo: The Possibility of Fiction* (2006), *Since Beckett: Contemporary Writing in the Wake of Modernism* (2009), *Twenty-First Century Fiction: A Critical Introduction* (2013) and *The Value of the Novel* (2015). He has edited a number of collections, including *Thinking Poetry* and *Beckett/Aesthetics/Politics*, and a recent edition of Beckett's novel *Malone Dies*. He is co-editor, with Bryan Cheyette, of volume 7 of the *Oxford History of the Novel in English*. He is also the editor of *Textual Practice*, and the series editor, for Cambridge University Press, of *Cambridge Studies in Twenty-First Century Literature and Culture*. He is currently completing a book entitled *The Prosthetic Imagination: A History of the Novel as Artificial Life*.

KEVIN BRAZIL is a Lecturer in Twentieth and Twenty-First Century Literature at the University of Southampton. He is the author of *Art, History, and Postwar Fiction* (2018), co-editor of *Doris Lessing and the Forming of History* (2016) and has published widely on modern and contemporary literature in *Modernism/modernity*, *Textual Practice* and the *Journal of Modern Literature*.

BRIDGET CHALK is Associate Professor of English at Manhattan College in the Bronx, NY. She is the author of *Modernism and Mobility: The Passport and Cosmopolitan Experience* (2014), as well as multiple essays and reviews on modernism and narrative in *Twentieth-Century Literature*, the *Journal of Modern Literature* and elsewhere. She is currently working on a book project that traces continuities among the novel of development, education and ethics from the nineteenth century to the present.

PATRICK DEER is Associate Professor of English at New York University, where he teaches modern and contemporary British, American and postcolonial literature and culture. His publications include *Culture in Camouflage: War, Empire and Modern British Literature* (2009; paperback edition 2016), 'Beyond Recovery: Representing History and Memory in Iraq War Writing', *MFS* (2017) and 'Mapping Contemporary American War Culture', *College Literature* (2016). His current book projects are *Surge and Silence: Understanding America's Culture of War* and *Deep England: Forging British Culture after Empire.*

JEROME DE GROOT teaches in the Department of English, American Studies and Creative Writing at the University of Manchester. He is the author of *Consuming History* (2008, 2nd edn 2016), *Remaking History* (2015) and *The Historical Novel* (2009), as well as numerous articles on historical fictions, re-enactment, manuscript studies and historiography.

CAROLINE EDWARDS is Senior Lecturer in Modern & Contemporary Literature at Birkbeck, University of London. She is author of *Utopia and the Contemporary British Novel* (2019), co-editor of *China Miéville: Critical Essays* (2015) and *Maggie Gee: Critical Essays* (2015), and a Founding Director of the Open Library of Humanities. Her work has appeared in *Telos, Modern Fiction Studies, Textual Practice, Contemporary Literature, ASAP/Journal, Subjectivity, New Statesman* and the *Times Higher Education.* She is currently working on a book about science fiction and extreme environments.

MARTIN PAUL EVE is Professor of Literature, Technology and Publishing at Birkbeck, University of London. Martin holds a PhD from the University of Sussex and is the author of five books, most recently *Close Reading with Computers.* As a result of his higher education policy work, Martin was named as one of *The Guardian*'s five finalists for higher education's most inspiring leader in 2017, and in 2018 he was awarded the KU Leuven Medal of Honour in the Humanities and Social Sciences.

GABRIELE GRIFFIN is Professor of Gender Research at Uppsala University in Sweden. She coordinates the Nordforsk-funded Nordic Centre of Excellence 'Beyond the Gender Paradox' (2017–2022), and a Vinnova-funded project on female entrepreneurship and decent work (UN Goal 2030). She is editor of the 'Research Methods for the Arts and Humanities' series. Her most recent publication is *Body, Migration, Re/Constructive Surgery: Making the Gendered Body in a Globalized World* (co-ed., 2018).

BEN MASTERS is Assistant Professor of English Literature at the University of Nottingham. He is the author of *Novel Style: Ethics and Excess in English Fiction since the 1960s.* He also writes fiction and has written for *The Times Literary Supplement, The Guardian, The New York Time, Literary Review* and *Five Dials.*

STEPHEN MORTON is Professor of English and Postcolonial Literatures at the University of Southampton. His publications include *States of Emergency: Colonialism, Literature, and Law* (2013), *Terror and the Postcolonial*, co-edited with Elleke Boehmer (2009), *Foucault in an Age of Terror*, co-edited with Stephen

Bygrave (2008), *Salman Rushdie: Fictions of Postcolonial Modernity* (2007), *Gayatri Spivak: Ethics, Subalternity and the Critique of Postcolonial Reason* (2006) and *Gayatri Chakravorty Spivak* (2003). He has also published articles in *Public Culture, Interventions, Textual Practice, New Formations, Ariel* and *Research in African Literatures*. He is currently completing two monographs on 'Allegories of the World–System: Dispossession and the Idea of the Commons in Postcolonial World Literature' and 'In the Debt Colony: A Cultural History of Colonial Debt'.

REBECCA POHL is the co-editor of *Rupert Thomson: Critical Essays* (2016). Most recently, she has published on Christine Brooke-Rose and on Ali Smith. Her work in progress includes a manuscript that examines the impact of gender on mid-century experimental writing by women in Britain. She is Honorary Research Fellow at the University of Manchester.

PETRA RAU is Senior Lecturer in Modern Literature at UEA. Her research interests are literature and film about war, fascism and forced migration, travel writing and memory studies. She is the author, most recently, of *Our Nazis: Representations of Fascism in Contemporary Literature and Film* (2013) and editor of *Long Shadows: The Second World War in British Literature and Film* (2016). She is currently working on a British- Academy funded monograph about flight and expulsion in post-war German literature and film and on a family memoir.

PIETER VERMEULEN is Assistant Professor of American and Comparative Literature at the University of Leuven, Belgium. He is the author of *Romanticism after the Holocaust* (2010) and *Contemporary Literature and the End of the Novel: Creature, Affect, Form* (2015), and a co-editor of, most recently, *Institutions of World Literature: Writing, Translation, Markets* (2015) and *Memory Unbound: Tracing the Dynamics of Memory Studies* (2017). He is currently writing a book entitled *Literature and the Anthropocene*.

LEIGH WILSON is Professor of English Literature at the University of Westminster. She is the author of *Modernism and Magic: Experiments with Spiritualism, Theosophy and the Occult* (2013), co-editor of *The Edinburgh Critical Edition of the Selected Writings of Andrew Lang* (2 vols, 2015) and series co-editor of the *Decades Series on Modern and Contemporary British Fiction* (2014 onwards).

CAROLINE WINTERSGILL is Visiting Lecturer in the Department of English, Creative Writing and American Studies at the University of Winchester, where she is completing a PhD on endings in the twenty-first-century novel, funded by a 175th Anniversary Studentship. Caroline moved to academia following a 25-year career in publishing and she continues to work as a consultant editor to several publishers. Her research is on contemporary fiction, with a particular interest in literary institutions, the contemporary history of the book, readers and readership, and the relationship of all three to narrative. She also writes on haptic approaches to film and literature.

CHRONOLOGY

Charlotte Terrell

Date	Events	Publications
1979	Conservatives win majority in general election, Margaret Thatcher becomes Prime Minister	
1980	Republicans win majority in US election, Ronald Reagan becomes President	
	'Right to Buy' scheme begins, enabling council house tenants to buy their houses	
1981	Riots in Brixton after the 'sus' law had been used to stop and search 1,000 people in 6 days, stirring tension in ethnic minority communities	**Alasdair Gray**, *Lanark* **Salman Rushdie**, *Midnight's Children*
1982	Falklands War	**William Boyd**, *An Ice Cream War* **Kazuo Ishiguro**, *A Pale View of the Hills*
1983	IRA car bomb kills six and injures hundreds outside Harrods, London First Dyson vacuum cleaner manufactured	**William Golding** wins the Nobel Prize in Literature **Terry Pratchett**, *The Colour of Magic* (first book of his 'Discworld' series) **Graham Swift**, *Waterland* First year of Granta's Best of Young British Novelist – a once-per-decade list of twenty novelists who hold promise to become the outstanding writers of their generation
1984	Coal miners strike for 12 months over threat of pit closures, nearly half of miners return to work by February the following year Unemployment reaches a record high of 3.3 million First year of the FTSE 100 First Virgin Atlantic flight British Telecoms privatised	**Martin Amis**, *Money* **J. G. Ballard**, *Empire of the Sun* **Christine Brooke-Rose**, *Amalgamemnon* **Anita Brookner**, *Hotel du Lac* **Angela Carter**, *Nights at the Circus* **Alasdair Gray**, *1982 Janine*
1985	Riots in Brixton, Tottenham and Peckham in London after Cherry Groce is shot in her home by police and left paralysed	**Iris Murdoch**, *The Good Apprentice* **Caryl Phillips**, *The Final Passage* **Jeanette Winterson**, *Oranges Are Not the Only Fruit*

(cont.)

Date	Events	Publications
	UK's first heart and lung transplant carried out	
	First mobile phone calls are made	
1986	GCSEs replace O Levels	Kazuo Ishiguro, *An Artist of the*
	London Stock Exchange is computerised	*Floating World*
1987	Remembrance Day bombing in Northern Ireland kills eleven	Penelope Lively, *Moon Tiger* Ian McEwan, *The Child in Time*
	General election sees Margaret Thatcher win a third term in office	Alan Moore, *Watchmen*
1988	Lockerbie bombing, kills 270	Stephen Hawking's *A Brief History of*
	IRA bombing kills a British solider in London and six in Belfast	*Time* is published David Lodge, *Nice Work* (the last book
	NHS nurses go on strike for higher pay	in the 'campus trilogy')
	Tate Liverpool opens to public	Salman Rushdie, *The Satanic Verses*
	Group known as 'Young British Artists' begin to exhibit together	
1989	Hillsborough disaster, ninety-six killed in crush at Sheffield football stadium	Martin Amis, *London Fields* Janice Galloway, *The Trick Is to Keep*
	Satellite TV becomes available via Sky TV	*Breathing* Kazuo Ishiguro, *The Remains of*
	Iran breaks off diplomatic relations with UK over the publication of Rushdie's *The Satanic Verses*	*the Day* Jeanette Winterson, *Sexing the Cherry*
1990	Aldi and Poundland open first stores in UK	A. S. Byatt, *Possession*
	Reunification of Germany	Hanif Kureishi, *The Buddha of* *Suburbia*
1991	First website goes online through the first web browser WorldWideWeb	Martin Amis, *Time's Arrow* Pat Barker, *Regeneration* (the first book
	Dial-up internet becomes available to the public	of a trilogy)
	Three IRA members killed in Northern Ireland by British Army	Christine Brooke-Rose, *Textermination* (considered one of Brooke-Rose's foremost 'anti-novels') Angela Carter, *Wise Children* Ben Okri, *The Famished Road*
1992	Further and Higher Education Act sees thirty-five polytechnics become universities	Victor Headley, *Yardie* Nick Hornby, *Fever Pitch*
	Damien Hirst's *The Physical Impossibility of Death in the Mind of Someone Living* included in an exhibition of Young British Artists' work in the Saatchi Gallery	
	Conservatives elected for fourth term, John Major is PM	

(cont.)

Date	Events	Publications
1993	Downing Street Agreement signed, promising the transfer of Northern Ireland to Ireland if voted for by its people, and the exclusive right of Ireland and Northern Ireland to determine its conflict resolution Racially motivated murder of Stephen Lawrence. The examination of forensic evidence in 2012 leads to the sentencing of his killers	**Toni Morrison** wins the Nobel Prize, simultaneously the first African American woman, and first African American ever to receive the award **Irvine Welsh**, *Trainspotting*
1994	Provisional IRA announce a ceasefire Coal industry privatised Russell Group formed, a collection of twenty-four research universities self-selected as 'elite' in the UK	**James Kelman**, *How Late It Was, How Late*
1995	Amazon.com, initially an online bookstore, launched by Jeff Bezos	**Diran Adebayo**, *Some Kind of Black* **Penelope Fitzgerald**, *The Blue Flower* **A. L. Kennedy**, *So I Am Glad* **Philip Pullman**, *Northern Lights* (first book of the 'His Dark Materials' trilogy)
1996	Provisional IRA ends ceasefire and conflicts continue into 1997 Dunblane school shooting, sixteen children and one teacher die, private gun ownership in the UK effectively banned by subsequent legislation Dolly the sheep – the first animal cloned using somatic cells – is born GMO foods go on sale Prince Charles and Princess Diana divorce	**Helen Fielding**, *Bridget Jones's Diary* **Graham Swift**, *Last Orders* **Meera Syal**, *Anita and Me*
1997	General election results in landslide victory for Labour, Tony Blair becomes PM Hong Kong becomes a Chinese territory again, as agreed in the Sino-British Joint Declaration of 1984 Diana, Princes of Wales, dies in a car crash Scotland and Wales vote in favour of devolved power from Westminster BBC launches an online news service	**J. K. Rowling**, *Harry Potter and the Philosopher's Stone* **Ali Smith**, *Like*
1998	Good Friday Agreement is signed, a major step in the Northern Irish peace process Larry Page and Sergey Brin's pet computer project receives first	**Rob Colson, Martin Cooper, Ted Curtis, Robert Dellar, Keith Mallinson, Emma McElwee and Lucy Williams**, *Seaton Point* (a collectively authored polemic novel against postmodernism)

(cont.)

Date	Events	Publications
	investment and officially becomes Google Inc.	Jackie Kay, *Trumpet* Ian McEwan, *Amsterdam*
1999	Scotland's devolved parliament at Holyrood, and the devolved National Assembly of Wales, hold their first meetings TV presenter Jill Dando shot and killed outside her home, shooter never found Series of nail bomb attacks in London by far-right terrorists SMS texts can be sent across different networks for the first time	J. M. Coetzee's *Disgrace* wins the Booker Prize, making him the only novelist to have won the award more than once
2000	Millennium Dome opens Tate Modern opens in London on the site of Bankside Power Station Damilola Taylor stabbed to death on way home from school First series of Big Brother airs on Channel 4	Zadie Smith, *White Teeth*
2001	9/11 attacks in US. Al-Qaeda hijack four planes, two of which are flown into the Twin Towers. Nearly 3,000 people are killed Launch of Wikipedia Foot and mouth disease outbreak *OED* revises its definition of 'meme' to include the internet joke format	Ian McEwan, *Atonement* David Mitchell, *Number9Dream* V. S. Naipaul wins the Nobel Prize Ali Smith, *Hotel World* Irvine Welsh, *Glue*
2002	Gibraltar holds referendum, votes in favour of remaining a solely British territory Euro tender enters into circulation	Maggie Gee, *The White Family* Jon McGregor, *If Nobody Speaks of Remarkable Things* Sarah Waters, *Fingersmith*
2003	Millions of citizens across UK march in protest of British military action in Iraq PM Tony Blair announces UK intervention in Iraq in support of the United States' search for weapons of mass destruction	Monica Ali, *Brick Lane* Hari Kunzru, *The Impressionist* Adam Thirlwell, *Politics*
2004	Social networking sites Myspace and Facebook both founded	Alan Hollinghurst, *The Line of Beauty* Andrea Levy, *Small Island* David Mitchell, *Cloud Atlas*
2005	7/7 bombings in London, fifty-two killed and over 700 injured	Kazuo Ishiguro, *Never Let Me Go* Tom McCarthy, *Remainder*

(cont.)

Date	Events	Publications
	MG Rover goes into administration, resulting in over 6,000 job losses at its Longbridge plant	Harold Pinter wins the Nobel Prize Zadie Smith, *On Beauty*
	Israel withdraws troops from Gaza, temporarily ending its occupation of Palestine	
	Gender Recognition Act comes into effect, meaning transgender people will have their reassigned gender recognised by law	
	First partial face transplant surgery takes place in France	
2006	Saddam Hussein, President of Iraq, is executed	Naomi Alderman, *Disobedience*
	Twitter launched	J. G. Ballard, *Kingdom Come*
	A whale is spotted swimming in the River Thames	Gautam Malkani, *Londonstani* Sarah Waters, *The Night Watch*
2007	First model of Apple's iPhone available to buy on the market	Nicola Barker, *Darkmans* Doris Lessing wins the Nobel Prize
	Amazon's Kindle released	Ian McEwan, *On Chesil Beach*
	Smoking ban stops smoking in enclosed public spaces	
2008	Global financial crash, believed to be the worst since the Great Depression of the 1930s, results in the collapse of investment bank Lehman Brothers and public bail-outs for financial institutions	James Kelman, *Kieron Smith, Boy* Salman Rushdie's *Midnight's Children* wins the 'Best of the Booker' award
	Barack Obama elected US President	
	Closure of the last working mine	
2009	MP expenses scandal: the illegitimate claims of MPs, ranging from income-generating second homes to duck houses for ponds, are exposed	Hilary Mantel, *Wolf Hall*
2010	Full body scanners introduced at UK airports	Andrea Levy, *The Long Song*
	General election results in a coalition between Conservatives and Liberal Democrats; Chancellor George Osborne announces Austerity to reduce deficit, involving drastic cuts to public services	Tom McCarthy, *C*
	The Equality Act requires employers to give equal access to jobs across different age groups, races, genders and religions	

(cont.)

Date	Events	Publications
2011	Mark Duggan shot and killed by police in Tottenham, London, on suspicion of possessing a gun. His death catalyses riots across London	First issue of arts and literary journal *The White Review*
		Julian Barnes, *The Sense of an Ending*
	Osama Bin Laden assassinated in Pakistan by US special forces	Luke Williams, *The Echo Chamber*
2012	Car manufacturer Ford closes its last UK production plant in Dagenham, East London	John Lanchester, *Capital*
		Zadie Smith, *NW*
	PM David Cameron issues apology over police misconduct in Hillsborough disaster	
	Scientists at the CERN Large Hadron Collider – the world's most powerful particle accelerator – observe proof of the Higgs Boson particle	
	After government cuts, universities allowed to raise tuition fees to £9,000 per year (later capped at £9,250), in comparison with £3,375 in previous years	
	Britain deploys troops to Syria	
2013	Same-sex marriage legalised in England and Wales. Scotland follow suit the following year and although public opinion polls show Northern Ireland in favour of same-sex marriage it has not been legislated	Goldsmiths Prize established for fiction that 'embodies the spirit of invention'
		Eleanor Catton, *The Luminaries*
2014	Scotland holds referendum for independence from the rest of UK, majority vote to stay in the UK	Helen Oyeyemi, *Boy, Snow, Bird*
		Ali Smith, *How to Be Both*
	First REF (Research Excellence Framework) takes place in UK universities, a controversial new system for measuring the 'quality' of research	
	'Selfie' is added to the *OED*	
2015	European Migrant Crisis begins. It is estimated that over 1 million people – displaced by conflict and climate change – have tried to reach Europe by crossing the Mediterranean Sea	University of East Anglia opens British Archive for Contemporary Writing, includes holdings of Nobel Laureate Doris Lessing
		Kazuo Ishiguro, *The Buried Giant*
	Jeremy Corbyn elected as leader of the Labour Party	Tom McCarthy, *Satin Island*
2016	Jo Cox, MP murdered in her Leicestershire constituency by far-right terrorist	Man Booker International Prize established
		Deborah Levy, *Hot Milk*

(cont.)

Date	Events	Publications
	UK holds EU referendum, majority vote to leave the Union beginning exit of the UK from the EU (dubbed 'Brexit'); David Cameron resigns and Theresa May becomes PM Department for Education adds TEF (Teaching Excellence Framework) to REF as a measure of teaching quality Scotland ends Right to Buy Junior doctors strike over proposed changes to working hours	**Ian McEwan,** *Nutshell* **Ali Smith,** *Autumn* (the first of a quartet) **Zadie Smith,** *Swing Time*
2017	May calls snap election and loses majority, creates coalition with Northern Ireland's Democratic Unionist Party (DUP) Fire at Grenfell Tower, London. Official death toll stands at seventy-one Donald Trump elected as US President Bomb at a pop concert in Manchester Arena kills twenty-two and injures over 100 people Film, TV, and music streams and downloads overtake physical sales for first time in UK	**Kazuo Ishiguro** wins the Nobel Prize **Jon McGregor,** *Reservoir 13* **Kamila Shamsie,** *Home Fire* Inaugural Republic of Consciousness Prize for small press publications
2018	'#metoo' campaign highlights the frequency of women's experiences of sexual assault Government privatises portion of its student loan books Volvo makes decision to stop developing new models of petrol engine and invest in electric motor development 'Despacito' by Luis Fonsi ft Daddy Yankee becomes the most viewed video on YouTube, accumulating over 5 billion views	

PETER BOXALL

Introduction: Framing the Present

When does the present begin?

An immediate answer to this curiously vexing question might be to suggest that the present *does not* begin. The present, one might argue, has no duration. It is the now, the passing moment, and as such cannot be truly said to have a beginning or an end, and cannot be measured, or regarded in any sense as having passed, or being to come. The present does not unfold or occur, but is the vanishing, fleeting medium of our immediate becoming.

If the question is a vexing one, however, this is because this answer, however plausible or even inescapable it is in one sense, is entirely inadequate in another. The present cannot have duration, because if it is so extended then it immediately becomes divisible, partaking of the past and the future, from which it is by definition distinct; but our experience of the present is nevertheless necessarily an experience of duration. The present is an experience of passing time, and the way that we give our time colour, substance and experiential weight depends upon the ways in which we frame the present, the ways in which we assign it parameters and coordinates. The present might begin with the opening of a sentence, or the break of a day, or the beginning of a life, or the emergence of a historical period or geological era, and the essential ephemerality of presentness as such is only thinkable – is only endurable – when it is located within this wider, extended timeframe. Consider Tom Stoppard's Rosencrantz and Guildenstern, characters exiled to an epistemologically evacuated present that will not attach itself securely to a wider history. 'What's the first thing you remember', Guildenstern asks Rosencrantz. Rosencrantz considers for a while, before replying, 'No, its no good. It's gone. It was a long time ago.'[1] To anchor ourselves in the present requires us to endow it with a beginning, an origin, as Guildenstern recognises; but the experience of the present itself allows no such originary stability, and requires us to abandon ourselves to Rosencrantz's hellish nontime, dramatised so tantalisingly by Stoppard, and by Beckett and Sartre before him.

This is a problem that attends all attempts to think about the present – a problem that is perhaps intrinsic to the ontology *of* the present. But it takes on a particular urgency, a particular critical freight, when one seeks to produce a historical picture of any period that ends with 'the present' – that has the immediately contemporary moment as its far horizon. To speak of a period which ends with one's own moment – to write in the last days of 2018 of a period which ends in 2018 – touches on the difficulty of capturing a time that is still in process, that is so close to us as to defy categorisation or focus. It is always difficult to fashion the historical or temporal frame through which the attributes of a given present might come to view. And what is more, it is perhaps the case that this is particularly difficult in our own time, when addressing *our own present*, given that one of our defining preoccupations is the ephemerality, the unthinkability of the present itself. Wendy Brown makes an exemplary argument when she writes, in 2001, that in our own time we have 'lost the thread of progress in history',[2] that the 'engine of historical movement' has stalled.[3] 'Ours', she argues, 'is a present that is hurtled into the future', 'a present that dishonours the past by erasing it with unprecedented speed and indifference', 'a present whose inevitable and rapid eclipse is uppermost in the political consciousness of its inhabitants'.[4] If there is any truth in this observation, then how can we produce a historical frame in which to locate the present – a present which owes its historical specificity to its resistance to, obliteration of, historical protocol, its refusal of what Brown calls the 'periodicity of this particular past-present-future'?[5]

To respond to this difficulty is to return to the question with which we began – where does the present, our present, begin? If Wendy Brown's comments sound somewhat out of focus, somewhat anachronistic, then this is perhaps because she is writing here at the turn of the millennium, before 9/11, before the wars in Afghanistan and Iraq, before the financial crisis of 2008 – before the unfolding of the historical events that have begun to give colour to a Western postmillennial present. It felt to Brown, at the dawn of the new millennium, that the present had folded into the future, that, as Don DeLillo puts it in the later twentieth century, the future has arrived 'ahead of schedule', 'It's backed into us. It's here';[6] but as she writes, she is unaware of the actual postmillennial future to come, the future that would give a different texture to the experience of 'our' present (as a character puts it in DeLillo's future haunted novel *Cosmopolis*, in the looming lee of 9/11 Brown is ironically unaware that 'something will happen soon, maybe today, to correct the acceleration of time'[7]). This gives Brown's comments a slightly anachronistic feel, but her observations nevertheless remain recognisable, maintaining a purchase on the texture of contemporary temporality.

The experience of historical, temporal life in the early decades of the twenty-first century remains, in Ursula Heise's terms, schismatic. Chronology is disrupted, still, by what Heise calls 'chronoschisms', that is, by the perception that temporality is no longer linear, that periodicity, in Brown's phrase, is no longer contained within a stable model of past-present-future.[8] The historical events of the twenty-first century have not restored us to a prior model of historiography, have not, in their massive implications, kick-started a stalled historical engine; rather they have ushered in a new historical structure of feeling, that is still difficult to measure, and that remains historically estranged and estranging. The question, then, the challenge that the quality of the present offers to the cultural historian, is how to find the roots of this historical quality, how to historicise a temporal structure of feeling, whose qualities are manifest in the political consciousness of a weakened historicity, of a present that cannot quite engage with the past, and that melts into a future that we cannot quite frame or shape.

The response taken, by this *Cambridge Companion*, to this question, is to find the genesis of a contemporary British condition, as it is reflected in and in part produced by the development of contemporary British fiction, at the turn of the 1980s, that decade which ushered in the cultural formations which still dominate cultural and socio-economic life today – the decade in which a certain conception of our present can be seen to begin. Existing accounts of the modern and contemporary British novel tend to fall either side of this watershed moment. There are a number of prominent and influential accounts of the modern novel which take the Second World War or its immediate aftermath as the originary moment – such as Steven Connor's *The English Novel in History: 1950–1995*,[9] Dominic Head's *Cambridge Introduction to Modern British Fiction: 1950–2000*,[10] Alistair Davies and Alan Sinfield's *British Culture of the Postwar*,[11] or *The Oxford History of the Novel in English*, edited by myself and Bryan Cheyette.[12] Conversely, many accounts of the contemporary novel, perhaps taking their cue from Robert Eaglestone's suggestion that 'the contemporary' should be measured 'as the last ten years',[13] bring a much tighter focus to bear on the near present. There are a number of studies which take the turn of the millennium as the moment when a recognisable contemporaneity began, such as my own *Twenty-First Century Fiction*,[14] or Sian Adiseshiah and Rupert Hildyard's *Twenty-First-Century Fiction: What Happens Now*,[15] and Eaglestone's 2013 study *Contemporary Fiction* obeys his own rule by declaring the contemporary to consist of 'the last ten years or so'.[16] Both of these horizons are perfectly justifiable ways of framing the period, but this *Companion* takes 1980 as its point of departure, because this is the moment, we will argue here, that saw the emergence of the structure of feeling which still shapes the angle at which we meet our present, and so telling a story of the development of the novel from 1980 to 2018 will best allow us to capture the terms in which modern and contemporary British fiction enters into a shaping dialogue with our living, changing present. It is 1980, David Harvey has recently argued, that marks what he calls a 'revolutionary turning point in the world's social and economic history'.[17] Where the period from the end of the Second World War to 1980 was characterised by a Keynesian economics, and by the development of the welfare state, several things come together, around 1980, to transform the socio-economic basis of the culture. The election of Margaret Thatcher in Britain in May 1979, along with the election of Ronald Reagan in 1980, changes to Chinese economic policy instigated by Deng Xiopenh in 1978 and changes to US monetarist policy instigated by Paul Volcker in the United States in 1979 came together, Harvey writes, to give birth to what we now call neoliberalism, at a moment which was to 'remake the world around us in a totally different image'.[18]

The emergence of a peculiarly disappearing present, the schismatic chronology outlined by Brown and by Heise, has its roots in this moment, as do so many of the features of contemporary British and Western culture that have been dominant in giving a shape to our time. Thatcher and Reagan, in their commitment to free trade as the basis of an emerging global marketplace, set in train the process by which local communities, embedded in their own discrete histories and practices, were dismantled, like cheap housing in the path of a rail route, in order to make way for the free movement of capital. As Fredric Jameson has brilliantly demonstrated, the mark of this transformation can be seen in the emergence of the shopping mall – the replacement of organic, slow-growing town centres with readymade, prefabricated market places, all of which are indistinguishable from one another.[19] Thatcherism, despite its nostalgic investment in Englishness, in the idea of a 'nation of shopkeepers', acted to weaken the concept of national sovereignty, as well as welfare-statism, in order to replace the model of parliamentary democracy endorsed by the nation-state with the model of global capital, overseen not by national governments, but by the international corporation. The major historical developments that have determined the passage of British culture over this time, from 1980 to 2018, have been shaped by this transformation. The miners' strike, from 1984 to 1985, and other industrial disputes such as the Wapping strike in 1986 were some of the more visible ways in which an older model of community struggled against the emerging logic of neoliberalism. In defeating the unions, the Thatcher government enabled what Harvey calls the 'process of neoliberalization'[20] that characterises contemporary Western modernity – that saw the mass privatisation of what Marx calls the 'means of production', the marketisation of the university, the collapse of the British left into the neo-conservative 'New Labour', and with it the emergence of a new electronic public sphere (exemplified by corporations such as Amazon and Google). Thatcherism leads, in Britain, to Blairism, and then to the conditions which determine British culture in the twenty-first century – such as Britain's adherence to US foreign policy in Afghanistan and Iraq, as a side effect of its ideological investment in US global capital. The crisis which has gripped UK cultural politics in the latter half of the current decade – marked by the referendum decision to exit the European Union, by the murder of the Labour MP Jo Cox, or the powerful symbolism of the Grenfell fire (sharply anatomised in a recent radio essay by Will Self) – seems in one sense to mark the end of the Thatcher-Blair period. Brexit appears in part to be a reassertion of national sovereignty in which Parliament 'takes back control' from the corporation as represented by Brussels; the grim spectacle of Grenfell tower stands as a rebuke to contemporary architecture, a peeling back of the cheap cladding that disguised the unequal distribution of wealth which is the real driver of global capitalism. But, rather than demonstrating the collapse of neoliberalism, it is equally if not more likely that the end of the second decade of the current century is seeing simply the intensification of the contradictions that have fuelled neoliberalism since 1980 – the contradiction between on the one hand the smooth spectacle of frictionless free trade and the political and cultural homogenisation that it requires (captured in the bland ubiquity of the 'barcode facade' that veneered Grenfell tower), and on the other the reality of deprivation and disenfranchisement that underwrites it, that led to the deaths of Grenfell residents, that provoked the xenophobic violence perpetrated against Jo Cox, and that inspired 52 per cent of those who voted on 23 June 2016 to defy both the logic of the market place, and the principle of liberal hospitality, by turning their backs on their neighbouring countries. As Self says, of the barcode facades that wrap around the exteriors of London's tower blocks, 'I wonder what price would be displayed if you were somehow to scan them'.[21]

1980 stands as a moment at which the historical structure of the present adopted its recognisable form – the form which still shapes development of the culture as I write. And if the Thatcher-Reagan era saw the birth of the political present, then the turn of that decade also sees the emergence of a new era in the history of the British novel. It was the later 1970s and early 1980s that saw the arrival, on a British scene that was up until then rather resistant to both European and American literary influence, of cultural post-modernism. The texture and feel of the British novel, immersed as it was in the stylistic and political conditions of realism, was fundamentally shifted by the arrival of a series of major figures at this time, all of whom were associated to some extent with the developing fiction of postmodernism. Angela Carter's *The Bloody Chamber* was published in 1979,[22] and was the first of her works to have a shaping influence on our understanding of the role of fiction in forging the basis upon which we establish gendered identity. Ian McEwan's work first started having an influence at this time also, with the publication of his early, macabre fictions such as *The Cement Garden*[23] and *The Comfort of Strangers*.[24] Martin Amis published *The Rachel Papers*[25] and *Dead Babies*[26] in the 1970s, but it was the publication of *Money* in 1984 that established his global reputation, and that also produced one of the most enduring literary depictions of the greedy superficiality of Thatcherism.[27] And perhaps most influentially of all, it was the publication, in 1981, of Salman Rushdie's *Midnight's Children* that suggested how fundamental a role fiction can have in determining the cultural forms – post-modern and postcolonial – in which we give expression to our history and to our identity.[28]

These four figures – Amis, McEwan, Carter and Rushdie – as well as a number of associated figures such as Julian Barnes, Kazuo Ishiguro, Milan Kundera and others, had a revolutionary impact on the British novel at the turn of the 1980s, just as David Harvey's neoliberal revolution began to 'remake the world around us in a totally different image'. As the Thatcher-Reagan period introduced a set of forces which dematerialised the culture, which loosened our grounding in material histories and environments in order to prepare the ground for the free movement of capital, so the British novel responded, to an extent, with its own act of dematerialisation, its own melting of all that is solid into air. The uncertain emergence of a postmodern influence in British fiction was in part a symptom of the very socio-economic forces that gave rise to neoliberalism – what drove Carter's revolutionary conception of gendered identity, what fuelled Rushdie's retelling of the history of India after the partition of 1947, was a sense that such historical and material forms were themselves modes of *fiction*, that the homelands we live in, to quote the title of Rushdie's 1992 collection of essays, are imaginary homelands.[29] But if British postmodernism (if it is valid to deploy such a term) came about in part as a reflection of Thatcherite economics, it is also the case that the novel at this time produced a set of resistances, a set of critiques of the culture which gave rise to it. Rushdie's development of a postcolonial form in which to capture the imaginary history of his home-land, in *Midnight's Children*, was an act of political resistance to the homo-genising power of global capital, as, in a more ambivalent sense, was Amis's *Money*, and the development of the British novel through the 1980s and 1990s was characterised by this difficult sense that it was at once enabled by, and resistant to, the global forces which shaped late twentieth-century

Western culture. Many of the most influential developments in the British novel of the 1990s were bound up with forms of regionalism, nationalism and decolonisation, which were conceived, quite directly, as a practice of resistance to the development of neoliberal globalisation. The Scottish Renaissance, for example, driven by writers such as Janice Galloway, A. L. Kennedy, James Kelman, Irvine Welsh and others, gathered pace over the 1990s, and, in extremely influential novels such as *Trainspotting*[30] and *How Late It Was How Late*,[31] pitted the specificity of a Scottish dialect and history against the imperial influence of Englishness, or the Anglo-American culture most hilariously dissected in Kelman's 2004 novel *You Have to Be Careful in the Land of the Free*.[32] These novels were committed to the retrieval of historical difference and specificity, but at the same time they were influenced to varying degrees by the postmodern mode, which itself was so closely bound up with the Anglo-American culture that they most fiercely resisted. These contradictions shaped the difficult and ambivalent relationship between postmodernism and nationalism in the British novel of the late century; and then, with the turn of the century, and with the decline of postmodernism as a global cultural dominant, one can see the emergence of a new generation of British writers, whose sensibility shifted from the ironic scepticism associated with Rushdian or Amisian postmodernism to a new kind of political commitment (sometimes known as 'the new sincerity'), which was nevertheless associated with the cultural experiments of postmodernism. Zadie Smith's enormously influential 2000 novel *White Teeth*[33] might mark the height of a form of postmodern cosmopolitanism, but this novel also has resonances with a new group of post-millennial writers, such as David Mitchell, Ali Smith, Tom McCarthy and others, who were deploying the formal innovations of late century fiction to produce newly vigorous commitments to the politics of form. There is, for example, a significant shift from the zany cosmopolitanism of *White Teeth* to the political seriousness of Zadie Smith's 2013 novel *NW*,[34] and works such as McCarthy's *Remainder*,[35] Gautam Malkani's *Londonstani*[36] and Ali Smith's *The Accidental*,[37] *Autumn*[38] and *Winter*,[39] however different in temperament and tone, all work through the production of new forms with which to critique the neoliberal culture which emerged in 1980, and which has determined the terms in which the British novel has given an expression to our present, the 'periodicity of this particular past-present-future'.

There is a close accord, then, between the development of a neoliberal globalisation, the rise and fall of a postmodern cultural dominant, and the history of the British novel in the period from 1980 to the present. The chapters of this *Companion* set out to trace this relationship, and to offer as full as possible an account of the ways in which the novel of the period engages with its political, cultural and literary contexts. In order to produce this account, what follows is broken into four parts.

Part I, 'Overview', breaks the period into three sub-periods – the 1980s, the 1990s and the literature of the new millennium. Bridget Chalk's chapter on the 1980s offers an account of the most significant figures and works of the 1980s – Amis, Carter, Rushdie and McEwan, as well as Barnes, Amitav Ghosh, Graham Swift, Jeannette Winterson, Pat Barker, Kazuo Ishiguro and writers such as Margaret Drabble and V. S. Naipaul, who wrote important works in the 1980s – to demonstrate the interweaving of the influence of Thatcherism, and the emergence of a postmodern strain in the British novel. Pieter Vermeulen offers a close and nuanced account of the passage, in the 1990s, from Thatcher, to Major, to Blair, to trace the difficult and uncertain ways in which the novel of the 1990s (in works by Caryl Phillips, Hanif Kureishi, A. L. Kennedy, James Kelman, Michael Ondaatje, Jeanette Winterson and others) captured a new kind of cosmopolitan excitement (bound up with 'Cool Britannia'), while also maintaining forms of resistance to or ambivalence about the postmodernism that influenced it. Leigh Wilson's chapter then covers the fiction of the two decades of the current century, from Zadie Smith to David Mitchell to Tom McCarthy to Nicola Barker, finishing with a reading of Paul Kingsnorth's novel *The Wake*[40] as a reflection on climate change. Deploying a term from Benedict Anderson – the 'meanwhile' of the novel – Wilson argues that the fiction of the twenty-first century crafts a new kind of temporality which gestures towards an emergent cultural imaginary – an imagined community, that might come to thought after the decline of postmodernism, but that remains for us difficult to conceive or codify.

This first part lays out the broad trajectory of the novel in the period; subsequent parts then offer a range of critical frames through which to view that trajectory. Part II, 'New Formations', focuses on some of the cultural, material and aesthetic formations that have produced and have been produced by the novel of the period. Gabriel Griffin's chapter on the 'limits of the human' reads the novel from 1980 to 2018 as it has been involved with the transformation of the human as a result of the development in the period of new forms of biotechnology. Exploring the inventive engagement with new biopolitical formations in J. G. Ballard, Tom McCarthy, Deborah Levy, Kazuo Ishiguro, Emma Rendel and Rob Davis, Griffin suggests the novel of the period offers a means of critically picturing forms of material and technologised life, after the paradigms that situated us with the realms of the human have lapsed. Griffin explores the relation between new biotechnological forms and new literary forms; Kevin Brazil's chapter offers a close history of the shifting ways in which literary form itself has produced pictures of reality. Beginning with the development of metafictional formal strategies in the 1980s, used to explore the relationship between fiction and history in writers such as Rushdie, Caryl Phillips, Timothy Mo, Graham Swift, Peter Ackroyd, Pat Barker and A. S. Byatt, Brazil traces the relationship between form and postmodernism over the course of the period. There is a shift, he argues, around the turn of the century, when the exhaustion of a postmodern strand of metafiction led to a rethinking of the relationship between form and the real – exemplified on the one hand by the new relationships between literature and science in the work of McEwan and Ishiguro, and on the other by inventive forms of realism developed by Zadie Smith and Tom McCarthy. Brazil and Griffin, then, in different ways, explore the relationship between cultural formations and literary formations; Caroline Wintersgill closes Part II by attending to the development of new forms that shape the production of the book as a material commodity – one of the shifts that has had a foundational effect on the ways that novels are produced and consumed. Combining an empirical history of the book in the period with a theoretical account of its contribution to the process of imagining our environments, Wintersgill traces five processes that have determined the transformations in the publishing industry from 1980 to 2018 – professionalization, commodification, globalisation, democratisation and digitisation.

Part III turns to 'genres and movements', to offer a critical account of the ways that shifts in our understanding of style, genre and periodicity have been reflected in the modern and contemporary novel. Martin Eve's chapter gives explicit theoretical attention to the question that runs through the *Companion* as a whole – that is, to the ways in which the period is shaped by the legacies of modernism, the powerful influence of postmodernism and the entry, in recent years, into a period that is variously defined as 'after' postmodernism. Caroline Edwards offers an analysis of the ways in which the balance between the generic and the experimental shifts in the fiction of the period. In relatively new genres such as steampunk and the 'new weird', as well as in more traditional genres such as horror, the crime thriller, and utopian and dystopian fiction, Edwards argues that the novel does not remain bound by genre conventions, but in fact offers a powerful and restless critique of them. As the period sees deep transformations in the way that we conceive of the boundaries that shape political identity as well as discursive forms, it is in the novel's critical engagement with the unstable genres that frame it that we see it at its most contemporary. Jerome de Groot's discussion of the historical novel, the genre in the period that has perhaps been the most productive of new aesthetic possibilities, extends Edwards's discussion of the relationship between the generic and the experimental. Offering a critical picture of the historical novel from Angela Carter's *Nights at the Circus*[41] to

Zadie Smith's *Swing Time*,[42] de Groot suggests that, while the historical novel has a generic tie to realism, this does not mean that it is trapped within temporal or formal conventions; on the contrary, it is the historical novel, he argues, that has allowed us the most inventive access to the ways in which temporalities, and our very access to the real, have been refashioned in the period. Part III closes with Petra Rau's analysis of the influence that the televisual and the cinematic has had on the novel of the period. In a chapter that resonates richly with Edwards and with de Groot, Rau argues that cinematic adaptations of the novel in the period are not simply aesthetically neutral or conservative, as has often been suggested; rather, Rau argues, the process of cinematic adaptation has given a new energy to our conception of the world-making powers of fiction, particularly as it relates to the generic parameters of the historical novel.

The final part, 'Contexts', zooms out to characterise some of the broader forces operating on the fictional imagination of the period. Ben Masters's chapter, 'The Mid Atlantics', offers an account of the pervasive influence of American culture on British culture, pitched at the level of style. Reading the influence of the major male American writers of the later twentieth century – John Updike, Normal Mailer, Philip Roth – on the British novel, and particularly on Martin Amis, Julian Barnes and Ian McEwan, Masters shows how the ethical, political and aesthetic currents that run through the British fictional imagination are directed by a difficult relationship with the American novelistic voice. Rebecca Pohl's chapter reads the relationship between fiction and forms of sexual dissidence and transgression, as it develops from Doris Lessing, Angela Carter, Alan Hollinghurst and Jeanette Winterson to Sarah Hall, Ali Smith and Joanna Walsh. The advances made in LGBT rights in the period might suggest that the battle for sexual equality and recognition has largely been won, and the adoption of writers such as Carter and Winterson in school syllabi might suggest that these works have lost some of their countercultural force; but Pohl demonstrates that the transgressive urge in this strain of British fiction remains a powerful means of critiquing all forms of cultural normativity, as the struggle for new ways of narrating identities continues in our own embattled present. The last two chapters of Part IV turn to forces that are actively shaping our own moment, at the end of the second decade of the twenty-first century. Stephen Morton offers an account of the 'Rushdie affair', to examine the tensions in British culture between cultural relativism and the right to free speech, that have worked through Rushdie's writing, from *Satanic Verses*[43] to *Joseph Anton*.[44] And this part closes with Patrick Deer's wide-ranging reflection on the purchase of cosmopolitanism in the fiction of the period. One of the contradictions of cosmopolitanism, Deer argues, is that it stages a particular struggle between nationalism on the one hand and utopian forms of globalisation and universality on the other. This contradiction has run through the British novel's engagement with cosmopolitanism, from Penelope Fitzgerald to Zadie Smith. It is an understanding of this history, Deer suggests, that allows us to reach a fuller and more nuanced understanding of the sharp political and cultural pressures that are at work in 'Brexit Britain'.

Throughout these four parts, the *Companion* demonstrates how powerful the neoliberal revolution at the turn of the 1980s remains as a way of framing our present, of containing its various contradictory drives. Even as the advent of Trump and Brexit threaten a paradigm shift, a collapse of the uneasy consensus that has marked the period from 1980 to the present, it is nevertheless the case that the episteme ushered in by Thatcher and Reagan looks set to survive this crisis – a crisis that is nothing other than a radicalisation of the contradictions that gave rise to it in the first place. But if this persistence of neoliberalism is the story of this period – and if it is this that leads us to 1980 as its originary point, the moment when our present begins – it is nevertheless the case, as has been demonstrated by all of the chapters in this volume, that the novel of the period harbours counter images, the stirrings of a new and different future, that might see past the contradictions of our time, the contradictions that are frozen in the blackened remains of Grenfell tower. My conclusion to the *Companion*, 'Imagining the Future', closes the volume by reading the capacity of the contemporary British novel to produce images of a future that lies beyond the dark horizons of our culture moment. The novel as a form has a power and a duty to offer images of the world as it is – to help us to see the outlines of our present. It also has a duty to invent pictures of a world that does not yet exist, a world that belongs not to 'is', but to 'ought'. It is this second duty, this second power, that is perhaps most pressing for us now, as 'the planet rolls', in Samuel Beckett's memorable phrase, 'eager into winter'.[45]

Notes

1. T. Stoppard, *Rosencrantz and Guildenstern Are Dead* (London: Faber & Faber, 1968), pp. 6–7.
2. W. Brown, *Politics Out of History* (Princeton University Press, 2001), p. 7.
3. *Ibid.*, p. 14.
4. *Ibid.*, p. 142.
5. *Ibid.*, p. 14.

6. D. DeLillo, *Players* (London: Vintage, 1991), p. 84.
7. D. DeLillo, *Cosmopolis* (London: Picador, 2003), p. 79.
8. U. Heise, *Chronoschisms: Time, Narrative and Postmodernism* (Cambridge University Press, 1997).
9. S. Connor, *The English Novel in History: 1950–1995* (London: Routledge, 1996).
10. D. Head, *Cambridge Introduction to Modern British Fiction: 1950–2000* (Cambridge University Press, 2002).
11. A. Davies and A. Sinfield, *British Culture of the Postwar: An Introduction to Literature and Society 1945–1999* (London: Routledge, 2000).
12. P. Boxall and B. Cheyette, *The Oxford History of the Novel in English: British and Irish Fiction since 1940* (Oxford University Press, 2016).
13. R. Eaglestone, 'Contemporary Fiction in the Academy: Towards a Manifesto' (2013) 27(7) Textual Practice 1089–1101, 1095.
14. P. Boxall, *Twenty-First Century Fiction: A Critical Introduction* (Cambridge University Press, 2013).
15. S. Adiseshiah and R. Hildyard, *Twenty-First-Century Fiction: What Happens Now* (Basingstoke: Palgrave, 2013).
16. R. Eaglestone, *Contemporary Fiction: A Very Short Introduction* (Oxford University Press, 2013), p. 5.
17. D. Harvey, *A Brief History of Neoliberalism* (Oxford University Press, 2005), p. 1.
18. *Ibid.*
19. See F. Jameson's essay, 'The Antinomies of Postmodernity', in *The Cultural Turn* (London: Verso, 1998), pp. 50–72, for an exemplary rendition of this argument.
20. *Ibid.*, p. 3.
21. W. Self, 'After Grenfell', available at www.bbc.co.uk/programmes/bo8v8vho (2017), np.
22. A. Carter, *The Bloody Chamber* (London: Victor Gollancz, 1979).
23. I. McEwan, *The Cement Garden* (London: Jonathan Cape, 1978).
24. I. McEwan, *The Comfort of Strangers* (London: Jonathan Cape, 1981).
25. M. Amis, *The Rachel Papers* (London: Jonathan Cape, 1973).
26. M. Amis, *Dead Babies* (London: Penguin, 1975).
27. M. Amis, *Money: A Suicide Note* (London: Jonathan Cape, 1984).
28. S. Rushdie, *Midnight's Children* (London: Jonathan Cape, 1981).
29. S. Rushdie, *Imaginary Homelands: Essays and Criticism 1981–1991* (London: Vintage, 1992).
30. I. Welsh, *Trainspotting* (London: Secker & Warburg, 1993).
31. J. Kelman, *How Late It Was How Late* (London: Secker & Warburg, 1994).
32. J. Kelman, *You Have to Be Careful in the Land of the Free* (London: Penguin, 2004).
33. Z. Smith, *White Teeth* (London: Penguin, 2000).
34. Z. Smith, *NW* (London: Hamish Hamilton, 2012).
35. T. McCarthy, *Remainder* (London: Alma, 2005).
36. G. Malkani, *Londonstani* (London: Fourth Estate, 2006).
37. A. Smith, *The Accidental* (London: Hamish Hamilton, 2005).
38. A. Smith, *Autumn* (London: Hamish Hamilton, 2016).
39. A. Smith, *Winter* (London: Hamish Hamilton, 2017).

40. P. Kingsnorth, *The Wake* (London: Unbound, 2014).
41. A. Carter, *Nights at the Circus* (London: Chatto & Windus, 1984).
42. Z. Smith, *Swing Time* (London: Penguin, 2017).
43. S. Rushdie, *Satanic Verses* (London: Penguin, 1988).
44. S. Rushdie, *Joseph Anton: A Memoir* (London: Jonathan Cape, 2012).
45. S. Beckett, *Molloy, Malone Dies, The Unnamable* (London: Picador, 1979), p. 46.

PART I

Overview

I

BRIDGET CHALK

The 1980s

In 1983, the journal *Granta* released its first 'best of' issue, featuring the twenty most promising British novelists under the age of 40. The *Granta 7* roster proved auspicious and laid the groundwork for the careers of some of the most successful British novelists of the late twentieth century. Based on a campaign run by the Book Marketing Council, the issue ran over 300 pages and included the work of such figures as Salman Rushdie, Pat Barker, Ian McEwan, Kazuo Ishiguro, Graham Swift and Julian Barnes. From Thatcherism to the expansion of British identity, and from gender inequality to newly flexible models of history, the issue's themes announced the main literary and cultural preoccupations of the decade.

In the later post-war period, the British novel had come to be seen as 'provincial, insular, and dominated by conventional forms of realism ... an exhausted form, in a state of terminal decline', particularly in comparison to the work of ground-breaking American novelists like Thomas Pynchon, Phillip Roth and Saul Bellow.[1] While retrospective accounts of the 1960s and 1970s, in which John Fowles and Iris Murdoch were writing, may overstate the dismal state of novel publishing, it is nevertheless true that the 1980s saw a rejuvenation of the novel in England and the emergence of many new writers whose work would continue to influence the writing of fiction in the decades ahead. Both formally and philosophically, the theoretical shift towards post-structuralism in the academy helped to shape this revitalisation. In many of the decade's best novels, ideas distilled from the work of Jacques Derrida, Michel Foucault and Roland Barthes were manifested in what Patricia Waugh calls 'a range of self-referential aesthetic practices involving playful irony, parody, parataxis, nestings and framings, self-consciousness, and the mixing and meshing of high and popular culture'.[2] While these postmodern formal strategies clearly emerged from the groundswell of academic interest in French post-structuralism, the 'overwhelming influence' of Samuel Beckett, whose 'closed space' novels (*Company* [1980], *Mal vu mal dit* [*Ill Seen Ill Said*] [1981] and *Worstword Ho* [1983]) were published in the

1980s, continued to guide literary experimentation.[3] Beckett's signature linguistic irony and reflexivity, as well as his focus on language as the creation, not the representation, of reality, resonates with the principles energising the decade's postmodern expression. Broadly, commitments to aesthetic innovation and political resistance characterise the clutch of writers that has become known as the 'Granta generation'.[4]

Resisting Thatcher

Formally defined by the expansion of postmodern style, many of the decade's novels concerned thematically the specific social and political conditions of the 1980s. Margaret Thatcher's tenure as Prime Minister (1979–1990) has become synonymous with a constellation of ideological and political positions that transformed English society, and it is difficult to overstate her centrality to 1980s British culture. Elected in 1979, and re-elected in 1983 and 1987, Thatcher ruled according to an ideology of economic self-interest, reversing the consensus-based governance and social support networks of the post-war period in favour of New Right principles. The first years of her reign saw surging unemployment, rising taxes and social unrest. Nevertheless, an outpouring of patriotism during the 1982 Falklands War helped to deliver her second victory at the polls. On returning to England during the days leading up to this election, Rushdie lamented, '(with) the near-inevitability of a more or less enormous Tory victory, my sense of alienation has blossomed into something close to full-scale culture shock'.[5] Rushdie's personal reaction extended to the 'tacitly liberal-left' cadre of new, exciting writers including Amis, Barnes, McEwan and Ishiguro, as well as many in the academic and literary worlds.[6]

No novel resists Thatcher's New Right values as directly and famously as Martin Amis's *Money* (1984). Son of the novelist Kingsley Amis, Martin Amis was regularly touted as a literary darling and celebrity in the 1980s, when his work was alternatively praised and critiqued for its lewd, bawdy and misogynistic elements. 'Widely accepted as a satire of Thatcher's England, a time that lives in the public imagination as one of self-absorbed materialism and cultural vacuity', *Money* follows the transatlantic travails of the ironically named John Self, who is engaged in the production of a vaguely defined film alternatively titled *Good Money* and *Bad Money*.[7] Uproariously funny as well as deeply cynical, the novel establishes many of the hallmarks of high postmodern fiction: playfulness, irony, self-referentiality, a mixture of high and low cultural elements, and a critique of literary conventions. Crass conspicuous consumerism permeates the world of the novel, in which the passion for money above all else has annihilated morality, identity, intimacy and productivity. Self is a destructive pleasure seeker whose romps with alcohol, drugs, food and sex, legendary as they are, sink him further and further into self-loathing and social alienation. The plot ultimately reveals that the film Self is working on is in fact a scam, and that all the funding for it has been pilfered from Self's account, bankrupting him.

The novel deconstructs character through Self's convoluted identity and alienating behaviour; he tells the reader early on, 'I want sympathy, even though I find it so very hard to behave sympathetically'.[8] This is one of multiple tongue-in-cheek references to the conventions of novel reading, which draw attention to the choreographed nature of literary fiction and its relationship to human interaction and understanding. In one of the novel's most clearly postmodern, self-referential details, the novelist Martin Amis features as a character, whom Self first describes as 'a guy who lives round my way who really gives me the fucking creeps'.[9] Martin plays a minor role in Self's story and provides a meta-commentary on the role of fiction in the creation and maintenance of identity. Indeed, narrative trickery, manipulation of temporality and character, and plots of deception and confidence tricks characterise much of Amis's oeuvre. His follow-up to *Money*, the murder-mystery *London Fields* (1989), extends his critique of the political climate of late capitalism and the nefarious, shallow world to which it has given rise. The novel follows the misadventures of the loathsome Keith Talent, a darts-playing, working-class knockabout who treats women shamefully and earns a paltry living as a 'cheat'. The rendering of Talent's dialect remains one of the novel's enduring elements, and, as in *Money*, Amis shows great dexterity in depicting characters of all classes, from black British immigrants to aristocrats, and working-class teenage girls to American professionals.

Amis stands as a representative figure of the decade due to his experimental style and perspicacious take on the political atmosphere of the time. Many other writers shared Amis's dissenting voice, and Rushdie urged his contemporaries explicitly to 'rage against the dying of the light that Thatcherism represents'.[10] Ian McEwan, whose popularity and broad appeal has surpassed that of Amis in the last twenty years, also began writing in the 1970s, producing fiction and drama marked by darkness, violence and sexual explicitness like the novel *The Comfort of Strangers* (1980). His next novel, *The Child in Time* (1987), links the larger national mood of the 1980s decisively to the individual suffering of its characters. Set in a 1990s future world of authoritarian conformist rule, this meditation on childhood and exploration of the relationship between science and the moral nature of being also functions as a scathing critique of the Thatcher administration. The novel imagines a nameless Thatcher figure in a fifth term at the helm of an increasingly stringent government dedicated to conservative, controlling principles: a 'nation ... to be regenerated by reformed child-care practice'.[11] Centrally focused on the kidnapping of Stephen Lewis's 3-year-old daughter five years earlier, the novel explores temporality in various imaginative and pseudo-scientific ways. In its marriage of contemporary scientific theory (the 'New Physics') and imaginative literature, McEwan's novel leaks beyond the boundaries of realism without abandoning its conventions entirely. The novel counterbalances its dystopic present with a political vision of flexible, alternative realities and the redemptive nature of human connection and unification.

Beyond Amis and McEwan, a variety of 1980s fiction reflects the Thatcherite world as a dark, vaguely apocalyptic and diseased place, often focusing on inequities of class, race and gender. Margaret Drabble's sweeping realist novel *The Radiant Way* (1987), for example, demonstrates the compromised state of liberal life under Thatcher. Cuts to social services and the arts, the loss of political ideals that comes with financial success, and violence against women in the form of a serial killer and a long-repressed memory of incestuous sexual abuse form the backdrop to this expansive, socially critical work. From a broad range of perspectives and subject positions, 1980s writers reinvigorated the novel as a site of protest and resistance, confirming Rushdie's proclamation that 'writers and politicians are natural rivals ... and the novel is one way of denying the official, politicians' version of truth'.[12]

Rewriting the Past

Deploying postmodern literary techniques, novelists of the decade offered competing versions of truth and reality, often by approaching historical narratives anew. Julian Barnes's *Granta* 7 contribution was an excerpt from *Flaubert's Parrot* (1984), a novel that follows doctor Geoffrey Braithwaite's quest to discover the hidden facts of Gustave Flaubert's life through material evidence and speculation. A journalist and reviewer in the late 1970s, Barnes published *Metroland*, a cynical *bildungsroman* in 1980, followed by *Before She Met Me* (1982), a noirish tale of a husband obsessed with his new wife's former sex life. *Flaubert's Parrot* employs a pseudo-archival methodology to construct a dizzying array of perspectives and versions of 'truth' about Flaubert, the 'writer who disdainfully forbade posterity to take any personal interest in him' through such mediums as chronology, concordance, dictionary and even a school examination.[13] The novel also mines the mysterious connections between the past and the present in the scant details provided of Braithwaite's relationship with his apparently adulterous late wife. 'I loved her; we were happy; I missed her. She didn't love me; we were unhappy; I miss her … I have to hypothesise a little. I have to fictionalize … We never talked about her secret life. So I have to invent my way to the truth.'[14] The subjectivism inherent in Braithwaite's recollections of his wife also defines the project of his research and Barnes's novel itself: we all must invent our way to the truth, and choose among a vast repository of evidentiary material to support our inventions.

After his foray into nineteenth-century France, Barnes once again delved into the past, this time broadening his scope to *A History of the World in 10½ Chapters* (1989). In a kind of bricolage, the chapters of the title form a series of loosely linked narratives with disparate themes and styles. In a now standard postmodern gesture, Barnes challenges the idea of the grand historical narrative with achronological accounts of Noah's Ark from the perspective of a woodworm, the story behind Théodore Géricault's painting 'The Raft of the Medusa', a sixteenth-century court case against woodworms that have damaged a church and the story of a woman in the near future fleeing a natural disaster, among others. In the chapter on the subject of love and history entitled 'Parenthesis', which takes the form of a direct address from implied author to reader, only love, due to the 'imaginative sympathy' necessary to experience it, stands in opposition to hegemonic, accepted accounts of history: 'We must believe in (love) … If we don't, then we merely surrender to the history of the world and someone else's truth.'[15] Love, and the flexibility of the novel form, allows us to take some kind of ownership over history and reality. The function of narrative in our sense of the past, in both *Flaubert's Parrot* and *History*, undermines available records to empower the individual to reimagine history and her place in it.

Emerging from and alongside the poststructuralist developments in the academy, historical novels deconstructed authorised narratives of the past in order to reveal the necessarily limited and partial truth of any given account. These novels represent a category of postmodern literature that Linda Hutcheon calls 'historiographic metafiction', characterised by 'overtly metafictional assertions of both history and literature as human constructs', that are both deceptive and necessary.[16] Far from nostalgia or reclamations of Old England, then, 1980s novels that engaged with historical events produced alternatives to the white, masculine, triumphantly imperial past. In *Liza's England* (1989), for example, Pat Barker filters major events of the century through the life of one working-class, ultimately dispossessed woman and the conflicted social worker sent to convince her to leave her flat. The novel traces Liza's individual development against larger ideological and political forces such as gender oppression and the casual violence of world war through to the divisive social attitudes of the 1980s. The feminist, popular historian protagonist of Penelope Lively's *Moon Tiger* (1987) recollects various phases of her life in England and Egypt throughout the twentieth century, subverting the patriarchal imperial power complex and normative assumptions surrounding the sexual lives of women. Peter Ackroyd's temporally complex novels *Hawksmoor* (1985) and *Chatterton* (1987), both popular successes, straddle contemporary and eighteenth- and nineteenth-century England to destabilise the reader's understanding of linear historical time in favour of a sense of simultaneity. The most successful novels of Angela Carter (*Nights at the Circus* [1984]), Rushdie (*Midnight's Children* [1981], *Shame* [1983]) and Ishiguro (*A Pale View of Hills* [1982], *An Artist of the Floating World* [1986], *The Remains of the Day* [1989]) fictionalise specific historical eras and recast the present by upending conventional national and global historical accounts.

One of the most influential historical novels of the decade is Graham Swift's *Waterland* (1983), an epic novel about generations of two families in the Fens, which presents history not as a series of facts, but as 'the fabrication, the diversion, the reality-obscuring drama'.[17] Swift's novels, including *Shuttlecock* (1981) and *Out of This World* (1988), filter the relationship between national history and quotidian life through first-person narration and temporally inventive formal strategies. The narrator, Tom Crick, is a history teacher on the brink of losing his job due to his wife's attempted kidnapping of a baby and because the school is 'cutting back on history'[18] in favour of a more contemporary, vocational vision of education, encapsulated in the question: 'What about Now?'.[19] In this way, the novel converses with the Thatcherite materialistic devaluation of the humanities and the past in favour of the thirst for measurable gain and professional success. In his heavily ironic and self-reflexive narration of his family's story, Crick reveals long-obscured secrets that have shaped generational and regional history and undermines conventional notions of a coherent past. He proclaims at one point, 'can I deny that what I wanted all along was not some golden nugget that history would at last yield up, but History itself: the Grand Narrative, the filler of vacuums, the dispeller of fears of the dark?'.[20] The novel plays on the relationships among fairy tale, fiction and history, and between the makers of history and the supposed 'non-participants'.[21]

Kazuo Ishiguro, another *Granta* 7 novelist who came to prominence during the decade and subsequently won the 2017 Nobel Prize for Literature, situates his novels in mid-century England and Japan to interrogate the historical events of the twentieth century for their illusory qualities. His first two lauded novels, *A Pale View of Hills* and *An Artist of the Floating World*, explore the connections between the political and cultural history of Japan and individual ethical conflicts. The slippery nature of memory and the gradual revelation of the implications of past actions by unreliable narrators mark his three novels of the 1980s, which are told in muted, elegant prose that belies the striking structural innovations of the fiction. His masterful, Booker-Award-winning *The Remains of the Day* examines the facade of English manners from a mid-century perspective, looking back on the politics of the aristocracy in the 1930s. Through Stevens, the butler who narrates the novel, Ishiguro suggests that conventional English class propriety displaces authentic emotional and moral life, and masks bigotry, racism and collaboration. In an illustration of the post-war waning of the manor lifestyle, Darlington Hall has been sold to an American eager to live the life of an English lord, but with a substantial downsizing in staff. Stevens tells his tale over the course of a motoring trip through the English countryside, which he undertakes in order to find his colleague from years ago, Miss Kenton, ostensibly to hire her back as head housekeeper. Over the course of this journey, snapshots of the past reveal that he has long suppressed his love for Miss Kenton. Evasions, blind spots and repression permeate the novel, constructing Stevens as a deeply layered character bound to performing a self in constant tension with his more human emotional instincts. Ultimately, Stevens's failures of intimacy and moral action in his relationship to the Nazi sympathiser Lord Darlington prompt a larger examination of England's connections to fascism in the 1930s.

Redefining Britishness

Ishiguro was born in Nagasaki, but moved to England at the age of 5 and was raised in a London suburb. While not from a former colony, his nationality and literary prominence in England illustrates the broader post-war expansion of the definition of Britishness. The British Nationality Act of 1948 granted citizenship to all members of the Commonwealth, and migration to England from the former colonies increased dramatically. The next few decades saw public resistance to the growing numbers of immigrants settling in the country, which engendered acts of racism and ethnocentric public discourse. Enoch Powell's sensationalistic and fear-mongering 'Rivers of Blood' speech in 1968 advocated ceasing immigration and instituting repatriation, and legitimised racism in the name of national interest. This tension persisted into the 1980s, exacerbated by Parliament's restrictive Nationality Act of 1981 and the Brixton riots of 1981 and 1985 between the Afro-Caribbean community and police. As Philip Tew suggests, 'issues of a pluralized ethnicity have extended an ongoing social and cultural dispute

BRIDGET CHALK

as to the direction, focus, representation, rewards, voicing and so forth of Britishness in all its forms'.[22]

Despite much debate over its political utility and accuracy, the term 'Black British' gained currency during the decade as a way to refer to 'the common experience of racism and marginalization in Britain and ... a new politics of resistance, amongst groups and communities with, in fact, very different histories, traditions and ethnic identities'.[23] Cultural theorists such as Stuart Hall and Paul Gilroy highlighted the complexity and intersections of race and Britishness in the later twentieth century and 'link(ed) postmodernism with questions of ethnicity and new identities'.[24] Citing the work of Hanif Kureishi and other writers as exemplars, Hall articulated the need for a new 'politics of ethnicity predicated on difference and diversity', not, as Englishness had historically been, based on 'marginalizing, dispossessing, displacing and forgetting other ethnicities'.[25] In his well-known essay 'The New Empire within Britain', Salman Rushdie concentrated his vocal resistance to Thatcherite policy on the mistreatment of minority groups: 'Britain is undergoing a critical phase of its post-colonial period, and this crisis is not simply economic or political. It's a crisis of the whole culture, of the society's entire sense of itself. And racism is only the most clearly visible part of this crisis.'[26]

In many ways, Rushdie epitomises the English literary world of the 1980s: his commentary in essays reveals the international scope of the issues facing the Anglo-Indian and the broader immigrant community in England; his specific tragicomic vision of postcolonialism and his fabulist postmodern style has set the tone for much subsequent work; and his notoriety exemplifies the decade's rise in literary celebrity. *Midnight's Children* is a magical realist national epic, which tells the tale of Saleem Sinai, born at the stroke of midnight on 15 August 1947, simultaneous with the birth of India as an independent nation. Informed by developments in the Latin American novel of the 1970s in the style of Gabriel Garcia Marquez and Central European novels like those of Gunter Grass, among countless other sources of inspiration, Saleem's story is therefore chronologically and metaphorically coterminous with the sixty years of the history of modern India, Pakistan and Bangladesh. Rushdie depicts the multiplicity of the country in its stories, regions, traditions and hybrid forms born of colonialism. Saleem functions as a metaphor for a polyglot and multi-faith India: he is the biological child of a Hindu mother and English father, but was brought up Muslim by a Catholic ayah. Featuring interjections of the fictional scene of composition, in which the impotent Saleem spins his tale in a pickle factory in the company of the muscular peasant woman Padma (his intimate companion), the novel draws ironic attention to its own construction. Saleem reveals that he was in fact

24

switched at birth with another baby, who becomes his enemy and double, Shiva, a poor Hindu with enormous knees to match Saleem's enormous ears. This deformity, an outward manifestation of Saleem's miraculous telepathy, allows him to serve as 'All India Radio' and communicate with all the other children of midnight, or those born on the day of India's independence. Signalling the arbitrary nature of identity categories such as paternity, religion and class, the novel undermines the principles on which Indian society is organised. Saleem contests our belief in the fiction of the unitary self with reference to the variety of lives and cultures that make up a postcolonial Anglo-Indian identity: 'I have been a swallower of lives; and to know me, just the one of me, you'll have to swallow the lot as well. Consumed multitudes are jostling and shoving inside me.'[27] His project, and the end of the novel suggests it is a failed one, is to 'mean something', to avoid being 'sucked into the annihilating whirlpool of the multitudes'.[28]

Shame, Rushdie's next novel, concerns the recent socio-political history of the subcontinent, this time exclusively in Pakistan. Smaller in scale than the immense *Midnight's Children*, *Shame* deploys tropes of oral story-telling and the fairy tale to dramatise military and criminal enterprises through the lives of two families based on political figures in Pakistan. While the novel's 'explicitly feminist' agenda was criticised as condescending, Rushdie's focus on the plight of women in the context of Islamic nationalism set it apart from his earlier work.[29] His next novel, *The Satanic Verses* (1988), follows two immigrants from India to England and portrays London as a potpourri of race, faith and class. Gibreel Farishta is a Bollywood actor undergoing a crisis of religious faith and Saladin Chamcha is an Anglophile Indian who specialises in voice-overs and grapples with the clash between the Eastern and Western parts of his identity. Almost immediately upon its publication, the novel sparked violent demonstrations on the subcontinent, in which people lost their lives, and in England, where the book was burned as blasphemous. The arguably heretical depiction of the origins of Islam in Gibreel's dream sequences fanned fury, and included prostitutes with the names of the wives of the Prophet Mahound and distorted versions of certain episodes of the Qur'an. The protests were followed in February 1989 by the Ayatollah Khomeini's issuance of a *fatwa*, or death sentence, on Rushdie's head and all those involved in the production of the book (his Japanese translator was murdered and others connected to the novel's publication were attacked). Rushdie later explained that the offending elements functioned to 'crystallize the opposition between the sacred and the profane' and question problematic aspects of the Muslim faith, in particular its treatment of women.[30] The affair, defined as it was by issues of free speech, religious fundamentalism and fragile diplomatic relationships, became a global crisis over the next few years. In a moving defence, Rushdie has called the novel a 'migrant's-eye view of the world ... written from the very experience of uprooting, disjuncture and metamorphosis ... (it) celebrates hybridity, impurity, intermingling, the transformation that comes of new and unexpected combinations of human beings, cultures, ideas, politics, movies, songs'.[31] Unfortunately, this 'mongrelisation' that Rushdie aimed to honour deepened the fissures among the world's religious and cultural positions, auguring decades of tensions between Islam and the West to come.

Other figures who illuminate the experience of migration and minority life in England in the 1980s include V. S. Naipaul, Timothy Mo, Buchi Emecheta, Hanif Kureishi and Amitav Ghosh. Naipaul belongs to an earlier generation of writers, and provides a counterpoint to Rushdie's virulent opposition to majority English culture. His novel-cum-memoir *The Enigma of Arrival* appeared in 1987, and concerns the relationship of the immigrant protagonist to the English countryside and literary tradition. Naipaul has been criticised for not being sufficiently resistant to imperial England, and Dominic Head contends that the novel 'fails to register the connection between the exercise of colonial power and the maintenance of traditional English tranquility'.[32] The irreverent early work of Hanif Kureishi focuses on the experience of England from the perspective of second-generation Pakistani immigrants, and engages with the urban unrest and racism of the previous twenty years. Although he did not publish his first novel until 1990, the brilliant and subversive *The Buddha of Suburbia*, Kureishi's plays and screenplays of the 1980s such as *My Beautiful Laundrette* (1985) and *Sammy and Rosie Get Laid* (1988) defy stereotypes of conservative immigrant communities with their heady mix of sex and drugs, and the challenges of straddling generations, racial categories and cultures. Amitav Ghosh, who was educated in India, Egypt and Oxford, wrote novels set on the subcontinent and in England that trace the complexities of history and the convoluted construction of identity in the wake of Empire and Partition. *The Shadow Lines* (1988), for example, was composed in response to the 1984 assassination of Prime Minister Indira Ghandi, which sent India into a period of protracted violence among religious groups. The novel probes earlier bloody conflicts in Europe and on the subcontinent such as the Blitz in London and the riots in Dhaka and Calcutta in the 1960s. Reversing the colonial gaze with an Indian protagonist who travels to England and observes hybrid postcolonial phenomena like Brick Lane in London, *The Shadow Lines* focuses on the convoluted imperatives of postcolonial (and post-Partition) belonging in England, India and East Pakistan/Bangladesh.

Nigerian immigrant Buchi Emecheta, a realist writer whose novels concern the plight of African and Caribbean women in their home countries and in

England after migration, was also featured in *Granta*. Informed by her own experiences, her early work depicts the struggles and strength of Nigerian women. *The Family* (1989, also published as *Gwendolyn*) tells the story of a young girl born in Jamaica and left by her parents, who emigrate to England and send for her three years later. The second part of the novel tracks her difficulties in acclimating to an alien culture and family. While racial difference figures in subplots and details of the immigrant story, the novel centrally illuminates the oppression of women by men who are empowered by cultural myths of superiority and privilege to exploit them. Gwendolyn is raped at age 9 by a lecherous family friend in Jamaica who is fairly easily forgiven by the community, and later raped again by her own father, who impregnates her. Her father justifies this incest by her mother's absence (she has gone back to Jamaica to fetch money for the family) and his sense that she is less his daughter due to her three-year absence from the family. This dark plot underscores the ruptures in the family unit and the identities it secures created by postcolonial migration and urban post-war economic hardship.

In addition to immigrant voices, the 1980s also saw an awakening of new figures in Scottish letters, who voiced a cultural identity long suppressed in British literary history. Alisdair Gray's ambitious *Lanark* (1981), for Gerald Carruthers 'the one undoubtedly great Scottish novel of the second half of the twentieth century', began the decade with a vision of urban decay and alienation set in Glasgow and earned much praise from the British literary establishment.[33] A focus on poor and working-class characters characterises much of the best Scottish writing of the period and can be linked to the disillusionment and disappointment surrounding questions of national and cultural identity within Great Britain. James Kelman's debut novel, *The Busconductor Hines* (1984), portrays the working-class alienation of his protagonist, and is set over the course of a few weeks in which the married Rab grapples with his disenchantment with his class position and professional subordination. Compared to that of Joyce and Beckett for the unflinching, coarse, stream-of-consciousness perspective of his city men, Kelman's work prioritises the quotidian and the disgruntled yet palpably human character of the working-class savant. Kelman gained international attention with his third novel, *A Disaffection* (1989), which was shortlisted for the Booker Prize, but his signature deployment of slang and Glaswegian dialect drives his early work as well. Uninterested in scheming for promotion like his 'typical fenian marxist fucking glory seeker' colleagues, Rab carries his challenges to the system and the men that run it to the point of his resignation at the end of the novel.[34] As a representative of contemporary Scottish identity, Rab brings together passivity and irreverence in the face of possible means of socioeconomic advancement with honourable resistance to forces of oppression and deep love and loyalty to his family.

Reassessing Inequity

Issues of identity beyond ethnicity, including gender, class and sexuality, also drive much of the rich fiction of the decade. While second-wave feminism had improved the social and legal standing of women in England by 1980, forms of patriarchal oppression persisted, and novelists approached the experience of women and the social structures that contained them from new angles. The subject of an explosion of critical attention in the 1980s, Angela Carter wed high-flying postmodern experimentation to feminist themes in her fiction in a career which lasted from the 1960s until her untimely death in 1991. While her eclectic writing style drew upon fairy tale, philosophy and popular culture from the beginning, it was not until the 1980s that 'a kind of highly stylised and conspicuously erudite postmodern writing that resembled Carter's had become the "next big thing"', and her reputation skyrocketed.[35] Her best known work, *Nights at the Circus*, reliant on pastiche and combinations of high and low cultural references, comments through the use of spectacle and showmanship on society's treatment of women as pleasure and thrill-delivering objects. Partially focalised through the American journalist Walser, the novel presents the beautiful and massive Sophie Fevvers, a *fin de siècle* aerial artist with feathered wings that may or may not be real, as an over-determined object of study set in various performative spaces: the brothel, the house for the monstrous, the vaudeville stage and the circus. At the brothel in which she grew up, she declares, 'I was a tableau vivant from the age of seven on ... I served my apprenticeship in *being looked at* – at being the object in the eye of the beholder'.[36] Carter explicitly and figuratively links Fevvers with the Winged Victory, Icarus, Helen of Troy and Zeus in the form of the swan, ensuring that she blurs the boundaries between genders as well as reality and illusion. While Fevvers in various ways subverts and claims power over the men and institutions that attempt to enclose her, the various failures, ruptures and uncertainties of the novel indicate with foreboding the struggles for female agency that lie ahead in the twentieth century.

Like Carter, Jeannette Winterson deploys strategies of metanarrative and magical realism to interrogate social structures surrounding gender and sexuality. Her novels of the decade, including *Oranges Are Not the Only Fruit* (1985), *The Passion* (1987) and *Sexing the Cherry* (1989), were publishing successes and quickly took their place in the developing canon of gay and lesbian fiction, as well as in the postmodern novel. Winterson's humorous and moving works weave together motifs of autobiography, myth, Christianity and fairy tale to destabilise the narratives that dictate identity. *Oranges* relies heavily and self-reflexively on autobiography, and tells the coming-of-age story of Jeannette, a young girl who realises and embraces her lesbian identity over and against the bullying protests of her church community. Like those of Sophie Fevvers, Jeannette's origins are mysterious and over-determined: her mother 'arranged for a foundling', in the manner of the Virgin Mary, and thus in the resemblance of her origins to those of Christ, Jeannette represents the promise of a new word and world to her mother.[37] The novel, like Winterson's later work, affirms and deconstructs dominant 'truths' about gender, faith and history through its combination of Jeannette's story and the interspersed sections of the fable of Winnet, a girl also exiled from her home for elements of her sexual awakening. *Sexing the Cherry* traverses space and time between seventeenth- and twentieth-century London and also plays upon the trope of maternal creation with the giant protagonist Dog-Woman and her adopted son, Jordan. With this novel, Winterson left behind the recognizable narrative structure of the novel of development to mount a more radical postmodern assault on the marginalisation of women and the normative classifications that regulate love and intimate relationships.

Best known for her award-winning First World War trilogy (*Regeneration* [1991], *The Eye in the Door* [1993], *The Ghost Road* [1995]), Pat Barker's 1980s fiction links the conservative political environment to the evacuation of dignity and security from women's lives. Encouraged to embrace her working-class upbringing in her writing by Carter, and influenced by D. H. Lawrence, Barker gives voice to women who are socially and politically marginalised in a time of national economic distress and high unemployment. Barker's work might be less overtly experimental and acrobatic than some other prominent novelists of the decade, but her novels are nonetheless formally inventive and purposeful. Her notion of the multi-perspectival 'compound eye', for example, models a collective voice for silenced working-class women, and her moving reconstruction of war history in her later trilogy strikes at the foundations of masculinity.[38] *Union Street* (1982) is a novel in seven linked stories about individual women who live on the same street in northern England. The novel evokes community structurally, then, even as it shows women estranged from those to whom they are most intimately connected. At times Barker is unsparing in her depiction of the indignities of female life: the first story features the rape of an 11-year-old child, and gruesome accounts of childbirth, abortion, domestic abuse, prostitution and starvation feature here and in her other novels of the period. In *Blow Your House Down* (1984), the novel excerpted for her contribution to *Granta 7*, Barker turns to an even more muted figure of society: the prostitute. Based on the recent case of a real serial killer, the novel is focalised through various women involved in sex work or surviving on the scraps of work available at the chicken slaughterhouse. Existing in an environment of 'back streets, boarded-up houses, [and] the smell of blood in a factory yard', these women are infused with spirit and depth by Barker, who refuses to paint them as objectified victims, as the newspaper coverage treats the murdered.[39] Evocative of a national atmosphere of depletion with a nameless killer identified only through his 'heavy scent of violets and decay',[40] *Blow Your House Down* condemns the society that preys upon the bodies of women and ignores their cries for help, whether on an individual or socioeconomic level.

While political and social critique specific to 1980s Britain forms the central subject matter of a good deal of the decade's finest novels, many of the writers who got their start at this time have continued to produce critically acclaimed work over the past 30 years. Barker, Barnes, Drabble, Ghosh, McEwan, Rushdie and Swift are just some of the 1980s novelists who have produced compelling new work in the late 2010s. The recent European and American resurgence of virulent nationalism and conservative values, moreover, suggests that today's cultural landscape resembles that of the 1980s in manifold ways, and that novelists new and familiar will continue to 'rage against the dying of the light' they see in the contemporary world.

Notes

1. D. Head, *The State of the Novel* (Malden, MA: Wiley-Blackwell, 2008), p. 10.
2. P. Waugh, 'Postmodern Fiction and the Rise of Critical Theory' in B. Shaffer (ed.), *A Companion to the British and Irish Novel* (Malden, MA: Blackwell, 2005), p. 68.
3. J. Brooker, *Literature of the 1980s: After the Watershed* (Edinburgh University Press, 2010), p. 50.
4. Approaching the key figures of the 1980s through *Granta 7* creates a canon of mostly male writers. Despite the achievements of Pat Barker, Jeannette Winterson and other female novelists, most of the decade's enduring work (cemented as such through publishing and prize-winning prospects) was produced by men. As this chapter, particularly the last section, should make clear, however, female writers likewise approached the political and social issues of the decade with experimental techniques and proffered powerful indictments of the patriarchal structures that limited women's opportunities in contemporary Britain.
5. S. Rushdie, 'A General Election' in *Imaginary Homelands: Essays and Criticism 1981–1991* (New York: Penguin Books, 1991), p. 159.
6. Brooker, *Literature of the 1980s*, pp. 51–2.

7. J. Ayres, 'Confirming the New Orthodoxy: Martin Amis's *Money* and Thatcherism' (2014) 60(1) *Twentieth-Century Literature* 59–78, 60.
8. M. Amis, *Money: A Suicide Note* (New York: Penguin, 2010), p. 32.
9. *Ibid.*, p. 61.
10. Rushdie, 'A General Election', p. 162.
11. I. McEwan, *The Child in Time* (London: Jonathan Cape, 1987), p. 191.
12. S. Rushdie, 'Imaginary Homelands' in *Imaginary Homelands*, p. 14.
13. J. Barnes, *Flaubert's Parrot* (New York: Vintage International, 1990), p. 16.
14. *Ibid.*, pp. 161, 165.
15. J. Barnes, *A History of the World in 10 ½ Chapters* (London: Jonathan Cape, 1989), p. 244.
16. L. Hutcheon, *A Poetics of Postmodernism: History, Theory, Fiction* (New York: Routledge, 1988), pp. 124–5.
17. G. Swift, *Waterland* (New York: Vintage International, 1992), p. 40.
18. *Ibid.*, p. 5.
19. *Ibid.*, p. 60.
20. *Ibid.*, p. 62.
21. *Ibid.*, p. 40.
22. P. Tew, *The Contemporary British Novel* (New York: Continuum, 2004), p. 36.
23. S. Hall, 'New Ethnicities' in B. Ashcroft, G. Griffiths and H. Tiffin (eds), *The Post-Colonial Studies Reader* (New York: Routledge, 2006), p. 199.
24. J. Skinner, 'Black British Interventions' in Shaffer (ed.), *A Companion to the British and Irish Novel*, p. 131.
25. Hall, 'New Ethnicities', p. 202.
26. S. Rushdie, 'The New Empire within Britain' in *Imaginary Homelands*, p. 129.
27. S. Rushdie, *Midnight's Children* (New York: Random House, 2006), p. 4.
28. *Ibid.*, p. 533.
29. T. Brennan, 'Salman Rushdie' in G. Stade and C. Howard (eds), *British Writers Supplement IV* (New York: Scribner's, 1997), p. 444.
30. S. Rushdie, 'In Good Faith' in *Imaginary Homelands*, p. 401.
31. *Ibid.*, p. 394.
32. D. Head, *The Cambridge Introduction to Modern British Fiction, 1950–2000* (Cambridge University Press, 2002), p. 177.
33. G. Carruthers, 'The Novel in Ireland and Scotland' in Shaffer (ed.), *A Companion to the British and Irish Novel*, p. 124.
34. J. Kelman, *The Busconductor Hines* (London: Polygon Books, 1984), p. 34.
35. N. Pitchford, 'Angela Carter' in Shaffer (ed.), *A Companion to the British and Irish Novel*, p. 410.
36. A. Carter, *Nights at the Circus* (New York: Penguin, 1993), p. 23 (emphasis in the original).
37. J. Winterson, *Oranges Are Not the Only Fruit* (New York: Grove Press, 1985), p. 3.
38. S. Carson, 'Pat Barker' in Stade and Howard (eds), *British Writers Supplement IV*, p. 46.
39. *Ibid.*, p. 168.
40. *Ibid.*, p. 64.

2

PIETER VERMEULEN

The 1990s

It is all too easy to forget that the 1990s were *not* just the decade of Cool Britannia. Tony Blair's New Labour only took power in 1997, and the major part of the decade consisted in the slightly embarrassed hangover of a decade of Thatcherism. The 1997 *Vanity Fair* article that launched the 'Cool Britannia' label identified the eminently forgettable face of that lukewarm Britannia as 'gray-flannel, beans-on-toast John Major!'.[1] Major's tenure as prime minister between 1992 and 1997 consolidated Thatcher's break with Britain's post-war consensus, yet failed to develop a national iconography to convert the fall-out of that rupture into a marketable national brand. This brand arrived later in the decade, when New Labour's Third Way spun the realities of imperial decline and rampant deindustrialisation as, somehow, good things – as occasions for entrepreneurialism and a patriotic embrace of a demotic national culture. This culture was emblematised by the Britpop phenomenon, as bands like Blur and Oasis indulged in their eclectic recycling of sounds, styles and fashions from three decades of British music – looking back, but not in anger so much as in nostalgic yearning. When, in one of the iconic images of the decade, Oasis's Noel Gallagher shook hands with Tony Blair at 10 Downing Street in July 1997, the neoliberal reorganisation of the nation that had started in the 1980s finally found its cool.

The major developments in British fiction in the decade, then, germinated in a tepid body politic that could not quite contain centrifugal forces. There was the drive for devolution in Wales and Scotland, culminating in the establishment of regional assemblies in 1997, and there was the increasingly multicultural make-up of Britain – two sociocultural developments that were reflected in a renewed literary interest in questions of identity and belonging. Yet there was another diffusive force that surreptitiously eroded customary notions of identity: as the 1980s had ravaged Britain's industrial basis, capital increasingly came to rely on profit from intangible goods – brands, symbols and cultural products. Literary fictions and the identities they shaped and interrogated increasingly came to operate within a marketplace that was rapidly colonising British culture. Indeed, the famed instability of identity is not just an aloof theoretical point, but a key feature of British writing and identity formation in the lukewarm interval between the onslaught of neoliberalism under Thatcher and its rebranding as Cool Britannia.

The erosion of national industries offered the backdrop for a resurgence of Scottish writing. Irving Welsh's 1993 debut novel *Trainspotting* illustrates the entanglement of identity affirmation and cultural consumption particularly well. The novel evokes the life world of a group of Edinburgh heroin users, whose diminished lives, as the title suggests, are reduced to that of passive bystanders, as the progress promised by modern industrialisation (symbolised by the train) has long passed them by. The novel is written in non-standard English, which is not to say that it is a straightforward expression of an authentic vernacular experience; in fact, the novel's language combines a transcribed (and thus less than authentic) Edinburgh vernacular, working-class demotic, various subcultural elements, as well as standard English. The characters' experience is thoroughly saturated by a globalised popular culture. The novel opens on a scene in which Mark Renton, the novel's main narrator, and his friend Sick Boy are watching a Jean-Claude Van Damme movie: 'As happens in such movies, they started oaf wi an obligatory dramatic opening. Then the next phase ay the picture involved building up the tension through introducing the dastardly villain and sticking the weak plot thegither.'[2] This insight into the genericity of such rote cultural products does not serve as a metafictional device that elevates the narrator or the novel above popular culture, but only as an index of that culture's pervasiveness. The novel's Scottishness, that is, is a thoroughly 'Americanised Scottishness' that makes it more easily accessible for broad audiences.[3] This is not unlike the strategy deployed in Nick Hornby's 1995 novel *High Fidelity*, whose narrator, music snob Rob Fleming, fills his story of relational alienation with pop-cultural signifiers and intermittent top five lists ('five best side one track ones of all time'! 'Top five subtitled films'!).[4] Rather than testifying to neurotic self-obsession, this display of cultural saturation ultimately comes to restore Rob's romantic relationship and his professional identity (as a DJ rather than a small record shop owner); at the same time, this curatorial (and inescapably backward-looking) mode invites readers to indulge their own cultural savvy. Already in 1992, Hornby's football fan memoir *Fever Pitch*, about his life as an Arsenal fan, had repurposed that other key vernacular of 1990s Britain, English football, as a marker of cool and a signifier of switched-on masculinity.

The afterlife of *Trainspotting* would bear out this pop cultural reach: the 1996 film version and the white and orange aesthetic of its posters became popular icons, while Welsh himself became a celebrity in Britain's booming magazine culture, which often promoted an anti-intellectual, alcohol-fuelled culture of 'laddism'. Such commercialisation does not equal outright diminishment, neither for *Trainspotting*'s characters nor for Welsh's literary project. For all the brutality, squalor and madness, the lives of the novel's skagboys intimate a tentative sense of togetherness and community – which is significant in the wake of Thatcher's infamous declaration that 'there is no such thing as society', only 'individual men and women' and 'families'.[5] Welsh himself continued to write challenging fiction: his 1998 novel *Filth* features the voice of a tapeworm, which also typographically comes to disturb the story of its host, the psychotic Detective Sergeant Bruce Robertson. If the silly text balloons in which this voice is captured save this playful device from high modernist seriousness, they yet evince Welsh's resistance to the easy consumption of his literary voices as authentic expressions of a particular ethos and identity.

Such an intimation of a sense of community that cuts across traditional families and social categories also emerges in Alan Warner's 1995 debut *Morvern Callar*. The novel begins with a radical evisceration of the couple form, as the eponymous protagonist, a young supermarket employee, wakes up next to the corpse of her boyfriend, who has committed suicide (and is ominously referred to as a capitalised 'He' and 'Him'). The result is a sense of release – 'He couldnt object so I lit a Silk Cut' – that yet remains vague: 'A sort of wave of something was going across me.'[6] Morvern walks out on her life in a remote Highland sea-port town and makes her way through the European rave scene – a trajectory sustained by her deadpan, blank and decidedly cool interior monologue. Morvern's short, clipped sentences record the actions of the omnipresent 'I', yet the story reaches out for a sense of togetherness beyond the death of 'Him'. The final scene finds Morvern 'all sicked up on [a] church floor' – a church, we assume, left evacuated by 'Him' – pregnant with '[t]he child of the raves', with 'both hands on [her] tummy at the life there, the life growing right there'. Morvern ends the novel by accepting this life, which the novel refers to as 'queerly familiar'.[7]

In a monologue made famous by the band Underworld on the *Trainspotting* soundtrack, Mark Renton formulates a comparable commitment to a somewhat queered life – a life of unemployment and excess in which traditional templates for masculinity have been rendered inoperative: 'Choose us. Choose life. Choose mortgage payments; choose washing machines; choose cars; choose sitting oan a couch ... Choose life. Well, ah choose no tae choose life. If the cunts cannae handle that, it's thair fuckin problem ... ah jist intend tae keep right on to the end of the road.'[8] Just as for Morvern, this constitutes a vague commitment rather than a definite plan, as becomes clear in Warner's beautiful train wreck of a sequel to *Morvern Callar*, *These Demented Lands* (1998), which finds Morvern on a Scottish island, surrounded by a cast of quasi-allegorical characters in a symbolically resonant landscape. Somehow, the child conceived in the early 1990s is finally born at the consummation of the millennium and is referred to as 'the Messiah';[9] the bloated symbolism is as much a mark of Warner's grandiose ambition as of the provisional nature of fiction's imagined alternatives to a demented society.

Like Morvern, the protagonist of James Kelman's Booker-Prize-winning *How Late It Was, How Late* (1994) wakes up in a 'queerly familiar' place: hungover, without a clear memory of the previous days, and wearing strange clothes on the streets of Glasgow (and not even knowing yet that his partner has left him), Sammy gets into a fight with two 'sodjers' (policemen), gets himself arrested and discovers he has become blind. Kelman's third-person stream-of-consciousness adopts a Glaswegian working-class accent, and it is more seriously committed to authentically rendering a raw vernacular experience (which is also Kelman's own, as a working-class Glaswegian who left school at the age of 15) than Warner's or Welsh's voices. The novel signals its resistance to commodification on its very first pages, when it shows how the defeated Sammy becomes part of an urban spectacle catering to 'tourists' or 'strangers to the city for some big fucking business event', 'courtesy of the town council promotion office', who consume the image of working-class debauchery as part of the gritty reality of city life.[10] The trope of blindness radically excludes Sammy, as the representative of working-class life, from such ocular consumption, and it allows Kelman to register his antagonism to the recuperation of working-class voices, cultures and experiences as part of the creative economy that began booming in the 1990s. The scene offers a surreptitious comment on Glasgow's status as a European Capital of Culture in 1990, which was just one example of a wave of inner-city renewal and city marketing that also radically altered the make-up and the demographics of places like Birmingham, Manchester and Cardiff. Such a capitalist colonisation of creativity, Kelman suggests, even converts suffering into a commodity (which is not to say that *How Late It Was, How Late* is not itself repackaging economic deprivation and social marginalisation as an experience to be consumed). The same antagonistic logic was on display in the controversy besetting the novel's election for the Booker Prize, in which one jury member and parts of the press objected to the vulgarity of the novel's language (especially its generous use of four-letter words) and the marginality and squalor of the life-world it depicted. The jury member complained that 'Kelman is deeply inaccessible for a lot of people',[11] showing that the literary field continued to resist a demotic writing style that stubbornly declines its unwritten rules.

This is not to say that that the literary field cannot accommodate difference: in between the seminal achievements of Salman Rushdie's *The Satanic Verses* (1988) and Zadie Smith's *White Teeth* (2000), the 1990s saw an increasing mainstreaming of ethnically diverse British writing. In his Booker Prize Acceptance Speech, Kelman situates his own working-class fiction as 'part of a much wider process – or movement – towards decolonisation and self-determination', a 'tradition' that assumes '[t]he validity of indigenous culture' and defends 'against cultural assimilation'.[12] That ethnic – and, as we will see, sexual – diversity were much more easily absorbed by the literary field than the non-middle-class experiences Kelman records testifies to the existence of different differences in a literary marketplace that found it easier to accommodate cultural diversity than class difference.

In Hanif Kureishi's 1990 novel *The Buddha of Suburbia*, ethnic differences are playful signifiers rather than stable identities. Having become a reluctant spokesperson for Asian Britain in the 1980s on the strength of successful plays and films like *My Beautiful Laundrette*, Kureishi launches his first novel as an exuberant refusal of a role 'as public relations officer, as hired liar'.[13] Instead, we get the messy and amusing complexity of the life of Karim, the novel's narrator of a mixed British and Indian background, and his father Haroon. Both are picaresque characters: Karim notes that his father 'taught [him] to flirt with everyone [he] met, girls and boys alike' and to see 'charm' as 'the primary social grace', a capacity that leads Haroon to a gig as a kind of therapeutic healer and to a marriage-destroying affair.[14] Both achievements, however questionable, capitalise on Haroon's ethnic identity. Most of the novel consists of the story of Karim's *Bildung*, which takes him from his South London suburb to London (with a dejected detour through New York), and which sees him aspire to a career in the theatre. This occupation is no coincidence: it underlines Kureishi's investment (echoing that of Rushdie in *The Satanic Verses*) in the volatile nature of identity – as something to be enacted rather than inherited. Still, this changeability is thwarted by hegemonic expectations and stereotypes, as Karim finds himself typecast as Mowgli in *The Jungle Book* because he is 'dark-skinned ... small and wiry'.[15] Forcing a loin-cloth and brown make-up on him, the producer reminds him he is 'cast for authenticity and not for experience'.[16] If the production gives Karim a first whiff of success, it leaves him open to criticism from his friend Jamila, who finds the play's depiction of race relations 'completely neo-fascist' and 'disgusting'.[17] If different identities are on offer, then, they are not necessarily compatible.

For all its brashness and humour, *The Buddha* remains ultimately undecided about the liberating potential of identity performances. The most
important element in the novel's famous opening sentence – 'My name is
Karim Amir, and I am an Englishman born and bred, almost'[18] – is not the
quaint obsolete Britishness of the phrase 'born and bred' or the clear echo of
Saul Bellow's *The Adventures of Augie March*, a resonance that yet underlines the importance of American literature and culture for Karim; it is the
'almost' that points to a residue of liberty and open-endedness, to a certain
freedom to escape birth and breeding, or indeed the compulsive force of
language suggested by the alliteration. Even if Karim finds himself slotted in
an identitarian niche, the novel gestures to the indeterminate yet essentially
open-ended forces of pop music and sexuality – to, that is, vibes, styles and
experiences rather than vision. It is pop music that allows Karim's teenage
crush Charlie to reinvent himself as a punk; it allows Karim and his later
girlfriend Eleanor to come together; and it allows the young Karim to
negotiate his own Englishness by 'study[ing] *Melody Maker* and *NME*'.[19]
Pop culture is not just an occasion for consumption (as in Welsh), for ecstasy
(as in Warner) or for snobbism (as in Hornby), but for cultural negotiation.
Apart from its investment in pop music, the novel also infamously represents
bisexuality and promiscuity; still, it registers its scepticism about the liberating potential of sexual and musical experience by ending at the election in
1979 – the election that would jumpstart the neoliberalisation of British
society.

This scepticism extends to Kureishi's 1995 novel *The Black Album*. Like
The Buddha, *The Black Album* drops its protagonist, Shahid Hasan, in
London; yet the earlier novel's flexible, smart and lively first-person narration makes way for a more didactic and analytical third-person perspective
(and such a sparse and gritty mode is more typical of literary engagements
with multiculturalism in the 1990s than, say, the exuberance of Rushdie or
the formal experiments of Windrush generation novelists such as Sam Selvon
and Wilson Harris). *The Black Album* is a 'condition of England' novel, and
the condition is a complicated one. Hasan is confronted by the twin tempta-
tions of sexual and intellectual liberation – personified by his university
lecturer Deedee Osgood – and communitarian belonging – embodied by
a group of fundamentalist Muslims who, in the novel's 1989, gather to
burn a book that remains unnamed yet is clearly Salman Rushdie's *Satanic
Verses*. Five years after *The Black Album*, the famous Bradford demonstration against the publication of Rushdie's book would become the object of
good-natured satire in Zadie Smith's *White Teeth*, but Kureishi emphasises
that ignorant fundamentalism (a topic also explored in his 1998 film *My Son
the Fanatic*) is rooted in the social and identitarian ills that plague Britain.

Neither the unbearable whiteness of left-wing cultural politics nor the bigotry of religious fundamentalism are tenable existential options, yet the novel makes them visible as regrettable but understandable responses to a sense of disorientation and rootlessness. It is this rueful insight that makes the novel's official commitment to hybridity and plurality less than confident; if Shahid's post-coital surroundings strike him as full of 'sexual tension', 'enticement and fascination ... everywhere', this offers only a temporary enchantment, no solution.[20]

One of the novel's main emblems of hybridity is the musician Prince, from one of whose albums the book takes its title. Prince's protean racial, artistic and sexual identity stands for a mode of hybridity the novel cannot fully bring itself to believe in. In the year *The Black Album* was published, Britpop bands Blur and Oasis fought a cynically staged and artificially hyped chart battle by releasing major singles on the same day that not only sold records, but also a particular version of Englishness that was decidedly less hybrid than the one *The Black Album* wants to believe in. When New Labour comes to institute that image of British cool on a political level, London is no longer figured as the complex, maddeningly contradictory multicultural site of Kureishi's novels, but what the *Vanity Fair* article that coined the 'Cool Britannia' label called 'a city in glorious thrall to a thriving youth culture', 'the place to which we must all look to learn how to act, think, and dress'.[21] Anticipating this contrived consensus, *The Black Album* ends by investing love – the love of Shahid and Deedee – with whatever redemptive value remains, '[u]ntil it stops being fun'.[22] Significantly, Kureishi's next novel, *Intimacy* (1998), is a barely disguised autobiographical work that chronicles the writer's painful divorce.

Caryl Phillips's novels of the 1990s offer an account of the plurality of Britishness that is not sublimated as midlife crisis. Born in the West Indies, Phillips in the 1990s divided his time between his native St Kitts, England, where he was raised and educated, and the United States, where he would end up teaching. Phillips's fiction and essays situate the question of British belonging in a resolutely transcultural perspective (even if he maintains that his 'primary axis of frustration' invariably lies between the Caribbean and Britain[23]); as such, he radically explodes the category of Black British literature, which in the 1980s often served as a catch-all phrase to name writing by people of Asian, West Indian and African descent. Often opposed to postcolonial and migrant writing traditions, the term loses its coherence when confronted with the vast scope of Phillips's imagination and archival labour. This resolutely dispersed approach is especially on display in *The Nature of Blood* (1997), which juxtaposes (without quite interweaving) different narrative strands: the story of Eva, a traumatised survivor of a Nazi concentration camp; a retelling of the story of Othello; an account of anti-Semitic violence in fifteenth-century Italy; and the story of Gerry, a British soldier who asks Eva to marry him, which uncomfortably connects the novel's history of violence to British history (and thereby revises a triumphalist imperialist nostalgia centring on 'two world wars and one world cup'). The novel does not make the relations between black suffering and Jewish oppression explicit – as a work of what has been called 'comparison literature',[24] it provides reflection and engagement rather than causal explanations. Phillips's novels share this commitment with the stories of displacement of W. G. Sebald, a German author who taught at the University of East Anglia. If *The Emigrants* (1992; English 1996) juxtaposes four loosely related stories of (mostly Jewish) German exiles in the war-torn twentieth century, *The Rings of Saturn* (1995; English 1998) strings together different episodes in a planetary history of suffering through the narrator's walking tour through East Anglia: British imperialism, modern science, the Holocaust, but also environmental devastation – 'many ages are superimposed here and coexist'.[25] Sebald's signature combination of meandering text and photographs serves to foreground questions of evidentiality and documentary veracity.

The earlier *Crossing the River* (1993) already showcases Phillips's talent for arranging voices in ways that evoke (rather than determine) entangled histories of suffering – in this case, the dislocations suffered by people of colour who have nominally escaped slavery, yet remain constrained by racial oppression. Ranging from the mid-eighteenth century to the post-war period, and expanding its geographical scope from Africa over the United States to Britain, the novel is as epic in scope as *The Nature of Blood*, even if its ending more optimistically gestures towards a diasporic community. *Cambridge* (1991), which combines the voices of the eponymous slave and his English mistress Emily, also invokes the suffering of uprootedness – an intuition that, as we saw, compromises Kureishi's affirmation of hybridity and that is central to Phillips's work.

Phillips's historical fiction crystallises a number of concerns around the tenuous place of postmodernism in British literature. Postmodernism was always a foreign import in Britain: having been developed in response to American socioeconomic realities in the 1970s, it found little traction in Britain until Thatcherism brought British socioeconomic life in line with that in the United States.[26] And even then, a postmodern emphasis on disorientation, uncertainty and the proliferation of images was more often than not framed by a realist commitment, as in the work of Julian Barnes or Peter Ackroyd. Phillips's novels, for all their experiments with historical formats – diaries, testaments, journals, history books, official reports – consist of eminently accessible and realistic voices (even if it is the realism proper to the psyche of traumatised Holocaust survivors).

What is more, Phillips's interest in history dovetails with the remarkable popularity in the 1990s of historical fiction (see Chapter 9), even if his history of the present runs deeper and broader than that in, for instance, Kureishi's novels of the recent past (the 1970s in *The Buddha*, the 1980s in *The Black Album*) or a novel like Jonathan Coe's *What a Carve Up?* (1994), a satire of Thatcher's break-up of the nation narrated through the disintegration of the Winshaw clan that indulges in genre elements (slasher film, detective story, comedy, Gothic) in a much more playful way than Phillips's novels. Yet a characteristic of postmodernism is that the question of literary seriousness becomes properly undecidable, as revisions of the past become indistinguishable from 'pastiche' or an indulgence in eclecticism – a tendency compounded in the 1990s by the unprecedented alliances between literature, film and television, which further blur the boundaries between art and mass entertainment (see Chapter 10). The clearest example of such confusion outside the literary domain is the rise of the Young British Artists. Damien Hirst's *The Physical Impossibility of Death in the Mind of Someone Living* consists of a shark in formaldehyde in a vitrine, and the question of whether this is a serious engagement with art history, a canny gimmick, an investment vehicle for art collector Charles Saatchi or all of these things at once becomes properly unanswerable. Which is annoying, but which is, as we will see, not necessarily unproductive.

A. S. Byatt's Booker-Prize-winning *Possession* (1990) indulges in postmodern pastiche and metafictional sophistication, yet mobilises these stylistic features for a decidedly traditional literary project. The book, subtitled 'A Romance', tells the story of how two contemporary scholars of Victorian literature discover the illicit love affair between their scholarly objects, the (fictional) Victorian poets Randolph Ash and Christabel LaMotte, only to show how that love spills over into the sexual attraction between the two contemporary scholars. The novel not only riffs on the template of the romance (or, indeed, of the confident omniscience of the Victorian novel), but it also presents impressively convincing pastiches of Ash's and LaMotte's poetry, diaries and letters. The novel's plot evinces a strong commitment to the potency of literature, which is compounded by the negative portrayal of literary theory, academic pettiness and cynical reading modes that resist the pleasures of literature – and, the novel suggests, disable love. Love of literature, and especially for its capacity to vividly evoke the past, for Byatt, becomes a placeholder for love as such, and the association between literariness, historical difference and romance exemplifies how British postmodernism often domesticates metafiction as nostalgic bookishness.

Byatt's later *The Biographer's Tale* (2000) tells the story of a Phineas G. Nanson, a graduate student who abandons the mortifying austerities of literary theory for the supposedly more visceral rewards of the study of biography; again, the textual nature of this interest does not spoil its reality effect (Phineas turns to biography because he feels 'an urgent need for a life full of *things* ... the shining *solidity* of a world full of facts'[27]), as his life comes to repeat the patterns of the life of the author he studies. Metatextual sophistication, again, comes to inform a keener sense of historical reality. This investment in pleasurable experiences of historical difference (which override metafictional scepticism) is ultimately not very different from the projects of two other mildly metafictional Booker-Prize-winning historical novel projects. Pat Barker's *Regeneration* trilogy (*The Ghost Road*, the third instalment, won the Booker in 1995) centres on a shell-shock treatment hospital during the First World War, where experimental psychiatrist W. H. R. Rivers treats, among others, poets Wilfred Owen and Siegfried Sassoon. The novels' reliance on written accounts of the war and the history of psychiatry (also, anachronistically, on elements that post-date the events depicted), while foregrounding textual mediation, also augment their reality effect. Especially in the first novel in the trilogy, the focus on trauma – a term that names a sudden, overwhelming, immediate experience that yet withdraws from clear knowledge – overrides concerns over historical authenticity and scepticism over the power of language to capture the horrors of war (much as the focus on love bridges historical distance in *Possession*).

Canadian author Michael Ondaatje's 1992 *The English Patient* similarly de-glamorises war through a revision of masculine ideals by centring on the mutilated, denationalised and immobilised body of a mysterious patient in the aftermath of the Second World War. Metafictional shifts and often classical intertexts (turning the Italian landscape into a palimpsest rather than a secure background) destabilise the account of a patient who turns out not to be English, but rather Almásy, a Hungarian who has collaborated with both British and German forces, and, like the rest of the scarred characters assembled in an Italian villa, has overcome national belonging. This transcendence is a curse as much as it is a liberation; it leads Kip, a servant of Indian descent, to almost kill Almásy in response to news about the bombing of Hiroshima, reasoning that '[w]hen you start bombing the brown races of the world, you're an Englishman' – which means that the non-English English patient is guilty by association after all.[28] The amnesic, traumatised body at the centre of the novel recalls Barker's mobilisation of trauma, while the painstaking reconstruction of his story through diaries (sometimes morphine-induced), memories and other forms of evidence combined with an authoritative omniscient narrator recalls Byatt's approach, as does the uncynical belief in the love-generating force of literature: Almásy's love for Katherine, the love of his life, is triggered by her voice as she reads aloud from *Paradise Lost* – an event that all at once turns him into a lover of literature. It was a small step, then, for the immensely successful movie adaptation to twist a metafictional text into a consummate love story.

The work of Jeanette Winterson tests the possibilities of postmodern form for more daring explorations of sexuality and gender. If her novels from the 1980s (especially *Oranges Are Not the Only Fruit* [1985] and *Sexing the Cherry* [1989]) already used playful postmodern techniques – fantasy and time travel, fairy tales and intertextuality – to unsettle gender norms and make visible a queer sexuality, her novels of the 1990s even more ambitiously position these concerns in terms of the struggle between literature and competing intellectual frameworks. *Written on the Body* is organised around the (somewhat too emphatically proclaimed) conceit of a genderless narrator, forcing readers to suspend their customary projection of gender stereotypes. Such a denaturalisation of extant categories and a search for novel discourses of the body inform the account of the narrator's affair with Louise, which ends when Louise's leukaemia forces her to return to her oncologist husband. If Ondaatje uses the traumatised body to invite the inscription of other people's stories, Winterson shows how a traumatised narrator draws on anatomic discourse to inscribe a diseased body it can no longer possess. The narrator begins to study anatomy, and '[w]ithin the clinical language, through the dispassionate view of the sucking, sweating, greedy, defecating self', the novel recovers 'a love-poem to Louise'.[29] At once lyrical and analytical, scientific and erotic, *Written on the Body* updates the history of romance to make room for the materialist language of biology and medicine. In this respect, it resembles Jim Crace's 1999 novel *Being Dead*, which reconstructs the love story of a couple of 'doctors of zoology' who are randomly killed on the beach and intertwines it with a surprisingly tender account of the disintegration of their bodies and their intermingling with dead matter.[30] The entanglement of human love and biological decomposition paradoxically offers what Crace calls '[a] narrative of comfort for atheists'[31] – the comfort that death is not the end, but simply more life, even if that life is no longer human.

Winterson's 1997 novel *Gut Symmetries* is even more intellectually promiscuous. It draws on post-Newtonian physics – string theory, quantum physics – and other explanatory thought systems – tarot cards, alchemy – to map the warped spaces in which gut meets GUT: the love triangle between Alice, Jove and Stella at the heart of the story is imbricated with the scientific ambition to draw up a General Unified Theory of everything. The different theories expound the unpredictability and instability of things: 'What should be stable, shifts. What I am told is solid, slips.'[32] Such volatility makes it possible for Alice and Stella to suddenly feel attracted to each other in what is the erotic equivalent of a quantum event. As in *Written on the Body*, Winterson enlists scientific discourses to design a new sensual language, one that codes sexuality and gendered life as fluid processes rather than fixed realities. Even if Winterson's novel is a much more playful and ironic exercise, this interest in the resonances between literature and science recurs in Nicholas Mosley's bewildering *Hopeful Monsters* (1990). The novel, the fifth and most celebrated part of Mosley's *Catastrophe Practice* series, covers nothing less than the main scientific, philosophical and sociopolitical shifts of the twentieth century. Much more cerebral than Winterson's work, the novel is nevertheless obsessed with the question of how to wrestle a residue of indeterminacy and freedom from a universe that becomes increasingly predictable and knowable – to find what the novel, in a term borrowed from evolutionary biology, calls a 'hopeful monster': a creature 'born perhaps slightly before [its] time', and thus offering a possible relief from the waste and loss that besets natural selection.[33] The experiment remains confined to salamanders, and there is little that indicates the sober comfort that a novel like *Being Dead* offers or the ecstasy that Winterson's fiction evokes.

A bio-literary experiment that tests the limits of sexuality and love: this is one way to characterise A. L. Kennedy's 1995 novel *So I Am Glad*. One of the freshest and most versatile voices to emerge from Scotland in the 1990s, Kennedy peoples her novels and short stories (she has also written drama, screenplays, and cultural and literary journalism, and is an accomplished stand-up comedian) with 'the emotionally and politically disenfranchised and dispossessed'.[34] *So I Am Glad* is narrated by Jennifer, a young woman who is disturbingly unemotional and uninvolved – 'unable to share in the emotional payoff, to feel the benefits of close company and sex'.[35] Yet the novel forces this unlikely test subject into a love relationship with a reincarnation of the seventeenth-century French writer and duelist Cyrano De Bergerac – an encounter between natural limitation and supernational invention that strains the protocols of human romance as we thought we knew it. The novel underlines that Jennifer's lack of emotion is a material fact – she imagines emotions as a colony of moles, a reference to Bergerac's quaint theory of 'universal mitology', which surmises that the human is basically a colony of smaller animals, but also to the molecules that make up humans' animal DNA.[36] The story, in other words, becomes a lab for the encounter of not-quite-human forces and desires. The result is that the narrator's deadpan and flat registration of events paradoxically activates a sense of affective unease and humour that exceeds the traditional emotional portfolio of the romance novel – the protocols of 'being furious and chipper, nostalgic, nauseous, glum and all the rest'.[37]

Kennedy's stories often generate a sense of intimacy through the power of fiction, lying or deceit, and through narrators' overt manipulation of information (as in the blending of past and present in her first novel, *Looking for the Possible Dance* [1993]).

As the novel ends on a metafictional twist that destabilises the parameters of the experiment that constitutes it, readers realise that the story, for all its ontological instability, has nevertheless performed its magic, and that they themselves have been part of this provisional affective community. In Kennedy's third novel, *Everything You Need* (1999), writing (and reading) serve as activities that bring an estranged father and his daughter together, which converts the text of the novel into an extended declaration of love. This mode of operation recalls the work of Janice Galloway, which similarly features emotionally derelict female characters – on a road trip to France reminiscing about dysfunctional past relationships (in *Foreign Parts* [1994]) or stuck in an armchair and almost too depressed to muster the courage to survive (in *The Trick Is to Keep Breathing* [1989]). As in Kennedy, wry humour and the creative potential of language (in the case of Galloway, often through collage and typographical experimentation) allow the novels (and, more conditionally, also the characters) to escape their emotional stultification. If Galloway's writing is, to adopt Winterson's phrase, writing 'on the body', it also involves overwriting the always already inscribed female body. In her first novel, for instance, Joy Stone, the main character, becomes anorexic and bulimic as a response to the gendered social injunction to be sexually attractive; the novel confronts this condition by mobilising the material elements of the literary text through the emphasis on irregular typography and various textual formats.

Imagining romance at the border of the human (in Kennedy) or patriarchy (in Galloway), and unflinchingly imagining forms of sexual violence, these novels find a tonality that is capacious and intractable rather than simply lukewarm or cool – and much too unsettling to be straightforwardly British or Scottish. The variety and intensity of literary production on the British islands in the 1990s testifies to a sense of disorientation that is both aesthetic and political. Aesthetic, in that the customary templates of, for instance, Black British writing and working-class fiction had lost traction, and the protocols of postmodernity often proved stale upon arrival. Political, in that the ascent of neoliberalism was, for most of the decade, not yet consolidated as a Third Way one could confidently join or oppose, and was more often celebrated for its role in revitalising Britain's creative industries than criticised for furthering the erosion of the post-war consensus. If the 1990s are indeed 'the most politically tedious decade in living memory',[38] their literary fiction is a rare place where that tedium is rendered memorable at all.

Notes

1. D. Kamp, 'London Swings! Again!', *Vanity Fair* (March 1997).
2. I. Welsh, *Trainspotting* (London: Vintage, 1999), p. 3.
3. R. Walkowitz, 'The Post-Consensus Novel: Minority Culture, Multiculturalism, and Transnational Comparison' in Robert Caserio (ed.), *The Cambridge Companion to the Twentieth-Century English Novel* (Cambridge University Press, 2009), p. 228.
4. N. Hornby, *High Fidelity* (New York: Riverhead Books, 2000), pp. 147 and 28.
5. D. Keay, 'Margaret Thatcher Interviewed in Women's Own' (1987), *Margaret thatcher.org.*
6. A. Warner, *Morvern Callar* (London: Vintage, 1996), p. 1.
7. *Ibid.*, pp. 227–9.
8. Warner, *Morvern Callar*, p. 187.
9. A. Warner, *These Demented Lands* (London: Vintage, 1998), p. 212.
10. J. Kelman, *How Late It Was, How Late* (London: Vintage, 1998), p. 2.
11. R. Winder, 'Highly Literary and Deeply Vulgar: If James Kelman's Booker Novel Is Rude, It Is in Good Company', *The Independent* (13 October 1994).
12. J. Kelman, 'Elitists Slurs Are Racism by Another Name', *Scotland on Sunday: Spectrum Supplement* (16 October 1994), p. 2.
13. H. Kureishi, 'Dirty Washing', *Time Out*, 795 (1985), p. 26.
14. H. Kureishi, *The Buddha of Suburbia* (London: Faber & Faber, 1990), p. 7.
15. *Ibid.*, p. 142.
16. *Ibid.*, p. 147.
17. *Ibid.*, p. 157.
18. *Ibid.*, p. 1.
19. *Ibid.*, p. 8.
20. H. Kureishi, *The Black Album* (London: Faber & Faber, 1995), p. 124.
21. D. Kamp, 'London Swings! Again!', *Vanity Fair* (March 1997).
22. Kureishi, *The Black Album*, p. 276.
23. C. Phillips, 'Interview with Maya Jaggi' in Susheila Nasta (ed.), *Writing across Worlds: Contemporary Writers Talk* (London: Routledge, 2004), p. 122.
24. R. Walkowitz, 'Comparison Literature' (2009) 40(3) *New Literary History* 567–82.
25. W. G. Sebald, *The Rings of Saturn* (London: Harvill Press, 1998), p. 36.
26. J. Murphet, 'Fiction and Postmodernity' in Laura Marcus and Peter Nicholls (eds), *The Cambridge History of Twentieth-Century English Literature* (Cambridge University Press, 2004), pp. 716–35; see Chapter 7.
27. A. S. Byatt, *The Biographer's Tale* (London: Vintage, 2001), p. 4 (emphases in the original).
28. M. Ondaatje, *The English Patient* (London: Bloomsbury, 2004), p. 304.
29. J. Winterson, *Written on the Body* (London: Vintage, 2001), p. 111.
30. J. Crace, *Being Dead* (London: Penguin, 2000), p. 1.
31. A. Lawless, 'The Poet of Prose: Jim Crace in Interview', *Three Monkeys Online* (no date).
32. J. Winterson, *Gut Symmetries* (London: Granta, 1998), p. 10.
33. N. Mosley, *Hopeful Monsters* (Elmwood Park: Dalkey Archive, 2000), p. 71.

34. S. Dunnigan, 'A. L. Kennedy's Longer Fiction: Articulate Grace' in Aileen Christianson and Alison Lumsden (eds), *Contemporary Scottish Women Writers* (Edinburgh University Press, 2000), p. 154.

35. A. L. Kennedy, *So I Am Glad* (London: Vintage, 2004), p. 4.

36. O. de Graef, '"I Know He Knows I Know He Knows I Am": Suspension of Disbelief in A. L. Kennedy' (2014) 12(2) *Partial Answers* 355–74, 363.

37. Kennedy, *So I Am Glad*, p. 5.

38. L. Segall, 'Theoretical Afflictions: Poor Rich White Folks Play the Blues' (2003) 50 *New Formations* 142–56, 142.

3

LEIGH WILSON

Post-Millennial Literature

Literary critics face particular obstacles in thinking about and interpreting the novels with which they share a period. As Robert Eaglestone has noted, because the archive from which literary critics of the contemporary choose is constantly expanding, because we lack the perspective which retrospect brings, our criteria of selection tend to be based on subjects we have already chosen: 'we choose the themes ... and then find books that explore these themes'.[1] However, it is possible to see that the selection of themes and the subsequent claims made have reached something of a critical consensus in contemporary literary studies. For many critics, the contemporary novel has rejected a postmodern playfulness that draws attention to textuality and exhibits a scepticism about the nature of representation. Instead, it attempts to reattach itself to what is usually called 'the real'[2] and a new seriousness in narrowing the gap between fictional representation and the world around it.[3] Even those critics who see a continuation of some of the claims of postmodernist thought argue that these are being forced into relation with a more recent desire for the 'real'. For Daniel Lea, the contemporary novel is involved in a 'striving to marry the desire for the real with the legacy of postmodernism's fascination with the simulacral'.[4] These claims about a 'return to the real' have very often also involved a reassessment of the contemporary British novel's engagement with the conventions of realism. For many critics, novels since 2000 have acknowledged that no easy return to a classic realism is possible. Instead they argue that what many do is challenge the 'simple opposition' between realism and experiment.[5] In this chapter, I will not be suggesting that this reading of the post-millennial novel is mistaken. Writers themselves – in interviews, articles and essays – are articulating their aims and concerns in such terms.[6] Rather, I want to suggest that parallel to a desire for a return to the 'real' there runs an anxious awareness of the limits of the novel in achieving such a return.

The history of the relation between the fictionality of the novel and its ability to represent and crucially to shape the world is key in Benedict

Anderson's *Imagined Communities* (1983). Anderson's argument is that two printed forms – the novel and the daily newspaper – both of which came into being in the eighteenth century in Europe, were intimately related to the idea of nation as it developed in the same period. The precise relation between these printed forms and the nation is not always clear in Anderson's work, and has been the subject of debate, but what the link between them grants Anderson is the revelation that the nation, like the newspaper and the novel, is a fiction. The nation has to be imagined by those who would make up its members, and this imagining is both an analogue of and made possible by the fictive elements of the novel and the newspaper.[7] While the importance of the fictive nature of these forms for Anderson has been less commented on than other aspects of his argument, it suggests a more nuanced way of thinking about the contemporary novel's ability to represent the 'real'. For Anderson the novel is fictional in two key ways. First, the primary characteristic of books, in contrast to other commodities, is their existence as discrete objects, and therefore their characteristic fiction is that what they contain is both bounded and cohered into some kind of unity.[8] It is the case that, since the late 1990s, technology has made very different forms of fictional narrative acts possible beyond the conventional form of the book, but the digital novel – in the form of either a straightforward ebook or in terms of novels which utilise the flexibility of the digital to stretch the link between novel and book – has not really yet taken off, and remains a tiny part of the market in comparison to conventional books.[9] So the novel still largely shares this particular fiction of coherence with all books, but, and this is the second element of the novel's fictionality, it is augmented by something which brings further coherence in place of the spatial arrangement of the newspaper page – the narrator. The narrator of the novel, in Anderson's later gloss, is able to 'represent synchronically [a] bounded, intrahistorical society-with-a-future' beyond the ability of any actual human being to do so.[10] It is this which produces what Anderson calls in *Imagined Communities* the 'meanwhile' of the novel;[11] the novel's ability, that is, through the coherence of its physical form and the coherence of its narrative act, to represent and to assert the 'real' of the world as one of coherence and connection. In *Imagined Communities* and in later works, Anderson, like many critics who have developed his argument, deviates from this insight into the effects of the novel's key form to discussion of the way that the content of novels links them to ideas of nation. However, some critics have kept this question of form to the forefront. For Timothy Brennan, in an influential chapter first published in Homi Bhabha's *Nation and Narration*, it is the novel as a 'composite but clearly bordered work of art', rather than any specific contents, which constitutes its link to the creation of nation.[12] Jonathan

Culler's reconsideration of the implications of Anderson's argument for literary critics also makes this point: 'The most important feature of the novel for Anderson's claim seems to be a narrative technique.'[13]

In *Imagined Communities*, it is for Anderson the 'old-fashioned novel'[14] that produces the simultaneity of place and time necessary to the creation of the 'meanwhile'. However, critics continue to use the implications of Anderson's 'meanwhile' to think about novels very far from the 'old fashioned'.[15] For these critics, contemporary novelists are continuing the important role of coherent imagining ascribed to them by Anderson. They acknowledge of course the pressures that the post-millennial world exerts on such a role. The world since the millennium has seen the destructive rise of populist nationalisms, numerous acts of genocide, the challenge to the nation-state from supra national forces, whether of global capital or religious fundamentalism, migration, the speedy rise in the power and effects of digital technology, and the planetary scale of climate change. If Anderson's 'meanwhile' is predicated on an act of fictional telling which, however intricate and self-aware, remains coherent through the object of the book and the very act of telling, the forces listed above are predicated precisely on an undoing of these. In other words, the forces which many critics have seen as ending postmodernism and as returning the novel to the 'real' are the very forces which also threaten the form of the novel. In the rest of this chapter I will suggest a variety of ways that these challenges to the form of the novel from the post-millennial world, while pushing novelists towards the representation of various types of 'real', have also been a significant challenge to the narrative acts which constitute the form.

The 'We' of *On Beauty*

Anderson's 'meanwhile' is crucially linked to the construction of a 'we'. Readers of novels and members of nations are able to share a plural yet unified subject position with those distant and unknown through the cohering work of the novel. Zadie Smith's *On Beauty* (2005) is alive to the ethical questions that surround the 'we' in the post-millennial world, but through the novel's narrative acts it clearly attempts such a coherence. As she makes clear in her acknowledgements, Smith attempts this through a rewriting of E. M. Forster's *Howards End* (1910).[16] Both novels represent their contemporary social milieu as riven with divisions – of class, wealth, education, ethnicity, politics, gender – through the interactions of two families, the Wilcoxes and the Schlegels in *Howards End*, the Belseys and the Kipps in *On Beauty*. The epigraph to Forster's novel urges us famously to 'only connect', and for both Forster and Smith the novel is a place in which not just to represent division, but to enact a connection and shared collectivity that is at the heart of

Anderson's 'meanwhile'. It is noticeable, however, that an analogue for the primary act of connection achieved in Forster's novel – the marriage between Henry Wilcox and Margaret Schlegel – is missing from *On Beauty*. This does not mean, though, that the achievement of such a connection is eschewed in *On Beauty*. Rather, the aspect of Forster's novel it repeats is the particular form of Forster's narrator: third person, insistent, prone to making what Frank Kermode has called 'announcements'.[17] It is, though, precisely in this repetition that *On Beauty*'s struggles with the 'we' can be most clearly seen.

On Beauty is set mostly on the campus of a liberal arts college on the east coast of the United States. Its protagonists are a couple – Howard Belsey, white and British, who teaches at the college, and Kiki Simmonds, an African-American nurse. The novel follows them and their children through scenarios which are produced in particular by the divisive legacies of colonialism, but the narrator from the beginning is a vehicle for connection and coherence. The opening scenes all deal with Howard and Kiki's eldest son, Jerome – who is in London living with and working for Howard's nemesis, Montague Kipps – and his brief affair with Kipps's daughter, Victoria. Chapter 4 ends with the awkwardness of Howard's trip to London to persuade Jerome against marrying Victoria. Despite these divisions, the narrator tells us at the beginning of chapter 5: 'We must now jump nine months forward, and back across the Atlantic.'[18] This narratorial 'we' articulates exactly the temporal and spatial connection across division and difference that is implied in Anderson's 'meanwhile', and explicitly claims the 'meanwhile' not just within a nation, but between nations.

Elsewhere, however, assertions by the narrator of 'truths' supposedly acknowledged by us all begin to reveal the problematic nature of the 'real' and of the narrator's creation of the 'meanwhile'. Some of these assertions are clearly ventriloquisms of a character's belief as is usual in free indirect discourse, but the claims are always left unchallenged by either the narrator or the events of the novel. Chapter 4, for example, begins: 'When it comes to the weather, New Englanders are delusional.'[19] The next sentence is explicitly about Howard's own experience, but utterly confirms rather than in any way ironises the preceding general claim. Frank Kermode, in his review of the novel, does justify such techniques as ironic acts of ventriloquism which serve to challenge or destabilise their truth claims.[20] Dorothy Hale, extending his claim, argues that such assertions in *On Beauty* are Smith's way of working out the tensions between her assertion of the voice of the author and the novel's ethical desire to acknowledge and represent the experiences and voices of others.[21] The 'we' claims of the narrator avoid the danger of drowning out the other, Hale claims, because they 'potentially emanate from three different enunciatory scenarios'. They are the views 'issued by an omniscient narrator who expresses the opinions of the author', they ventrilo-quise a character, as Kermode argues, and they bring 'a poetic quality that stands out from the rest of the prose'.[22] However, what is key about all these aphorisms – whether they are ventriloquised or not – is that they are meant to be shared, by the narrator, the character and the reader. Near the end of the novel, Kiki, who has throughout been deciding on whether or not to leave Howard after learning of his adultery, is sorting through her children's old belongings in the storeroom. She packs things no longer needed in bin bags as she thinks about her family and her marriage. The bags split: 'She had packed them too heavy. The greatest lie ever told about love is that it sets you free.'[23] That characters we are supposed to identify and sympathise with, such as Kiki, have banal thoughts does not undermine or ironise the thought within the narrative economy of *On Beauty*. The banality is the point. It is what *can* be shared.

This assumption of shared experience and assertion of collectivity is familiar from Smith's first and most famous novel, *White Teeth* (2000). Dominic Head has noted that the earlier novel 'is artfully constructed as the definitive representation of twentieth-century British multiculturalism'.[24] In the years between the two novels, of course, the world changed. The difficulties these changes presented to Smith's favoured form of narrative construction, to its attempt to construct the 'we' of the 'meanwhile', is made visible in *On Beauty*.[25] If the overall effect of the narrative position of *On Beauty* is to assert a shared belief and experience through the repetition of things most likely to be shared, the contemporary impossibility of such an assertion is illustrated through scenes early in the novel where the 'real' of the post-millennial world intervenes. As can be seen in Anderson's later work on the novel and nation, the 'meanwhile' of the novel, its gathering, cohering function, is often represented thematically through the staging of a party and formally through the way such events are heard of and spoken about.[26] Near the beginning of *On Beauty*, Howard and Kiki throw a party to celebrate their thirtieth wedding anniversary. Earlier, as they invite people, the date of the party is never revealed to the reader, but when Kiki mentions it to her invitees it produces in them 'that tiny, involuntary shudder with which Kiki had, in recent years, become familiar'.[27] At the party itself Howard too is faced with reactions to its date.

> 'Strange date for it, though,' he heard somebody say. And then the usual response: 'Oh, I think it's a wonderful date for a party. You know it's their actual anniversary, so . . . And if we don't reclaim the day, you know . . . then it's like they've won. It's a reclaiming, absolutely.' This was the most popular conversation of the night. Howard had had it himself at least four times since

the clock struck ten and the wine had really kicked in. Before that no one liked to mention it.[28]

The party, it gradually dawns on the reader, takes place on 11 September, as had the Belseys' wedding thirty years before. The novel is set in 2003. The awkwardness around and therefore attention given to the date of the party is an indication of how important it is as a frame for the novel's own act of narration, but also how it blocks the narrator's ability to make 'announcements' that are easily shared. The overheard party conversation produces 'we' truth claims from the guests of the same order as those of the narrator, but the usually loquacious narrator is silent about them, both in its own terms and in terms of any acts of ventriloquising. Neither Howard nor Kiki express an opinion about either the shudders or the conversations of their guests. Even more crucially, in clear contrast to the rest of the novel, in which the narrator never fails to inform, share and include, at this point the reader is held at arm's length. While in *On Beauty*, as in many, many novels through the history of the European novel, a party acts as an attempt to literalise the 'meanwhile' of the novel form as such – from the picnic on Box Hill in *Emma* (1815) to the party at the end of *Mrs Dalloway* (1925) – the date of Howard and Kiki's party brings awkwardness not just to the guests, but to the narrator's position and the coherence of the novel.

The 'Meanwhile' and Digital Technology

Mieke Bal has argued that the possible obsolescence of the novel (and the newspaper) is due in part to the fact that 'if any medium works by means of "meanwhile", it is the Internet, that enemy of the novel'.[29] The meanwhile of the internet does not, however, work to fortify the nation-state: 'Instead, arguably it mitigates, perhaps even destroys, it. As a result new imagined communities emerge based on all manner of communities. No generalizations about what "meanwhile" connects seem possible at this time.'[30] Scepticism about the nature of this new 'meanwhile' has also been recently voiced by the novelist and essayist John Lanchester. In a *London Review of Books* article, he has argued that the 'filter bubbles' of social media mean that '[o]ur conception of "we" is becoming narrower', and that the subsequent fragmentation is directly responsible for the phenomena of 'fake news' and 'post-truth' which, he argues, 'were made possible by the retreat from a general agora of public debate into separate ideological bunkers'.[31] While cultural work and theoretical positions designated as postmodern celebrated the demise of a grand 'meanwhile' and replaced it with numerous smaller ones, the internet, according to Lanchester, shows that this might lead not to positive multiplicity, but to a destructive fragmentation. If the narrator is the central producer of the 'meanwhile' of the novel, the possible challenge to the creation of the 'meanwhile' that comes from digital technology, and any possible resistance, must be looked for, then, in the narrative acts of post-millennial novels.

David Mitchell's *Ghostwritten* (1999) consists of interlocking stories – nine, plus one at the end which reprises all those preceding it – set in various locations around the world. The chapter titles name these locations – 'Okinawa', 'Tokyo', 'Hong Kong' and so on. All are narrated in the first person (apart from the ninth, 'Night Train', which consists entirely of dialogue) by a wide variety of characters who ostensibly have little to do with one another. Unlike Mitchell's later novel, *Cloud Atlas* (2004), in which individual chapters are temporally, spatially and generically very different, but are connected through a clear patterning, the narrators of *Ghostwritten* are separated by place, culture and language in a way that is not easily cohered and would seem to strain the construction of the 'meanwhile'. However, rather than asserting the breakdown of narrative coherence and the celebration of multiple stories against the grand narratives, Rita Barnard, in her consideration of *Ghostwritten*, has described the novel's mode as that of the 'hyperlink' which produces 'a kind of synthetic or sutured omniscience that transcends any single individual's experience and spans *Ghostwritten*'s disjunct mise-en-scenes'.[32] This is an indication of the importance of digital technology for the narrative coherence of Mitchell's novel. However, its particular use of the 'hyperlink' not only makes possible a new kind of omniscience; it also threatens the place of the novel as the pre-eminent form of the construction of the 'meanwhile'. In Mitchell's novel the 'meanwhile', as well as being an effect of formal construction, is a character who represents a globalised digital technology as both saviour and nemesis.

The multiple stories in the novel are intricately interwoven: the narrators of each chapter appear as minor characters in others. Indeed, the structure of Mitchell's novel, while describable as one of hyperlinks, is also a repetition of episode 10 of James Joyce's *Ulysses* (1922), 'Wandering Rocks'. What is different in Mitchell's novel, however, are the implications of his version of this structure for the 'meanwhile'. In 'Wandering Rocks', the various stories are held together by time and space – they occur simultaneously between 3pm and 4pm on the streets of Dublin on 16 June 1904 – but also, beyond this, the stories are held together by a narrative position that mimics the 'mechanical eye' of the film camera. From above, it pans Dublin. It is significant of course that in *Ulysses*, at the moment of modernist re-evaluation, the 'meanwhile' of the novel could also not be taken for granted – it needed the extra-literary terms and tropes of film in order to work. In *Ghostwritten* the ability of the novel to provide the 'meanwhile' is even less secure. The 'mechanical eye' is literalised in the world of the novel in its attempt to reassert the possibility of authoritative narration and the connectivity of the 'meanwhile'. It is turned into a character whose first-person narration is able to connect and cohere.

One of the voices involved in the dialogues that constitute chapter 9, 'Night Train', is an AI who has been programmed with four laws – versions of the three laws of robotics developed by the science fiction writer Isaac Asimov in the 1940s[33] – which mean that it cannot harm humans and must actively work to protect them. While the AI is not the single narrator of this story (the story's narrator is a kind of recording machine, more akin to the camera eye of 'Wandering Rocks'), it is a kind of narrator of the world. The AI moves through 'ultrawave transmission' and uses satellites to view events all around the globe; it enters computer programmes and internet sites in order to carry out its global duties.[34] Its ability to see and know all is supposed to enable the world to operate coherently and to achieve justice.[35]

The AI calls a late-night phone-in show on a New York radio station, Night Train FM, and the DJ, who it is using as a kind of confessor, names it Zookeeper. It is in the conversations between the DJ and Zookeeper that the threat of such an achievement of coherence becomes clear. 'Night Train' ends with the DJ signing off his show after a night in which the world has celebrated the aversion of nuclear disaster which the reader knows was down to the AI's intervention. Unbeknown to the DJ, however, his conversation with the AI during the night has convinced it to let a comet destroy the world as the only way for it to keep all of its four laws. The narrative coherence made possible by the AI's omniscience is finally the cause of apocalypse.

The structure of *Ghostwritten* is in the end ambiguous about the desirability of coherence, however. The narrative of the novel is circular – chapter 10 returns to the topic and narrator of chapter 1, and the final words take us back to the novel's beginning – so appearing to alleviate anxieties about apocalyptic endings and to achieve a formal coherence, but the present of the final chapter is before the events of 'Night Train'. Within the present of 'Night Train', though, the continuing existence of the familiar tugs against the knowledge of impending disaster. As the sun rises over New York, the DJ signs off his show with much narrative irony, yet the possibility of the familiar and safe remains: 'The stars are going out over Staten Island, and Night Train FM is pulling in to a new morning.'[36]

Cohering narratives abound in Tom McCarthy's *Satin Island* (2015), but in the end the novel's own narrative form eschews safe spaces either of circularity or the familiarity of Staten Island. McCarthy's first-person narrator, known only as 'U', is an anthropologist who works for a shady corporation – 'the Company' – whose work involves the construction of narrative fictions.[37] U's hero is the anthropologist Claude Lévi-Strauss, whose work he sees as a kind of supranational novel, taking the detail of human culture and linking it to a larger system which lies 'behind not just a single tribe but also the larger one of all humanity'.[38] At the opening of the novel, the Company begins work on a project for an even shadier client, Koob-Sassen.[39] Although the exact nature of the project is kept mysterious by the narrator, his descriptions of it show that it has much in common with the internet as a kind of super-narrative: 'Koob-Sassen involved many hook-ups, interfaces, transpositions … It was a project formed of many other projects, linked to many other projects.'[40] At the same time, the narrator compiles numerous dossiers – on oil spills, on the deaths of parachutists, on shark attacks[41] – which he believes will eventually cohere and unite into the 'Great Report' that the Company wishes him to write: 'the Book. The First and Last Word on our age'.[42]

Anthropology, the Koob-Sassen Project and the 'Great Report' all stand in for another cohering narrative not actually mentioned in McCarthy's novel – that of the novel itself. U's anxiety about the unwritten 'Great Report' articulates questions about the possible form and shape of any novel that attempts to take on and respond to the realities of the contemporary world: 'It was all a question of form. What fluid, morphing hybrid could I come up with to be equal to that task? What medium, or media, would it inhabit? Would it tell a story? If so, how, and about what, or whom? If not, how would it all congeal, around what cohere?'[43] U comes to realise that the 'Great Report' is *unwritable*; it is 'unplottable, unframeable, unrealizable',[44] but then worries that it is not so much unwritable as already written. The cohering narrative of Zookeeper in *Ghostwritten* morphs into the existing possibilities of the internet itself. It is the internet that is the 'fluid, morphing hybrid' which connects and coheres:

> that tabulates and cross-indexes what we buy with who we know, and what they buy, or like, and with the other objects that are bought or liked by others who we don't know but with whom we cohabit a shared buying- or liking-pattern.[45]

If a cohering narrative can no longer be written by human beings, whether anthropologists or novelists, then it cannot be read by them either: 'Only another piece of software could do that.'[46] The truth of the world is beyond human telling, and narratives, when they exist, cannot be made to cohere meaningfully. The story U's girlfriend tells him about what happened to her in Genoa in 2001 when she was there as part of the anti-globalisation protests is unassimilatable by him as meaningful narrative; it is, he says, 'just fucking weird'.[47] Of course, while the 'Great Report' remains unwritten, *Satin Island* does exist as a novel, but as a novel whose structural coherence exists through the very form of the report – the novel is formed of numbered sections, in the way that a corporate report might be. An anxiety about the relation between this form and the form of the novel may be detected in McCarthy's (or the publisher's) choice of title. The full title of the novel is *Satin Island: A Novel*.

If *Ghostwritten*'s narrative form permanently defers apocalypse, and Staten Island remains as a safe haven, in *Satin Island* no such safe place remains. U has a dream about his Great Report which leaves him with two words, '*Satin Island*'.[48] He sees these as linked to a promise of 'significance' and ultimate meaning.[49] In Manhattan for a conference, he discovers that, from a certain perspective, the sign for the ferry to Staten Island reads 'Satin Island'.[50] He decides to travel on the ferry in expectation of discovering 'something rich, strange and miraculous'.[51] However, U is unable to make the journey when he realises that both going and not going are in the end meaningless.[52] As he watches the ferry he was to take disappear across the Upper Bay, the dazzle on the water produces 'a holocaust of light' which erases 'the departed ferry, Staten Island, all the other landmarks and most of the sky',[53] as if the end to all narratives engineered by the great narrator, deferred in *Ghostwritten*, has come about.

Responses to the challenge of digital technology, and to the challenge of the internet in particular, to the act of narration should not, however, be seen as a gradual shift from Mitchell's drawing back from apocalypse to McCarthy's 'holocaust of light'. Nicola Barker's *H(A)PPY* (2017), for example, suggests that any response is determined more by different conceptions of the role and possibility of the novel than distance from the beginnings of the digital age. *H(A)PPY* is a post-apocalyptic dystopia set in a totalitarian society ruled by 'the System' where perfection and balance are achieved through the constant surveillance made possible by digital technology. Ever-present screens continuously relay an information stream comprised of an individual's thoughts, dreams, emotions, temperature and so on, and all members of the society censor and control themselves constantly in response to this stream. Narration is a threat to the stasis demanded by the System. The novel's protagonist is a young woman, Mira A, whose obedience to the System is gradually undermined, and whose rebellion is enacted through a release of language arranged in narrative form. Because the control of words is key to both the System and to Mira A's rebellion, there is little attempt in the novel to construct a conventional story world or to worry about the relation between the 'real' world and the digital; rather, the struggle over language is written into the physical object of the book itself.

The novel contains images, words coloured as if hyperlinks, blank pages and pages composed of a single repeated word mimicking a malfunctioning computer screen. Mira A's most crucial act of rebellion is to construct – mentally, in her information stream – a Cathedral of information and imagery into which she can retreat.[54] The Cathedral is made up of words, symbols and equations and is the means for Mira A's escape into 'the Unknown', the world beyond the System where the latter's control does not reach, but neither does its management of hunger, hatred and pain. Not only is Mira A's own final apocalyptic act – her escape from the System – an ambiguous move into narration, but the Cathedral itself is linked to the very technologies which make possible the System's totalitarian control. As Mira A attempts to flee Kite – the novel's main representative of the System – as he chases her through the Cathedral, he describes her creation as '[t]his giant, swarming edifice of contradictory words and empty echoes and meaningless quotations'.[55] But, of course, she has shaped this mass into something meaningful, a Cathedral. The modes of the internet – its construction through the symbolic – both constitute the technologies of control within the System and the way of escape from it.

War, Terrorism and the 'Meanwhile' of Genre

In the years following the attacks by Al-Qaeda on Washington and New York in September 2001, many novels, in contrast to *On Beauty's* refusal to name it, have directly addressed the effects of terrorism on the possibilities for the 'meanwhile' of the novel. These attempts to reshape the narrative possibilities of the novel have very often, however, led writers to question the ability of the literary novel to do just this, and to turn to the possibilities of genre instead. Martin Amis saw the attacks initially as a challenge to the role of the literary novel. They turned the novelist's work in progress into 'pitiable babble' and following them 'a feeling of gangrenous futility had infected the whole corpus' of novels. Rather than the 'pitiable babble' of the literary novel, what brought coherence after the attacks was cliché: 'actually we can live with "bitter cold" and "searing heat" … We can live with cliché. What we have to do now, more testingly, is live with war.'[56] While Amis argues that eventually the claims of 'literature' reasserted themselves to counteract what he calls the 'stock response' of religious belief – for him the cause of the terror attacks – in the years since, the greatest effect on the British novel has been not so much a reassertion of the power of 'literature' against cliché, but a move towards the conventions of genre in order to maintain the 'meanwhile' of the novel. Whereas postmodernist novelists of the 1980s and 1990s incorporated genre conventions into their novels in order to fragment them, novelists since 2000 have rather moved towards the writing of genre, but it is a move that is often troubled and anxious.[57]

In James Meek's *We Are Now Beginning Our Descent* (2008), the competing claims of the literary and genre fiction in representing war and terror are part of the plot, but the novel's own narrating acts reveal how difficult this question is for the contemporary novel. The protagonist, Adam Kellas, is a British journalist who has reported from Afghanistan during its invasion by the United States and its allies following the 9/11 attacks. Roger Luckhurst has argued that Kellas's job as a journalist is key in 'marking a sense of crisis about the ethics of fictional representations of the violence of modern war'.[58] However, for Kellas, and for Meek's novel, the key contrast is not between journalism and fiction, but between the literary novel and genre fiction. One of the central plots in the 'present' of the novel is about Kellas's travel to the United States to sign a contract with the publisher of his thriller, *Rogue Eagle Rising*, about a war in the future between the United States and Europe. Kellas has begun this novel after setting aside his aims to write more serious fiction, and throughout Meek's novel *Rogue Eagle Rising* is contrasted with the novel, *The Book of Form*, written by Kellas's best friend, Pat M'Gurgan. *The Book of Form* is described as a poet's novel and is the winner of a prestigious literary prize: 'It was dazzling, lovely, like exquisitely tooled, streamlined, burnished parts of a flying machine that hadn't been put together because they'd never been designed to be, couldn't fit, and would never fly.'[59] The title of M'Gurgan's novel and this description of it suggest that novels which interest themselves in questions of form are as useful in representing the truth of the contemporary world as flying machines that cannot fly.

If the poet's novel is beautiful but useless, Kellas has no illusions about the clichéd nature of his thriller, however. Despite their clichés, though, what the conventions of the thriller do facilitate is a 'meanwhile'. Thrillers generally both use coherent and seamless realist conventions – including a unified narrative voice – and rely too on the assumption that the world is an ordered or organised place, even if the originators of that order are the CIA, the Illuminati or an international criminal organisation. Kellas is fully aware of this in his own novel, and of its problems. His aim in writing the novel had been to commit an act of 'deliberate misimagining',[60] to write a novel that successfully managed a 'meanwhile' through the justification of cliché by sincerity. His aim is: 'To take a real, complicated country, in this case, the United States, and to simplify it to a set of caricatures so blatant, and so crude, that few readers would doubt his sincerity. A naïve entertainer, but sincere.'[61]

Kellas finally discovers – when he reaches the nadir at the end of his 'descent' – the consequences of such a novelistic lie. In New York he discovers from his editor that his publisher has been taken over by a French industrial conglomerate which no longer wants to publish his novel. Now penniless and jobless, Kellas leaves New York for a journey on a Greyhound bus to Virginia to find a fellow journalist, Astrid, with whom he had an affair in Afghanistan. During the trip he reads his now rejected novel to his fellow passenger, Lloyd, who by his own account is 'not a great reader',[62] but whose naive responses make visible the gap between the conventions of the thriller and lived experience. Kellas justifies his novel to the sceptical Lloyd through a distancing of it from the real world: 'It's a thriller. It's fiction. It's entertainment.'[63] Lloyd, however, refuses to be mollified and collapses back the distance between the novelistic and the real: 'My sister's best friend is in Kuwait right now with the Marines. That ain't much of an entertainment.'[64]

If neither the literary novel nor the thriller is adequate to represent the truth of the world through a credible 'meanwhile', a scene at the heart of the novel suggests what might be. Against the novel's traditional use of the party to assert the 'meanwhile', as we see however problematically in *On Beauty*, Meek uses a party to question the form's ability to represent a coherent picture of the contemporary world. Kellas attends a dinner party in Camden, north London. The hosts and guests represent politics, the media, the arts, science and finance, a good sweep of the power of London. The tensions begin when, trying to smooth over a disagreement between Kellas and another guest, Liam, the host, claims of his house: 'This is no man's land. There has to be one of those so we aren't killing each other and screaming at each other all the time.'[65] Kellas's response is to ask 'who's we?'.[66] The traditional function of the party as a literalised 'meanwhile', bringing the disparate and the diverse into some kind of coherence, begins to crumble. The climax of the scene occurs when Kellas is asked by Liam what Afghanistan is really like. Kellas tells Liam that he will show him. He destroys his host's kitchen, smashing crockery, pictures and furniture, finally shouting into the terrified face of their young daughter: 'THAT'S WHAT IT'S LIKE!'[67] In this scene, where the question of the representation of war and terror is central, the party cannot constitute the 'meanwhile'; indeed, its destruction questions the role and ethics of the 'meanwhile'.

However, Kellas's mimesis of destruction that is itself destructive is less happily transferred to the novel's own form. In chronological order, the events of the novel are as follows: Kellas spends time embedded with US troops during the invasion of 2001, returns to London no longer able to accept the banalities of bourgeois metropolitan life, destroys the dinner party, flies to New York to sign the book contract, then travels on to Virginia to find Astrid. We finally we see him and Astrid in Iraq in March 2003. This account of the events of the novel is, however, very hard for the reader to reconstruct when reading for the first time. The ordered simultaneity that the 'meanwhile' historically brought to the events of the novel and through that to the events of the world itself is shattered by the attempt, both by the novel and in the novel, to connect the world of British bourgeois 'reality' to the effects of US and UK political and military decisions in Afghanistan. More problematically, the ability of the novel finally to represent the 'real' of the world is made shaky by its own reversion to the worst aspects of genre. A review of the novel in *The Guardian* suggested that at the end, as we see Kellas and Astrid in Iraq during the invasion in 2003, Meek returns to the bad writing of commercial thrillers as if to say that what happened there can only be written about in that way: 'It is as if Meek were saying: the modern Anglo-American wars are so stupid, you can only write stupidly about them.'[68]

Such narrative uncertainty of the effects of terror and war on the cohering possibilities of the 'meanwhile' of the novel can also be seen in different ways in two other post-millennial novels, and again they circle around the question of the literary and genre. Glen Duncan's *A Day and a Night and a Day* (2009) draws on the conventions of the thriller to represent terror, but attempts in the end to work them into a literary novel.[69] Its protagonist, Augustus Rose, has endured torture carried out by the United States in north Africa through the processes of extraordinary rendition. However, Rose knows that the atrocious cannot be narrated, and the novel agrees by breaking off its account of this torture at the moment of maximum horror: 'It's the nature of horror: you've got to half-see it for it to work.'[70] However, the novel's mixing of thriller conventions with the literary novel's attention to the problem of representation of torture in particular, as Alice Bennett has noted, led to some disappointment among reviewers at the novel's 'half-seeing' and accusations of 'exhausted contempt for the kind of writing that seems to be called for'.[71] In comparison, if Duncan produced a thriller that did not tell enough because of its awareness of problems of representation in response to the atrocious, Nadeem Aslam's *The Wasted Vigil* (2008) is an intensely literary novel whose lyrical coherence sits uneasily with its narration of the most violent and destructive happenings. One of its protagonists, Marcus, is an English doctor who has lived in Afghanistan for decades. A description of his abilities as a perfumier show the novel as aligning itself to Salman Rushdie's variety of magical realism. We are told that his sense of smell was so accurate that 'he could discern a word written with colourless perfume on a sheet of paper'.[72] Further, the novel's structure, alternating between the novel's present, narrated in the present tense, and the past horrors experienced by the Afghan people under the Soviet occupation, the rule of the Taliban and following the US invasion in 2001, narrated in the past tense, reproduces a now conventional understanding of the relation between the past and the present where the use of retrospective narration attempts to heal or overcome the past. Because of this, the novel cannot admit in the end that the act of telling is complicated and threatened by the horror it narrates. While Duncan's thriller-ish novel explicitly discusses the relation between torture and language and refuses to narrate the horror of the former, Aslam's literary novel is still confident that violence can be beautifully and fully told. Marcus has lost both his daughter, Zameen, and his Afghan wife, Qatrina, also a doctor, the first to the Soviets and then to warlords, the latter to the Taliban. Just over half way through the novel we learn what had been Qatrina's ultimate fate. She is stoned by the Taliban for refusing to renounce either her husband or her medical knowledge. The public stoning does not actually kill her, and, injured following it, she is then thrown into a cell:

> That was where she died several days after the stoning. A man at the mosque was sent to see her, to ask if she would beg Allah's forgiveness for a lifetime of sin. She wouldn't respond to him. But as she sat there she sometimes raised her burka and pursed her swollen lips and spat out something white into a corner. Maggots had developed in her nasal cavity and were dropping into her mouth.[73]

In contrast to the reticence of Duncan's narrator and narrative, both totalitarian demand and horrible injury stop Qatrina's language, but not the linguistic facility of the narrator.

The Impossible 'Meanwhile': Narrating Climate Change

The difficult relation between the literary novel and genre fiction in the post-millennial world can be seen too in debates about the representation of the contemporary's most pressing 'real', climate change. Amitav Ghosh has recently argued that what he calls the 'serious novel' has failed to take this on, in part because the 'meanwhile' of the novel precludes the scale necessary in order to properly represent it.[74] In addition, Ghosh worries that 'the mere mention of the subject is often enough to relegate a novel or a short story to the genre of science fiction'.[75] Writing in response to Ghosh, McKenzie Wark also sees the relation between the novel and climate change as primarily a problem of genre, but for him the serious novel has already lost: 'science fiction has responded more strongly to the Anthropocene ... Serious fiction, like bourgeois culture, now seems rather unserious, indeed frivolous'.[76]

However, both Ghosh's argument and Wark's response suggest that a consideration of the novel as a narrative act – rather than the details of its theme and content – has been ignored. Ghosh argues that even literary writers seriously involved in debates about and activism in response to climate change usually write about it only in the pages of non-fiction. As an example, Ghosh cites the British novelist Paul Kingsnorth, whose novel *The Wake* was published in 2015 and who before that was closely involved in activism against climate change. Ghosh argues that, despite this involvement, 'as of the time of writing [Kingsnorth] has yet to publish a novel in which climate change plays a major part'.[77] However, such a charge can only be based on a very restricted idea of what novels are 'about', that is, of the relation between novels and the world in which they appear. Ghosh's argument is one which considers characters, events and themes as more important than the novel as a narrative act. A consideration of *The Wake* as a narrative act suggests instead that this novel is in fact deeply invested in the possibilities of and problems surrounding the form's engagement with climate change.

The Wake is set at the time of the Norman invasion of England in 1066 and is narrated in the first person by Buccmaster, an Anglo-Saxon who has lost everything through Norman violence and who retreats, with a few others, into the great woods from where they carry out acts of insurgence against the Normans. Kingsnorth has made the telling of his novel as different from contemporary English as possible while retaining legibility through the creation of a pseudo Old English, what he calls a 'shadow tongue'. He uses no words in Buccmaster's telling that would not have been available to inhabitants of England in 1066. In one way, this is a kind of authenticity, an attempt at a link to the 'real' of an apocalyptic moment in the life of the country at the turn of the last millennium. However, the reader's struggle to read on beginning the novel, and the difficulties in reading acknowledged by the inclusion of paratextual material such as a preface and a glossary, challenges any idea that a 'return to the real' can be straightforward. If the 'shadow tongue' causes difficulty, this is complicated further by Buccmaster's role as narrator. What motivates Buccmaster is his connection to the old Anglo-Saxon gods. He rejects Christianity as a religion of 'the book'[78] and clings to the old beliefs which are rooted in the physical reality of the natural world. As a child, Buccmaster is shown a submerged forest by his grandfather, who also believes in the old gods, and who believes that the trees are the gods themselves:

> he telt me that in the time before the crist angland was ham to a hus of gods what was born of this ground and what lifd in it among the folc. and these gods he saed was not lic the crist they was not ingenga gods bound about in lies and words ... these was gods of the treows and the water lic we is folc of them.[79]

At the heart of *The Wake*, then, are the relations between humans and the natural world. Buccmaster wishes to save England from the 'ingenga' Normans and to return to the old beliefs which produce a harmonious relation between the gods, the land and the people. However, it gradually becomes clear that Buccmaster is a liar and a bully. Indeed, he is a murderer whose actions in the past have produced results analogous to the Normans' violent destruction. Buccmaster claims to 'speak for' the land, which he sees as a living being, but his act of narration is duplicitous. Kingsnorth's novel does not mention climate change, but its construction of the narrative act questions the establishing of a cohering 'meanwhile' between human beings and the natural world, while at the same time producing a vision of the pre-Norman world – one of 'blithe lif'[80] – that is in many ways far preferable to the one brought in by the invaders. The novel articulates a yearning for a relation to the physical world other than that of late capitalism, while at the same time acknowledging the problematic role of the narrative act in achieving this.

In all the novels discussed in this chapter we can see the powerful desire expressed in the post-millennial British novel to reconnect with a 'real' that was jettisoned by postmodernist epistemological scepticism. However, by paying attention to the narrative acts of the novels as understood through Anderson's concept of the 'meanwhile', we can also see a remaining hesitancy and disquiet about the role of the novel in such a reconnection. The post-millennial 'real' – shot through as it is with forces and challenges which threaten the coherence that is at stake in the 'meanwhile' – produces in the novels which yearn for it a formal conundrum that is both productive and fragmenting.

Notes

1. R. Eaglestone, 'Contemporary Fiction in the Academy: Towards a Manifesto' (2013) 27(7) *Textual Practice* 1089–101, 1095.
2. See, e.g., P. Boxall, *Twenty-First Century Fiction: A Critical Introduction* (Cambridge University Press, 2013); P. Boxall, *The Value of the Novel* (Cambridge University Press, 2015); and P. Vermeulen, *Contemporary Literature and the End of the Novel: Creature, Affect, Form* (Basingstoke: Palgrave, 2015).
3. See L. Konstantinou, *Cool Characters: Irony and American Fiction* (Harvard University Press, 2016).
4. D. Lea, 'The Anxieties of Authenticity in Post-2000 British Fiction' (2012) 58(3) *Modern Fiction Studies* 459–76, 461; see also D. Lea, *Twenty-First Century Fiction: Contemporary British Voices* (Manchester University Press, 2016).
5. A. Gasiorek and D. James, 'Introduction: Fiction since 2000: Postmillennial Commitments' (2012) 53(4) *Contemporary Literature*, Special Issue on Fiction since 2000, edited by A. Gasiorek and D. James, 609–27, 617; see also D. James, 'A Renaissance for the Crystalline Novel?', *Contemporary Literature*, Special Issue, 845–74.

6. See, e.g., D. Shields, *Reality Hunger: A Manifesto* (London: Hamish Hamilton, 2010); A. O'Hagan, 'Don Delillo, *Underworld* and *Falling Man*' in L. McIllvanny and R. Ryan (eds), *The Good of the Novel* (London: Faber & Faber, 2011); I. McEwan, 'When Faith in Fiction Falters', *The Guardian* (16 February 2013), www.theguardian.com/books/2013/feb/16/ian-mcewan-faith-fiction-falters; H. Kunzru, 'Karl Ove Knausgaard: The Latest Literary Sensation', *The Guardian* (7 March 2014), www.theguardian.com/books/2014/mar/07/karl-ove-knausgaard-my-struggle-hari-kunzru; and R. Cusk, Interview with Kate Kellaway, *The Guardian* (24 August 2014), www.theguardian.com/books/2014/aug/24/rachel-cusk-interview-aftermath-outline.

7. B. Anderson, *Imagined Communities: Reflections on the Origin and Spread of Nationalism*, 2nd edn (London: Verso, 2006), pp. 24 ff.

8. *Ibid.*, pp. 34–5.

9. See J. Thompson, *Merchants of Culture: The Publishing Business in the Twenty-First Century*, 2nd edn (Cambridge: Polity, 2012), pp. 314–15.

10. B. Anderson, 'El Malhadado Pais' in *The Spectre of Comparisons: Nationalism, Southeast Asia and the World* (London: Verso, 1998), p. 334.

11. Anderson, *Imagined Communities*, p. 24.

12. T. Brennan, 'The National Longing for Form' in B. Ashcroft, G. Griffiths and H. Tiffin (eds), *Postcolonial Studies Reader* (London: Routledge, 1995), p. 172.

13. J. Culler, 'Anderson and the Novel' (1999) 29(4) *Diacritics* 19–39, 22.

14. Anderson, *Imagined Communities*, p. 25.

15. See, e.g., M. Bal, 'Meanwhile: Literature in an Expanded Field' in I. Hoving, F.-W. Korsten and E. van Alphen (eds), *Africa and Its Significant Others: Forty Years of Intercultural Entanglement* (Leiden: Brill, 2003), pp. 183–97; and R. Barnard, 'Fictions of the Global' (2009) 42(2) *The Novel: A Forum on Fiction* 207–15.

16. Z. Smith, *On Beauty* (London: Hamish Hamilton, 2005), p. vii.

17. F. Kermode, 'Here She Is', review of *On Beauty* (2005) 27(19) *London Review of Books* n.p., www.lrb.co.uk/v27/n19/frank-kermode/here-she-is.

18. Smith, *On Beauty*, p. 42.

19. *Ibid.*, p. 27.

20. Kermode, 'Here She Is', n.p.

21. D. Hale, '*On Beauty* as Beautiful? The Problem of Novelistic Aesthetics by Way of Zadie Smith', *Contemporary Literature*, Special Issue, 814–44, 820; see also Z. Smith, 'Zadie, Take Three', Interview conducted by Jessica Murphy Moo, *Atlantic Monthly* (October 2005), www.theatlantic.com/magazine/archive/2005/10/zadie-take-three/304294/.

22. Hale, '*On Beauty* as Beautiful?', p. 840.

23. Smith, 'Zadie, Take Three', p. 424.

24. D. Head, 'Zadie Smith's *White Teeth*: Multiculturalism for the Millennium' in R. J. Lane, R. Mengham and P. Tew (eds), *Contemporary British Fiction* (Cambridge: Polity, 2003), p. 106.

25. The way that the attacks on 9/11 led novelists to assert shared values and clichés about love can be found too in Ian McEwan's article written days after the attacks on the Twin Towers and the Pentagon, 'Only Love and Then Oblivion', *The Guardian* (15 September 2001), www.theguardian.com/world/2001/sep/15/september11.politicsphilosophyandsociety2.

26. B. Anderson, 'The First Filipino' in *The Spectre of Comparisons: Nationalism, Southeast Asia and the World* (London: Verso, 1998), p. 227.
27. Smith, *On Beauty*, p. 68.
28. *Ibid.*, p. 107 (ellipses in original).
29. Bal, 'Meanwhile', p. 183.
30. *Ibid.*, pp. 183–4.
31. J. Lanchester, 'You Are the Product' (2017) 39(16) *London Review of Books*, 3–10, 5. The terms 'fake news' and 'post truth' rose to prominence in public debate in 2016, and were made 'words of the year' by the *Macquerie Dictionary* and the *Oxford English Dictionary* respectively. See www.theguardian.com/australia-news/2017/jan/25/fake-news-named-word-of-the-year-by-macquarie-dictionary and https://en.oxforddictionaries.com/word-of-the-year/word-of-the-year-2016.
32. Barnard, 'Fictions of the Global', pp. 209, 212.
33. I. Asimov, 'Runaround' (1942) *Astounding Science Fiction* 94–103.
34. D. Mitchell, *Ghostwritten* (London: Sceptre, 1999), pp. 389–90, 397–8.
35. *Ibid.*, pp. 386 ff.
36. *Ibid.*, p. 429.
37. T. McCarthy, *Satin Island: A Novel* (London: Vintage, 2016), pp. 16, 55.
38. *Ibid.*, p. 35.
39. It has been suggested that the project is named after the artist and friend of McCarthy's, Hilary Skoob-Sassen, whose mother, Saskia Sassen, is a Dutch-American sociologist whose books include *The Global City* and *Globalization and Its Discontents*.
40. *Ibid.*, p. 15.
41. *Ibid.*, p. 40.
42. *Ibid.*, p. 70.
43. *Ibid.*, p. 90.
44. *Ibid.*, p. 145 (emphasis in original).
45. *Ibid.*, p. 153.
46. *Ibid.*
47. *Ibid.*, p. 203.
48. *Ibid.*, p. 164 (emphasis in the original).
49. *Ibid.*, p. 204.
50. *Ibid.*, p. 205.
51. *Ibid.*, p. 210.
52. *Ibid.*, p. 213.
53. *Ibid.*, p. 216.
54. N. Barker, *H(A)PPY* (London: William Heinemann, 2017), p. 253.
55. *Ibid.*, p. 261.
56. M. Amis, 'The Voice of the Lonely Crowd', *The Guardian* (1 June 2002), n.p., www.theguardian.com/books/2002/jun/01/philosophy.society.
57. Some examples include the historical fiction of Sarah Waters, David Peace's Red Riding Quartet (1999–2002), which are crime novels, Toby Litt's *Corpsing* (2000) and *Journey into Space* (2009), which are a crime novel and a science fiction novel respectively. Benedict Anderson argued in his later work that the fragmentation of the novel into genres in the twentieth century weakened the 'meanwhile' of the novel (see Anderson, 'El Malhadado Pais', p. 335). For

a challenge to this claim on grounds other than the one made here, see Culler, 'Anderson and the Novel'.

58. R. Luckhurst, 'In War Times: Fictionalizing Iraq', *Contemporary Literature*, Special Issue, 713–37, 720.

59. J. Meek, *We Are Now Beginning Our Descent* (Edinburgh: Canongate, 2009), pp. 34–5.

60. *Ibid.*, p. 114.

61. *Ibid.*

62. *Ibid.*, p. 190.

63. *Ibid.*, p. 191.

64. *Ibid.*

65. *Ibid.*, p. 94.

66. *Ibid.*

67. *Ibid.*, p. 111.

68. J. Buchan, 'Once More Unto the Front', review of *We Are Now Beginning Our Descent*, *The Guardian* (9 February 2008), n.p., www.theguardian.com/books/2008/feb/09/featuresreviews.guardianreview19.

69. Like *Satin Island*, this novel also asserts its claims to being a novel in its title. While the subtitle 'A Novel' is used fairly frequently by US publishers, especially by publishers of genre fiction, both parodying it (as in the experimental novel by US novelist David Markson, *This Is Not a Novel*, from 2001) and appropriating it for a literary novel, as in *Satin Island*, draws attention to uncertainty around the limits of the form in the contemporary. Glen Duncan moved, after being dropped by his agent following the global economic crash of 2008, from writing novels with literary aspirations, such as *A Day and a Night and a Day*, to writing genre fiction (see, for an account of this, Bennett, 'Remaindered Books'.). As my analysis of the novel makes clear, however, *A Day and a Night and a Day*, while from Duncan's 'literary' period, contains a number of elements of the thriller.

70. G. Duncan, *A Day and a Night and a Day: A Novel* (New York: HarperCollins, 2009), p. 35.

71. A. Bennett, 'Remaindered Books: Glen Duncan's Twenty-First Century Novels' in S. Adiseshiah and R. Hildyeard (eds), *Twenty-First Century Fiction: What Happens Now* (Basingstoke: Palgrave, 2013), p. 73.

72. N. Aslam, *The Wasted Vigil* (London: Faber & Faber, 2009), p. 174.

73. *Ibid.*, p. 267.

74. A. Ghosh, *The Great Derangement: Climate Change and the Unthinkable* (University of Chicago Press, 2016), pp. 58–63. On the question of scale in connection with the relations between human beings and the natural world, see M. McGurl, 'Gigantic Realism: The Rise of the Novel and the Comedy of Scale' (2017) 4(2) *Critical Inquiry* 403–30.

75. *Ibid.*, p. 7.

76. M. Wark, 'On the Obsolescence of the Bourgeois Novel in the Anthropocene' (16 August 2017), n.p., www.versobooks.com/blogs/3356-on-the-obsolescence-of-the-bourgeois-novel-in-the-anthropocene.

77. Ghosh, *The Great Derangement*, p. 8.

78. P. Kingsnorth, *The Wake* (London: Unbound, 2015), p. 68.

79. *Ibid.*, p. 52.

80. *Ibid.*, p. 194.

PART II

New Formations

4

GABRIELE GRIFFIN

British Writing and the Limits of the Human

Introduction: Time and Technology Shifts

In 1980 I did not have a computer. Neither did anyone else I knew. E- as a prefix to anything such as e-passports was not in use then; in 2017 the capture of biodata in many different forms such as iris recognition has made e-passports a norm. Similarly, the ability to manipulate biodata and bio materials through biotechnological innovation, for instance in the context of fertility, has revolutionised ideas of kinship[1] and can, in 2017, accommodate notions of multiple biological parents to a single child.[2] The driverless car is being tested.[3] Paro, the robot seal, is being used to comfort the elderly as robot carers for the elderly are being developed.[4] Technology-enhanced surveillance is becoming ever more sophisticated, with the state and corporations submitting to and exploiting the self-learning algorithms of artificial intelligence systems that pervade the everyday.

This world of seismic shifts in the diversity, speed, reach and ubiquity of technology finds its counterpart in a range of British fiction from the 1980s onwards that responds to those shifts and thereby engages with the question of the limits of the human. These limits might be understood both in terms of what lies beyond the human and what the human can endure.

One way in which these limits take shape in contemporary British writing is through an exploration of how environments, bio- and communications technologies, and neoliberal agendas of deregulation, marketisation, (self-) surveillance, processulisation, the so-called democratic deficit, and changing social and late(?)-capitalist realities impact on notions of community and individual. Drawing on a range of fictions, predominantly from the 1990s and the post-2000s, I argue that these texts do not display 'rampant technophilia' as Madelena Gonzalez[5] suggests in relation to Jeanette Winterson's *PowerBook* (2000), among others. Rather, and more in line with Sonya Andermahr's thinking,[6] technology figures as a conceit,[7] mobilised mostly thematically but at times structurally, and in graphic novels also visually, in order to explore the necro- or thanatopolitics that comes with the refusal of difference and the failure to take moral responsibility that the texts I discuss elucidate. These texts do not tend to celebrate the collapse of boundaries, the notion of distributed and machinic identities, or the construction of endless self-learning feedback loops that function as emblems of the digital age. Rather, they offer a critique of the moral vacuum that the ontological uncertainty fostered through technologisation has created. In that sense they are at least partly old-fashioned morality tales, possibly nostalgically and implicitly harking back to a before that might be imaginary. The texts I am referring to and which I shall explore here are G. J. Ballard's *Cocaine Nights* (1997) and *Super-Cannes* (2000), Tom McCarthy's *Remainder* (2005), Deborah Levy's *Diary of a Steak* (1997) and *Hot Milk* (2016), Kazuo Ishiguro's *Never Let Me Go* (2005), and the graphic novels *The Vicar Woman* by Emma Rendel (2013) and *The Motherless Oven* by Rob Davis (2014). In their different ways all of these fictions engage with questions of the limits of the human.

Coordinates of the Limits of the Human

'Crossing frontiers is my profession. Those strips of no-man's land between the checkpoints always seem such zones of promise, rich with the possibilities of new lives, new scents and affections. At the same time they set off a reflex of unease that I have never been able to repress.'[8] Thus begins *Cocaine Nights*, one of J. G. Ballard's many works which chart a male first-person narrator's navigation between an alienating terrain, its inhabitants, and the protagonist's proclivities to be both attracted and repelled by these. Ballard's depiction of this non-place,[9] with its sense of opportunities and uncertainties, gestures towards the importance of cartographic thinking in contemporary fiction, particularly in writing by men that engages with challenged masculinities. Such challenges, often coupled with physical problems, may come in the form of professional redundancy: Paul Sinclair in Ballard's *Super-Cannes* roams the business park for lack of occupation and significantly starts his narrative with the assertion: 'it seems only too apt that my guide to this "intelligent city" in the hills above Cannes should be a specialist in mental disorders'.[10] Or they may manifest themselves as hyper-masculinised quasi-testosterone-fuelled 'hunting expeditions' of groups of men destroying those who seem other, justified by the ludicrous notion that: 'Our latent psychopathy is the last nature reserve, a place of refuge for the endangered mind.'[11] Here structures, grids, networks, fault lines, patterns and organisation as the establishment of order function as bulwarks against the unrepressed, or the repressed which threatens to surface in the face of seemingly unconquerable hyper-orders (material and symbolic) that appear to govern a new technologised reality in which time-space compression is set to outstrip human capacity. The limits of the human seem to become evident here – but without a clear sense of what exactly this phrase means. If one googles this phrase the first hits are all concerned with corporeality – the limits of the human body, understood in terms of athletic capabilities and defying bodily death. Corporeality is there interpreted in strictly material terms, the body as flesh. But Ballard's introduction to *Cocaine Nights* also indicates an immaterial cartography, one of promise and of unease, an affectscape. Given this mapping of the hypermodern[12] as materialised space and of a repressed interiority as immaterial territory, I want to propose that certain post-1980s British fictions work to a cartography of the limits of the human that encompasses both material and immaterial coordinates while exploring four domains which inter-relate and which function as the four sub-sections to this chapter:

- circumscribed hypermodern spaces which challenge the meanings of social and of power structures;
- the collapse of boundaries;
- notions of the cyborg and of the companion species; and
- the post-humane, or the loss of empathy in the hypermodern.

This hypermodern is characterised by a biopolitics which seeks dominion over every aspect of human life, material and immaterial, but in that very process threatens that life's viability. Unsurprisingly, much of the writing about this is either dystopic or, at the very least, ambivalent about contemporary manifestations of the hypermodern. In British artist Grayson Perry's (2016) words,[13] this writing might be described as being about 'the descent of man', man or men in particular, but also, as I shall discuss in relation to Emma Rendel's graphic novel *The Vicar Woman*, about women's inability or incapacity to intervene, the limits of the kindness of women. In their rendition of the descent of man, Ballard's diptych fictions *Cocaine Nights* and *Super-Cannes* have their antecedents in texts as different as John Milton's *Paradise Lost* and William Golding's *Lord of the Flies*. They are, in a sense, texts about wanton boys killing for their sport.

The Socio-Cultural Meanings of Hypermodern Spaces

J. G. Ballard's fiction, as has been much discussed, is populated with recurring motifs such as 'hyper-organizational spaces'[14] and figures such as the charismatic tempter who appears like God to know the answer to everything, but turns out to be the Devil wreaking havoc, the seduced violent follower/s and the uncertain interloper, all male and forming an unholy trinity which begins and ends in violence. This fiction tackles the limits of the human in a secular world in terms of a quasi-religious motif: the creation of a seemingly perfect, materially comfortable and supposedly secure world, a kind of assumed paradise or Eden, undone by the imperfections of those inhabiting it. These imperfections, often a submission to escalatingly violent demands of those who hold sway, result in either expulsion or death. In *Cocaine Nights*, the paradise is a sports complex on the Spanish coast for British ex-pats, the charismatic tempter a sports pro, and the interloper the brother of the sports complex manager, come to rescue the latter from going to prison for having burned five people to death. In *Super-Cannes* the paradise is a business park, the charismatic leader figure engaged in a 'social experiment' the resident psychiatrist, and the interloper the husband of a woman come to work at the business park. In this homosocial triangular field,[15] women function as objects of exchange and victims, as well as collaborators. The space, a manufactured landscape where 'unreality thrived on every side',[16] acts as *agent provocateur* in that its unitary purpose impacts on its inhabitants such that an antidote is supposedly needed to counteract its effects. This is provided through the guru-like leader figure with a mission to stimulate the inhabitants, in *Cocaine Nights* to engage in community endeavours, in *Super-Cannes* to enhance their creative work potential. The nature of the stimulant is the same in each case: licensed transgression, supposedly 'for the public good'.[17] As a character in *Cocaine Nights* puts it: 'what else is there to do in paradise? ... Believe me, everyone here is trying to lie down with the serpent.'[18] Lying with the serpent in both novels takes the forms of violence against property, women, children, migrants and all those considered in some way 'other'. Transgression is made possible through the evacuation of the moral and the regulatory sphere. Politics, the state and its institutions are constructed as irrelevant. Crawford, the tempter in *Cocaine Nights*, states: 'Politics are a pastime for a professional caste and fail to excite the rest of us',[19] a notion born out in actuality by the voter apathy of the last quarter of the twentieth century.[20] In both novels private police or vigilante forces are established whose role it is to facilitate transgression, thus giving a new meaning to the notion of organised crime. This is accompanied by extensive surveillance apparatuses, cameras everywhere, supposedly in the name of security. But their function is to facilitate the enactment and consumption of the disinhibition that accompanies licensed transgression. This 'quicken[s] the nervous system and jump[s] the synapses deadened by leisure and inaction',[21] and in *Super-Cannes*, by overwork.

Although Ballard has described himself as 'a scout ... sent ahead to see if the water is drinkable or not',[22] the parallel worlds to contemporary reality set up in his novels constitute an astute measure of the contemporary, thus lodging them in recognisable historical moments. Importantly, his tempter figures are always convinced that the present represents the future, even if only for a circumscribed privileged group of people. Thus, the tempter in *Cocaine Nights* confidently argues:

> Our governments are preparing for a future without work, and that includes the petty criminals. Leisure societies lie ahead of us, like those you see on this coast. People will still work – or, rather, some people will work, but only for a decade of their lives. They will retire in their late thirties, with fifty years of idleness in front of them.[23]

By 2000 and *Super-Cannes* this had turned into the recognition that:

> Years ago people took for granted that the future meant leisure. That's true for the less skilled and less able . . . Talk to senior people at Eden-Olympia. They've gone beyond leisure . . . Work is where they find real fulfilment . . .[24]

One might wonder what this means for the 'less skilled and less able', but they are not at the centre of Ballard's concern. Both novels subscribe to the same diagnosis regarding the middle class, whether constructed as newly leisured or as massively over-worked: 'The twentieth century ended with its dreams in ruins. The notion of a community as a voluntary association of enlightened citizens has died for ever. We realise how suffocatingly humane we've become, dedicated to moderation and the middle way. The suburbanisation of the soul has overrun our planet like the plague.'[25] While the tempter in *Super-Cannes* no longer believes in community, his counterpart in *Cocaine Nights* still asks the question: 'how do you energize people, give them some sense of community?'[26] And the answer in both instances is licensed transgression or psychopathy, 'a carefully metered violence'.[27]

Both novels, as is variously repeated in critical writings on Ballard,[28] may be read as rooted in Ballard's childhood experiences in a Japanese internment camp in Shanghai. Here adults could be 'stripped of all garments of authority'[29] and the 'fragility of civil society'[30] was exposed. Unreality and provisionality indeed reign in Ballard's novels. Nonetheless, explanations for the loss of moral compass are gestured towards; these invariably lie in childhood. As Paula, a character in *Cocaine Nights*, says: 'Unhappy parents teach you a lesson that lasts a lifetime.'[31]

Ballard's fictional exploration of community occurred at a time when the topic of community was very much discussed, especially by French and Italian philosophers such as Jean-Luc Nancy, Giorgio Agamben and Roberto Esposito. Hence a less individualist explanation for the alienated worlds conjured up in *Cocaine Nights* and *Super-Cannes* might be found in the work on community by the Italian theorist Roberto Esposito, especially his *Terms of the Political* (2013). Here he describes community as constituted by beings-in-common, based on the notion of a shared obligation towards the other, *munus*: a 'task', 'duty' or 'law'.[32] The tempter in *Cocaine Nights* argues exactly this: 'What makes a community but that duty we all owe to each other as neighbours.'[33] In the novel it is never spelt out what precisely that duty is. But Esposito does have an answer. He is interested in an affirmative biopolitics that rescues community from the potential of becoming a thanatopolitics as it emerges in *Cocaine Nights* and *Super-Cannes*. Esposito suggests that community is both fundamental to humans – we can only be in common – but also that which threatens the individual since what is common is by implication that which is not proper to the individual. Community thus requires that the individual give up his individuality through meeting the demands of community. This drive towards unity which Esposito sees as immanent in community may lead to a situation, such as occurs in the two novels, where the ruling order is 'founded on the subjects' renouncing of every power and turning it over to one who, in order to defend their lives [or in the novel perhaps better "life styles"], is also authorized to kill them.'[34]

Esposito argues that *communitas* stands in relation to *immunitas* through *munus*, the obligation that binds community, dividing what belongs from what does not. Belonging grants immunity both in the sense of protection and of exemption. It seals off community from the other as a divisive measure, a form of socio-cultural and geopolitical spatialisation. Protected by the tempter figure and his accomplices, the inhabitants of the Costa del Sol and of the business park become immune from all but the order of their community which entitles them to violence. Tellingly when the interloper in *Super-Cannes*, not yet fully immunised, asks, 'Where are the moral compass bearings that hold everything together?',[35] the tempter responds: 'They fall away. We shed them . . .'.[36] Instead the multinationals which decide everything for the individual provide freedom, 'freedom from morality'.[37] This freedom is equated by the tempter with man's base 'nature': 'Homo sapiens is a reformed hunter-killer with depraved appetites . . . We need to revive him, give him back the killing eye and the dreams of death.'[38] The tempter here articulates biopolitics as thanatopolitics, where people's great dream is 'to become victims'.[39] He wants to 'play on people's deep-rooted masochistic needs built into the human sense of hierarchy'.[40] Following his vision to create monolithic enclaves or communities of people 'free from morality' leads to a deadly scenario in which psychopathy is allowed to rule the community, at once protected by and exempted from obligation.

Against the monolithic imperative that creates the logic of the one, that is of sameness, which characterises the fully immunised (self-)destructive community, Esposito, following Heidegger, posits *munus* as an obligation of *care* for the other, both in terms of looking after and in terms of identifying with the other. The agonistics between the demands of the community and the self-preservation of the individual which might be construed as counterpunctual are thus resolved through community-in-difference, an affirmative biopolitics that views the other not as a source of threat to the individual and to community, but as the one for whom one should care. In this Esposito's *munus* is driven not by the insistence on the sameness which monolithic communities desire, but by the recognition of difference.

One effect of the submission of the subject to a sovereignty or power which may decide about both life and death[41] is the estrangement of self from self. In Ballard's novels this manifests itself inter alia in an alienation from emotion. Typically people's faces tend not to display emotion. They are described, as one woman is, for example, as having 'a pleasant but toneless face from which all emotion had long been drained'.[42] This kind of alienation from self through a certain surrender to the demands of a power or parent figure is the subject of psychoanalyst Alice Miller's *The Drama of the Gifted Child* (1981). Miller argues that a parent's demands that her child focus on the parent's needs, and the lack of recognition of the child's needs and desires by that same parent lead to the child, especially the gifted sensitive child, being alienated from self. But reciprocal recognition which requires the acceptance of difference and distinction between self and other is necessary to provide space for the individual to develop a sense of her self. Such recognition, unless it is on the tempter's terms, is not fostered in Ballard's new Edenic communities which thus turn into a kind of futuristic hell of enclosure and repression, ruled by the tempter as puppeteer who dehumanises those around him.[43]

The Issue of Boundaries

In *Terms of the Political* Esposito argues that we live in a world where: 'Everywhere we look, new walls, new blockades, and new dividing lines are erected against something that threatens, or at least seems to, our biological, social, and environmental identity.'[44] Donald Trump's proposed wall against Mexico, the closing of European borders against refugees from Africa and the Middle East, the UK vote to leave the European Union, also known as Brexit, and the newly (re-)emerging notions of the 'deserving poor' in light of the withdrawal of state-sponsored welfare services are just some contemporary examples of this phenomenon. Such walling in and keeping out acts as a form of immunisation which, in Esposito's terms, ultimately becomes auto-destructive. We need, he argues, to protect ourselves from too much protection.

This reading of the contemporary world assumes certain kinds of agency modelled in part on Foucauldian notions of distributive power, but also particular interpretations of the world as not necessarily threatening to self. Agency, however, acquires a different meaning in a context where the affectscape has been deadened. In Tom McCarthy's *Remainder* the protagonist has had a brain-damaging accident: 'It involved something falling from the sky. Technology. Parts, bits.'[45] Paid off by the multinational corporation involved in return for his silence, the protagonist uses the pay-off to create and re-enact situations which he imagines or has witnessed. These situations involve escalating violence, met by the protagonist with complete indifference other than in aesthetic terms. Thus, as he physically probes the shot gun wounds of a dying man his response is 'Beautiful!'.[46] With 'zero degrees of empathy',[47] he resembles the psychopathic tempters in Ballard's fiction. Like them he inhabits manufactured scenarios where he seeks to control and manipulate both the material environment and those who inhabit it. But whereas Ballard's artificial hypermodern landscapes are spaces one might commonly find in actuality and that exist at least partially independently of their protagonists (although towards the end of *Super-Cannes* the tempter is imagining building a much larger Eden II, and *Cocaine Nights*' tempter likewise intends to move on to ever larger leisure and retirement complexes), in *Remainder* the spaces the protagonist occupies are actually purpose-(re)built, constructed for him to re-enact particular scenes and experiences over and over. Built like film sets in disused hangars and cordoned-off areas, they are simulacra representing different sign-orders,[48] ranging from being microscopically faithful reproductions of a space the protagonist has encountered to having seemingly no material origin.

The re-enactments have their origin in the violent moment of the protagonist's accident. In this he resembles Sigmund Freud's traumatised man 'who has experienced some frightful accident – a railway collision, for instance' and who, in subsequent weeks, 'develops a number of severe psychical and motor symptoms'.[49] Trauma is here constituted as 'an *event* that assaults the subject from the outside',[50] a 'breaching of the protective shield'[51] where 'the traumatic experience involves a fragmentation or loss of unity of the ego resulting from the radical unbinding of the death drive'.[52] The tendency in much writing on trauma is to focus on the notion of the traumatic event as a quasi-singular or, in the case of abuse, often as a repeated but the same kind of experience, and the debate is frequently about whether or not trauma is the result of external violence or of a psychic or internal process.[53] In McCarthy's *Remainder*, this either/or scenario is resolved in favour of a tripartite structure, another unholy trinity we might argue, of the experience of the initial violent traumatic event, i.e. the accident, its consequences for the victim in whom particular prior tendencies become augmented, and the implications of the resolution of these consequences for the victim and the others involved in the resolution. The protagonist in this novel is not interested in reconstructing his accident, nor does he remember it. But the severe physical wounds inflicted by the accident lead to a splitting of self involving a consciousness of his embodied materiality over which, on first recovering, he finds he has lost substantial control. He has to relearn '[e]verything, every movement: I had to learn them all',[54] breaking down all bodily activities 'into each constituent part, then execut[ing] them'.[55] For the protagonist this process denaturalises his corporeal demeanour and has a self-alienating effect: 'Recovering from the accident, learning to move and walk, understanding before I could act – all this just made me become even more what I'd always been anyway, added another layer of distance between me and things I did.'[56] Already previously alienated from his self, his subsequent quest, materialised in his re-enactments, is to get back to a state when he was 'the least artificial, the least second-hand'.[57] This state involves, from his point of view, unselfconsciousness about his actions, the supposed re-naturalisation of his behaviour by reassembling the self into a seamless imbricated performance. The world around him seems unreal, with everybody performing their roles[58] and hence being inauthentic and fraudulent. He has a memory that in certain spaces, 'all my movements had been fluent and unforced. Not awkward, acquired, second-hand, but natural ... I'd merged with them ... until there was no space between us ... I'd been real – *been* without first understanding how to try to be: cut out the detour.'[59] He wants to re-experience the merger of consciousness and bodily action into a state of un(self)conscious bliss where: 'My body seemed to glide fluently and effortlessly through the atmosphere around it – gracefully, slowly, like a dancer through water.'[60] The analogy to being in the womb is rather obvious here, a state and space outside the social since the symbiotic relation to the mother is not consciously experienced as such by the foetus (we assume). The protagonist's desired state of a pre-social undifferentiated blissful oblivion is granted him variously, but only momentarily, in his re-enactments. These are based on repetitive actions that lose their meaning in the very act of repetition until they acquire the monotony of pure iterative activity.[61] The 'hum of infinite self-repetition without origin or end'[62] is what he is after, a state where 'time became irrelevant, suspended, each instant widening into a huge warm yellow pool I could just lie in, passive, without end'.[63]

Such circumscription of being is, however, ultimately auto-destructive since its implicit immunisation from the other, secured through the other's exclusion by the absolute focus on self, produces entropy. The protagonist describes his reassembly of self as stripping away surplus matter, thus viewing the material rather than the psychic as the obstacle to his desired state of un-differentiation. In this he resembles the monolithic worldview informing the tempters' perspectives in Ballard's fictions. His ultimate undoing is the effect of matter (bits of technology) on matter – his brain and psyche.

Combining psychoanalysis and neuroscience Catherine Malabou has explored material changes to the brain which lead to permanent psychic changes. In *Ontology of the Accident* (2012) and other works[64] she discusses 'destructive plasticity', arguing that 'phenomena of coldness and indifference are characteristic of destructive plasticity, of this power of change without redemption, without teleology'.[65] Here brain damage 'interrupts the economy of our affects'[66] exactly as is the case in *Remainder*. In early dialogues in *Remainder* McCarthy plays with the two meanings of plastic, plastic as rigid and plastic as false or unreal – two versions of destructive plasticity that sidestep the actual issue faced by the protagonist. He is told by his physiotherapist that his 'muscles are still plastic ... Plastic. Rigid. It's the opposite of flaccid. With time they will go flaccid: malleable, relaxed. Flaccid, good; plastic, bad.'[67] Commenting on watching the actor Robert De Niro perform in a film the protagonist later explains to his friend: 'He's natural when he does things. Not artificial like me. He's flaccid. I'm plastic.'[68] His friend replies: 'He's the plastic one, I think you'll find ... being stamped onto a piece of film ...'.[69] The vocabulary is telling in terms of challenged masculinity; flaccidity, commonly associated with an un-erect penis (a penis that does not represent the phallus as masculine power), is not, within the conventional frame of masculinity, 'good'. Prowess, particularly sexual prowess, has in *this* depiction of late capitalist high individualism been replaced by money which 'speaks', or rather commands. The protagonist makes ample use of this prosthesis, wielding absolute control over his creations, the re-enactments, to the point of absurdity. At various points he reiterates to his re-enactors, 'I was paying [them] to do what I said',[70] a mantra of the absolute power of money. He never shows any concern for those trapped as re-enactors in his scenarios. In this he manifests the same perversion or absence of moral compass, in fact destructive plasticity, as certain characters in Ballard's novels do. McCarthy's protagonist wants just 'to be'. This is what he considers to be 'natural'. But such unselfconsciousness is not only rarely achieved, but also involves costs, the costs of oblivion to self and to other, a kind of death.

Cyborgs and Companion Species

The thanatopolitics of Ballard's and McCarthy's fictions are given a rather different slant in Deborah Levy's brilliant experimental fiction *Diary of a Steak*.[71] Here the collapse of boundaries is constructed as an effect of consumer desire. This collapse of boundaries, in the first instance between species, is semiotically and semantically invoked in the heteroglossia of the text itself which refuses distinctions between different kinds of discourse. It is a six-day anti-creation narrative, told by a piece of meat, during which a calf is turned into a steak, then minced beef as it decays. The antecedent to this text is in many ways Franz Kafka's monologue[72] by an ape addressing a learned society, 'A Report for an Academy', in which the ape details his/ its denaturalisation as a captive of humans. Making himself into a quasi-human spectacle and deliberately aiming to end up performing in a variety show rather than ending his life in a zoo, the ape conflates his humanisation and humans' dehumanisation in the species-defying assertion that 'your apehood, gentlemen, in so far as you have anything of the sort behind you, cannot be farther removed from you than mine is from me'.[73] Such equivalence is also produced in *Diary* when the steak asserts, 'Gentlemen ... We do have something in common after all. You eat sheep and I eat sheep.'[74] The text then draws explicit parallels both linguistically and semantically between the calf's descent into bovine spongiform encephalopathy (BSE), the effects of new variant Creutzfeldt-Jakob disease (vCJD) on humans, humans' self-poisoning through cross-species feeding of domestic animals and then eating those cross-fed animals, *and* the ways in which female hysterics were encouraged to display certain symptoms not dissimilar to those of BSE and vCJD to spectators in asylums in the late nineteenth century. Meat and hysterical women are here equated in complex ways to indict uncensored desire for embodied flesh, female or animal: 'Do you want to hear my erotic music?' asks the sign stuck into the steak that graces the original edition of the text. 'Just a piece of meat' turns out to be much more than that; playing to and on human desire as generative of death, the steak as carrier of a deadly disease startles the limits of the human as it asserts, through its history of denaturalised production, the importance of boundaries and the consequences of the failure to maintain these.

This, on the surface, flies in the face of notions of the 'reinvention of nature'[75] that Donna Haraway, for example, promotes in texts such as *Simians, Cyborgs, and Women, When Species Meet* and *Staying with the Trouble*. Like Esposito, Haraway regards the immune system as 'an elaborate icon for principal systems of symbolic and "material" difference in late capitalism ... a map drawn to guide recognition and misrecognition of self and other in the dialectic of Western biopolitics ... a plan for meaningful action to construct and maintain the boundaries for what may count as self and other in the crucial realms of the normal and the pathological'.[76] In *Diary of a Steak* the normal and the pathological collapse into each other as the 'fully denaturalized'[77] process of meat production generates a circular system of auto-destruction among humans by way of domestic animals whose humanly controlled creation and feeding processes render them toxic to humans and to themselves. The workshop of filthy creation[78] produces a 'fragmented post-modern subject'[79] which, however, refuses the usual suppression of 'the plane of political and moral discourse ... in scientific writing'.[80] Instead it asks whether the seductions of late capitalism, the production and repeated re-renderings of products (if you can't sell it as steak, turn it into mince – the mark of indistinction) whose 'erotic music' beckons the consumer, are an appropriate means to handle the 'constraint and possibility for engaging in a world full of "difference", replete with non-self'.[81]

Haraway's work, just like Levy's, asks how we know and understand, and hence deal with, difference, perhaps the key socio-political question of our time. This issue also engages Kazuo Ishiguro in *Never Let Me Go*, where the focus, however, is on the 'farming' of people rather than animals, this time for organs. Cloning has become an increasingly realistic possibility since the first cloning of Dolly the Sheep at the Roslin Institute in Edinburgh in 1996.[82] Its practice remains contested, not just on scientific, but also and importantly on ethical grounds.[83] Hence in *Never Let Me Go* 'ideas about difference ... are enacted and disturbed, in the performance of technoscience'[84] as the text portrays the clones' perspective on their lives, rather like Levy's *Diary* features the steak's view of its existence. The very fact of this focalisation grants this narrative perspective a pathetic humanity since having a voice is considered uniquely human. Its pathos resides in the 'techno-logic of fore-closure of opportunity'[85] that the clones, just like the steak which as calf could not choose what it was fed, suffer as a function of their fate as organ donors – their preordination for an engineered death. Regarded by those who rear them in the main as organ providers and hence effectively non-human, the clones live in a world where the material *qua* material in the form of the clones as whole entities is seemingly worthless, precisely because they suppo-sedly lack the quintessential human 'soul'. However, the clones' organs are highly prized and, as such, valued. Thus, while animated materiality (the clones) is abjected, inanimate fragmented materiality is desired. Both the clones and the calf fulfil service functions in relation to humans in providing them with body parts that are incorporated or ingested by the latter. Through that process as much as through the narrative perspectives adopted by the texts, any clear distinction between animal and human or clone and human is, however, refused. *Never Let Me Go* and *Diary* thus challenge 'conceptions of difference as absolute categories'.[86] Constructed as companion species or cyborgs, animals and clones in their fabricatedness and denaturalisation constitute in Haraway's words 'our ontology ... our politics'.[87] While this leads Haraway to produce 'an argument for *pleasure* in the confusion of boundaries and for *responsibility* in their construction',[88] in the fictional texts which portray the limits of the human, pleasure as a good is less evident than the often implicit notion of ethical responsibility as a necessity, threatened by extinction. Thanatos seems to prevail over Eros or Agape; community manifests itself mainly as a defensive reaction against intruders, against risk, against infection – against that and those who might undo the prevalence of a singular vision of the world. Unsurprisingly, in his discussion of cloning Baudrillard describes the latter as 'the hell of the same'.[89] It leaves 'the self purged of the other, deprived of its divided character and doomed to self-metastasis, to pure repetition'.[90] Comparing cloning to cancerous growth in its proliferation of cells,[91] Baudrillard views clones as 'enucleated of their being'[92] and no longer confronting the other, thus ultimately becoming 'an antibody to [themselves]'.[93] In Baudrillard's writings we find the same preoccupation with corporeal and psychical immunity as in Haraway's and Esposito's work, and a similar notion of the operations of the death drive at the heart of contemporary biotechnological developments: 'what, if not a death drive, would ... impel us ... to deny all otherness, to shun any alteration in the same, and to seek nothing beyond the perpetuation of an identity, nothing but the transparency of genetic inscription no longer subject even to the vicissitudes of procreation?'.[94]

Difference and the Post-Humane

The preoccupation with difference and, importantly, differentiation has continued to haunt contemporary British writing well into the twenty-first century. In Deborah Levy's novel *Hot Milk*, for example, that preoccupation manifests itself in the exploration of a mother–daughter relationship, a common and much explored trope in feminist writing and literary criticism from the late 1960s onwards. Here the limits of the human are articulated as questions of how much the human can endure, psychologically or physically. *Hot Milk* confronts its characters with finitude as the mother's toxic hysterical hypochondria, mobilised to tie her daughter to her side following her abandonment by her husband, transforms, unexpectedly and soberingly, into the prospect of the mother's imminent actual bodily death from oesophageal cancer. In *Hot Milk* we revisit the Spanish costas already familiar from Ballard's work, where the mother–daughter combo are seeking help for the mother's hysterical paralysis.

The guru doctor they consult rightly diagnoses a failure of separation on the part of mother and daughter. Significantly the novel's epigraph is a quote from Hélène Cixous's famous feminist classic 'The Laugh of the Medusa': 'It's up to you to break the old circuits', and the novel begins with a depiction of the symbiotic relation of the daughter and her laptop (the motherboard?): 'My laptop has all my life in it and knows more about me than anyone else. So what I am saying is that if it is broken, so am I.'[95] The indirect personification of the laptop since it knows more than 'any*one* else'[96] is telling here. It gestures towards a cyborgian fusion between, in this instance, woman and machine which functions as an analogy to the daughter's relation with her mother. The latter fusion, repeatedly expressed in the text as a corporeal equation (e.g. 'her head is my head'[97]), is both an articulation of a state, evidenced by the use of the verb to be, *and* in its sheer bodily impossibility (humans cannot be identitarian in the way suggested by the just referenced state) a form of auto-destruction: it makes the mother psychosomatically ill and maintains her in that state, and prevents the daughter from becoming an adult independent of her mother. In classic quasi-Freudian fashion the text suggests that female intra-familial interdependence as a reaction to male abandonment impedes both women's ability to move on. Classically, also, it is through the help of a male doctor that mother and daughter come to understand their dilemmas. However, in a more contemporary gender-bending twist the doctor's clinic 'resemble[s] a spectral, solitary breast ... [with] a maternal lighthouse ...'.[98] The maternality of the doctor as saviour has its counterpart in the daughter's sense that 'we are all lurking in each other's sign' such that 'a daughter can be a sister or a mother to her mother who can be a father and a mother to her daughter ...'.[99] For all these claims of merger, the novel finally comes down in favour of an also classic separation: the mother has to die so that the daughter may live. Differentiation remains a necessity, but the pull of biological kinship also remains; the smashing of technology signals the refusal of fusion. The kindness of women has its limits.

This limit is also only too evident in one of the new fiction forms to emerge fully in the 1990s, graphic novels for adults.[100] Graphic novels for adults, and especially ones for and by women, emerged in Britain somewhat later than in the United States. They are part of the 1980s and 1990s 'epidemic of signification'.[101] In this epidemic the AIDS/HIV crisis, the related use of immunological metaphors and critiques, the rise and spread of information and communication technology, and the move towards neoliberalism, market cultures and global aggressivity in the form of multiple wars in which Britain actively participated, altogether conjoined to lead to new forms and uses of visualisation. These ranged from memory quilts for those dead from AIDS to computer and video games encouraging active, if 'not real' killing online, a mode of communication later replicated in the online dissemination of actual killings of hostages by Islamist factions of different kinds. One might argue that the mother's psychosomatic ailments in *Hot Milk* are but one expression of how women's limits of kindness translate into (self)abandonment when and as they are unable to effect change. Significantly, quite a number of British graphic novels by women (and to some extent by men) have taken up this theme.[102] I shall briefly discuss two: Emma Rendel's *The Vicar Woman* and Rob Davis's *The Motherless Oven*.

The Vicar Woman centres on a female pastor newly employed on an island who discovers that her role appears to be to help its community atone for their turning a collective blind eye to violent sexual child abuse. The community itself maintains silence about those events, and the vicar woman only gradually discovers what appears to have happened. The distortion of the truth this involves is visually signalled through several devices: the elongated noses and mouths of many of the characters, reminiscent of Pinocchio's nose elongation for lying, but also suggestive of grotesque phalluses; the use of unusual, oblique visual perspectives, particularly from above and from below, to gesture towards the lack of direct engagement between characters, and the inaccessibility of the truth; whole-page panels involving large numbers of characters to indicate community connivance, including by the island's core institutional representatives: the teacher, the doctor, the previous vicar. Like Ballard, Rendel makes use of the self-enclosed and hence lawless, ungoverned community to suggest that the post-humane is fostered by this kind of geo-social separation. There is a map for abuse. It is enclosure. The narrative implicitly references a number of child sexual abuse scenarios that gained worldwide media attention in the 1990s and 2000s: the abuses in children's homes, the Catholic church, boarding schools, girls' imprisonment for sexual exploitation for years in family homes and on islands. Rendel renders her figures less than human, or other than human, through morphologically visualising them as having on the one hand certain exaggerated bodily parts (e.g. leading the vicar by their noses – intended pun!) and, on the other, lacking others (e.g. no arms in some panels, perhaps to indicate that they are 'sitting on their hands', i.e. doing nothing, or closing up, or acting in consort). This dehumanising visual effect suggests performance, here understood as a stylisation of interaction that sequesters guilt from view. Rejected by the congregation because she fails to go along with their desire to be absolved by her for their inhumane treatment of a little girl who was sexually abused by her father, the vicar woman leaves the island, effectively allowing the congregation to get away with their bystander attitude, and indicting a world that fails to intervene.[103]

Abusive or antagonistic relations between authority figures and their offspring, literally and symbolic, have been the long-standing subject of mythic and religious, as well as secular, tales as a way of imbuing the socio-material world with meaning. At the centre of *The Motherless Oven* is a group of three teenagers, two boys and a girl, rather like in the *Harry Potter* tales, all strange in a strange world.[104] Scarper, Vera and Castro live in the Death Age where their death day is preordained and known. They study subjects such as Mythmatics, God Science, Theory of Switches and Circular History at school. Their parents are all machines, made from ancient and unfamiliar parts, which the teenagers have to maintain. When Scarper's machine dad disappears, Castro's bedside lamp tells them that 'he went in search of the motherless oven where all the mums and dads are baked by the children of the world'.[105] This inversion of genesis, where children supposedly make parents, projects a dark necropolitics reinforced by the use of black gutters, the borders around the panels, on many pages. Male and female adult authority figures are equally implicated in the necropolitics of this graphic novel which condemns its characters to perish by their death date.

Conclusions

One of the cultural manifestations of contemporary (bio)technological changes in British writing is the construction of worlds that explore the limits of the human. However, instead of projecting the ludic, celebratory possibilities of these changes that much critical writing heralds,[106] many of the texts raise questions regarding the ethical implications of living in worlds that shift the limits of the human. These limits may be understood in material or immaterial terms, usually as effects of changing environments, fusions across material entities or imbrications of the material in the human. Arguing against the collapse of boundaries, these texts reflect on the ethical implications of the drive towards sameness and ultimately entropy that this collapse implies, a kind of necropolitics. In writings by men this is associated with a male over-reacher syndrome, a drive towards complete, technologically facilitated control which is meant to act as a counterpoint to the actual ontological uncertainty that accompanies contemporary (bio)technology. Here control is possible through the fragmented and segmented social worlds that the texts showcase, akin to technology in its algorithmic structuring. It is achieved through segregated spaces that permit the exclusion of and total lack of empathy for others. Postulating somewhat parallel worlds to the actual one we inhabit, and exploring the relation between individual and community, these texts suggest that the ability to tolerate difference is key to an ethical engagement with the other, that such tolerance tests the limits of the human, understood as what we are ready to do and willing to endure, but that evacuating the scene of difference is not the answer.

Notes

1. S. Franklin and S. McKinnon (eds), *Relative Values: Reconfiguring Kinship Studies* (Durham, NC: Duke University Press, 2001).

2. I. Sample, 'First UK Licence to Create Three-Person Baby Granted by Fertility Regulator', *The Guardian* (16 March 2017), www.theguardian.com/science/2017/mar/16/first-licence-to-create-three-person-baby-granted-by-uk-fertility-regulator.

3. M. Hogan, 'Horizon: Dawn of the Driverless Car Is an Entertaining Spin Around Driverless-Car Technology: Review', *The Telegraph* (29 June 2017), www.telegraph.co.uk/tv/2017/06/29/horizon-dawn-driverless-car-entertaining-spin-around-driverless/.

4. M. Hanson, 'Robot Carers for Elderly People Are "Another Way of Dying Even More Miserably"', *The Guardian* (14 March 2016), www.theguardian.com/lifeandstyle/2016/mar/14/robot-carers-for-elderly-people-are-another-way-of-dying-even-more-miserably.

5. M. Gonzalez, 'The Aesthetics of Post-Realism and the Obscenification of Everyday Life: The Novel in the Age of Technology' (2008) 38(1) *Journal of Narrative Theory* 111–33, 111.

6. S. Andermahr, 'Cyberspace and the Body: Jeanette Winterson's *The PowerBook*' in N. Bentley (ed.), *British Fiction of the 1990s* (London: Routledge, 2005), pp. 108–21.

7. *Ibid.*, p. 110.

8. J. G. Ballard, *Cocaine Nights* (London: Harper Perennial, 2006), p. 9.

9. M. Augé, *Non-Places: Introduction to an Anthropology of Supermodernity*, trans. J. Howe (London: Verso, 1995).

10. J. G. Ballard, *Super-Cannes* (London: Harper Perennial, 2001), p. 3.

11. Ballard, *Cocaine Nights*, p. 264.

12. G. Lipovetsky, *Hypermodern Times*, trans. A. Brown (Cambridge: Polity, 2005).

13. G. Perry, *The Descent of Man* (London: Allen Lane, 2016).

14. Z. Zhang, A. Spicer and P. Hancock, 'Hyper-Organizational Space in the Work of J. G. Ballard' (2008) 15(6) *Organization* 889–910.

15. E. Kosofsky Sedgwick, *Between Men: English Literature and Male Homosocial Desire* (New York: Columbia University Press, 1985).

16. Ballard, *Super-Cannes*, p. 17.

17. *Ibid.*, p. 181.

18. *Ibid.*, pp. 89–90.

19. *Ibid.*, p. 180.

20. P. Norris, *Electoral Engineering: Voting Rules and Political Behaviour* (Cambridge University Press, 2004); and D. S. Glasberg and D. Shannon, *Political Sociology: Oppression, Resistance, and the State* (London: Sage, 2010).

21. Ballard, *Cocaine Nights*, p. 180.

22. T. Elborough, 'An Investigative Spirit: Travis Elborough Talks to J. G. Ballard' in Ballard, *Cocaine Nights*, pp. 17–18.

23. Ballard, *Cocaine Nights*, p. 180.

24. Ballard, *Super-Cannes*, p. 94.

25. *Ibid.*, p. 263.

26. Ballard, *Cocaine Nights*, p. 180.

27. Ballard, *Super-Cannes*, p. 264.
28. See J. Baxter, *J. G. Ballard* (London: Continuum, 2008); A. Gasiorek, *J. G. Ballard* (Manchester University Press, 2005); and R. Luckhurst, *The Angel between Two Walls: The Fiction of J. G. Ballard* (Liverpool University Press, 1997).
29. Elborough, 'An Investigative Spirit', p. 15.
30. *Ibid.*
31. Ballard, *Cocaine Nights*, p. 193.
32. R. Esposito, *Terms of the Political* (New York: Fordham University Press, 2013), p. 14.
33. Ballard, *Cocaine Nights*, p. 256.
34. Esposito, *Terms of the Political*, p. 30.
35. Ballard, *Super-Cannes*, p. 95.
36. *Ibid.*
37. *Ibid.*
38. *Ibid.*, p. 263.
39. *Ibid.*, p. 365.
40. *Ibid.*
41. A. Mbembe, 'Necropolitics' (2003) 15(1) *Public Culture* 11–40.
42. Ballard, *Super-Cannes*, p. 134.
43. Elborough, *An Investigative Spirit*.
44. Esposito, *Terms of the Political*, p. 59.
45. T. McCarthy, *Remainder* (London: Alma Books, 2005), p. 5.
46. *Ibid.*, p. 260.
47. S. Baron-Cohen, *Zero Degrees of Empathy* (London: Penguin, 2012).
48. J. Baudrillard, *Simulacra and Simulation*, trans. S. Glaser (Ann Arbor, MI: University of Michigan Press, 1994).
49. S. Freud, *The Origins of Religion* (Harmondsworth: Penguin, 1986), vol. 13, pp. 309–10.
50. R. Leys, *Trauma: A Genealogy* (University of Chicago Press, 2000), p. 33 (emphasis in the original).
51. *Ibid.*
52. *Ibid.*, p. 34.
53. C. Caruth, *Trauma: Explorations in Memory* (Baltimore, MD: Johns Hopkins University Press, 1995); and Leys, *Trauma*.
54. McCarthy, *Remainder*, p. 20.
55. *Ibid.*
56. *Ibid.*, p. 23.
57. *Ibid.*
58. See, e.g., *ibid.*, pp. 48, 54.
59. *Ibid.*, p. 60 (emphasis in the original).
60. *Ibid.*, p. 129.
61. See, e.g., *ibid.*, pp. 144–5.
62. *Ibid.*, p. 186.
63. *Ibid.*, p. 196.
64. C. Malabou, *The New Wounded* (New York: Fordham University Press, 2012); and A. Johnston and C. Malabou, *Self and Emotional Life* (New York: Columbia University Press, 2013).
65. C. Malabou, *Ontology of the Accident* (Cambridge: Polity Press, 2012), p. 24.

66. Johnston and Malabou, *Self and Emotional Life*, p. 58.
67. McCarthy, *Remainder*, p. 21.
68. *Ibid.*, p. 22.
69. *Ibid.*
70. *Ibid.*, p. 135.
71. For a detailed reading of this text, see R. McKay, 'BSE, Hysteria and the Representation of Animal Death: Deborah Levy's *Diary of a Steak*' in The Animal Studies Group, *Killing Animals* (Urbana, IL: University of Illinois Press, 2006), pp. 145–69.
72. F. Kafka, 'A Report for an Academy' in J. A. Underwood (trans.), Franz Kafka: Stories 1904–1924 (London: Futura Macdonald & Co., 1981), pp. 219–28.
73. *Ibid.*, p. 219.
74. D. Levy, *Diary of a Steak* (London: Book Works, 1997), pp. 6–7.
75. D. Haraway, *Simians, Cyborgs, and Women: The Reinvention of Nature* (London: Free Association Books, 1991).
76. *Ibid.*, p. 204.
77. *Ibid.*, p. 209.
78. Buckley, 2009.
79. Haraway, *Simians, Cyborgs, and Women*, p. 211.
80. *Ibid.*, p. 213.
81. *Ibid.*, p. 214.
82. See the National Human Genome Research Institute's website for latest updates: www.genome.gov/25020028/cloning-fact-sheet/ and www.roslin.ed.ac.uk/public-interest/dolly-the-sheep/a-life-of-dolly/.
83. F. Bowring, 'Therapeutic and Reproductive Cloning: A Critique' (2004) 58(2) *Social Science & Medicine* 401–9; and A. Fiester, 'Ethical Issues in Animal Cloning' (2005) 48(2) *Perspectives in Biology and Medicine* 328–43.
84. W. Anderson, 'Introduction: Postcolonial Technoscience' (2002) 32(5–6) *Social Studies of Science* 643–58, 644.
85. G. Griffin, 'Science and the Cultural Imaginary: The Case of Kazuo Ishiguro's Never Let Me Go' (2009) 23(4) *Textual Practice* 645–63, 655.
86. *Ibid.*, p. 653.
87. Haraway, *Simians, Cyborgs, and Women*, p. 150.
88. *Ibid.* (emphases in the original).
89. J. Baudrillard, *The Transparency of Evil: Essays on Extreme Phenomena*, trans. J. Benedict (London: Verso, 2009), p. 129.
90. *Ibid.*, p. 140.
91. *Ibid.*, pp. 137–8.
92. *Ibid.*, p. 138.
93. *Ibid.*, p. 139.
94. *Ibid.*, pp. 130–1.
95. D. Levy, *Hot Milk* (London: Hamish Hamilton, 2016), p. 1.
96. *Ibid.* (emphasis added).
97. *Ibid.*, p. 11.
98. *Ibid.*, p. 211.
99. *Ibid.*, p. 159.
100. Relatively little has been written on this new form which has its antecedents in comic books for children and teenagers, and what there is comes mostly from the

United States. For a brief history, see S. Weiner, *Faster than a Speeding Bullet: The Rise of the Graphic Novel* (New York: Nantier, Beall, Minouchstchine Publishing, 2003).

101. P. Treichler, 'AIDS, Homophobia, and Biomedical Discourse: An Epidemic of Signification' (1987) 43 *October* 31–70.

102. See, e.g., K. Green, *Lighter than My Shadow* (London: Jonathan Cape, 2013); Una, *Becoming Unbecoming* (Brighton: Myriad Editions, 2015); and B. Yelin, *Irmina* (London: Selfmadehero, 2016).

103. It is worth noting that in 2016 the UK government set up an Independent Inquiry into Child Sexual Abuse (see www.iicsa.org.uk), following overwhelming evidence of the rise of this phenomenon, and the emergence of significant so-called historical abuse, including in the British Broadcasting Corporation (BBC) by entertainers, etc.

104. For a review, see E. Szep, 'The Motherless Oven', *The Comics Journal* (2016), www.tcj.com/reviews/the-motherless-oven/.

105. R. Davis, *The Motherless Oven* (London: Selfmadehero, 2014), p. 75.

106. See, e.g., N. K. Hayles, *How We Became Posthuman* (Chicago University Press, 1999); and N. K. Hayles, *My Mother Was a Computer: Digital Subjects and Literary Texts* (Chicago University Press, 2005).

5

KEVIN BRAZIL

Form and Fiction, 1980–2018

Form is one of the more slippery concepts in literary criticism: elusive of definition, unavoidable in practice. Even the most doctrinaire of political critics, questioned as to why they are writing about novels to expose economic injustice, rather than about the more obvious evidence of income distribution, must justify their choice, in the end, by claiming there is something distinct about the novel as a form that offers insights unavailable elsewhere. That distinction has often been a dubious one. In a claim that set the tone for attitudes towards form at the beginning of the period covered by this *Companion*, Fredric Jameson argued that form named a special kind of deception: 'the production of aesthetic or narrative form is to be seen as an ideological act in its own right, with the function of inventing imaginary or formal "solutions" to unresolvable social contradictions'.[1] This inverted the tradition, beginning with Kant and Schiller, of using form to name what distinguished literature in a positive sense from other uses of language. This use of form was dubious in its own way, acquiring so many contradictory meanings that it became, as Angela Leighton observes, 'a noun lying in wait of its object'.[2] Yet whether the target of censure or praise, literary critics have never strayed far from using form to talk about the relationship between what Raymond Williams identified as two persistent but different meanings: a 'visible and outward shape' and an 'essential shaping principle'.[3] The attempt to talk about both at once is what makes the concept of fictional form so slippery. In trying to analyse as tangible that which can only be virtual, form must always evade our grasp. You can't point to linear causality, just as you can't touch first-person narration, but these are the shapes and shaping principles we use form to name. Form is an attempt to talk about what enables language to mean by imagining something tangible and material lying between words and their referents, be they themselves real or imaginary.

An embrace of the slippery nature of form has marked its return to prominence as a topic of debate in literary studies. No longer the purest distillation of ideological deception, form has come to be regarded as the record of an 'act-event'[4] identifying the uniquely literary at the same time as it has declared to be 'patterns of socio-political experience ... at work everywhere'.[5] Form is a discipline-specific 'notion bound pragmatically to its instances' of textual explanation;[6] form is a property shared across art and nature: 'the shape matter (whether a poem or a tree) takes'.[7] It is the 'tiny enigmatic pivot in much of the current debate about literary studies';[8] it is the focus of an exclusive 'new formalism'.[9] Strange as it may seem when these definitions so flagrantly contradict each other, form has been hailed as what will give literary studies new purpose after years of historical contextualisation and subservience to cultural studies.[10] But maybe this elusiveness is the point. Form is not something that needs a definition, but the precipitant of new questions – or of old questions newly asked. What uses of language should we value, and why? What political effects do we want literary criticism to have? Or do we just want to linger in literature as a source of pleasure, and not feel guilty about it?

In surveying British fiction's relationship to form from 1980 to 2018, this chapter will not attempt an exhaustive taxonomy of the different forms deployed by different writers, nor a merely descriptive stylistics. Instead, it will offer a history of moments when form surfaced as a question that became particularly pressing for certain writers at certain times, analysing these moments in order to give an account of the motivations and consequences of these changes. Sometimes fiction changed in tune with changes in criticism and theory, sometimes not; but because the history of theory in this period is amply documented elsewhere,[11] this chapter will foreground the statements and practice of novelists out of the conviction that they are too often neglected in studies of contemporary fiction. Not all writers are concerned with the question of form, even when they are committed to reflecting on how meaning is made. A fiction's 'visible outward shape' and 'shaping principle' can be determined by something else: textuality, discourse, structure, ideology, myth, the unconscious. At the beginning of the 1980s, the question of fiction's form was seen as less important than how fiction was defined by such concepts, since they seemed to be what opened fiction up to questions of politics, subjectivity, the limits language placed on knowledge. Yet as the decades passed, a number of writers with very different aims, from investigations of life-writing to the renewal of realism, turned not so much away from these questions, but towards seeing them as inescapably bound up with the question of their fiction's form.

Myths, Structures and Discourses

'I'm in the demythologizing business': so declared Angela Carter in a 1983 essay about the relationship between gender and writing in her work.[12]

Despite her familiarity with the theorists guiding these debates in the 1980s, she was no theorist *manqué*: 'What I *really* like doing is writing fiction and trying to work things out *that* way.'[13] From *The Passion of the New Eve* (1977) onwards she was attempting to demythologise the 'social fictions that regulate our lives – what Blake called the "mind forg'd manacles"', above all 'the social fiction of my "femininity"'.[14] Her understanding of myth was influenced by how 'Roland Barthes uses it in *Mythologies* – ideas, images, stories that we tend to take on trust without thinking what they really mean'.[15] To expose them she turned to folklore and fairly tales because '[i]t turned out to be easier to deal with the shifting structures of reality and sexuality by using sets of shifting structures derived from orally transmitted traditional tales'.[16] Her writing was 'applied linguistics', because 'language is power, life, and the instrument of culture, the instrument of domination and liberation'.[17] Only from within fiction can the structures that produce us be exposed. Fevvers' desire in *Nights at the Circus* (1984) to liberate women from their 'mind forg'd manacles' sees her burlesque the 'simulacra' of feminine archetypes from Sleeping Beauty to 'S-O-P-H-I-A', the symbol of knowledge itself.[18] The novel's own burlesque of fairy-tale tropes guides its exposure of the linguistic production of femininity: 'As a symbolic woman, she has a meaning, as an anomaly, none.'[19] 'Woman' only exists as a consequence of the symbolic pursuit of meaning, and gender is a product of symbolic structure. Carter's linking of textual and sexual politics was hardly new, but if for a previous generation this was, as Doris Lessing's Anna Wulf claimed, 'a question of *form*', for Carter it was a question of myth, structure and language.[20] Instead of fiction being a form through which new expressions of selfhood can be realised, it is a means for exposing the linguistic structures that produce the myths of our subjectivity.

Carter was not the only British writer in the demythologising business during the 1980s. Salman's Rushdie's *Midnight's Children* (1981) is about 'India, the new myth – a collective fiction in which anything was possible', and like Carter he saw myth as enabled and exposed by the manipulation of linguistic structures.[21] The governing principle of *Midnight's Children* is that Saleem Sinai is 'linked to history both literally and metaphorically'.[22] His narrative literalises the metaphors of the nation in order to expose them as just that: mere metaphors. This is the principle to which Saleem refers when he declares: 'There is no escape from form.'[23] These literalised metaphors are produced by Saleem himself, but we only read the error-strewn chapters that are revisions of drafts read by his wife Padma. Demythologisation is achieved not by revealing the real truth of history, but by the metafictional exposure that all histories are fictions – an exposure that is itself a fiction. The aim, as Rushdie wrote in his subsequent novel *Shame* (1983), was 'the substitution of a new myth for the old one'.[24] All history for Saleem is a product of 'chutnification', a pickling that distorts as it preserves, a mixture of myth and fiction.[25] All we can do is choose the myths we live by, just as we choose the chutneys that suit our taste.

The use of metafictional strategies to expose history as a fiction was pervasive in British fiction in the 1980s and 1990s. As A. S. Byatt observed, although one impetus for the 'polemical revisionist tales' by Rushdie, Caryl Phillips and Timothy Mo were the consequences of colonisation, this was preceded by the scepticism about Britain's own national story shown by Anthony Burgess, William Golding and John Fowles. Graham Swift's *Waterland* (1983), Peter Ackroyd's *Hawksmoor* (1985) and Byatt's own *Possession* (1990) continued this debunking of national histories.[26] Summing up this demythologising decade, the narrator of Julian Barnes's *A History of the World in 10 ½ Chapters* (1990) declared: 'History isn't what happened. History is just what historians tell us ... Our panic and our pain are only eased by soothing fabulation; we call it history.'[27] For Barnes, the 'multiplicity of subjective truths we assess and fabulate into history' demands a leap of faith akin to love: 'We must believe in it, or we're lost.'[28] As with Rushdie, we must accept the loss of even provisional objectivity: 'Myth will become reality, however skeptical we might be.'[29] The dissolving of the boundaries between fiction and history, and fiction and reality itself, leads to a scepticism focusing on the identity of authors and writers. In deciding what to believe, what matters is the identity of the teller, not the coherence of the tale. Or as Jeanette Winterson's *The Passion* concludes: 'I'm telling you stories, trust me.'[30]

The controversy surrounding Rushdie's *The Satanic Verses* (1988) so quickly became the medium for political conflict that Gayatri Spivak declared it was 'impossible' to read the novel apart from the controversy it caused.[31] But part of that controversy was a return to claims that fiction was a form that must be read differently from the discourses of history, religion or politics. Accusations of misinterpretation were frequently accusations of being insufficiently attentive to form. Aamir Mufti faulted critics outside 'the Muslim public sphere' for failing to grasp the novel's '*ambivalence* of form';[32] according to Edward Said, the novel was 'not just *about* the mixture' and hybridity of contemporary culture, 'it *is* that mixture'.[33] One of Rushdie's own earliest responses focused neither on a legal right to free speech nor on issues of identity, but on the novel as a form. The novel was not just another language like politics or religion; rather, 'the novel has always been *about* the way in which different languages, values, and narratives quarrel, and about the shifting relations between them, which are relation of power. The novel does not seek to establish a privileged language, but it insists upon the freedom to portray and analyse the struggle between the different contestants for such privileges.'[34] The novel is 'the form created to discuss the fragmentation of truth', the acceptance 'that reality and morality and not givens but imperfect human constructs'.[35] Citing the authority of Richard Rorty, Jean-François Lyotard and Michel Foucault, Rushdie offered a theory of the novel as 'the crucial art form of . . . our post-modern age'.[36] The novel was 'the most freakish, hybrid, and metamorphic of forms', and thus it is 'the arena of discourse, the place where the struggle of languages can be acted out . . . where we can hear *voices talking about everything in every possible way*'.[37]

This postmodern theory of the novel, one that recalls Mikhail Bakhtin's theorisation of the novel as the site of linguistic *heteroglossia*, posits fiction as a form outside relations of power that can reveal the work of other discourses. Yet by assuming a specific view of that work – that language constructs the world – its claim to be a neutral platform staging the drama of discourse is an exercise in bad faith: all voices can speak so long as they speak on the terms of a secular relativism, and staged debate takes the place of democratic conflict. This tension is manifested in the form of Rushdie's own fiction. As Neil ten Kortenaar observes, while Rushdie's novels feature a carnival of voices, they contain precious little dialogue between characters.[38] The reason for this can be explained by way of Franco Moretti's critique of Bakhtin, who points out that heteroglossia and dialogism actually exist in inverse proportion to one another: 'If people don't speak the same language, after all, how is dialogue going to be possible?'[39] The controversy surrounding *The Satanic Verses* showed critics and authors relying upon the concept of literary form in order to account for the novel's political effects in an age when British fiction was part of an unequally structured global literary field, a field fractured by differences that could not be resolved by invocations of cultural hybridity and epistemic relativism. Yet it also showed that reductions of the work of form to enacting demythologising critique or staging a carnival of discourse were unable to account for form's effects at a moment when they had become more consequential than ever.

Forms of Life, Forms of Fiction

'How do we seize the past?' If the question Geoffrey Braithwaite asks in Julian Barnes's *Flaubert's Parrot* (1984) animates much late-twentieth-century British fiction, so too does the answer he discovers: 'the past is autobiographical fiction pretending to be a parliamentary report'.[40] As the novel's mock paper in literary criticism notes: 'It has become clear to the examiners in recent years that candidates are finding it increasingly difficult to distinguish between Art and Life.'[41] In Rushdie's *Midnights Children*, Swift's *Waterland*, Carter's *Wise Children* (1991), Pat Barker's *Regeneration* trilogy, or A. S. Byatt's *Possession* and *The Biographer's Tale* (2000), seizing the past takes the form of autobiographical and biographical fictions: fictions where a narrator is engaged in autobiographical writing, or fictions incorporating partial or whole biographies. The assumption that seizing the past can be achieved through the story of a life echoes shifts in historiography during the 1980s, when oral histories, microhistories, testimony and memory all assumed new prominence. In the same way such fictions suggest the past doesn't exist outside of the fictions we write about it, so too they explore the extent to which the self might be nothing more than fiction.

The relativist tendencies Rushdie identified as characterising a 'postmodern age' also influenced auto/biographical practice and theory, and their interactions with fiction. What is the referent of auto/biography when it is not a self expressed in writing, but what Roland Barthes calls a 'subject [that is] merely an effect of language'?[42] Paul de Man and Jacques Derrida's deconstructions of the rhetorical and generic markers separating autobiography from fiction aimed to show, as de Man wrote, that 'the distinction between fiction and autobiography ... is undecidable'.[43] Judith Butler's performative account of identity suggested autobiographical writing as an ambivalently constitutive and constraining practice for the articulation of subject positions.[44] The cumulative effect of these theorists led many autobiography critics to claim that 'the self that is the center of all autobiographical narrative is necessarily a fictive structure'.[45] Yet as Laura Marcus has observed, claims that the auto/biographical self is a literary fiction only displaces the question as to what that fiction is: 'Cultural postmodernism, while endorsing fictionalism and conventionalism, has to an extent relativized the sphere of the "literary" and thus troubled the concept of literary identity.'[46] For a range of writers writing in the wake of postmodernism, the troubling of the literary effected by the elision of the difference between self and text, autobiography and fiction, became a way to raise new questions about fiction as a form by probing its scope and limits for writing lives.

The late careers of Britain's two Nobel laureates for fiction in this period, V. S. Naipaul and Doris Lessing, were characterised by a juxtaposition of fictional, historical and auto/biographical modes that exemplify a version of late style defined by Edward Said 'not as harmony and resolution but as intransigence, difficulty, and unresolved contradiction'.[47] Naipaul's *A Way in the World* (1994) consists of a 'sequence' trying to make sense of a self born into a landscape 'wiped clean' of the past by colonisation. The sequence features a writer adopting the autobiographical perspective of being 'strangers to ourselves';[48] the 'historical bird's eye view'[49] provided by archival research; imagining fictionalised biographies of past lives; and reading the literary criticism of the radical Lebrun. The relationship between these different modes of writing is left unresolved, and this formal parataxis is the narrator's relationship to history: what is the connection between the past and his present? An unresolved conflict between the forms of fiction and autobiography also structures Lessing's *Alfred and Emily* (2008). In a final attempt to get free of the 'monstrous legacy' of war that 'squatted over my childhood', the book begins with a novella imagining the lives of her parents had they never met, followed by an auto/biographical reflection on the life they lived in colonial Rhodesia.[50] The latter section figures the relationship between mother and daughter in terms of lives enabled and denied, with Lessing imagining her mother's thoughts: '*You won't let me live through you, you won't let me be you, you're killing me.*'[51] Fiction might be able to atone for the death all children inflict on their parents by assuming their own life, but that this atonement is a life where Lessing's parents do not marry means it is a life bought at the cost of her own death. If this makes the 'monstrous legacy' squatting over the book ambiguously war, her parents, or the original violence of being born, as with Naipaul's attempt to make sense of a self born from colonial violence, *Alfred and Emily* refuses to elide fiction and auto-biography by showing the costs of how both forms make sense of the self.

A sense of historical lateness shadowed the work of another writer whose interweaving of fiction, life-writing and photography was credited as invent-ing 'a new literary form' that has had an important influence on British fiction: W. G. Sebald.[52] In what Sebald cagily called his 'semi-documentary prose fiction', especially *The Emigrants* (1993) and *Austerlitz* (2001), the writing of lives rather than traditional logics of plot and genre structure and shape the narrative.[53] These life stories are conveyed through what Sebald called a form of perioscopic narration: inverting the creative writing mantra of 'show, don't tell', a narrator recounts what other people reveal about themselves and the lives of others, so that one life story is always mediated by another. Woven through these narratives are reproductions of photographs, with one of their many effects being to introduce the questions of reference, testimony and evidence raised by photography's indexical relationship to its referent. Sebald's works derive their form from life-writing and make the act of narrating lives their theme, but in seeming to hew so close to telling the stories of lives and history, the moments when they slide into fiction are charged with implications for how we understand the ethics of fictional form. One example is Ambros Adelwarth's diary in *The Emigrants*: presented as evidence for the source of the narrative, it was in fact written by Sebald himself.[54] Such manipulations aimed to throw up 'one of the central pro-blems of fiction writing, which is that of legitimacy and arrival at the truth on crooked route'.[55] What are the truths provided by fiction as a form – and how are they different from those of history, memory or auto/biography? What are the responsibilities of the novelist – and to whom? After a decade when fiction's imaginary solutions were deemed as suspect as they were unavoidable, by turning to life-writing and photography, Sebald revealed new capacities for remembrance, as well as new dangers of deception, in the illusion that is fiction as a form.

Sebald's entangling of fiction and life-writing has been so influential that Hari Kunzru saw it producing 'an emerging genre, the novel after Sebald, its 19th-century furniture of plot and character dissolved into a series of passages, held together by occasional photographs and a subjectivity that hovers close to (but is never quite identical with) the subjectivity of the writer'.[56] Engagement with forms of life-writing and its epistemological and ethical claims characterises writers across the globe: Teju Cole, Sheila Heti, Karl Ove Knausgaard, Chris Krauss and Edouard Louis. In Britain the recent work of Rachel Cusk shares this concern with the relationship between life and fiction, while being distinctively preoccupied with how it is complicated by the effect of form. In her memoir *Aftermath* (2012), the aftermath of the title is at once her life after a divorce and the narrative of that life: 'I no longer have a life. It's an afterlife; it's all aftermath.'[57] Her novels *Outline* (2014), *Transit* (2016), and *Kudos* (2018) are structured around a largely silent narrator, Faye, who conveys the conversations of others – a form similar to Sebald's *The Emigrants* and *Austerlitz*. But if for Sebald one person's autobiographical confession enables another, for Faye the stories of others produce an 'anti-description' and a 'corresponding negative': other life-stories only enable her 'to see herself as a shape, an outline, with all the details filled in around it while the shape itself remained blank'.[58] In *Transit*, she reflects that 'I had found out more by listening than I had ever thought possible'; but she learns not self-knowledge, but 'how to read that fate, to see the forms and patterns in the things that happened'.[59] For Cusk – as for the classical figures of Oedipus and Medea haunting her stories – the creation of a story of one's life is a moment of loss, the retrospective fixing in form of a fate unknown at the time. As she reflects in *Aftermath*: 'Form is both safety and imprisonment, both prosecutor and dissembler: form, in the end, conceals truth, just as the body conceals the cancer that will destroy it.'[60] Far from collapsing life into fiction by assuming an inherently fictive autobiographical self or a performative constitution of identity, Cusk's work, as in many interactions between life-writing and fiction after postmodernism, is haunted by the distance between life and literary form while pursuing their ever close fusion.

Contemporary Realism: 'The Demanding Re-enactment of the Plausible'

If the exhaustion of postmodern demythologisation led one strand of recent British fiction to turn inwards to explore the forms of writing the self, it led another to turn outwards to attempt with fresh eyes what Henry Perowne, protagonist of Ian McEwan's *Saturday* (2005), calls 'the difficulties and wonders of the real, of the demanding re-enactment of the plausible'.[61] Even at the height of postmodernism's prominence in 1990, David Lodge could rightly observe that realism remained the dominant mode of British fiction.[62] While established writers like Kingsley Amis or Iris Murdoch continued to produce expansive realist fiction over the course of the 1980s and 1990s, their conceptions of realist form were fixed in an earlier post-war moment, defined by a rejection of modernism and an embrace of humanist commitment. In Murdoch's later novels, for example – *The Good Apprentice* (1985), *The Book and The Brotherhood* (1987) and *The Message to the Planet* (1989) – the 'respect of the contingent' that enables fiction to mirror the incompleteness of reality demands inexplicable deaths, unresolved coincidences and inexplicable decisions: plot and character being the anchors of her formal realism.[63] However, the most consequential debates about contemporary realism as a form, and the most ambitious attempts at expanding its range, have been driven by a new generation of writers who are informed by metafiction's critique of mimetic illusions, yet refuse to believe that the transformations of twenty-first-century life are beyond the purview of realism.

The question of realism as a literary form is never merely a question of literary form alone, since realism, as Fredric Jameson writes, is 'a peculiarly unstable concept owing to its simultaneous, yet incompatible, aesthetic and epistemological claims, as the two terms of the slogan, "representation of reality," suggest'.[64] This coupling of aesthetics and epistemology is what makes it impossible for realism to ever find a fixed and final form, since changes in our understanding of both terms means their pairing must ever 'be reformulated in a productive way, as a tension to be solved and resolved over and over again, in a series of fresh innovations'.[65] If epistemological realism is the belief that there exists and we can know a mind-independent reality, aesthetic realism is a representation of our experience of that reality. As Elizabeth Deeds Ermarth argues, what makes these illusions convincing is not simply a panoply of technical features – linear causality in neutral space and time, a narrating agent absent from the action – but the ability of these beliefs to engender consensus within the fiction and without.[66] For Rushdie the lack of such a 'consensus about the world' was why '[t]he fiction of the Victorian age, which was realist, has been to my way of thinking inadequate as a description of the world for some time now'.[67] For contemporary realists this scepticism about consensus has itself come to be unconvincing, ignorant of the advances in science and technology that have redefined each term of the phrase 'mind-independent reality'. And the formal model perfected in the nineteenth century for the coupling of epistemology and aesthetics has remained a touchstone in debates about the possibility of achieving a representation of that ever-transforming reality.

While many British novelists have responded to transformative scientific discoveries in genetics, neuroscience, quantum physics and climate science – from Maggie Gee in *The Ice People* (1998) to Kazuo Ishiguro in *Never Let Me Go* (2005) – the work of Ian McEwan stands out for the depth of his engagement with contemporary science, and his conviction that it offers new foundations as well as new challenges for realist form. For McEwan, scientific discoveries do more than redefine the reality the novel represents. Drawing on his 'hero' E. O. Wilson, McEwan sees his fiction as engaged in a project of consilience between literature and science, 'the linking of facts and theories to create a common framework of explanation' – the source of new grounds for the consensus demanded by realist form.[68] In *Saturday*, the neurosurgeon Henry Perowne extemporises on the connection between scientific knowledge and realist form: 'A man who attempts to ease the miseries of failing minds by repairing brains is bound to respect the material world, its limits, and what it can sustain – consciousness, no less ... If that's worthy of awe, it also deserves curiosity; the actual, not the magical, should be the challenge.'[69] As with Murdoch, representing contingency is central to the challenge of the actual, but Perowne's reflections on whether the actions of his assailant were determined by incipient Huntington's disease show neuroscience and genetics transforming what we understand contingency and causality to be. The controversy caused by *Saturday*'s treatment of its other great actuality, the protests over the 2003 invasion of Iraq, showed that while science can revitalise the claims of realist epistemology, it alone cannot ensure the consensus upon which realist form depends. Perowne's curiosity about consciousness does not extend past the clothing of the Muslim women he passes on the street, the novel's realism unable to extend empathy across ethnic and religious difference.

These aspirations of realist form have been central to the work of Zadie Smith, whose novels and essays have been lodestars for debates about contemporary realism. The 'hysterical realism'[70] that James Wood identified in her first novel, *White Teeth* (2000), as emphasising plot connection over contingency, information over the individual, has over time been smoothed into a realism deployed in service of the ideals of sympathy and consensus she locates in the nineteenth-century novels of George Eliot: 'Author, character, and reader all striving in the same direction.'[71] As with McEwan, the ethics and politics of her realism are informed by yet reject postmodernism's claim that 'the world has collapsed into language',[72] with *On Beauty* gently satirising the academic Howard Belsey's demythologising exposure that 'Art is a Western myth'.[73] What makes Smith such an insightful critic of realism is how uncertain she is in her chosen coupling of epistemology and aesthetics. In 'Two Directions for the Novel' (2008), she declared that 'lyrical realism', her 'own tradition', has dominated Anglo-American fiction and yet is a 'form in long term crisis'.[74] Beyond her specific critique of Joseph O'Neill's *Netherland* (2008), Smith identifies two developments that have led to realism becoming a form in crisis. The intensified consciousness of historical change in the twenty-first century – for which 9/11 is a metonym – makes it seem suspect that the 'nineteenth-century lyrical realism of Balzac and Flaubert' feels like 'the closest model to our condition'.[75] But Smith's problem is also epistemological, a problem with the model of the self nineteenth-century realism proposes: 'Do selves always seek their good, in the end? Are they never perverse? Do they always want meaning? … Is this really realism?'[76] Smith's critique of contemporary realism aims at its reinvigoration rather than its rejection, the expansion of its technical means to capture historical change and more perverse notions of the self explored in *NW* (2012). Thus, for all that *NW* contains gestures at concrete poetry and defamiliarising metaphors, it remains an attempt to represent 'the way of things in reality, as far as I am able to see and interpret them, which may not be especially far'.[77]

Conclusion: Forming the Present

For Smith, representing 'the way of things in reality' is only one direction for the future of the novel, and the least necessary. The other is the kind of 'avant-garde challenge[s] to realism' exemplified by Tom McCarthy's *Remainder* (2005), 'one of the great English novels of the past ten years'.[78] *Remainder*'s avant-gardism, she writes, lies in its emptying out of character interiority, its creative deconstruction of realist conventions and its dialogue with post-structuralist thought. But 'avant-garde' is a sociological – not an aesthetic – concept, and opposing it to realism risks re-introducing an opposition between avant-garde experimentation and arrière-garde realism that has long plagued criticism of British fiction. Walter Benn Michaels, in contrast, argues that *Remainder* opens up a new direction for the novel in its posing of the question of form in ways distinct from modernism or postmodernism, in part because the novel is a reflection upon them. For *Remainder*'s narrator: 'Forensic procedure is an art form, nothing less. No I'll go further, its higher, more refined than any art form. Why? Because its real.'[79] For Michaels the novel is about this tension between the affective significance created through re-enacting and the frustration of that significance by the reality of matter: the non-identity between meaning and matter that is his definition of aesthetic form. While the novel – and McCarthy's authorial pronouncements – might see matter as disrupting form, the novel itself is made possible by denying the most fundamental law of matter: gravity. It ends with the narrator in a plane circling the sky, a plane that cannot have fallen to the ground, killing the narrator, in order for the previous narrative to have been told in the past tense.[80] As Smith also observes, *Remainder* fails to simply let 'matter matter', and it is this trick of form that enables the difference between form and matter, art and reality, to be articulated at all, and for the tension of that difference to be charged with an affective significance unavailable in the 'real'.

Remainder shows that finding new ways to pose the question of form is a way to make literature contemporary – the obsession of McCarthy's subsequent *Satin Island* (2015). It shows that it is in terms of form, rather than plot, setting or the interests of characters like Perowne, that fiction can engage contemporary intellectual currents; in McCarthy's case, the interests in materiality, ontological realism and non-human agency loosely grouped as new materialism. Claire-Louise Bennett's genre-blurring *Pond* (2015) similarly exemplifies how the work of literary form can be an expression of a preoccupation with: 'Material. Matter. Stuff.'[81] *Pond*'s narrator is trapped in a comic war with the language she uses because of the work of metaphor, of having something 'stand for something': 'I don't want to be in the business of turning things into other things, it feels fatal for some reason.'[82] When visiting the *Pond* of the book's title, her childish facility for 'moving about in deep and direct accordance with things' is frustrated by the erection of a sign saying 'pond'.[83] This makes us ask: what is a sign? A thing in the world, like a piece of wood; or a 'meddlesome' thing that turns things into other things? Or is it both at the same time: the interlinking of meaning and matter whose gap is the condition for fiction, but which prevents us from being 'at home' in the world of things? The formal concerns of recent fiction extend beyond these questions of matter and meaning. For Jacqueline Rose, the syntax of Eimear McBride's *A Girl Is a Half-Formed Thing* (2013) helps us to think about the violence against women that is 'the hallmark of the modern world' not by rendering it traumatically unspeakable, but by giving it form so that we can think about what that violence might entail.[84] This is not, however, achieved by a stream of consciousness, a more mimetically faithful representation of thought. If in McBride's work we see syntax break to express thought, we also see grammar and sound shape how subjectivity can be proposed at all: 'I'm lying. I am not I am.'[85] As the novel's title suggests, the girl's 'I' can only be half-formed, existing neither as an antecedent consciousness nor as an effect of language, but in an interaction that is brutal and in the end unbearable.

This interest in literary form as exploring the relationship between meaning and materiality is not the sole purview of new writers; the story of recent fiction's relationship to form is not the return of the repressed. James Kelman's work, for example, has long explored the relationship between narrative form, monologue and consciousness, although this aims at the depiction of ethnic and class identity rather than the more destabilising use of form in McBride. The parading inventiveness of Ali Smith's fiction is matched by her concept of form. Form, for Smith, divides 'form and formlessness' ... 'form, the shaper and moulder, acts like the other thing called mould, endlessly breeding forms from forms'.[86] In Smith's writing, metaphor and simile are modes of thought, and her linking of these two moulds, the artificial and the natural, serves the triumph of artifice over nature. Form 'sorts the shape from the shapeless – not that the shapeless doesn't have a form too, it does, because nothing doesn't. Even formlessness has form.'[87] Nothing lies outside the range of form, not even the deaths that haunt works like *Artful* (2012) and *How to Be Both* (2014). This is the polar opposite of McCarthy's understanding of form, according to whom there is always a remainder – matter, death – that evades form and thus defines it. What is revealing is less this difference than the fact that competing notions of aesthetic form have become central to the practice of contemporary British writers.

Form might be newly salient for the work of contemporary novelists, but as this chapter has hoped to show, form is always a question readers can ask of fiction, whether it is attempting the re-enactment of the plausible, the writing of a life or even its own demythologisation into linguistic structures. As this chapter has also shown, in posing the question of form we are also asking about gender difference, about the long history of colonisation, of the ethics of remembrance, the implications of neuroscience and the politics of violence. Perhaps what is different about post-millennial fiction is a reversal of the terms of address, so that it is fiction that poses new questions about form to its readers. After all, as David Shields reminds us: 'The etymology of *fiction* is from *fingere* (participle *fictum*), meaning "to shape, fashion, form, or mold."'[88] In returning to its roots, contemporary fiction might also be discovering the forms of the future.

Notes

1. F. Jameson, *The Political Unconscious* (London: Routledge, 2002), p. 64.
2. A. Leighton, *On Form: Poetry, Aestheticism, and the Legacy of a Word* (Oxford University Press, 2007), p. 1.
3. R. Williams, *Keywords: A Vocabulary of Culture and Society* (New York: Oxford University Press, 1985), p. 134.
4. D. Attridge, *The Singularity of Literature* (London: Routledge, 2004), p. 111.
5. C. Levine, *Forms: Whole, Rhythm, Hierarchy, Network* (Princeton University Press, 2015), p. 2.
6. J. Kramnick and A. Nersessian, 'Form and Explanation' (2017) 43(3) *Critical Inquiry* 650–99, 661.
7. S. Macpherson, 'A Little Formalism' (2015) 82(2) *English Literary History* 385–405, 390.
8. S. Otter, 'An Aesthetics in All Things' (2008) 104(1) *Representations* 116–25, 119.
9. M. Levinson, 'What Is New Formalism?' (2007) 122(2) *PMLA* 558–69.
10. E. Rooney, 'Form and Contentment' (2000) 61(1) *Modern Language Quarterly* 17–40; I. Armstrong, *The Radical Aesthetic* (Oxford: Wiley-Blackwell, 2000); and P. Boxall, *The Value of the Novel* (Cambridge University Press, 2015).
11. T. Eagleton, After Theory (London: Allen Lane, 2003); and D. Attridge and J. Elliot, 'Introduction: Theory's Nine Lives' in *Theory after 'Theory'* (London: Routledge, 2011), pp. 1–16.
12. A. Carter, *Shaking a Leg: Collected Journalism and Writings* (London: Vintage, 2013), p. 47.
13. *Ibid.*, p. 53 (emphases in the original).
14. Carter, *Shaking a Leg*, p. 47.
15. A. Katsavos, 'A Conversation with Angela Carter' (1994) 14(3) Review of Contemporary Fiction 11–17, 12.
16. Carter, *Shaking a Leg*, p. 47.
17. *Ibid.*, p. 53.
18. A. Carter, *Nights at the Circus* (New York: Penguin, 1993), p. 285.
19. *Ibid.*, p. 161.
20. D. Lessing, The Golden Notebook (London: Panther, 1972), p. 406 (emphasis in the original).
21. S. Rushdie, *Midnight's Children* (London: Jonathan Cape, 1981), p. 111.
22. *Ibid.*, p. 232.
23. *Ibid.*, p. 221.
24. S. Rushdie, *Shame* (London: Jonathan Cape, 1983), p. 251.
25. Rushdie, *Midnight's Children*, p. 443.
26. A. S. Byatt, *On Histories and Stories: Selected Essays* (Cambridge MA; London: Harvard University Press, 2001), p. 12.
27. J. Barnes, *A History of the World in 10 ½ Chapters* (London: Jonathan Cape, 1989), p. 242.
28. *Ibid.*, p. 245.
29. *Ibid.*, p. 181.
30. J. Winterson, *The Passion* (London: Vintage, 2001), p. 160.
31. G. C. Spivak, 'Reading *The Satanic Verses*' (1989) 2(1) *Public Culture* 79–99, 79.

32. A. Mufti, 'Reading the Rushdie Affair: An Essay on Islam and Politics' (1991) 29 *Social Text* 95–116, 98 (emphasis in the original).

33. L. Appignanesi and S. Maitland (eds), *The Rushdie File* (London: Fourth Estate, 1989), p. 117 (emphases in the original).

34. S. Rushdie, *Imaginary Homelands: Essays and Criticism 1981–1991* (London: Granta Books, 1991), p. 420 (emphasis in the original).

35. *Ibid.*, p. 422.

36. *Ibid.*, p. 424.

37. *Ibid.*, p. 427 (emphasis in the original).

38. N. ten Kortenaar, *Self, Nation, and Text in Salman Rushdie's Midnight's Children* (Montreal and Kingston: McGill-Queen's University Press, 1994), p. 46.

39. F. Moretti, *The Way of the World: The Bildungsroman in European Culture* (London: Verso, 2000), p. 194.

40. J. Barnes, *Flaubert's Parrot* (London: Jonathan Cape, 1984), p. 90.

41. *Ibid.*, p. 171.

42. R. Barthes, *Roland Barthes by Roland Barthes*, trans. R. Howard (London: Macmillan, 1977), p. 79.

43. P. de Man, 'Autobiography as De-Facement' (1979) 94(5) MLN 919–30, 921.

44. J. Butler, *Gender Trouble: Feminism and the Subversion of Identity* (London: Routledge, 1990).

45. P. J. Eakin, *Fictions in Autobiography: Studies in the Art of Self-Invention* (Princeton University Press, 1985), p. 3.

46. L. Marcus, *Auto/Biographical Discourses: Criticism, Theory, Practice* (Manchester University Press, 1994), p. 239.

47. E. Said, *On Late Style* (London: Bloomsbury, 2006), p. 7.

48. V. S. Naipaul, *A Way in the World* (London: Heinemann, 1994), p. 208.

49. *Ibid.*, p. 9.

50. D. Lessing, *Alfred and Emily* (London: Fourth Estate, 2008), p. viii.

51. *Ibid.*, p. 183 (emphasis in the original).

52. J. Wood, 'W. G. Sebald, Humorist', *The New Yorker* (5 June 2017), www.newyorker.com/magazine/2017/06/05/w-g-sebald-humorist.

53. Quoted in K. Brazil, 'W. G. Sebald's Revisions of Roland Barthes' (2017) *Textual Practice*, p. 1, http://dx.doi.org/10.1080/0950236X.2017.1308961.

54. W. G. Sebald, *The Emigrants*, trans. M. Hulse (London: The Harvill Press, 1996), pp. 130–1.

55. W. G. Sebald, 'The Questionable Business of Writing', interview by Toby Green (December 1999), www.amazon.co.uk/gp/feature.html?ie=UTF8&docId=21586.

56. H. Kunzru, 'Impossible Mirrors', *The New York Times* (7 September 2014), p. 12.

57. R. Cusk, *Aftermath: On Marriage and Separation* (London: Faber & Faber, 2012), p. 91.

58. R. Cusk, *Transit* (London: Jonathan Cape, 2016), pp. 239–40.

59. *Ibid.*, p. 243.

60. Cusk, *Aftermath*, p. 55.

61. I. McEwan, *Saturday* (London: Jonathan Cape, 2005), p. 68.

62. D. Lodge, *The Practice of Writing* (London: Vintage, 2011), pp. 9–10.

63. I. Murdoch, 'Against Dryness' (1961) 88 *Encounter* 16–20, 20.

64. F. Jameson, *Signatures of the Visible* (London: Routledge, 1992), p. 158.
65. F. Jameson, 'A Note on Literary Realism' in M. Beaumont (ed.), *A Concise Companion to Realism* (Oxford: Wiley-Blackwell, 2010), pp. 279–89, 280.
66. E. Deeds Ermarth, *Realism and Consensus in the English Novel: Time, Space, and Narrative* (Princeton University Press, 1983).
67. S. Rushdie, Conversations with Salman Rushdie, ed. M. Reder (Jackson, MS: University Press of Mississippi, 2000), p. 57.
68. I. McEwan, 'Move Over Darwin', *The Observer* (20 September 1998).
69. McEwan, *Saturday*, p. 68.
70. J. Wood, 'Human, All Too Inhuman', *The New Republic* (24 July 2000), https://newrepublic.com/article/61361/human-inhuman.
71. Z. Smith, *Changing My Mind: Occasional Essays* (London: Hamish Hamilton, 2009), p. 38.
72. *Ibid.*, p. 115.
73. Z. Smith, *On Beauty* (London: Hamish Hamilton, 2005), p. 115.
74. Smith, *Changing My Mind*, pp. 72–3.
75. J. O'Neill, *Netherland* (London: Fourth Estate, 2008), pp. 72–3.
76. *Ibid.*, p. 81.
77. A. Smith, *Artful* (London: Penguin, 2013).
78. Smith, *Changing My Mind*, pp. 84, 93.
79. McCarthy, *Saturday*, p. 185.
80. W. B. Michaels, *The Beauty of a Social Problem: Photography, Autonomy, Economy* (University of Chicago Press, 2015), pp. 72–3.
81. C.-L. Bennett, *Pond* (London: Fitzcarraldo Editions, 2015), p. 86.
82. *Ibid.*, pp. 164–5.
83. *Ibid.*
84. J. Rose, 'Feminism and the Abomination of Violence' (2016) 94 *Cultural Critique* 4–25, 22–3.
85. E. McBride, *A Girl Is a Half-Formed Thing* (Norwich: Galley Beggar, 2013), p. 57.
86. Smith, *Artful*, p. 67.
87. *Ibid.*, p. 73.
88. D. Shields, *Reality Hunger: A Manifesto* (London: Hamish Hamilton, 2010), p. 10 (emphasis in the original).

6

CAROLINE WINTERSGILL

Institutions of Fiction

In 1924, Virginia Woolf wrote memorably of the birth pangs of a new literary era: 'we hear all round us, in poems and novels and biographies, even in newspaper articles and essays, the sound of breaking and falling, crashing and destruction. It is the prevailing sound of the Georgian age.'[1] Debates have raged on whether the period around 1980 should be seen as a comparable moment of epochal transition for the novel. In his introduction to the third issue of the newly (re-)launched *Granta* magazine in 1980, the issue in which the first extract of Salman Rushdie's *Midnight's Children* appeared, Bill Buford famously announced that we were seeing 'at last, the end of the English novel and the beginning of the British one'.[2] The narrative of a moribund English novel, transformed in the 1980s as the empire 'wrote back' (in Rushdie's phrase), has shaped the teaching of modern and contemporary fiction.[3] For Robert Eaglestone, the publication of *Midnight's Children* is a 'literary event' that marks the 'beginning [of] the contemporary' for two reasons: it represents the flourishing of postmodernism, while opening up a wholly new thematic landscape for the novel, and it achieved huge international publishing success as the first truly 'global' novel.[4] It is the second of Eaglestone's reasons for considering *Midnight's Children* to be a transitional literary event that is central to this chapter: the unprecedented international publishing success of a groundbreaking literary novel, the context for that success and its effects. Rushdie's novel was published in spring 1981 with very modest advance orders of 639 copies. Its Booker Prize success, in the first year that the prize announcement was televised, boosted hardback sales by 17,000 copies in three months.[5] Since then, *Midnight's Children* has been garlanded with the accolade of 'Booker of Bookers' not once, but twice: for the best book in twenty-five years in 1993 and for the best book in forty years in 2008. It was chosen for the BBC's Big Read in 2003, and it has now sold over a million copies.

But alongside his championing of Rushdie and his new generation in *Granta* 3, Buford heard, as Woolf had earlier done, the sound of breaking and falling, crashing and destruction. His essay examined the pervasive narrative of dismal disillusionment with the English novel of the late 1970s and, citing an article by Robert McCrum, then an editor at Faber, the widely held perception of a 'Current Crisis in Publishing ... of unprecedented proportions, and ... noisy with terrible doomsday pronouncements'.[6] Buford's view was that this crisis was wholly self-inflicted, the result of the stultifying parochialism of a 'sweet, old fashioned and self-protected' publishing industry, idly waiting for the new Conrad to roll up, rather than recognising a brave new world of literary energy and innovation outside its garden wall. He was far from the only critic of the publishing industry of this period. In 1978, John Sutherland wrote that the British book trade was 'founded on discipline, self-control and protectionism – sometimes with a fierceness reminiscent of the Catholic Church in its most militant phase',[7] a control that had created stability and professional dignity, but also halted progress (such as paperback reviewing or engaging the youth market). To Sutherland, just as to Buford, it was clear that a crisis was imminent, whether 'an apocalypse or a periodic adjustment'.[8]

There was undeniable hubris in Buford's promotion of a relaunched Cambridge undergraduate quarterly as the vital new institution that would spearhead both a literary and a publishing revolution. However, nearly forty years later we know the influential group of novelists who personify the energy of 1980s literary fiction as the 'Granta Generation', signalling the centrality of this upstart literary institution to the demarcation of an era. As with Rushdie's novel, so Granta's influence has become global: the magazine has editions in twelve languages across three continents and it publishes influential lists of the Best of Young Novelists in Britain, America, Brazil and Japan, in addition to a Best of Young Spanish Language Novelists list. Faber's influence persists, but many of the old established imprints of the publishing landscape Buford condemned have gone, or have at least been subsumed into vast publishing corporations. Taking Buford's challenge to the literary establishment of 1980 as its starting point, this chapter examines the transformation of the institutional context of literary fiction in the intervening years. Whether or not we see 1980 as the birth of the contemporary novel in a formal or thematic sense, the material conditions of its production and consumption changed beyond recognition in this period and perhaps one of the defining features of the contemporary novel may be its relationship to this furious pace of change.

The first question to ask is what is meant by a literary institution. This chapter ranges across the organisations and structures, commercial and non-commercial, that define, enable and support literary production and consumption. Clearly the very use of the terms 'production' and 'consumption' are problematic in the context of the literary novel: its 'success' is tied, additionally, to a complex series of concerns around aesthetic and cultural value, innovation and longevity – qualities that are rarely immediately apparent. So my definition of 'literary institutions' also includes the structures through which the novel is validated, judged and indeed canonised: what James English and John Frow refer to as the 'literary value industry'.[9] The chapter focuses on publishers and literary agents, booksellers and book prizes, but it also touches on public literary events, the literary media both on and offline, and universities. Some of the institutions discussed are of long-standing influence, pre-dating the period covered by this book, but many of them developed or at least significantly changed during this period.

For Buford, the publishing industry of 1980 was still little altered from the nineteenth century:

> [T]he book, in more than one sense is a handmade art in an economy no longer able to accommodate it . . . The real censorship taking place is not political but economic, has little to do with writers and everything to do with the way their writing is produced, distributed and sold. Hardback publishers are this culture's most influential arbiters of taste: they determine what we value if only because they determine what we will have the opportunity to judge. It is urgent to distinguish the current state of publishing and bookselling from the actual state of fiction.[10]

Buford's claim is typically overstated – Allen Lane's revelation at Exeter station in 1934 leading to the creation of the sixpenny Penguin paperback, and the arrival of a generation of Jewish émigré publishing entrepreneurs in the 1940s, had shaken up the industry a few decades earlier – but his contention that publishers (rather than book reviewers, for example) were the chief arbiters of 'literary value' does point to an important shift in attitude from 1980 to the present. Bourdieu claimed that the literary and artistic field has always been shaped by a struggle between the *heteronomous principle* and the *autonomous principle* and he demonstrated this by reference to nineteenth-century French literary culture.[11] In this respect at least the nineteenth-century culture prevailed, even in 1980. Literary fiction was distinct: it was art rather than commerce and it reflected the cultural standing of the publishing house. Victor Gollancz considered it his duty to publish books because he believed they deserved publishing even if they would lose him money.[12] John Calder, publisher of Samuel Beckett, William Burroughs and Henry Miller and a vocal critic of the creeping philistinism of publishing culture, is described as having 'squandered fortunes on difficult, uncommercial writing'.[13] While it is fair to say that there remains a sense that the literary novel has value for the publisher beyond its immediate commercial success, the professionalised publishers of today would generally be seen as institutions of commerce first; their role as institutions of 'literary value' has, at least, been very much diluted.

The way in which novels acquire value now is complex, involving a network of actors, including literary agents, fellow authors, reviewers, literary prize-judges, bookshops, bloggers, academics and, above all, readers. Buford's critique of prevailing forms of literary valuation has a direct lineage from Woolf's in 'Mr Bennett and Mrs Brown'. Woolf is clear that the impact that matters is the impact of the novel on the reader: 'It is this division between reader and writer, this humility on your part, these professional airs and graces on ours, that corrupt and emasculate the books which should be the healthy offspring of a close and equal alliance between us.'[14] Authors have always been driven by a desire to communicate as directly as possible with their readers. Mark McGurl notes that even in their strenuous promotion of the novel as high art, Henry James and his circle remained committed to its acceptance within the mass market and the continuing cultivation of their relationship with the reader.[15] In her publishing memoir, *Stet: An Editor's Life*, Diana Athill suggests that '[t]he person with whom the writer wants to be in touch is his reader: if he could speak to him directly, without a middleman, that is what he would do. The publisher exists only because turning someone's written words into a book (or rather, into several thousand books) is a complicated and expensive undertaking.'[16] One of Buford's most vehement criticisms of the publishing industry was its construction of a monolithic chimera of a Great British Public to sustain its own archaic publishing practices: 'a mythic beast of extraordinary proportions – with puffy white arms, sustained by McVitie's chocolate biscuits and books about the Queen Mother'. He is no politer about the book trade: there are too few bookshops and those that there are stock the wrong books: 'I am not urging booksellers to create a "market". I am saying that the market exists and has existed for some time: it's made of people not getting the books they need, and everybody – from author to reader – is suffering.'[17] Perhaps one of the ways in which literary institutions have changed most in the past forty years is in their attentiveness to the reader, the recognition that publishing success is predicated on loyal audiences, rather than on elite critical approbation.

Andrew Nash suggests that the oil crisis of 1973–74, following which production costs escalated rapidly and public library cuts led to a dramatic reduction in sales of hardback novels, was a defining moment of transition in British fiction publishing.[18] Certainly the recession of the mid-1970s was an early causal trigger, but the institutional changes that revolutionised the literary industry were slow to come about. Although publishing corporations had been snapping up independent fiction publishers since the 1960s, the publishing landscape of 1980 still included some of the distinguished independents of the mid-twentieth century – André Deutsch, Victor Gollancz,

Weidenfeld & Nicholson – although none was performing particularly well. Other independents had entered into mergers to preserve their autonomy: the union of Chatto & Windus, Jonathan Cape and The Bodley Head endured until 1987 when it was acquired by the US corporation Random House. Some of the twentieth century's most legendary editors were still active: Diana Athill (editor of Jean Rhys, Philip Roth and V. S. Naipaul) at André Deutsch; Charles Monteith (editor of Samuel Beckett, William Golding and Philip Larkin) at Faber – although he retired that year; Tom Maschler (editor of Joseph Heller, John Fowles and Doris Lessing, and the founder of the Booker Prize) at Jonathan Cape. Athill recognised that her senior status within the industry was unusual: 'All publishing was run by many badly-paid women and a few much better-paid men.'[19] Publishers were still divided into the prestigious hardback imprints, which Clark and Phillips describe as inhabiting 'fine but slowly decaying Georgian houses in Bloomsbury'[20] and mass-market paperback presses – Penguin, Pan, Corgi, Panther and others – which obtained paperback rights to the more successful books and issued reduced format editions, often of throwaway quality, in monthly batches. The former held the prestige, lunching authors at the Garrick, editing manu-scripts, nurturing literary careers and obtaining the heavyweight reviews in the literary press, but they also carried the risk – John Feather explains that hardback publication was seen as a means of market testing a new book or author: 'In the early 1980s it was still axiomatic that original publication of fiction … in paperback was likely to fail.'[21] The latter were much more aggressive in their sales and marketing strategies, printed high and sold cheap. Book clubs were successful throughout the 1970s and 1980s; they bought bulk stock of new hardback books in advance of publication, enabling very high discounts to their members – recruited via adverts in the Sunday newspapers – who received regular parcels of books by mail order. By far the largest provider was Book Club Associates (BCA), part–owned by WH Smith, with 1.7 million members by 1987 across their various clubs.[22] Literary agents existed in the 1970s and they represented best-selling authors with serious advances to be negotiated – the Stephen Kings and Judith Krantzes – but literary novelists were often unrepresented, indeed some publishers would not consider agented books. The writer Terence Blacker described agenting as 'a back-room trade, largely populated by the tweedy or the seedy'.[23] There was little money for most literary authors. According to Robert McCrum, an editor at Faber in 1980, novels were regularly signed up for £500 and short-story collections for £200 or £300,[24] although the most celebrated novelists of the day could command more: Nash records that Anthony Burgess's UK advance for *Earthly Powers* in 1980 was £40,000,[25] which was certainly generous at the time (although perhaps less so when compared, for example, to Martin Amis's headline-grabbing £500,000 advance for *The Information* in 1995).

McCrum remembers bookshops of the period as 'gloomy, inhospitable places, smelling of stewed meat' and claims that the manager of WH Smith in Hampstead used to turn off the lights when there were no customers to save electricity.[26] WH Smith was the dominant force in British bookselling, controlling approximately 40 per cent of the retail market for books by the 1970s.[27] The more significant players for readers of literary fiction were the hundreds of independent booksellers around the United Kingdom, ranging from well-established traditional booksellers such as Hatchards of Piccadilly to quirky local institutions, often rather eccentric and badly run. A handful of the independents of the 1970s still exist, but others were taken over by book chains in the 1980s and 1990s. Some went the other way: Dillons in London and Blackwell's in Oxford extended their brands into book chains during this period and Foyles did so from 2005. Public libraries were central to reading culture. At the end of the 1970s they supplied a reading public of approximately 30 per cent of the adult population of the United Kingdom;[28] by 2013–14, the number of regular borrowers had dwindled to 15.3 per cent of the population, and this figure included children, who borrow more.[29] Until the mid-1970s, it was simply expected that public libraries would order hardback stock of new literary novels from the major publishers on release; hardback publishers were dependent on them doing so. However, with the oil crisis and the subsequent recession in 1973–74, book prices had risen quickly and public spending had been slashed, throwing library budgets into crisis and exacerbating, in turn, the crisis in hardback literary publishing.

The Booker Prize had been launched in 1968 and the Whitbread in 1973, although neither could be read as 'literary institutions' until well into the 1980s. McCrum describes the Booker in the1970s as 'a humdrum dinner at which a cabal of dowdy Oxbridge literati rewarded one of their peers for an interesting new addition to the English novel. The only time anyone paid any attention to the Booker was in 1972, the year John Berger, the author of the novel G, donated his prize-money to the Black Panthers.'[30] Literary reviews were much more significant, reaching a vast readership in 1980: Sutherland estimates it as 10 million.[31] In addition to the daily and Sunday newspapers there were reviews in weekly journals, including *The New Statesman, The Listener, The Spectator* and the *Times Literary Supplement*, and periodicals including *Books and Bookmen, The New Review, Encounter* and *The London Magazine*. Radio and television book programmes reached an even wider audience. Despite this extensive coverage of the book scene, Sutherland was sceptical about the influence British reviewers had as leaders of literary discourse or even in discriminating good from bad. He attributed this partly to the 'coterie-dilettantism' of British reviewers and partly to the fact that new novels were reviewed in group round-ups – reviewers rarely had time to do more than glance through each book and there was never an adequate sense of literary context.[32] Sutherland's critique fanned the flames of a long-standing (and still pervasive) antagonism between literary studies and the literary establishment. From the academy, F. R. Leavis attacked the 'concerted and conscienceless misguidance' of newspaper book reviewers,[33] while Peter Ackroyd, writing in *The Spectator*, claimed that academic literary criticism was 'now all but paralysed . . . There has been nothing original from them in ten years. I have yet to read a contemporary academic critic who could write more intelligently, or read more carefully, than a good book reviewer.'[34] Although academics were frequently recruited as book reviewers by the leading periodicals, there was the perception of an unbridgeable divide with university critics seen as fusty and abstruse, literary journalists as diverting but lightweight. It should be borne in mind that many university English departments in 1980 taught a chronologically organised literary canon that started with *Beowulf* and petered out either before, or shortly after, the Second World War. It was only with the 'theory wars' of the 1970s and 1980s that modern and contemporary literature began to be seen as a respectable subject for scholarship and to make a significant impact on the teaching curriculum.

The public literary culture of year-round festivals and events was in its infancy in 1980. There were prestigious literary societies (the Royal Society of Literature, for example, or the many Literary and Philosophical Societies across the United Kingdom dating back to the late eighteenth and early nineteenth centuries) and there were book readings and signings in libraries, arts centres and independent bookshops. But there were only two UK literary festivals (Cheltenham and Ilkley), while there are now over 350; there were only two International Book Towns (Hay-on-Wye and Kanda-Jinbōchō in Japan, which preceded Hay by two centuries), while there are now forty, there was no World Book Day, no UNESCO Cities of Literature and no established culture of reading groups, let alone mass-mediated events such as *The Big Read* or *Richard and Judy's Book Club*.

Yet, things were beginning to change. In addition to the relaunch of *Granta*, two new literary periodicals were launched in 1979: *The Literary Review* and the *London Review of Books* (*LRB*). *The Literary Review* had a particularly high profile from 1986 until 2001 when it was edited by Auberon Waugh of whom – notwithstanding his tendency to treat reviewing as a 'blood sport'[35] – even Sutherland generally approved for his fearlessness in breaking reviewing conventions. The *LRB* was distinctive in standing between the poles of academic and journalistic reviewing. It was co-founded, with an Arts Council Grant and initial support from *The New York Review of Books*, by Karl Miller, who simultaneously held the Lord Northcliffe Chair of English at UCL, Susannah Clapp, who had been an editor at Jonathan Cape, and Mary-Kay Wilmers, who had been an editor of *The Times Literary Supplement* (Wilmers still edits the *LRB* thirty-eight years later). Aided by its launch at a period when the *TLS* had been closed for a year due to industrial action, it quickly established a reputation as an arbiter of literary taste of consistently high quality, with early contributors including Martin Amis, Julian Barnes and Angela Carter given space to write much more substantial critical essays than had appeared previously in periodical form. 1980 also saw the creation of a British Book Marketing Council headed by Desmond Clarke, later sales and marketing director at Faber. Clarke's first venture was a promotion of the Best of British Writers, who were photographed by Lord Snowdon and promoted in the *Sunday Times*. There was certainly no indication in the writers selected – who included Graham Greene, Laurie Lee, Beryl Bainbridge, V. S. Pritchett and John Betjeman – that epoch-shifting change was afoot in the British literary scene. It was the promotion itself that was radical according to Ian Jack, who notes that 'we were still in the time when writers were private figures, their public lives mainly confined to what was printed on the page'.[36] In 2013, Clarke remembered that '[a] few of the literati were a little sniffy about marketing campaigns to promote literary fiction'.[37] Clarke's new initiative was the first of three such promotions. The second, three years later, was the Best of Young British Novelists list. Clarke chose the judges (Michael Holroyd, Beryl Bainbridge, Martyn Goff, who was the administrator of the Booker Prize, and Alison Rimmer, the fiction buyer at Heffers in Cambridge), who agreed on a famously prescient list of writers, only two of whom (Amis and McEwan) had any real reputation at the point the list was published. Clarke garnered unprecedented support from the book industry: 2,000 booksellers, including WH Smith and John Menzies, agreed to feature the books prominently on their shelves and in window displays and they were also stocked by 1,000 public libraries. Publishers and booksellers were given advance intelligence of the featured writers so they could ensure adequate stock or announce paperback editions. In terms of book sales it was an enormous success: 250,000 additional copies of the featured novels were sold. *Granta*'s involvement came after the list was announced. Buford decided to publish an issue excerpting forthcoming work from each of the listed novelists. *Granta 7* was very successful, reprinting six times in ten years. This success prompted *Granta* to launch its own once-a-decade list from 1993. Literary fiction was becoming more visible and it was becoming aspirational.

In *Liquid Modernity* (2000), Zygmunt Bauman argues that we have moved from a solid phase of modernity to a 'liquid' phase, in which nothing holds its shape for long and institutions are constantly in flux. Bauman acknowledges that in many ways modernity has been fluid since its inception: 'the self-confident and exuberant modern spirit awarded the society it found much too stagnant for its taste'[38] and sought to melt the solids of tradition. But the difference for Bauman between prior modernity and present modernity is that the 'melting' was previously 'to clear the site for *new and improved solids* ... a solidity which one could trust and rely upon and which would make the world predictable and therefore manageable'.[39] When, in 1978, John Sutherland asked whether the crisis in publishing was 'an apocalypse or a periodic adjustment'[40] he bargained on the eventual construction of a new norm for the fiction industry; what happened instead was that at some point in the 1980s, the industry entered a state of furious and seemingly ceaseless flux, with far-reaching effects for both authors and literary publics.

At the centre of the development of this new era of what might be termed 'liquid modern publishing' are a series of complex and interrelated processes, driven initially by the political and economic climate of the late 1970s and early 1980s. The first of these processes was the *professionalisation* of both publishing and bookselling. Claire Squires cites a speech given by Tony Godwin on his departure from Penguin in 1967, in which he discussed the decline of the long-standing notion (promulgated by Frederic Warburg in his memoir *An Occupation for Gentlemen*) that publishers should be the 'custodians of culture' and the move towards a more professionalised publishing culture in keeping with the democratisation of culture of the 1960s.[41] This took more time to come about than Godwin expected, but it was accelerated by the recession of 1980–82, which forced redundancies and the cutting of lists, a new wave of mergers and acquisitions by both European and US corporate publishers, and the vertical restructuring of the industry, enabling hardback and paperback editions to be published by the same company. The growing importance of agents was a further feature of a process of rationalisation that transformed the traditional editorially led field of literary fiction publishing into a market-oriented culture in which sales and profitability were the primary goal, and analysis of sales figures and accurate forecasting were seen as more reliable means to reach it than the publisher's instinct. The 1980s also saw the rise of the book chains, starting with the establishment of Waterstones in 1982 which revolutionised the landscape of high street bookselling.

The second development was the *commodification* of literary fiction. With the professionalisation of the publishing industry, the institutional separation between literary fiction and mass-market fiction began to crumble. Nash notes the development of 'best-sellerdom' in the 1970s, with writers of genre fiction increasingly marketed as brand names.[42] From the 1980s, writers of literary fiction – Martin Amis, Sebastian Faulks, Jeanette Winterson, Louis de Bernières, Zadie Smith – entered the best-seller lists. Literary authors gained celebrity status, regularly appearing in newspapers and on TV, as cultural commentators and as newsworthy in their own right (whether for the size of their advances or the unwanted attentions of the Ayatollah). They attracted sell-out audiences at literary events. The Booker Prize announcement was first televised live in 1981; by 1989 it was being covered by *Channel 4 News, Newsnight* and *The Late Show* and was discussed in all the broadsheets, on radio news and on all the main art shows.[43] In 2003, the BBC's search for the United Kingdom's best-loved novel, *The Big Read*, drew 2.5 million viewers. Shortly afterwards, drawing on the success both of *The Big Read* and Oprah Winfrey in the United States, the chat show hosts Richard Madeley and Judy Finnigan launched a televised book club as a biannual feature of their daily Channel 4 show, involving both 'on-air' discussion of the selected books with celebrity guests and interaction from 'off-air' book groups around the country. These shows regularly drew 2 million viewers. *Richard and Judy's Book Club* was so successful that their producer, Amanda Ross, was named by *The Observer* as the most powerful person in publishing in 2006.[44] Commodification is also linked to an increasingly short-termist mentality in the publication of literary fiction. Prior to the 1980s, popular novelists – Dick Francis or Catherine Cookson, for example – habitually put out a new book each year, but the same was not expected of literary novelists. It was assumed that the novels of Margaret Drabble or William Golding, for example, would be long-term backlist sellers and produce a reliable, long-term income for their publishers. The rise of corporate publishers seeking higher profits for their shareholders, the transformation of the retail industry and the mediatisation of literary fiction led to a much curtailed shelf-life for new titles, putting significant pressure on both authors and publishers to produce the Next Big Thing. In this renewed emphasis on frontlist over backlist, the dominance of the paperback began to ebb. The new, vertically integrated publishers pushed the mass-marketing energies that had previously driven paperback sales, into promoting new hardbacks and their price came down.[45] These rapid moves from hardback dominance, to decline, to renewed dominance, illustrate the fluidity of the industry over this period.

The third development was *globalisation*, which affected both the character of the British novel and the institutional context in which it appeared. In 1980, Bill Buford argued that '[t]oday ... the imagination resides along the peripheries'.[46] An examination of the Booker Prize lists of the 1980s bears out Buford's pluralist instinct: from 1969 to 1979, ten out of thirteen winners were British born; while from 1980 to 1997 only eight out of seventeen were British born.[47] London became the hub for the global Anglophone novel; the Booker, with an eligibility criterion that included Britain, the Commonwealth, Ireland, Pakistan and Bangladesh (and from 2014 has included America), was part of this changing perception of what the 'British' novel might be. Richard Todd argues that: 'Booker eligibility has gradually enabled the literary energy that was once at the former Empire's centre and directed outwards to the colonial periphery, by a process of post-colonial transference to be directed back at the enfeebled centre. The result is a literature that is significantly different in kind, tone and experience from the mainstream serious literary American novel.'[48] A further facet of globalisation was that as multinational corporations developed their publishing empires, global markets became ever-more important. Fiction publishing has traditionally been territorial (unlike academic or children's picture-book publishing, for example, in which publishers usually require world rights). Publishers acquire English language rights for the United Kingdom and Commonwealth, but US rights and foreign language rights tend to be sold separately. Increasing pressure to acquire rights in valuable intellectual property internationally led to both British and US publishers wishing to acquire imprints on the other side of the Atlantic and, later, to continental European publishers wishing to acquire both British and American publishers.[49] However, the rise of literary agents in this period, professionally committed to obtaining the best terms for their authors in each territory, has exerted a significant counter-pressure. These tensions have been exacerbated by the rise of digital content, which is free from the traditional distributive restrictions of print publishing and makes attempts to contain rights territorially particularly problematic.

The fourth development was *democratisation*. In the 1970s there was a perception of literary fiction as an elite, middle-aged preserve. According to Ian Jack: 'Few people in Britain connected serious fiction with youth ... Cartoonists drew publishers as men in tweed waistcoats who smoked pipes, and the typical successful novelist as a well-settled householder in Hampstead, Oxford or a country rectory.'[50] Bill Buford reported a conversation with Martin Amis about the 1970s in which he said: 'if you were a literary fiction writer and you were a kid, your horizon was empty, there was really nothing else going on. People weren't writing fiction or talking about it – everyone wanted to work for the BBC.'[51] In the 1980s, with the media spotlight on the Young British Novelists, literary fiction opened up to a wider and younger audience of both readers and writers. The 1990s saw the rapid growth of the reading group phenomenon; three-quarters of a million people voted in *The Big Read* and new literary festivals were launched. The Hay Literature Festival started in 1987: it now draws 250,000 visitors annually and the organisers run other literary festivals around the world from Colombia to Bangladesh. In 2003, the notoriously anarchic Elephant Fayre in Cornwall reinvented itself as The Port Eliot Literary Festival. Both Hay and Port Eliot (and many other high-profile festivals) are organised with extensive collaboration from publishing companies: they are forums for direct communication between the literary industry and literary publics. There has been a huge expansion in creative writing courses: in 2011, *The Guardian* reported that over ninety British universities were offering postgraduate degrees and that there were around 10,000 short creative writing classes.[52] Publishers have contributed to this development: the Faber Academy was launched in 2009, announcing in 2017 that sixty-two of their alumni had obtained publishing deals.[53] Bloomsbury runs writers' courses as part of the outreach activity from the *Writers' and Artists' Yearbook* and arranges public literary events at their Bloomsbury Institute. Digital developments have promoted this culture of reader engagement, enabling direct contact with authors and with other readers through social media, a plethora of online book groups, fan-fiction sites and Lit blogs, and popularising reviewing sites such as *goodreads.com, lovereading.com* and *librarything.com*, with advance proofs of forthcoming novels available to regular reviewers through *NetGalley.com*. Readers have become, as Buford suggested they should, a significant institution of literary valuing. Some of the most successful literary institutions of the twenty-first century bought in early to this democratisation of literary communication. One of Amazon's central innovations is that the organisation has never aimed to be seen as a 'cultural gatekeeper': their commercial success is built on a role as an enabler, bringing readers into contact with books and authors into contact with readers in new ways. But smaller enterprises too have built on this urge to democratise. The crowd-funding publisher Unbound was launched under the slogan 'Books are now in your hands', with a business model in which writers share their ideas for new work and readers offer to fund projects they wish to read.[54]

The fifth development is *digitisation*. Since the 1990s, digital developments have revolutionised every aspect of the book business. In bookshops, electronic point of sale (EPOS) systems were introduced in the 1980s, and the launch of Nielsen's BookScan in 2000 allowed the collation of point of sale data, which made publishing sales histories and authors' track records public knowledge. For readers, in addition to the emergence of the new internet book culture outlined above, the most radical change has been the shift in reading technology, with the partial supplanting of the codex by the eReader from 2007. Online bookselling has revolutionised the availability of a much wider range of fiction, including offerings from tiny independent presses and from foreign publishers, self-published books, backlist titles no longer stocked in high street bookshops, and even long-out-of-print books from second-hand booksellers. For both authors and publishers there is the capacity to reach out directly out to their readers through social media; there are new possibilities for self-publishing and there are innovations in form such as the evolution of hypertext fiction and online storytelling. In 2012, Jennifer Egan released *Black Box*, a short story involving a character from her Pulitzer Prize-winning novel *A Visit from the Goon Squad*. It was published by the *New Yorker* in the form of tweets sent out one a minute for an hour over ten days and only later released as an eBook.[55] The novelist Claire Fuller uses flash-fictions as a way of combating writers' block and clarifying particular episodes or characters within her fiction, publishing them on her website and disseminating them via social media. A selection of these was published as an appendix to her 2017 novel, *Swimming Lessons*.[56]

A closer examination of the trajectories of particular sectors of the literary industry since the 1980s reveals the dynamics, the interrelationships and the tensions of these five processes: professionalisation, commodification, globalisation, democratisation and digitisation.

The 1980s saw a massive cultural shift in publishing, as fiction publishers changed from small-scale operations – most privately owned, some part of larger media organisations,[57] but almost always independently run – to much larger, transnational organisations. Many of the prestigious, hardback imprints had faced problems of succession for some years, as the mid-twentieth-century generation of owner-publishers – George Weidenfeld, Allen Lane, Jonathan Cape *et al.* – retired or died. Diminishing library sales, rising book prices, book clubs, the increasing space for paperbacks in the new bookshop chains and the more aggressive marketing of the paperback houses meant that by the mid-1980s publishers were making almost no profit from their own hardback sales; their profit came, increasingly, from rights and co-edition sales. The sensible solution for both hardback and paperback imprints was vertical restructuring, ensuring that hardback and paperback editions were published by the same company (even if under a different imprint). In 1985, Penguin acquired the hardback imprints Hamish Hamilton and Michael Joseph from Thomson, while Vintage Paperbacks was launched in the United Kingdom in 1990 to publish the paperback editions of Chatto, Bodley Head and Jonathan Cape. Corporate ownership offered benefits of scale to small publishers, including centralised warehousing, distribution, sales and production services; and the financial clout of these much larger companies protected publishers against the increasing risks of publishing in a climate of ever-growing advance payments. John Thompson explains that: 'In earlier decades they could deploy both their symbolic capital and their economic capital to attract and retain authors, but with the changes taking place in the field, they now needed a much greater quantity of economic capital to stay in the game.'[58]

The financial climate of the time encouraged the process of merger and acquisition: the deregulation of the financial markets had led to the increasing availability of long- and short-term equity and debt-financing, giving large players the capital to take over medium-sized companies,[59] and allowing new, smaller players (such as Bloomsbury and Fourth Estate) to enter the market. Observers at the time, such as John Sutherland, may have assumed that there was an optimal size for a publishing company seeking to marry editorial integrity and economy of scale, but since the 1980s the narrative has been one in which publishing corporations have sought to increase their market share through a relentless process of acquisition: an examination of the Russian doll-like structure of the major players in fiction publishing today reveals their intricate business histories. It also reveals a shift in the dominant players from large American corporations, who simply could not make enough money from the mature publishing market, to European companies, notably Bertelsmann and Holtzbrinck in Germany and Lagardère – owner of Hachette Livre – in France. For example, the American corporation Random House acquired Chatto, Bodley Head and Jonathan Cape in 1987 and subsequently bought Century Hutchinson, Heinemann and Secker & Warburg. In 1998, Random House was itself acquired by Bertelsmann, which already owned Transworld. Meanwhile, Penguin, backed by Pearson capital, had been expanding into a major multinational, purchasing Viking, Hamish Hamilton and Michael Joseph among others. In 2013, Penguin and Random House merged, with Bertelsmann holding a majority stake.[60] The company now has 12,500 employees, nearly 250 imprints, publishes 15,000 new titles and sells 800 million books annually.[61] It is the largest player in the UK consumer book market and indeed globally. Its closest rival in the United Kingdom is Hachette Livre, originally an illustrious French publisher founded in 1826, which has expanded globally with the respective acquisitions of Orion (which owned Weidenfeld & Nicholson and Cassell, through which it had acquired Victor Gollancz), the Octopus Publishing Group, Hodder Headline (formed following the acquisition of Hodder & Stoughton by Headline and also the owner of John Murray), the Time Warner Book Group (which owned Little, Brown and through them, Virago) and the Perseus Books Group.[62]

The UK book market may be dominated financially by the global conglomerates, but there is also a notable culture of British independent publishing. The longest-standing literary independent is Faber & Faber, founded in 1929. The combination of an illustrious reputation including connections with T. S. Eliot, an extensive backlist in fiction, poetry and biography, and six Booker prize-winners draws in authors and ensures Faber's reputation as an elite cultural institution, but its survival in a corporate publishing landscape has required innovative business practice. In 2005, Faber established its Independent Alliance, a consortium of leading independent publishers, including Atlantic, Canongate and Profile Books,[63] who share sales representation, distribution and administrative functions. By 2006, the Faber Alliance was the sixth largest publishing group in the United Kingdom,[64] able to negotiate with Amazon, the big retail chains and the supermarkets on the same basis as the corporates. Other innovations at Faber have included Faber Digital and the Faber Academy, which teaches creative writing. Faber CEO Stephen Page has described Faber's attempts to pull in revenue from other sectors as 'a riot of cross-dressing'.[65] The other medium-sized independent with serious clout in literary fiction publishing is Bloomsbury, founded in 1987. The company's extraordinary financial growth in the 1990s and 2000s came from the success of the Harry Potter series, but its continuing independence and its reputation as a literary institution owe just as much to the swift acquisition of a roster of highly regarded literary authors, including Nadine Gordimer, Margaret Atwood, Howard Jacobson and Donna Tartt, the kudos of four Booker prize-winners and some notable best-sellers in adult fiction – Khaled Hosseini's books *The Kite Runner* and *A Thousand Splendid Suns* have sold more than 38 million copies worldwide, for example.[66] The last twenty-five years have seen a renaissance in independent publishing, with a number of small imprints garnering particular notice in the major literary prizes. Canongate was founded in the 1970s as a publisher of Scottish fiction, but gained a higher profile following its management buyout by Jamie Byng in 1994 and its 2002 Booker success with Yann Martel's *Life of Pi*; Granta Books, launched in 1989,[67] was the publisher of Eleanor Catton's 2007 Booker prize-winner *The Luminaries*; Oneworld, founded in 1986, began publishing fiction in 2009 and has had two successive Booker winners in Marlon James and Paul Beatty.[68] The rise of small independent publishers in this period is, in part, a response to a sense that the corporate culture of the conglomerates had taken power away from editors and stultified creativity, preventing the discovery of new and independent voices. One of the interesting effects of this resurgence of independent publishing has been a desire by the corporates to set up 'boutique imprints' of their own. Penguin launched their Fig Tree imprint in 2005, while Headline launched Tinder Press in 2013. These niche literary imprints are intended partly to help readers and booksellers navigate what Philip Jones describes as the 'publishing thicket'[69] and partly to prevent authors feeling commodified by the anonymity of the corporation. Benedicte Page of *The Bookseller* suggests that they reflect the individual taste of the editors behind them and 'put the quirkiness back into publishing'.[70] The trend for literary 'micro-imprints' has spread to independent publishers – for example, Tuskar Rock Press (2005) is an imprint 'curated' by the novelist Colm Tóibín and the agent Peter Straus – a team seen as having high cultural capital. It was initially an imprint of Atlantic Books and later moved to Serpent's Tail. Pushkin Press has a literary micro-imprint called One; Bloomsbury has Bloomsbury Circus.

If agents were an optional extra for literary novelists in the 1970s, by the 1990s they had become a necessary point of entry for authors seeking a major trade publisher.[71] Demand for agents grew throughout the 1980s for a variety of reasons. The consolidation of publishing made this a turbulent time for both publishers and authors. There was increasing job mobility: some editors were forced out following corporate acquisitions, some decided they didn't like corporate culture and decamped to smaller publishers, others were poached by ambitious new companies. Long-standing relationships between authors and editors were disrupted. Authors needed agents with extensive knowledge of an ever-more complex industry to protect their interests and as a point of stability in a sector in flux, to help them develop their literary career. At the same time, corporate culture meant more bureaucracy and less time for editors to sift through book proposals or discover new authors. Publishers began to rely on agents as gatekeepers: turning down unpromising submissions and working with promising authors to develop their pitches. Claire Squires notes that a trend in the 1990s and 2000s for editors to move from prestigious literary publishers to agencies may suggest that the agent–author role has, in some ways, replaced the traditional editor–author role.[72]

As the rise of the book chains and e-retailers increased the potential audience for literary best-sellers, so the rise of the publishing corporations led to greater availability of capital to fund substantial advance payments for leading authors and the costly publicity and marketing required by 'lead titles'. Agents were needed to negotiate both and, with increasing frequency, to auction books in which more than one publisher was interested, making final decisions not just on the basis of advance and royalty payments, but also on the publisher's marketing commitment to the book. John Thompson points to the role of the so-called 'super-agents' of the 1970s and 1980s in changing some of the comfortable publishing assumptions of the preceding decades.[73] Of particular influence in literary fiction was the New York agent,

Andrew Wylie, widely known as 'The Jackal' for his ruthless poaching of other agents' clients – Marianne Macdonald in *The Independent* reported that 'one story is that he sidles up to famous authors at parties … and whispers: "Would you like \$1 m for your next novel?"' [74] Wylie established his agency in 1980, setting himself apart from his contemporaries in his interest in pursuing literary novelists. According to Wylie: 'The best business is to have on your roster one hundred authors who will be read in a hundred years, not two authors who will be read in a hundred days.' [75] He was aggressive in pursuing spectacular advances for his clients, arguing that they were the best way of ensuring that the publisher made the book a success. This tactic remains controversial: while, reportedly, a majority of literary novels do not earn out their advances, [76] the late Pat Kavanagh, a distinguished London literary agent, noted that very high advances create artificial expectations for writers and may harm their future careers. She cited Gautam Malkani's £300,000 advance for his first novel *Londonstani*, which received vast pre-publication hype, but only sold very modestly. [77] Wylie was also distinctive in his insistence on operating globally: he developed expertise not only in international English language markets, but also in foreign language markets and would, as far as possible, sell rights in each territory and language separately to maximise the author's – and agent's – income. In an era when publishing companies too were becoming ever-more global in outlook, Wylie's new model created tensions, which have become still more fraught in an era of digital publishing (which could, in principle, operate completely outside traditional publishing territories). Above all, Wylie disdained the notion of publishing as 'a business peopled by members of a social elite who have a sort of gentlemanly game going, and the gentlemanly game was played to the disadvantage of the writer'. [78] Wylie's closest counterpart in London publishing was the flamboyant Ed Victor, founding director of the Groucho Club and trustee of the Hay Festival, who set up his agency in 1977 and ran it until his death in 2017, playing as significant a role as Wylie in the change of status of publishing from gentleman's profession to hard-selling business. Unlike Wylie, Victor deplored poaching, but he was ruthless in obtaining high advances for his clients. In return, he required a 15 per cent commission rather than the then standard 10 per cent and he was also one of the first London agents to stop accepting submissions for the 'slush pile', and take only personal introductions to new clients.

The number of literary agents in London rose from around eighty in 1975 to 138 in 1995, [79] while the number of authors represented rose exponentially. The rise of agents is one of the results of an increasingly professionalised and complex business; it is also connected to the globalisation of fiction markets and to the mediatisation of fiction: agents generally handle TV and film rights as well as foreign rights on the author's behalf. The developing role of agents has been a factor in the shift of cultural authority away from the publisher: agents function as literary gatekeepers, they often do substantial editing of their authors' work and they are usually more instrumental in developing literary careers than publishers, especially since it is common in literary publishing – as opposed to genre fiction for example – for publishers to contract only one book at a time.

Perhaps the most visible sign of an industry in transition to 1980s book buyers was the establishment of Waterstones in 1982. Tim Waterstone had a vision of a bookshop unlike anything that existed in Britain at the time, a shop with 'a sort of messianic desire to sell books, independent bookselling at its best, but to have them as a chain'.[80] Waterstones shops were designed for lengthy browsing, with well-read staff, evening and Sunday opening, extensive stock including unprecedented numbers of backlist titles and prime high street locations. They celebrated the book as a desirable commodity and fiction publishing as part of a fast-growing media leisure sector. In 1986, the Pentos Group followed suit, opening sixty-one Dillons branches across the United Kingdom in a three-year period and in 1987 Ottakers opened stores across southern England. For nearly a century, UK book pricing had been regulated by the Net Book Agreement (NBA), established in 1900 to ensure commercial stability for publishers and booksellers and a fair return for authors. Following years of fierce argument within the book trade – the Publishers' Association was a defender of the NBA, while the anti-NBA lobby included the supermarket Asda and the book chain Dillons (whose protest included an attempt in 1990 to discount the Booker Prize shortlist) – it was finally declared illegal by the Restrictive Practices Court in 1997. 1997 was also the year that the US-owned Borders chain arrived in the United Kingdom, buying the London chain Books Etc. and opening twenty-one book superstores across the country. But the most far-reaching change for the book industry came the following year, with the UK launch of Amazon. Amazon had been established in the United States since 1994, but had yet to turn a profit – indeed, that didn't happen until the last quarter of 2001. Amazon's focus was on building a large and loyal consumer base and excelling in the logistics of supply. Its business model depended on massive stockholding, and it benefited hugely from the collapse of the NBA, allowing it to negotiate unprecedented discounts from publishers. By 2005, Amazon controlled 10 per cent of overall UK book supply[81] and was by far the largest online retailer. Amazon's significant investment in developing its eBook market has also paid enormous dividends. The first-generation Kindle was launched in 2007, with initial competition from the launch of Barnes & Noble's Nook in 2009, and the Kobo reader in 2010. The consumer eBook market grew from £20 million in 2010 to £275 million in 2014[82] – although it has since fallen, to £204 million in 2016, while print sales of consumer books have grown. Since the launch of the Paperwhite in 2012, Amazon has had a virtual monopoly, controlling 79 per cent of the UK eBook market by 2013.[83]

Following the collapse of the NBA, consumer spending on books, which had been in marked decline from 1994 to 1996, almost immediately turned a corner, due to aggressive pricing from the chains and the emergence of supermarkets as outlets for mass-market paperbacks. Independent booksellers, unable to compete on price, were hit hard from the start, but as Amazon and other online retailers grew, their survival was threatened. In 2017, the number of independents fell for the eleventh consecutive year; 668 shops closed between 2005 and 2017, leaving only 867 independent booksellers in the United Kingdom.[84] The success of American-style mall bookselling was relatively short-lived too; Borders had pulled out of the United Kingdom completely by 2009. Waterstones had its difficulties too. From 1993 to 1998, it was owned by WH Smith, expanding rapidly both organically and by integration with the smaller Sherratt & Hughes chain. In 1998, it was acquired by HMV, which also owned Dillons, enabling Waterstones to absorb its key competitor, but the company suffered from HMV's strategies of aggressive pricing promotions, reduced inventory and central purchasing practices. In combination with the growing competition from Amazon, including rising eBook sales, Waterstones was on the brink of administration by 2011: eleven of its stores closed in the first two months of the year. But the chain was acquired by the Russian billionaire Alexander Mamut, who appointed James Daunt – owner of the small, upmarket, eponymous, London book chain – as managing director. Freed from corporate ownership, Daunt put in place a radical strategy that, ironically, given the struggles of independent bookshops in this period, was to start operating Waterstones stores like independent community bookshops. Central buying had allowed Waterstones to charge publishers for space in their stores and to sell popular books at high discount, but the level of returns was very high and there were few opportunities to promote local authors or small publishers. Daunt put buying into the hands of local store managers again, allowing them to buy the books they thought they could sell locally and dramatically reducing the level of returns from an industry standard of 25 per cent to 3 per cent by 2017.[85] In some locations, the chain has opened unbranded stores, allowing them to blend into towns with a strong independent retail sector. This 'mock-independent' strategy has been successful – in 2017, the chain went into profit for the first time in seven years, paving the way for the acquisition of a controlling share of Waterstones by the UK arm of American hedge fund Elliott Advisors in 2018 and the company's subsequent acquisition of the Foyles chain, in what James Daunt referred to as an act of resistance to 'Amazon's siren call'.[86] Following years of bland centralisation, Waterstones has become a hub for literary events: its branches have close relationships with local authors, host regular readings and book signings, and run in-store book clubs. In 2013, the Booksellers' Association and the Publishers' Association collaborated on the launch of the 'Books Are My Bag' promotion aimed at supporting high-street booksellers in a particularly difficult climate. In 2016, the campaign extended to include a series of Book Awards, with shortlists selected by booksellers and winners voted for by readers, consolidating the idea of the bookshop as a hub for a democratic literary culture, distinct from the 'elite' valuing of awards such as the Booker and Folio prizes.

Nonetheless, the 'elite' literary prizes have had an enormous impact in this period, both in terms of 'literary valuing' and commercially. There are a plethora of prizes, each with a distinctive remit, including the Nobel Prize for Literature, The Costa Book Awards (formerly the Whitbread) and the Bailey's Prize for Women's Fiction (formerly the Orange Prize). The Nobel is a lifetime achievement award, to an author of any nationality, writing in any language and in any genre; since 1980, it has been awarded to three British novelists: William Golding in 1983, Doris Lessing in 2007 and Kazuo Ishiguro in 2017. The Costa is explicitly pitched as a popular prize recognising 'the most enjoyable books of the year';[87] it is open only to writers resident in the United Kingdom and Ireland, awarding prizes in five categories (two of which are fiction), which are then pitted against each other for the Costa Book of the Year. The Bailey's honours a full-length novel by a woman of any nationality writing in English. In literary fiction, the prize seen as pre-eminent by the industry itself, by authors and by the public is undoubtedly the Booker: Amit Chaudhuri describes it as having 'a stranglehold on how people think of, read, and value books in Britain'.[88]

The Booker was established in 1968 by the publisher Tom Maschler and the managing director of Booker McConnell, Michael Caine, with the explicit intent of replicating France's illustrious Prix Goncourt and it was generously funded, with prize money of £5,000 in 1969, which rose by stages to £50,000 in 2002.[89] The annual selection of five judges by the Booker management committee gives an interesting perspective on those considered to be the 'literary elite' of the contemporary era. Martyn Goff, the prize's administrator from 1968 until 2006, described the ideal team as 'a respected academic (not necessarily a literature specialist), a literary editor of a quality newspaper, a writer (preferably two) and a qualified reviewer', but argued that booksellers should be excluded as they were likely to have a vested interest in the outcome.[90] During the 1980s, the judges frequently included a representative of 'the man [sic] on the street', but that element was quietly dropped in the 1990s, not least because they had become less 'street' and more 'media celebrity'.[91] Goff was adamant that there should be 'none of Whitbread's doubtful employment of some non-reading celebrities'.[92] The prize's archetypal 'person on the street' has now been replaced by observation of the effects on real book buyers. Given the commercial origins of the prize, it is unsurprising that the prize committee tracked its effect on sales from the outset, believing that the effect on sales and the status of the prize were linked. Thus, we know that the prize was thought to have added 1,000 copies to sales of John Berger's *G* and 5,000 copies to J. G. Farrell's *The Siege of Krishnapur*.[93] By 1980, the 'Booker effect' was more pronounced: of 52,000 UK sales of William Golding's *Rites of Passage*, 17,000 were attributed to the Booker.[94] The following year, the prize announcement was made on BBC2 in a live 25-minute programme, which included interviews with both judges and bookies.[95] The prize-winner, Salman Rushdie, was much less known than Golding: his first novel, *Grimus*, had been ignored by critics and sold fewer than 800 copies. On the eve of the award, sales (which had been bolstered already by the book's appearance on the shortlist and some high-profile reviews) stood at 3,152 copies. The award was announced on 20 October 1981; by 13 November, sales were 10,072 and by the end of January 1982 the book had sold over 21,000 copies, with an additional 11,000 copies in book club orders. The paperback print run a year later was 50,000 copies.[96] Since Rushdie's victory, the Booker effect has often been dramatic for winning titles and substantial for shortlisted titles, especially those by less-known authors. Sales reports from Nielsen Bookdata show weekly sales for Julian Barnes's *The Sense of an Ending* (2011) at 2,535 in the week before the prize announcement and 14,534 in the week of the announcement (a rise of 473 per cent). For the less established Yann Martel, *Life of Pi* (2002) sold 587 in the preceding week and 7,150 in the Booker week (a rise of 1,118 per cent) and there was an enduring effect on sales which reached 1.3 million copies ten years after the award, making this the Booker's most successful winner to date. In 2010, Howard Jacobson's *The Finkler Question* saw a weekly increase in sales of 1,918 per cent, from 2,535 to 14,534.[97]

Given the commercial backing of Booker McConnell and, since 2002, of stockbroking company, the Man Group, the Booker has always had its detractors, most famously John Berger in his 1972 tirade against the exploitative nature of Booker McConnell's trading interests in the Caribbean. Such criticisms have been deflected by the status the prize has acquired in establishing a widened post-imperial definition of British literature as a coherent body of work and a contrast to the American tradition. The prize had drawn attention to the work of authors from the Commonwealth from its inception, but before Rushdie these tended to be written from the point of view of the coloniser (e.g. Ruth Prawer Jhabvala's *Heat and Dust* or Paul Scott's *Staying On*). Since Rushdie, the prize has acted as a showcase for hitherto marginalised postcolonial voices.[98] When the Man Group took over sponsorship of the prize in 2002, there was immediate discussion of opening the prize to US authors;[99] in the event that didn't happen until 2014,[100] but the decision was controversial and criticised by authors, in particular, as a commercial move that is likely to have a detrimental effect on the prize's distinct identity.[101] Others have argued that the profile of the prize is indicative of an imbalance in literary valuing that is damaging to the long-term development of a literary oeuvre: Amit Chaudhuri laments that the prize 'has become most literary publishers' primary marketing tool. Publishing houses were once homes to writers; the former gave the latter the necessary leeway to create a body of work. Today there's little intellectual or material investment in writers.' He argues that the random nature of the Booker lottery 'confirms the market's convulsive metamorphic powers, its ability to confer success unpredictably'.[102] Indeed, some of the new prizes created since the rise of the Booker have been in response to its perceived limitations: the provocation for the Orange Prize was the Booker's 1991 shortlist, which contained no women; the Folio Prize was inspired by the perception of almost indecent populism in the 2011 Booker shortlist, while the Goldsmiths Prize in 2014 was launched to 'reward fiction that breaks the mould': its co-sponsor, the *New Statesman*, suggested that the Booker used to do this, but the Man Booker no longer did.[103]

Richard Todd suggests that one of the distinguishing features of the contemporary literary landscape is that 'a process of "canon-formation", guided but not dictated by consumer forces, in ways that have not been seen before, has come into being'.[104] The Booker is a clear example of this process: it is an award that has gained symbolic capital as its commercial impact has increased. We may see this, in Bourdieusian terms, as the systematic erosion of the cultural sphere by structures of power, or as a reification of the demands of the consumer and the undermining of old sources of 'expert' authority; a more optimistic interpretation might be that the literary industry has always been built on personal relationships and the current institutional structure attempts to bring readers into that relationship. In the 1980s and 1990s, publishing companies were consolidated and bookshop chains came to dominate the market, but, in the twenty-first century, we have seen a new rise in independent publishers and micro-imprints; in bookselling the 'mock-independent' strategy of Waterstones has kept the company afloat. Amazon's success is not predicated on undercutting its competitors' pricing of best-sellers, it is based on ferociously good logistics which allow consumers to get precisely what they want with great efficiency, whether that is the latest audiobook, a long out-of-print novel, a forum for reader engagement or a platform for their self-published fiction.

The commercialisation of literary fiction may have addressed the stultification perceived by Sutherland in the 1970s and proved nimble in facing some of the challenges of a liquid modern age, but there are clearly perils in an institutional structure that is continually battered by the winds of the market, as there are in the categorisation of literary fiction as just another part of the media-entertainment complex. Back in 1996, Richard Todd calculated that between 150 and 200 books by sixty-five to seventy authors were commercially supporting the fiction lists of London's major literary publishers at any one time,[105] while a 2007 survey by the Writers' Workshop revealed that the top 10 per cent of professional authors in the United Kingdom earned 60 per cent of the total income and the bottom 50 per cent earned only 8 per cent.[106] In December 2017, Arts Council England released a still more sobering report showing that the plummeting sales and stagnant prices of the past decade had led to a crisis for authors, publishers and by extension readers, with marginal voices and experimental fictions repressed and all but best-selling authors now, effectively, part of the precariat.[107] Prophecies of the death of the novel have been around for almost as long as the novel itself; back in 1980, Bill Buford argued that the well-entrenched 'vocabulary of termination has suddenly acquired a significance which has authoritatively dropped it from the theoretical to the base, real court of the marketplace'.[108] What is most interesting in the Arts Council England report is, first, that it emphasises the vitality rather than the moribundity of the sector within a very difficult climate: celebrating, in particular, the vibrancy of independent publishers and acknowledging that there is a powerful appetite for narrative, but that, increasingly, literary fiction struggles against competition from gaming and Netflix; and second, that it was not released until Arts Council England had decided precisely how to respond.[109] Their published response (2017) states: 'historically, there has been an assumption that literary fiction fell within the sphere of commercial publishing, and therefore required little in the way of direct intervention from the Arts Council';[110] however, in the light of the report and subsequent consultations they propose to allocate new funding to the development of literary fiction of £38 million annually from 2018 to 2022.[111] This is a significant commitment, given the UK home market for all fiction (including genre and mass market fiction) in print and eBook form was £356 million in 2016.[112]

Certainly it may be hard to mythologise the literary novel as 'the prince of art forms ... the true Wagnerian *Gesamtkunstwerk*' (as Will Self ironically termed it in one of the more recent essays anticipating its demise[113]), when the

Gesamtkunstwerk in question is the subject of fervid betting at Ladbrokes, on '3 for 2' in the local high street, or, conversely, struggling for crowd-funding, but there is a long history of claims that literary integrity is threatened by being 'dumbed down' in reaching to a commercial audience[114] and the novel has fought back with the creation of astonishing new worlds in new forms. The 2017 Booker prize-winner, *Lincoln in the Bardo* by George Saunders,[115] illustrates the agility of the form, with its multiple, cacophonous narrators, all of which turn out to be voices of the dead, helping to guide Abraham Lincoln's son through the passage between life and death. Saunders's novel is far from the only formally inventive best-seller of recent years: the highly elaborate structure of David Mitchell's *Cloud Atlas* did not prevent it from becoming the Richard and Judy Book of the Year in 2004, defying claims that contemporary readers lack the attention span required for immersion in a literary text, or that, in the age of the eBook, novels require a more straightforward 'storytelling' structure than the codex demanded.[116] Still, Eimear McBride's experimental, stream-of-consciousness novel, *A Girl Is a Half-Formed Thing*, was rejected as too much of a risk by every literary agent and publisher she approached in 2004; it was taken up nine years later by one of the independent publishers cited in the Arts Council England report, the tiny Galley Beggar Press, with an initial print run of 1,000 copies. It went on to win the inaugural Goldsmiths Prize, the Kerry Group Prize and the Bailey's prize, prompting a Faber co-edition printing of 25,000 copies. The ability of the contemporary literary marketplace to publish 'difficult' work with both commercial success and critical approbation is surely something that Bill Buford, back in 1980, would have celebrated. The hope is that new sources of central funding can support the vigour that already exists in the sector in finding new voices, bringing them to a wide readership and enabling a much more diverse range of writers to build literary careers.

Notes

1. V. Woolf, 'Mr Bennett and Mrs Brown' (1924), www.columbia.edu/~em36/MrBennettAndMrsBrown.pdf.
2. B. Buford, 'Introduction: The End of the English Novel', *Granta* 3 (1980), https://granta.com/the-end-of-the-english-novel/.
3. Much to the chagrin of A. S. Byatt, for example, who wrote of her irritation that the English novel was seen as so much in need of enlivening: 'a body of writing that included Burgess, Golding, Murdoch and Lessing, to start with, carries weight' (A. S. Byatt, *On Histories and Stories: Selected Essays* (Cambridge, MA: Harvard University Press, 2001), p. 3.
4. R. Eaglestone, 'Contemporary Fiction in the Academy: Towards a Manifesto' (2013) 27(7) *Textual Practice* 1089–1101.

5. Todd also notes that, despite the fact that it was joint favourite for the prize, its publisher, Jonathan Cape, was unprepared for its success and the book was out of stock for 10 days following its prize victory. R. Todd, *Consuming Fictions: The Booker Prize and Fiction in Britain Today* (London: Bloomsbury, 1996), p. 104.
6. Buford, 'Introduction', p. 1.
7. J. A. Sutherland, *Fiction and the Fiction Industry* (London: Bloomsbury, 2013 [1978]), p. xxi.
8. *Ibid.*, p. xxv.
9. J. F. English and J. Frow, 'Literary authorship and celebrity culture' in J. F. English (ed.), *A Concise Companion to Contemporary British Fiction* (Oxford: Blackwell Publishing, 2006), pp. 45–6.
10. Buford, 'Introduction', p. 4.
11. P. Bourdieu, *The Field of Cultural Production: Essays on Art and Literature* (Cambridge: Polity, 1993), pp. 37–61.
12. A. Bartram, *Making Books: Design in British Publishing since 1945* (London: The British Library Publishing Division, 1999), p. 9, cited in G. Clark and A. Phillips, *Inside Book Publishing*, 5th edn (London and New York: Routledge, 2008), p. 19.
13. J. O'Mahony, 'Publishing's One-Man Band', *The Guardian* (20 July 2002), www.theguardian.com/books/2002/jul/20/society.
14. Woolf, 'Mr Bennett and Mrs Brown', p. 20.
15. M. McGurl, *The Novel Art: Elevations of American Fiction after Henry James* (Princeton University Press, 2001).
16. D. Athill, *Stet: An Editor's Life* (London: Granta Books, 2001), p. 132.
17. Buford, 'Introduction', pp. 3–4.
18. A. Nash, 'The Material History of the Novel II: 1973–Present' in P. Boxall and B. Cheyette (eds), *The Oxford History of the Novel in English*, vol. III: *British and Irish Fiction since 1940* (Oxford University Press, 2016), p. 401.
19. Athill, *Stet: An Editor's Life*, p. 56.
20. Clark and Phillips, *Inside Book Publishing*, p. 16.
21. J. Feather, *Communicating Knowledge: Publishing in the 21st Century* (Berlin and New York: Walter de Gruyter, 2003), p. 84.
22. G. Greenfield, *Scribblers for Bread: Aspects of the English Novel since 1945* (London: Hodder & Stoughton, 1989), p. 235, cited in Nash, 'The Material History of the Novel II', p. 406.
23. T. Blacker, 'In Celebrityville Even the Fixers Are Famous Now', *The Independent* (23 November 2001), www.independent.co.uk/voices/commentators/terence-blacker/terence-blacker-in-celebrityville-even-the-fixers-are-famous-now-9196337.html.
24. R. McCrum, 'The Best Book Club', *The Guardian* (30 May 2004), www.theguardian.com/books/2004/may/30/biography.features.
25. Nash, 'The Material History of the Novel II', p. 403.
26. McCrum, 'The Best Book Club'.
27. J. B. Thompson, *Merchants of Culture* (Cambridge: Polity, 2010), p. 53.
28. Sutherland, *Fiction and the Fiction Industry*, p. xxvi.
29. The Reading Agency, 'Library Facts' (2017), https://readingagency.org.uk/about/impact/001-library-facts/.

30. McCrum, 'The Best Book Club'.
31. Sutherland, *Fiction and the Fiction Industry*, p. 84.
32. *Ibid.*, pp. 92–7.
33. F. R. Leavis, *Nor Shall My Sword: Discourses on Pluralism, Compassion and Social Hope* (London: Chatto & Windus, 1972), p. 221, cited in Sutherland, *Fiction and the Fiction Industry*, p. 91.
34. P. Ackroyd, 'The Slow Death of Cambridge English', *The Spectator* (6 March 1976), p. 26, cited in Sutherland, *Fiction and the Fiction Industry*, p. 90.
35. Q. Oates, 'Quentin Oates' Column', *The Bookseller* (8 May 1976), cited in Sutherland, *Fiction and the Fiction Industry*, p. 99.
36. I. Jack, 'Best of Young British Novelists 2003: Introduction', *Granta 81* (2003), https://granta.com/introduction-boybno3/.
37. D. I. Clarke, 'Up for Promotion', *The Bookseller* (11 April 2013), www.thebookseller.com/blogs/promotion.
38. Z. Bauman, *Liquid Modernity* (Cambridge: Polity, 2000), p. 3.
39. *Ibid.* (emphasis in the original). From Bauman's perspective, writing in 1999, 'present modernity' referred to the effects of a confluence of economic, social, cultural and philosophical shifts of the previous two decades. As an example of this transformation Bauman cited the tepid response to the 1984 celebration of George Orwell's canonical text: 'an inventory of the fears and apprehensions which haunted modernity in its "heavy" stage' (*ibid.*, p. 26), but which no longer appeared threatening in 'the post-Fordist, "fluid modern" world of freely choosing individuals' (*ibid.*, p. 61).
40. Sutherland, *Fiction and the Fiction Industry*, p. xxi.
41. C. Squires, *Marketing Literature: The Making of Contemporary Writing in Britain* (Basingstoke: Palgrave Macmillan, 2009), pp. 44–7.
42. Nash, 'The Material History of the Novel II', pp. 403–4.
43. J. Street, 'Showbusiness of a Serious Kind': A Cultural Politics of the Arts Prize' (2005) 27(5) *Media, Culture & Society* 819–40, 824.
44. R. McCrum, 'Our Top 50 Players in the World of Books', *The Guardian* (5 March 2006), www.theguardian.com/books/2006/mar/05/features.review.
45. Thompson, *Merchants of Culture*, pp. 37–41.
46. Buford, 'Introduction', p. 5.
47. Todd, *Consuming Fictions*, pp. 79–80.
48. *Ibid.*, pp. 77–8.
49. Clark and Phillips, *Inside Book Publishing*, p. 19.
50. I. Jack, 'Best of Young American Novelists 2: Introduction' (2007) *Granta 97*, p. 1, https://granta.com/introduction-boyan-2/.
51. Quoted in S. Garfield, 'From Student Rag to Literary Riches', *The Guardian* (30 December 2007), www.theguardian.com/books/2007/dec/30/culture.features.
52. J. Murray, 'Can You Teach Creative Writing?' *The Guardian* (10 May 2011), www.theguardian.com/education/2011/may/10/creative-writing-courses.
53. P. Nicol, 'Can You Teach Someone to Write a Bestseller? Judging by the Faber Academy's Record the Answer Is Yes', *Evening Standard Magazine* (16 August 2017), www.standard.co.uk/lifestyle/esmagazine/can-you-teach-someone-to-write-a-bestseller-judging-by-the-faber-academy-s-record-the-answer-is-yes-a3612021.html.

54. A. Clark, 'The Novelists of 1993 Had It Easy. How Will Today's Young Novelists Publish Their Work?' *The Guardian* (14 April 2013), www.theguardian.com/books/2013/apr/14/novelists-1993-easy-young-writers-publish.
55. *Ibid.*
56. Fuller, personal communication, 6 November 2017.
57. E.g. Hutchinson, which was owned by London Weekend Television from 1978. See Clark and Phillips, *Inside Book Publishing*, p. 15.
58. Thompson, *Merchants of Culture*, p. 108.
59. Clark and Phillips, *Inside Book Publishing*, p. 15.
60. Which it increased further in 2017. See G. Chazan and D. Bond, 'Bertelsmann Takes Greater Control of Penguin Random House', *Financial Times* (11 July 2017), www.ft.com/content/2bef8202-6602-11e7-8526-7b38dcaef614.
61. Publishers' Weekly, 'Global Publishing Leaders 2016: Penguin Random House' (26 August 2016), www.publishersweekly.com/pw/by-topic/industry-news/publisher-news/article/71304-global-publishing-leaders-2016-penguin-random-house.html.
62. I am indebted to John B. Thompson for his detailed history of UK publishing acquisitions (*Merchants of Culture*, pp. 119–26).
63. The other founding members were Portobello Books, Icon and Short Books. Others, including Granta Books, Serpent's Tail (part of Profile Books) and Quercus joined in 2007, although the latter has since taken its sales representation back in house, and a third tranche of members joined in 2013.
64. Thompson, *Merchants of Culture*, p. 181.
65. S. Unerman, 'Turning Old Media Around', *Campaign* (7 July 2016), www.campaignlive.co.uk/article/turning-old-media-around/1401509.
66. K. Hosseini, 'Biography' (2017), http://khaledhosseini.com/biography/.
67. Although they only published six books a year until their expansion in 1997.
68. Other successful independent publishers of literary fiction launched in this period include Salt Publishing in 1999, Atlantic in 2000, Alma Books in 2005 and the subscription-funded not-for-profit And Other Stories in 2010, publisher of twice Booker-shortlisted novelist Deborah Levy.
69. C. Armistead, 'Covers Story: Why Are There So Many New Publishing Imprints?' *The Guardian* (21 June 2016), www.theguardian.com/books/2016/jun/21/covers-story-why-are-there-so-many-new-publishing-imprints.
70. Page, personal communication, 22 September 2017.
71. Thompson, *Merchants of Culture*, p. 73.
72. Squires, *Marketing Literature*, p. 34.
73. Thompson, *Merchants of Culture*, pp. 63–71.
74. M. Macdonald, 'A Layman's Guide to Being Wylie', *The Independent* (12 April 1997), http://www.independent.co.uk/arts-entertainment/a-laymans-guide-to-being-wylie-1266821.html.
75. Quoted in *ibid.*, p. 67.
76. M. Meyer, 'About that Book Advance…', *The New York Times* (10 April 2009), www.nytimes.com/2009/04/12/books/review/Meyer-t.html.
77. Kavanagh, quoted in K. Kellaway, 'That Difficult First Novel', *The Guardian* (25 March 2007), www.theguardian.com/books/2007/mar/25/fiction.features7.
78. Wylie, quoted in Thompson, *Merchants of Culture*, p. 68.

79. Squires, *Marketing Literature*, p. 36, cites M. Legat, *An Author's Guide to Literary Agents* (London: Robert Hale, 1995).

80. Waterstone, quoted in Thompson, *Merchants of Culture*, p. 53.

81. Nash, 'The Material History of the Novel II', p. 409.

82. P. Jones, 'What We Have Learned from eBooks 2014', *The Bookseller* (8 May 2015), www.thebookseller.com/futurebook/what-we-have-learned-e-books-2014.

83. L. Campbell, 'Amazon Has 79% of eBook Market in UK', *The Bookseller* (12 September 2013), www.thebookseller.com/news/amazon-has-79-e-book-market-uk.

84. L. Campbell, 'Indie Bookshop Presence in the UK Contracts for an 11th Consecutive Year', *The Bookseller* (3 March 2017), www.thebookseller.com/news/indie-bookshop-presence-uk-contracts-11th-consecutive-year-499776.

85. W. Dunn, 'How a New Attitude to Work Saved Britain's Bookshops', *The New Statesman* (10 July 2017), www.newstatesman.com/microsites/skills/2017/07/how-new-attitude-work-saved-britain-s-bookshops.

86. Quoted in Z. Wood 'Waterstones Buys Foyles "in Face of Amazon's Siren Call"' The Guardian (7 September 2018), https://www.theguardian.com/business/2018/sep/07/waterstones-buys-foyles-in-face-of-amazon-siren-call.

87. Costa, 'Costa Book Awards' (2013–18), www.costa.co.uk/costa-book-awards/welcome/.

88. Chaudhuri, 'My Fellow Authors'.

89. It remains £50,000 at the time of writing.

90. Goff, quoted in Todd, *Consuming Fictions*, pp. 68–9.

91. Todd, *Consuming Fictions*, p. 68.

92. Goff, 1990, cited in Todd, *Consuming Fictions*, p. 69.

93. Minutes of Booker Management Meeting, 18 January 1974, cited in B. Driscoll, *The New Literary Middlebrow: Tastemakers and Reading in the Twenty-First Century* (London: Palgrave Macmillan, 2014), p. 119–51.

94. Minutes of Booker Management Meeting, 9 June 1981, cited in Driscoll, *The New Literary Middlebrow*, pp. 119–51.

95. Driscoll, *The New Literary Middlebrow*, pp. 119–51.

96. Todd, *Consuming Fictions*, p. 104; Nash, 'The Material History of the Novel II', p. 414.

97. Figures from Nielsen Bookdata, cited in The Guardian Datablog (2012).

98. John Sutherland argues that Berger's outburst too had 'a palpable influence in politically correcting the shortlist' (J. A. Sutherland, 'Exceptionally Wonderful Book', *London Review of Books* (6 October 1994), cited in Todd, *Consuming Fictions*, pp. 78–9).

99. Or as the Booker Prize Committee carefully say – opening the prize to all writers in English, regardless of nationality.

100. The Man Group opted to launch The Booker International Prize at this point, stalling the decision to expand the entry criteria of the original prize for 10 years.

101. Following Paul Beatty's Man Booker success in 2016, the *Daily Telegraph* reported that Julian Barnes and Peter Carey had spoken out against the inclusion of US authors (S. Knapton, 'Julian Barnes: Americans Should Be Barred from Booker Prize', *Daily Telegraph* (28 November 2016), www .telegraph.co.uk/news/2016/11/28/julian-barnes-americans-should-barred-

booker-prize/). In February 2018, it was reported that a letter was in circulation which had, to date, been signed by thirty publishers urging the Booker Prize Foundation to reverse the decision (V. Ward, 'Publishers Urge about Turn on Decision to Include American Authors in Man Booker Prize', *Daily Telegraph* (2 February 2018), www.telegraph.co.uk/news/2018/02/02/pub lishers-urge-about-turn-decision-include-american-authors/).

102. A. Chaudhuri, 'My Fellow Authors Are Too Busy Chasing Prizes to Write about What Matters', *The Guardian* (16 August 2017), www.theguardian.com/com mentisfree/2017/aug/16/booker-prize-bad-for-writing-alternative-celebrate-literature.

103. L. Robson, 'All Must Have Prizes! How the Goldsmiths and Folio Prizes Are Changing the Literary Landscape', *New Statesman* (1 October 2014), www .newstatesman.com/2014/09/all-must-have-prizes.

104. Todd, *Consuming Fictions*, p. 3.

105. *Ibid.*, p. 17.

106. Cited in A. Phillips, *Turning the Page: The Evolution of the Book* (London & New York: Routledge, 2014), p. 3.

107. M. Bhaskar, I. Millar and N. Barreto, 'Literature in the 21st Century: Understanding Models of Support for Literary Fiction', Arts Council England (15 December 2017), www.artscouncil.org.uk/publication/literature-21st-cen tury-understanding-models-support-literary-fiction.

108. Buford, 'Introduction', p. 1.

109. According to one of its authors, Nick Barreto, the report was completed a year before its release (Barreto, personal communication, 2 February 2018).

110. Arts Council England, 'Models of Support for Literary Fiction' (15 December 2017), https://www.artscouncil.org.uk/document/models-support-literary-fic tion-response.

111. This includes support for individual authors and for independent publishers, investment in strategies to increase diversity and take advantage of the opportunities presented by new technologies, and funds for reader development – including work with libraries and independent bookshops.

112. *PA Publishing Yearbook* (London: The Publishers Association, 2016), p. 29. Bhaskar, Millar and Barreto calculate that 'general fiction' (the closest approximation for literary fiction that the data allows) amounted to 42% of overall fiction sales in 2016 ('Literature in the 21st Century', p. 16).

113. W. Self, 'The Novel Is Dead (This Time It's for Real', *The Guardian* (2 May 2014), www.theguardian.com/books/2014/may/02/will-self-novel-dead-lit erary-fiction.

114. With the advent of mass literacy in the nineteenth century, for example.

115. G. Saunders, *Lincoln in the Bardo* (London: Bloomsbury, 2017).

116. See, e.g., J. Scott, 'The Virtues of Difficult Fiction', *The Nation* (30 July 2015), www.thenation.com/article/the-democracy-of-difficult-fiction.

PART III

Genres and Movements

7

MARTIN PAUL EVE

Late Modernism, Postmodernism and After

Postmodernism and Nationalism

To write of 'postmodernism' is both to skate on thin ice and to tread familiar ground. Almost every piece of scholarship that uses this classification must begin, by convention it seems, with a lengthy tract on what precisely is meant by 'the postmodern'. It is precarious 'thin ice' because these definitions are not always aligned with one another and are sometimes delicate. For instance, many of the tropes that one might call 'postmodern' and to which I will shortly turn are clearly exhibited in Romantic-era writing or in the epic of Melville's *Moby Dick* (1851). Such definitional work is 'familiar ground', though, because the procedure has become so routinised as to appear mundane.

I am afraid that this chapter will not be the exception to the rule. For the structural grouping of this piece under the section 'Genres and Movements' poses some initial problems. This is because, when postmodernism is couched in terms of a progression from 'late modernism', through 'postmodernism', to 'after', there is the ever-present temptation to consider it solely as a periodising movement as opposed to a set of stylistic techniques that have merely received additional emphasis in recent years. Yet the 'post' prefix here can be considered within multiple frames: it can mean 'after' modernism or it can mean 'a mutated continuation of' modernism. It could even mean 'an intensification of' modernism. Furthermore, the term 'postmodernism' is also used to refer discretely to the set of cultural, economic and political conditions that emerged in the latter half of the twentieth century. In Jean-François Lyotard's famous tract, *The Post-Modern Condition: A Report on Knowledge,* he described this socio-cultural phase as an 'incredulity toward metanarratives'.[1] In other words, the totalising logic of positivism that fuelled the early twentieth century gave way to a 'postmodern' ethos: in physics through quantum mechanics, in politics through the collapse of the British Empire and in literary production through a proliferation of destabilising narratological techniques. Certainly the continued destabilisa-tion of economic certainties along Marxist lines and the protracted unveiling of a structured unconsciousness through psychoanalytic tools also played a role. But this literary postmodernism is at once woven between broader globalised shifts in cultural postmodernism, while also possessing its own specificities.

The other side of the 'postmodern' definition that we must never neglect, though, is the fact that a straightforward claim of a progression from mod-ernism to postmodernism to 'something-after-postmodernism' also holds within it the possibility of a domineering or totalising chronology that neglects the vast quantity of fiction writing that falls outside of such a scheme. For instance, modernism and postmodernism never replaced lit-erary realism, they merely supplemented it. Furthermore, a range of genre forms, explored by Caroline Edwards in this volume, have been and continue to be read by a larger number of readers than avowedly postmodern works ever reached. Indeed, we should be cautious about our framing of postmo-dernism as a dominant literary narrative from the 1980s. Certainly, *a* strand of highbrow literary fiction can be classed under such a rubric. However, the degree to which postmodernism is often hailed as the *major* literary descrip-tor for this period is perhaps exaggerated.

That said and now turning to the geographical specificities of the term, literary postmodernism is often considered a predominantly Northern American phenomenon. Indeed, John Barth, Thomas Pynchon, Don DeLillo, Donald Barthelme, Kurt Vonnegut, Bret Easton Ellis, Richard Powers, Toni Morrison, Ishmael Reed, Joseph Heller, Hunter S. Thompson, Vladimir Nabokov, William Gaddis, Philip Roth, William Burroughs, Kathy Acker and the early works of David Foster Wallace, among many others, might be considered exemplary of postmodernism in the United States. We also see a marked dominance in this space by the ethnographic portrait that Wallace once summed up as, for the most part, 'the Great [white] Male Narcissists'.[2]

The literary traits that can be found within this group of American novelists can be concisely, albeit reductively and far from completely, summarised as: a focus on narrative indeterminacy; fragmentation and temporal distortion; a degree of irony and/or playfulness; a referential or intertextual structure; a destruction of the distinction between creative and critical practice; a post-secularism; a wariness about technology; pastiche; metafictive elements (that is, a narrative focus on the text's own textuality or the act of writing); magical realism; historiographic remarks; and a tendency towards either maximalist or minimalist writing (sometimes seen simultaneously within a single author's canon, as with David Foster Wallace). Furthermore, in one of the most prominent definitions of the American postmodern scene, Brian McHale has distinguished between modern and postmodern writing through reference to a 'change in dominant' from a focus on epistemology (knowledge) in the former to a centrality of ontology (being) in the latter.[3] For McHale, the central difference is that modernism poses (solvable) epistemological questions of the reader: for instance, 'what are the limits of readerly knowledge?'. On the other hand, in McHale's account, postmodern writing becomes about the limits of the world: 'Which world and whose reality?'

The British scene of postmodern writing since the 1980s exhibits almost all of the aforementioned traits, albeit with some given more space at the expense of others. For while the continued prominence in the twenty-first century of writers such as Ian McEwan, Kazuo Ishiguro, Pat Barker and Zadie Smith might suggest that there is an underlying connection between British writing and some kind of realism, that British writers are at their best when writing in a form that has its roots in the realism of Thomas Hardy and George Eliot, there is also a marked development of what might be called a postmodern aesthetic in British writing, which is sometimes entangled with British realism, but often diverts from it.

From Late Modernism to Postmodernism

In order to understand British postmodernism, it is first necessary to have some grasp of the transformations in late modernism that sculpted the immediately preceding era (despite the warnings above regarding this chronology). The term 'late modernism' is conventionally used to refer to works that exhibit modernist traits published after the 1930s, although it is also a contested phrase that has begun to telescope historically.[4] Among such figures, the most overshadowing author, though not British, was Samuel Beckett, whose shift in prose style is instructive for understanding British postmodern fiction since the 1980s.

Beckett is best known for his trilogy of novels, *Molloy* (1951), *Malone Dies* (1951)[5] and *The Unnamable* (1953), and for his plays *Waiting for Godot* (1953), *Endgame* (1957), *Krapp's Last Tape* (1958) and *Happy Days* (1962). Certainly Beckett's drama always exhibited a minimalist quality. Sparse barren landscapes or bare rooms with few characters are the hallmarks of these works. By contrast, though, the prose of *The Unnamable* overflows in its exhaustive oscillation between the narrator's self-obliteration and self-construction.

By any account, however, both Beckett's prose and his drama take a decisively minimalist turn towards the extreme end of his career (what Edward Saïd might term his 'late style'[6]). The late prose piece *Worstward Ho*

(1983), for example, is written in short staccato sentence blasts, while still maintaining the absence of setting pioneered in the earlier novels: 'On. Say on. Be said on. Somehow on. Till nohow on. Said nohow on.'[7] Likewise, the drama from around 1966 onwards becomes more contracted even than in Beckett's previously minimalist structures. *Come and Go* (1966) marks the ascent of this style (although *Not I* (1969) is verbose in its speech if not its setting) that works towards the culminating duologue playlet of *Ohio Impromptu* (1981) and the monologue of *Rockaby* (1981).

Such a minimalist style – even while noting that a precise definition of literary style that does not rely upon a crude form/content divide remains elusive – seems to generate a degree of backlash from certain British literary quarters. While Beckett's late prose and drama (and subsequent rigorous oversight by his estate) veer towards a desire for tight and precise control of voice, or even its excision, several works of British postmodern literary fiction exhibit the counter-tendency of an anarchic openness.

Perhaps the foremost example of this diametrically opposite take on style is best seen in John Fowles's 1969 novel, *The French Lieutenant's Woman*. This text features many of the classic tropes of postmodern fiction that will appear in mutated form in the British novels of the 1980s, most notably: metatextual authorial interventions; a historical setting and a focus on historiographic techniques; intertextual references; and a plurality of endings. Indeed, throughout the novel the 'narrator' frequently intervenes, citing scholarship and Darwinian science from the Victorian period.[8] The text is set in the Victorian age, yet is uncomfortable with any claim to accurately represent the period from a position of retrospection (a historiographic mode where the focus is upon how history is constructed, rather than the history itself). The novel also makes reference to works of literary theory, such as those by Roland Barthes and Alain Robbe-Grillet.[9] Most famously, the ending of the novel splits into three divergent narrative paths, with different outcomes permuted between the romantic attachments between Charles, Sarah and Ernestina.

The broad sense of proliferation that is conveyed in Fowles's novel – with its overloading of narratives, histories and voices – stands in stark contrast to those of Beckett. It is as though there is a chiastic (cross-shaped) structure at work here in which, as Beckett and others contract, a second group of writers are seeking a type of maximalism in the very opposite fashion. This fits neatly with the theorisation yielded by John Barth of a 'literature of exhaustion'; an attempt to embody 'an age of ultimacies' in which the realist form is collapsed and we head towards an omega point.[10] Whether Barth was historically correct is beyond debate: he was wrong and the persistence of the realist form continues unabated. But it is of note that this thinking was 'in the air' in the late 1960s.

As a counterpoint, though, it is also of interest that several of the classic American postmodernists, such as Thomas Pynchon and Don DeLillo, have moved, Beckett-like, towards a contracted late phase in their own writing. There is a sense, then, in which the maximalist proliferation that spins out of late 1960s postmodern is a phase. What I will turn to now, with this background sketch fleshed out, is how these contrasting movements found their way into the contexts that have informed some British fiction since the 1980s.

Postmodernism in the 1980s

Joe Brooker has written, amid the paradoxical and contrasting contexts for the fiction of the 1980s, that the political environment was shaped by Margaret Thatcher, but that the pop group Duran Duran was exemplary of at least part of a cultural scene manufactured to reproduce a 'glossy sound' that held 'loose connotations of cultural Thatcherism' embodied in a 'lifestyle of high consumption and excess'.[11] This is also twinned, though, as Brooker notes, with a paradoxical counter-movement that can be seen in various politicised forms of art that embody a more critical (or perhaps just liberal/left-wing) approach.

Of the novels in the 1980s that exhibit postmodern tendencies but that also have the Duran Duran factor of glossy Thatcherite complicity, Martin Amis's *Money* (1984) stands out as the foremost representation. Narrated by John Self – whose name is at least part of Amis's nod towards postmodern narratorial intrusion, but whose presence is complicated by the appearance of another writer within the text called 'Martin Amis' – *Money* is a 400-page-long *tour de force* of ostentatious literary over-writing.[12] It is also, though, a difficult text to place politically. Amis has never been known as the most progressive writer of gender politics, yet gender and sex are key to this text, which is saturated with similar questions: 'Got laid recently?'[13]

Given the transatlantic context for postmodernism that I have been tracing, it should come as no surprise to find that *Money* is a novel that deals with and that has been influenced by America. For instance, Finn Fordham has traced the ways in which, in particular, the shadow of the Russian-American novelist, Nabokov (but also Bellow) hangs over the road to Amis's text, even if the novel does eventually hit a limit in its Nabokovian tropes. More importantly, though, in reading the novel through Amis's famous assertion that 'style is morality', Fordham adeptly traces how *Money* can be seen as a text about the relationships between 'readers, writers, and their characters'.[14] As the character Martin Amis within the text asks: 'Is there a moral philosophy of fiction?'[15]

Despite this self-referentiality, though, and the fact that a range of critics have read the text as distinctly postmodern, not everyone shares this view.[16] David James, for example, points towards the fact that the ostentatious metafictive devices within the novel may distract us from viewing it as 'one in which inventiveness and traditionalism coexist in important ways that have often been sidelined'; that is, this could be a resurgent modernism rather than a postmodernism.[17] Notwithstanding the fact that, for James, there is a politics of style that runs through *Money* that is not just postmodern, James's eventual claim that 'what Amis tries to do is take our aesthetic infatuation, the pleasures of witnessing his virtuosity, and align it with the more puerile infatuations that Self indulges' does nonetheless sound somewhat metafictional.[18]

Despite the stylistic range of the novel, perhaps where we might most class *Money* as a postmodern text, however, is in its relationship to ethics. Critics such as Jane Flax, but also others, have noted that there has been a consistent 'association of postmodernism and amorality' in the critical literature, centred around purported claims for moral relativism.[19] *Money*, though, is a novel that satirises consumer culture and ultimately (morally) rails against it; including the disparaging of an environment that Amis feels possesses 'moral unease without moral energy'.[20] Yet the way in which this plays out is through a glossy stylistic framework that, in many ways, embodies the consumer-capitalist dynamic that Amis seems to satirise. Certainly, *Money* is a complex text when it comes to an ethical stance.

Yet other works of postmodern British fiction of the 1980s are more clearcut with regard to ethics and morality, intersecting with the strong postcolonial movement in force at that time. At the forefront of this movement – at least in the popular imagination in Britain – sat Salman Rushdie, who has continued to publish even as the discourse of postcolonialism may, in more recent days, be seen as giving way to a paradigm of 'world literature'.[21] In particular, Rushdie's novels *Midnight's Children* (1981) and the controversial *The Satanic Verses* (1988) can be said to represent an intersection between postmodern stylistics and postcolonial concerns.

Midnight's Children, for instance, explicitly deals with the aftermath of the British Empire in India and the partitioning of the newly decolonised space into India and Pakistan. Indeed, the character Saleem is born at midnight on 15 August 1947, the precise moment at which the partition came into effect. It soon becomes apparent, though, within the novel's plot, that all such 'midnight's children' possess extraordinary magical powers, such as telepathy, that vary in intensity the closer to midnight they were born.

The magical realism of this complex and dense novel, which begins by playfully questioning the fairy-tale premise of 'once upon a time' while also yoking the primary characters in a mysterious 'handcuff[ing] to history', is one of the many instances wherein British postmodernism becomes linked to postcolonialism.[22] For, although it might seem that what could be needed in the aftermath of the British Empire is a strong, coherent and unified identity for the former colonies – one that perhaps should be supplied by British realism instead of by 'open sesame' and 'a magic spell' – the entanglement of linear storytelling with a British history that led to empire complicates such a relationship.[23] It is not enough for Rushdie to re-appropriate a narrative style from British literary history, but instead he seeks to pluralise identity through postmodern stylistics of overload and historical rewriting. In Rushdie's writing it is, instead, the case that '[r]eality is a question of perspective' and, as his narrator metatextually remarks, one has the feeling that he is 'somehow creating a world'.[24]

Such a stance was also present in the most contentious of Rushdie's novels, *The Satanic Verses*. Although this work received high critical acclaim in Britain and was a Booker Prize finalist while also winning the Whitbread Award, it also came at a high personal cost to Rushdie, who was subjected to a fatwa issued by Ayatollah Khomeini, the Supreme Leader of Iran, calling for Rushdie's murder. The book begins aboard a hijacked, exploding airliner, from which the novel's two protagonists are miraculously saved and reincarnated respectively as an archangel and a devil. A series of dream narratives (including the controversial retelling of the life of Mohammed) are then narrated amid a range of 'cinematic' storytelling techniques that add up to a disorientating swirl that represents the immigrant experience.[25]

Rushdie's fourth novel trades, though, in aesthetic currencies of modernist (or, at least, Poundist) 'newness'. At least one critic has noted that Rushdie's forms of 'making it new' are of a different postcolonial variety in which a 'postcolonial hybridity' of 'hotpotch' is what, now, we call 'the new'.[26] This postmodern aesthetic technique of assemblage or *bricolage*, especially when cycling around its contentious politico-religious subject matter, questions the boundaries between the religious and the secular, the sacred and the profane. In many ways, as with much postmodern literature and postmodern culture more generally (such as the sociological field of science and technology studies), it is a straining at the boundaries of the enlightenment, calling on us to ask which boundaries of rationality and art it is possible to transgress.

Such political postmodernisms, though, had also been emerging just before the 1980s in Britain in other contexts, such as feminism, which can be seen clearly in the later writings of Angela Carter (although it is important to note here that 'feminism' is not a unified, single phenomenon). These political, feminist strains can be seen both in Carter's short story writings (such as *The Bloody Chamber* (1979)), but also in her penultimate novel,

Nights at the Circus (1984). The former of these works is a collection of reworkings, or 'extractions of latent content', as Carter preferred to term them, of fairy tales.[27] Indeed, this framing here poses, I contend, a core definition of postmodern fiction, in Britain and elsewhere, that often goes unremarked. That is: a blurring of the boundaries between creative and critical practice.

If, as Carter claims, her stories are *extractions* of the *latent content* of fairy tales, then what, we must ask, is the difference between literary criticism and literature itself? For how else would we define the procedures of much hermeneutic literary criticism but as 'extractions of latent content'? This merging of literature with literary studies, as with Fowles's citation of literary theory, was certainly also pronounced in the surge of author-critics (Woolf, Eliot, Lawrence, Pound, etc.) in the modernist period.[28] It is, though, in the postmodern 'era' that this slippage has most thoroughly progressed, leading Peter Boxall to remark that 'the distinction between creative and critical writing is becoming harder to sustain'.[29] Alternatively framing this same idea, Mark Currie writes that '[t]he postmodern context is not one divided neatly between fictional texts and their critical readings, but a monistic world of representations in which the boundaries between art and life, language and metalanguage, and fiction and criticism are under philosophical attack'.[30] As a result, I have argued, we 'should expect to see, in such a limited space, conflicts of legitimation, often played out through metafictional devices, where literary texts jostle with the academy for the authority to comment upon fiction'.[31]

And, in truth, it was Carter's own critical work translating the fairy-tale collection of Charles Perrault that led to her creative-critical feminist reworkings of the classic stories in *The Bloody Chamber*, including the well-known female rescue scene of the titular story. Yet, if *The Bloody Chamber* holds out this creative-critical paradigm, in a feminist tradition, then it is in *Nights at the Circus* in which Carter's postmodern sensibilities are most prominently articulated.

This novel wheels around the character Sophie Fevvers, an *aerialiste* (trapeze artist), who claims to have been hatched from an egg and to have sprouted wings at puberty. On top of this magic realism, the narrative possesses many of the common aesthetic traits of postmodern writing: the novel is extremely disorientating, with timings and truths rendered indeterminate throughout. For instance, we are told that 'Big Ben', on the same night, 'once again struck midnight'.[32] Perhaps one of the most curious features of the text, though, is its early intersection with a movement that is now termed 'post-secularism'.[33]

Indeed, the embrace of a partial spirituality, or post-enlightenment sensibility, that sits at odds with a purely rationalist approach and that was born in the postmodern period is tied closely to magical realism. However, in Carter's novel this relationship between enlightenment, secularity and faith/ the supernatural/the magical is also explicitly articulated when the narrator remarks (of Fevvers's claiming that her wings are real, even while the public believes them to be fake) that 'in a secular age, an authentic miracle must purport to be a hoax, in order to gain credit in the world'.[34]

This statement – at once apt for the way in which our current era of 'Brexit' and Donald Trump, at the time of writing, has been deemed 'post-factual' – is also, though, a metafictional riff. For what is fiction, itself, but a self-purported hoax in which, by some aesthetic miracle, we might see a clearer truth of reality through its dark glass? Of these glasses, though, few come as dark as the works of J. G. Ballard, the final British 'postmodernist' to whom I will now briefly turn.

Ballard made his name with a series of dark, transgressive fictions such as the experimental short-story cycle *The Atrocity Exhibition* (1970), the novel *Crash* (1973), focusing on automotive accident fetishisation (a symphorophilia) and earlier science/speculative fiction novels such as *The Drowned World* (1962). From the 1980s onwards, though, Ballard's oeuvre follows a generically unstable path through the quasi-autobiographical novels, *Empire of the Sun* (1984) and its sequel *The Kindness of Women* (1991), novels about dystopian elite social enclaves and their psychological dark secrets such as *Cocaine Nights* (1996) and *Super-Cannes* (2000), and fictions that are broadly concerned with the possibilities of resistance/rebellion within late capitalist paradigms, such as *Millennium People* (2003) and *Kingdom Come* (2006).

Ballard's work has always had an experimental quality, both aesthetically and politically. Indeed, the short story 'Why I Want to Fuck Ronald Reagan', later incorporated into *The Atrocity Exhibition*, led to the prosecution of the publisher, Bill Butler, for obscenity.[35] Yet, as with other writers of the British postmodern period, these political sensibilities are woven within a tapestry of disorientating prose and extreme metaphor. Indeed, it would be fair to say, at the level of Ballard's career, that his works exhibit that very 'resistance to metanarratives' that runs through so much postmodern theory; it is simply difficult to place his writings within any one single history.

... and After

When asking what has succeeded 'postmodernism' as a term to describe a particular brand of British literary fiction, we are left with many of the same problems as defining the 'genre' or 'period' itself. Has postmodernism gone anywhere? Did it ever really exist? (A most postmodern question.) Certainly for some critics, such as Charles Altieri as far back as 1998, the tropes, styles and even the name of postmodernism had faded or even become an embarrassment.[36] Yet, for Robert Eaglestone, a term such as post-postmodernism, popularised by Jeffrey Nealson, is potentially 'silly'.[37]

So, what has happened? In the first place, even while postmodernism continued to grow as a critical currency, a proliferation of generic suffixes of the '-modernisms' variety has spread far and wide, beyond a mere post-modernism. For we have had altermodernism, metamodernism, neomodern-ism, hypermodernism, remodernism and transmodernism, among others, to describe more recent literary fictions. For my own part, I have become unconvinced that such generic labels are actually helpful to describe any specific literary practice given that the underlying definition of modernism is itself plural and polyvalent. It also seems strange that a literary sensibility of modernism that is, in its high form, inflected by Pound's famous cry of 'make it new' should find its own critical terminologies and vocabularies so constantly reworked and recycled.

Yet, despite these modernist futures, as David James has referred to them, postmodern stylistics and themes never faded. Even throughout the late 1990s and 2000s writers such as Will Self, Russell Hoban, Ali Smith, Zadie Smith, Tom McCarthy, David Mitchell and James Kelman, among others, could be said to continue in the traditions of postmodern writing.

The arguments, however, continue to rage, both in and out of the printed page. David Mitchell's *Cloud Atlas* (2004), for example, both signals its own generic placement within a postmodern frame and situates the form as a historical relic when it speaks of 'backflashes' to the '1980s with MAs in Postmodernism and Chaos Theory'.[38] Tom McCarthy's *C* (2010) is, like-wise, a novel that possesses many traits that one would expect from post-modern literature – a ludic mode, proleptic and disorientating narrative structures, clever game playing, a critical stance towards technology – but has also been described as a 'forensic' excavation of 'modernism', not postmodernism.[39] This may be unsurprising since, for Lyotard, 'the post-modern is undoubtedly part of the modern'.[40] It does, however, raise ques-tions about what we mean by an 'after' to postmodernism.

The list goes on. Ali Smith's *The Accidental* (2005) opens with an epigraph citation of the centre-left author and journalist Nick Cohen, who writes that '[s]hallow uniformity is not an accident but a consequence of what Marxists optimistically call late capitalism'.[41] In this way, Smith not only straddles the creative-critical divide (in addition to the fact that she was previously a lecturer of Scottish, English and American literature at the University of Strathclyde), but also yields a novel that focuses on the nature of narrative and representation itself.[42] Indeed, whether in the work of Ian McEwan, which has often had an air of postmodern historiography about its practices (most strongly pronounced in the 2001 novel *Atonement*), or in Will Self's language and time-bending *The Book of Dave* (2006) and his gender-twisting *Cock and Bull* (1992), postmodernism continues to live on, even while some authors, such as the Irish writer Eimar McBride in *A Girl Is a Half-Formed Thing* (2013), seek a return to the contracted prose style of some late modernism.

The question that I believe we now face, though, is slightly different from where this chapter began. It is possible, as I have done here, to chart the ascent of postmodern stylistics as emerging from late modernist practices and persisting to the current day. The problem is, though, that so much literary fiction is now indebted to this historical movement that the vocabulary of postmodernism – and, even, modernism – begins to lose much of its critical force. That is: the effect of labelling contemporary fiction as falling within a postmodern or modern frame does not seem particularly helpful as either a generic or period classification. That is why, I suggest, we need to redefine our critical lexicon and taxonomies of contemporary fiction, British and worldwide. Perhaps what we need most is a call to stop. A call for 'no more-modernisms'.

Notes

1. J.-F. Lyotard, *The Postmodern Condition: A Report on Knowledge*, G. Bennington and B. Massumi trans. (Minneapolis, MN: University of Minnesota Press, 1984), p. xxiv.
2. D. F. Wallace, 'John Updike, Champion Literary Phallocrat, Drops One; Is This Finally the End for Magnificent Narcissists?' (13 October 1997), n.p., retrieved from http://observer.com/1997/10/john-updike-champion-literary-phallocrat-drops-one-is-this-finally-the-end-for-magnificent-narcissists.
3. B. McHale, 'Change of Dominant from Modernist to Postmodernist Writing' (1986) 21 *Approaching Postmodernism* 53–79, passim.
4. See T. Miller, *Late Modernism: Politics, Fiction, and the Arts between the World Wars* (Berkeley, CA: University of California Press, 1999), passim.
5. First published in English in 1956.
6. E. W. Saïd, *On Late Style* (London: Bloomsbury, 2006), passim.
7. S. Beckett, *Worstward Ho* (London: John Calder, 1983), p. 7.
8. For instance, J. Fowles, *The French Lieutenant's Woman* (London: Vintage, 2007), p. 53.
9. *Ibid.*, p. 95.
10. J. Barth, 'The Literature of Exhaustion' in *Friday Book: Essays and Other Non-Fiction* (Baltimore, MD: Johns Hopkins University Press, 1984), p. 67.
11. J. Brooker, *Literature of the 1980s: After the Watershed* (Edinburgh University Press, 2012), p. 19.
12. J. Brooker, 'Introduction: Listen to *Money* Singing' (2012) 26(1) *Textual Practice* 1–10, 2–4.
13. M. Amis, *Money: A Suicide Note* (New York: Penguin, 2010), p. 73.

14. F. Fordham, 'Nabokov on the Road to *Money*' (2012) 26(1) *Textual Practice* 43–62, 60.

15. Amis, *Money*, p. 260.

16. For just one such postmodern reading, see J. Diedrick, *Understanding Martin Amis*, 2nd edn (Columbia: University South Carolina Press, 2004).

17. D. James, *Modernist Futures: Innovation and Inheritance in the Contemporary Novel* (New York: Cambridge University Press, 2012), p. 12.

18. *Ibid.*, p. 23.

19. J. Flax, 'Soul Service: Foucault's "Care of the Self" as Politics and Ethics' in N. Brooks (ed.), *The Mourning After: Attending the Wake of Postmodernism* (Amsterdam: Rodopi, 2007), p. 80; see also D. James, '"Style Is Morality"? Aesthetics and Politics in the Amis Era' (2012) 26(1) *Textual Practice* 11–25, 10; and C. Levine, *Forms: Whole, Rhythm, Hierarchy, Network* (Princeton University Press, 2015), p. ix.

20. J. Begley, 'Satirizing the Carnival of Postmodern Capitalism: The Transatlantic and Dialogic Structure of Martin Amis's *Money*' (2004) 45(1) *Contemporary Literature* 79, citing Amis.

21. See E. Boehmer, 'The World and the Postcolonial' (2014) 22(2) *European Review* 299–308.

22. S. Rushdie, *Midnight's Children* (London: Picador, 1981), p. 3.

23. *Ibid.*, p. 629.

24. *Ibid.*, pp. 229, 241.

25. For more on the cinematic side, see H. Ramachandran, 'Salman Rushdie's *The Satanic Verses*: Hearing the Postcolonial Cinematic Novel' (2005) 40(3) *Journal of Commonwealth Literature* 102–17.

26. N. ten Kortenaar, 'Fearful Symmetry: Salman Rushdie and Prophetic Newness' (2008) 54(3) *Twentieth-Century Literature* 339–61, 343.

27. J. Haffenden (ed.), *Novelists in Interview* (London: Methuen, 1985), p. 80.

28. R. McDonald, *The Death of the Critic* (London: Continuum, 2007), p. 81.

29. P. Boxall, *The Value of the Novel* (Cambridge University Press, 2015), p. 5.

30. M. Currie, 'Introduction' in M. Currie (ed.), *Metafiction* (London: Longman, 1995), pp. 17–18.

31. M. P. Eve, *Literature against Criticism: University English and Contemporary Fiction in Conflict* (Cambridge: Open Book Publishers, 2016), p. 35.

32. A. Carter, *Nights at the Circus* (London: Vintage, 2006), p. 53.

33. See J. A. McClure, *Partial Faiths* (Athens, GA: University of Georgia Press, 2007).

34. Carter, *Nights at the Circus*, p. 17.

35. For more on the general culture of obscenity trials during the postmodern period, see L. Herman and S. Weisenburger, *Gravity's Rainbow, Domination, and Freedom* (Athens, GA: University of Georgia Press, 2013), pp. 52–60.

36. C. Altieri, *Postmodernisms Now: Essays on Contemporaneity in the Arts* (University Park, PA: Pennsylvania State University Press, 1998), p. 1.

37. R. Eaglestone, 'Contemporary Fiction in the Academy: Towards a Manifesto' (2013) 27(7) *Textual Practice* 1089–101, 1099; see also J. T. Nealon, *Post-Postmodernism, or, the Cultural Logic of Just-in-Time Capitalism* (Stanford University Press, 2012).

38. D. Mitchell, *Cloud Atlas* (London: Sceptre, 2004), p. 152.

39. See M. P. Eve, 'Structures, Signposts and Plays: Modernist Anxieties and Postmodern Influences in Tom McCarthy's *C*' in D. Duncan (ed.), *Tom McCarthy: Critical Essays* (London: Gylphi, 2016), pp. 183–203; and J. Nieland, 'Dirty Media: Tom McCarthy and the Afterlife of Modernism' (2012) 58(3) *Modern Fiction Studies* 569–99.
40. Lyotard, *The Postmodern Condition*, p. 79.
41. A. Smith, *The Accidental* (London: Penguin Books, 2006); and N. Cohen, *Cruel Britannia: Reports on the Sinister and the Preposterous* (London: Verso, 2000), p. 126.
42. For more on this, see R. Bradford, *The Novel Now: Contemporary British Fiction* (Malden, MA: Blackwell, 2007), p. 72.

8

CAROLINE EDWARDS

Experiment and the Genre Novel
British Fiction, 1980–2018

Introduction: Evaporating Genres

In a widely cited 2008 review entitled 'Two Paths for the Novel', Zadie Smith tackled the perennial question of the death of the Anglophone novel as a viable literary form for articulating contemporary experience. Joseph O'Neill's *Netherland* (2008) and Tom McCarthy's *Remainder* (2005), Smith wrote, represent divergent trajectories for novelistic style in the twenty-first century. On the one hand, O'Neill's complacent lyrical realism in the tradition of Balzac and Flaubert perpetuates the foundational myth that 'the self is a bottomless pool' and wields this anachronism into a new era of ontological and technological entanglement. On the other, McCarthy's deconstructive 'anti-novel' unceremoniously dismantles bourgeois depth psychology to reveal the chaos beneath – that indivisible remainder, which cannot be processed or made to cohere.[1] Smith's critique draws sustenance from the opposition in theories of the novel between realism and experimentation: a dichotomy that, as Dominic Head notes, has unhelpfully persisted in British literary criticism. The drawing-up of boundaries in the post-war period between writers like Kingsley Amis and Margaret Drabble on the side of realism, and figures such as B. S. Johnson and Christine Brooke-Rose on the side of experimentation, has thus simplified novelistic practices that might more productively be read as occupying some messy middle ground.[2]

There is, of course, another approach to the realism-experimentation continuum: the question of genre. And by genre I do not mean the novel as a literary genre (in contradistinction to drama or poetry), nor its sub-genres of the picaresque, the *bildungsroman*, the romance, the confessional, the historical novel and so on. I mean the tribe-splitting notion of *genre fiction* – written for self-defined, participatory readerships in a vibrant cultural milieu that boasts its own publishing houses, literary awards and prizes, and the magazines and websites that map its para-canons and alternative literary histories. Taxonomic arguments divide readers and scholars as to how the genres of science fiction, fantasy, horror and crime fiction might be parsed and sorted, but all are united in the felt effects of an ongoing marginalisation that has systematically prevented genre fiction from joining the hallowed ranks of 'mainstream', 'literary' and 'serious' fiction. This distinction, as a critic for *The Huffington Post* puts it, is between works that give readers pleasure and provide entertainment (genre) and works that delve *into* reality, rather than escaping *from* it (serious fiction).[3] In the twenty-first century, however, you'd be forgiven for confusing these two definitions. Our highly mediated, imbricated digital lifeworld of multiple overlapping public and private realms means that a single morning commute can encompass online newspapers and their live comments sections, digital magazines, podcasts and RSS feeds, email notifications and work reminders, as well as algorithmically selected Facebook news items and Twitter conversations that lead down rabbit holes of hyperlink-hopping and purposeless scrolling. Under these circumstances, a 'literary' novel of lyrical realism might offer a welcome escape from hyper-mediated reality, while a work of near-futuristic science fiction feels more compellingly 'real' to our current rush of instantaneity. As Kim Stanley Robinson has recently observed, science fiction has now become 'the realism of our time'.[4]

If some critics persist in a cherished distinction between the literary and the generic that overlooks these dramatic transformations to contemporary realism, we should note that since the 1980s many novelists – both from the 'literary' and the 'genre' tribes – have been paying less attention to generic boundaries and aesthetic fiefdoms. As Gary K. Wolfe writes, we are witnessing a period of 'evaporating genres' in which it becomes harder to differentiate clear parameters. This requires 'revisiting not only what is written under the various rubrics of science fiction, fantasy, and horror, but what is *read*, and how it is read, and how certain selective vacancies of sensibility have distorted our capacity to receive the fantastic as a viable mode of literary exploration'.[5] At a time when genre fiction is flourishing it's perhaps no surprise that our 'serious' literary novelists are turning to fantasy, horror, crime and science fiction to push the novel in new directions. In British literature, as elsewhere in the Anglophone world, an increasing number of 'literary' writers are incorporating genre tropes into their texts. As Theodore Martin argues in *Contemporary Drift: Genre, Historicism, and the Problem of the Present* (2017), 'one of the distinguishing aspects of twenty-first-century culture is art's transformed relationship to genre'.[6] And so the distinction between 'literary fiction' and 'genre fiction', which has always been rather difficult to sustain, has become particularly unstable in recent decades. This has been accompanied by what I will call a 'dark turn' across many of speculative fiction's sub-genres in this period. Since the 1980s we have seen the hardening of crime fiction in serial killer narratives and true crime by Ian Rankin, Susan Hill, David Peace and Gordon Burn; this has been contemporaneous with horror fiction's implosion of species boundaries, which has given rise to dark and urban fantasy in experimental works by Neil Gaiman[7] and Kim Newman,[8] and the hybridised avant-garde surrealism of the New Weird in M. John Harrison, China Miéville, Steph Swainston, Justina Robson and Hal Duncan. Earlier utopian narratives became replaced by dystopian fictions during the Thatcher-Reagan years, evident in texts such as Russell Hoban's *Riddley Walker* (1980), Alasdair Gray's *Lanark: A Life in Four Books* (1981), John Christopher's *When the Tripods Came* (1988), James P. Hogan's alternate history *The Proteus Operation* (1985) and P. D. James's demodystopia *The Children of Men* (1992).

Much of the experimental energy of the writing of the period has therefore been generated by the writers of genre fiction, and many writers who are identified as 'literary' themselves employ genre forms and techniques. In what follows, I will trace this crossover between the literary and the generic, to suggest that the novel in the period 1980 to 2018 requires us to rethink our understanding of the relationship between literary experimentalism and genre conventions.

Virtual Realms: From Cyberpunk to Post-Cyberpunk

The development of cyberpunk across this period is a good place to start in thinking about this 'dark turn'. Of all the types of genre experimentation with which I am concerned in this chapter, cyberpunk is most closely dedicated to exploring a world that could still be considered science fictional in the early 1980s, but has become, by the 2010s, lived reality. The signature neologistic prose style of early cyberpunk's cautionary tales about cyberspace and corporatisation thus came of age as technological innovation inched us ever closer to the Singularity – the point at which it becomes no longer possible to wield, or control, the technologies we have long dreamed of. The term cyberpunk was first coined by Bruce Bethke in a short story published in the November 1983 issue of *Amazing Stories*,[9] but became popularised by the American author William Gibson in his influential novel *Neuromancer* (1984). As anti-heroes of the cybernetic era, Gibson's console cowboys and rogue hackers charted a new frontier of human-machinic interaction that required networking the human brain with virtual reality (VR), physically 'jacking in' through brain sockets, neural plugs and connecting wires.

Although primarily an American sub-genre, cyberpunk influenced a generation of British science fiction writers, such as Neal Asher, Gwyneth Jones, Paul McAuley, Ken MacLeod, Justina Robson and Charles Stross.[10]

Gwyneth Jones's proto-cyberpunk novel *Escape Plans* (1986), for example, examined the future of cyberspace and its dystopian potential for tranquilising the masses into a stupefied 'low resolution happy-juice entertainment to keep [them] quiet'.[11] Written in a blank style punctuated by neologisms and acronyms that dot the text like an illegible machine code, this late-1980s vision of the future drew on George Orwell's *Nineteen Eighty-Four* (1949) for its dystopian setting, as well as Orpheus's journey to rescue Eurydice from the underworld in classical antiquity. Jones's lesbian protagonist produced a queering of predominantly heterosexual cyberpunk, also undertaken by Jones's American counterparts Mary Rosenblum, Maureen McHugh and Melissa Scott. Other British writers played on early cyberpunk's Californian settings to relocate the genre to decidedly downbeat British settings. Wilhelmina Baird and Kim Newman, for instance, both imagine noirish, rain-sodden versions of near-future England: Baird in her Cass sequence, *Crashcourse* (1993), *Clipjoint* (1994) and *Psykosis* (1995), and Newman in his first novel *The Night Mayor* (1989), which returns the genre to its roots in detective pulps.

If the early literary movement of cyberpunk was preoccupied with loner and outsider figures hacking the system, in the 1990s and 2000s the genre became interested in how infotech and biotech might affect entire populations as part of everyday life. As James Patrick Kelly and John Kessel write in *Rewired: The Post-Cyberpunk Anthology* (2007), 'we are no longer changing technology; rather it has begun to change us'.[12] Justina Robson's debut novel *Silver Screen* (1999) brings 'grrrl-style' American cyberpunk closer to home, specifically the near-future world of Bradford, England. Gifted with an eidetic memory, the protagonist Anjuli offers a fuzzy sense of the human, in which computer-like mental abilities pitch her into the corporate world of robotics and cyborg technology. Evolving ever-more sophisticated modes of machine consciousness, the data stream and artificial intelligences in *Silver Screen* assume independent life forms and Robson's novel offers a studied reflection upon transhumanism, reformulating Alan Turing's question 'can machines think?' for the post-millennial period. As Lula asks: 'Where does life end and the machine begin?'[13] Returning to first-generation cyberpunk's fascination with the digitisation of human consciousness, Scottish author Richard K. Morgan's hardboiled Takeshi Kovacs trilogy (*Altered Carbon* [2002], *Broken Angels* [2003] and *Woken Furies* [2005]) reconsiders the question of memory for a post-millennial readership, examining the long-term effects of uploading human consciousness into digital storage. In the galactic distant-future of *Altered Carbon*, life-extension technology means that the affluent can prolong their existence after their human bodies have perished by downloading their digitised consciousness into new 'sleeve' bodies. Morgan's trilogy moves between different genres – from the noirish detective narrative of *Altered Carbon* to the military SF atmosphere of *Broken Angels* – updating Gibson's *Neuromancer* during the high-frequency zeitgeist of pre-2008 algorithmic capitalism.[14]

Revisiting the narrative propulsion of late 1980s cyberpunk, Ren Warom's action adventure *Escapology* (2016) features a digital heist in which a talented hacker is press-ganged into service for a crime outfit stealing corporate data in the devastated post-apocalyptic wastelands of what used to be Asia. In Warom's pastiche novel, gangsters, assassins and AIs all converge in an electronic realm known as 'the Slip', a space of surreal cosmic horror that is as much an inheritor of the New Weird (more on this below) as it is of the classic cyberpunk of Gibson and Cadigan. Similarly, Jeff Noon's *Vurt* trilogy (1993–97) shifts Gibsonian cyberpunk in the genre-melding direction of the border-crossing Weird. Noon, a playwright and former punk musician, turned his hand to science fiction for the first novel in the sequence, *Vurt* (1993), which relocates cyberpunk's countercultural Californian *locus classicus* to a phantasmagoric rendering of near-future Manchester. The virtual realm (or 'vurt') is accessed by sucking hallucinogenic feathers, sidestepping the physical 'jacking in' required in earlier cyberpunk narratives. *Vurt* offers an acid trip retelling of Lewis Carroll's *Alice in Wonderland* (1865), in which characters tumble into a freaky underworld that blends the ecstasy-charged confusion of late 1980s acid house rave culture with science fiction monsters and an Orphic quest narrative for the protagonist Scrabble's missing sister, Desdemona (transplanted from Shakespeare's tragic play). Noon's sequel *Pollen* (1995), and the later prequel *Nymphomation* (1997), expanded this dystopian Mancunian world and confirmed cyberpunk's resilience as a genre that could withstand mind-bending experimentation while maintaining its popular appeal.

The New Weird: Post-Seattle Fiction

In the 1990s, British science fiction underwent an impressive resurgence that came to be known as the 'British boom'. Science fiction, fantasy and Gothic, as Roger Luckhurst notes, experienced a revitalisation 'because they could still find spaces outside the general de-differentiation or "mainstreaming" effect sought by the strategy of cultural governance' aggressively pursued by Thatcher's government.[15] Many of the writers associated with the British boom, such as M. John Harrison, Steph Swainston, China Miéville, Justina Robson and Hal Duncan, were hailed as exemplars of the New Weird, which took its inspiration from H. P. Lovecraft's 'Weird' stories of supernatural terror. As Jeff VanderMeer writes, the genre-blurring 'New Weird' came to define a group of writers who fused contemporary science fiction with fantasy, blending urban horror with secondary-world narratives in which complex, frequently anarchic metropolitan settings gave rise to visceral and surreal tales of alien races and transgressive body horror.[16]

In addition to the aesthetic of cosmic fear that Lovecraft had uncovered in a shadowy parallel version of historic New England, authors such as Harrison, Miéville, Swainston and Robson also drew on a British tradition of Weird fiction. This recalled Gothic's uneasy relationship with the sublime, the Victorian ghost stories of Charles Dickens and Wilkie Collins, and the threatening pulse of the numinous that writers like Arthur Machen, Algernon Blackwood, M. R. James, Lord Dunsany and William Hope Hodgson borrowed from religious visionaries. Drawing on this British tradition, M. John Harrison's Viriconium novels (1971–85) came to be identified as an important precursor to the twenty-first-century New Weird. The goal, as Harrison saw it, was 'the liquefaction of boundaries'[17] and his engagement with the surreal aspects of New Wave science fiction produced a futuristic dark fantasy in which the Earth's toxic surface and decaying cities are littered with the technological ruins of previous generations.

In the early to mid-2000s, the epic sweep of Miéville's Bas-Lag trilogy – *Perdido Street Station* (2000), *The Scar* (2002) and *Iron Council* (2004) – was regarded as exemplary of the New Weird. With its Baroque prose, surrealist conjugations of bodies and ideas, and its richly imagined neo-Victorian, steampunkish architecture, New Crobuzon offers an early twenty-first-century example of London in the visionary tradition of Blake and de Quincey. Although he subsequently abandoned the term, Miéville initially celebrated the political impulse of the New Weird, arguing that its literary sensibility was informed by the damaging effects of globalisation.[18] Protests at the WTO conference in Seattle in 1999 inaugurated a new period of activism, as a successful campaign organised huge demonstrations that gave fresh impetus to the anti-capitalist *mouvement altermondialiste* (the movement for another globalisation). Indeed, Miéville's early work is clearly informed by the language of leftist political discourse, with references to contingency and revolution popping up across his novels in descriptions of 'nomad' cities, 'hybrid' cultures, 'indeterminate' political possibilities, and the 'rugged, contingent democracy' of non-hierarchical political tactics.[19]

Although distancing himself from his earlier engagement with the New Weird, Miéville's work continues to excite and provoke critics with his characteristic genre slippage, as evidenced in the phantasmagoric ambiguity of his 2016 novella *This Census-Taker*. This bringing together of the elements of dark fantasy, science fiction and literary experimentation is also evident in Steph Swainston's *The Year of Our War* (2004), a novel that updates Robert A. Heinlein's military SF novel *Starship Troopers* (1959) for the post-millennial genre-blurring age. Swainston's baroque fantasy is set at a time of centuries-old warmongering between a variety of species, including bugs, humans and alien-human hybrids. Protagonist Jant Comet is admitted into an elite political cadre, but his addiction to the hallucinogenic alternate reality of 'the Shift', which is accessed by narcotics, has led one reviewer to describe it as 'fantasy's answer to *Trainspotting*'.[20] Swainston's anachronistic assemblage of medieval elements, contemporary technologies and steampunk touches echoes M. John Harrison's phantasmagoric Viriconium books and China Miéville's Bas-Lag trilogy. The fractured non-linear narrative of Hal Duncan's debut novel *Vellum* (2005) similarly resists generic classification. The titular Vellum is a timeless realm of meta-reality replete with angels, demons, Sumerian and Greek mythology, virtual reality, nanotechnology and proliferations of alternate selves that evoke the parallel versions of the narrator in Joanna Russ's *The Female Man* (1975). The novel borrows freely from cyberpunk, the Lovecraftian Weird, fantasy and horror and, in the process, transcends parochial genre territories. In its neo-Joycean borrowings, Duncan's novel is self-consciously aligned with writers such as Michael Moorcock and Samuel R. Delany, for whom the New Wave offered science fiction the chance to move away from 'hard' science and galactic settings and engage with the literary avant-garde.

Crime Fiction and the State of the Nation

The New Weird reveals how genre experimentation can offer writers a politicised aesthetic capable of articulating the fears and anxieties of a newly emergent socio-historical moment. This is also true of the crime fiction series, which presents the opportunity of examining national consciousness at a primal, phantasmagoric level. Where the realist 'state-of-the-nation' novel collapses under the weight of its own representational dilemma – capturing the panoramic sweep of a collective national psyche – crime fiction can harness generic form to address pressing questions of British identity. As Ian Rankin notes, it is a genre rooted in specific locations that encourages readers to reflect upon present-day society: 'I wanted to write about contemporary urban Britain, and couldn't think of a better way of doing it than through the medium of the detective novel: I would, after all, be positing questions about the "state we're in," and reckoned a cop could act as my surrogate.'[21]

The spy fictions of John le Carré (the pen name of David Cornwell) offer a salient illustration of how genre can accommodate the ever-fluxional anxieties that characterise the national mood. During the 1980s, le Carré's books continued to be immensely popular, with readers and critics alike. The sheer volume of sales and translations of his work positions le Carré as 'arguably the most successful serious British author since World War II'.[22] Drawing on his experience in the British secret service during the 1950s and 1960s, le Carré's treatment of espionage has lent a literary quality to the derided form of the spy thriller. As John L. Cobbs notes, this contempt for the genre can be attributed to 'a legacy of the generations of realist writers and literary commentators who, from the middle of the nineteenth century, pilloried romanticism in general and "derring-do" romanticism in particular'.[23] Having already released nine novels since his early 1960s spy thrillers were first published (such as *The Spy Who Came in from the Cold* [1963]), three of which were made into successful films, le Carré's work experienced a surge of interest from the late 1970s into the early 1990s when several books were adapted for television: including *Tinker Tailor Soldier Spy* (BBC, 1979), *Smiley's People* (BBC, 1982), *A Perfect Spy* (BBC, 1987) and *A Murder of Quality* (Thames Television, 1991). These TV adaptations of le Carré's work helped British spy dramas move out of a period in the 1970s of spoofs and geopolitical caricature into challenging works 'more akin to Samuel Beckett or Harold Pinter than James Bond'.[24]

The 1980s also saw a revived interest in the police procedural in British crime fiction. Borrowing from the American figure of the private eye, two major new detectives entered the scene: Ian Rankin's John Rebus in *Knots and Crosses* (1987) and Michael Dibdin's Aurelio Zen in *Ratking* (1988). Set in Edinburgh, Rankin's novels draw readers into a darker side of the city. By the 1990s, Rankin's Rebus novels had become best-sellers and put Scottish crime fiction on the map: painting, as David Martin-Jones observes, 'a grim, dark, rainy, murderous image of contemporary Edinburgh for worldwide consumption'.[25] This was cemented with the long-running TV crime series set in Glasgow, *Taggart* (which began in 1983), and BBC Scotland's murder mystery series, *Hamish Macbeth* (1995–97), which takes place on Scotland's picturesque West Coast and was adapted from the novels by M. C. Beaton (pen name of Scottish writer, Marion Chesney). Indeed, Scottish hard crime writing became so successful that by the late 1990s the appellation 'Tartan noir' gained currency, describing the combination of grim urban settings and social critique raised in the detective series of Rankin, Val McDermid, Christopher Brookmyre and Denise Mina. If Scottish crime fiction in this period proved to be one of the country's most successful international cultural exports, it also reflected the increasingly dark turn of genre fiction during the 1980s and into the 1990s. As Martin Priestman suggests: 'Perhaps in response to the 1980s' domination by the strongly right-wing Thatcher and Reagan governments, much of the decade's crime fiction explores the fracture between glossy, wealth-driven appearances and hidden histories of oppression and abuse'.[26]

British crime fiction in this period thus offers another frontier in which the struggle between literary realism and genre fiction played itself out. P. D. James is one of the most significant British crime writers of the second half of the twentieth century, having pioneered the clue-puzzle form in the 1960s along with writers such as Ruth Rendell and Colin Dexter. However, literary critics considered her detective fiction rather too plot-driven to be deserving of sustained critical attention: a prejudice against the genre which sees her crime writing oeuvre almost entirely overlooked in favour of scholarly appraisals of her 1992 novel *Children of Men*, which is considered an important example of the literary dystopia.[27] If James is a crime writer whose engagement with the more 'literary' genre of the dystopia garnered a notable increase in critical interest, then Susan Hill is a good example of a literary novelist whose turn to crime fiction (after her successful intervention into the ghost story with *The Woman in Black* [1983]) has helped 'confer literary status on [this] popular genr[e]'; something which, Andrew Hoberek suggests, creates a feedback loop in the absorption of genre elements into 'high-cultural' literary texts.[28] Reviews of Hill's Simon Serrailler novels (2004–14) reveal the battle lines critics draw between literary and genre fiction. Andrew Taylor's *Spectator* review of *The Soul of Discretion* (2014), praised Hill's treatment of crime fiction: 'When literary novelists turn to crime fiction (as they so often do these days), the results are not always happy. Susan Hill is a welcome exception';[29] while Robert Edric's review for the *Guardian* of the earlier *The Various Haunts of Men* (2004) berated Hill for moving into a genre that didn't match her previously established literary credentials: 'It's disappointing ... that Hill has followed so closely the conventions of this increasingly outmoded style and at the same time added so little of her own.'[30] Written a decade apart, we might ascribe these opposing reviews to changing attitudes towards genre fiction in recent years; indeed, Edric's charge of Hill's 'miscalculation' in entering genre territory now sounds out of step with much recent scholarly criticism which has laboured to reposition crime fiction 'as a significant participation in the international sphere of world literature', a claim made in the edited collection *Crime Fiction as World Literature* (2017).[31]

The rise of interest in true crime since the 1980s also coincides with an explosion in life writing and literary non-fiction over the past three decades. Journalist Andrew Hankinson's recent non-fiction narrative *You Could Do Something Amazing with Your Life* (2016) tells the story of the final days of Raoul Moat's life during the mammoth police hunt for the murderer in Rothbury, Northumberland. David Peace's true crime *Red Riding Quartet* (1999–2002) has achieved popular and critical success for its narrative excavation of West Yorkshire in the years 1974–83, during the search for the Yorkshire Ripper. Combining historical fact with speculation, fictionalisation and his own rooted sense of place, Peace's novels have modified crime fiction into a new bricolaged form. Alec Charles calls this 'dystopian realism', suggesting that 'through its elaboration of an extreme form of human experience, [*Red Riding Quartet*] becomes a history of its time, and specifically of its location, a history accentuated by the intensity of its subject matter, a nightmarish and phantasmagorical history'.[32] Gordon Burn's novels also draw on newspaper reportage and police records to examine the high-profile criminal figures of the Yorkshire Ripper and Fred and Rosemary West in *Somebody's Husband, Somebody's Son* (1984) and *Happy Like Murderers* (1998). Other British novelists have explored similar territory: Blake Morrison tells the story of James Bulger's murder in *As If* (1997), Maggie Gee's *The White Family* (2002) took the murder of black teenager Stephen Lawrence as its inspiration, and Irish author Emma Donaghue's 2010 novel *Room* narrates the horrifying experience of Elisabeth Fritzl's imprisonment and long-term abuse in a secret basement of her Austrian family home by her father Josef Fritzl. Donaghue's novel has received widespread critical and scholarly acclaim, not only for her handling of this internationally known story, but also for her nimble use of generic instability, as the narrative slides between the otherworldliness of fairy tale and Gothic horror to the mundane details of domestic naturalism.

As we have already seen in the 'evaporating genres' of cyberpunk and Weird fiction, crime fiction in recent years has also been subject to the literary experimentation of generic sampling that characterises much contemporary fiction. This is evidenced in works that dissolve the boundaries between science fiction and crime writing. Jeff Noon's noirish *A Man of Shadows* (2017) relocates the pulp cliché of a private eye investigating a serial killer to the distinctly science fictional setting of an alternate 1950s neon city. Here, every inhabitant lives according to their own individual timescale: a queasy desychronisation that literalises the modernist novel's fascination with undoing the distinction between public and private time. China Miéville's *The City and the City* (2009) similarly uses the crime sub-genre of police procedural to reveal a surreal tale of two ambiguously *Mitteleuropa* cities, Beszel and Ul Qoma, locked into a kind of ontological apartheid in which neither side can acknowledge the existence of the other. Inspector Tyador Borlú's investigation of a murdered woman draws him into a growing awareness of the other side, bringing the non-Euclidean geometry of the

Lovecraftian Weird to bear on the estranging effects of divided real-world cities like Berlin, Jerusalem and Belfast.

In the same year that Noon turned to crime fiction after a career marked by his revitalisation of cyberpunk (in the *Vurt* trilogy, discussed above), fellow British science fiction writer Adam Roberts also crossed genres with *The Real-Town Murders* (2017). Roberts had already experimented with the locked-room mystery in the first section of his award-winning novel *Jack Glass* (2012), and in *The Real-Town Murders* he pairs the narrative propulsion of a conspiracy thriller with a science fictional near-future setting (the murder occurs in a fully automated car factory in Reading). People spend almost all their conscious hours in an online environment so immersive they take to wearing 'body-mesh' suits to prevent bedsores and muscle atrophy; a vision that echoes E. M. Forster's memorable anticipation of flaccid humanity in 'The Machine Stops' (1909). Inspired by Hitchcock's idea for a film set in a car factory tended only by robots, Roberts's whodunit delivers a compelling vision of science fictional futurity that reflects on full automation, one of the pre-eminent anxieties of our time.

The End We Start From: Dystopian and Post-Apocalyptic Fiction

Over the course of the past three decades, as British literature's generic cross-fertilisations have become increasingly tricky to navigate, the planet has succumbed to what Gerry Canavan and Andrew Hageman call 'the ecological weird': a term that borrows from the literary Weird to express the increasingly uncanny weather patterns of global warming, with its unpredictable and severe meteorological events, and the uneven impact of climate change.[33] The profusion of climate change novels (what the commentariat terms 'cli-fi'), narratives of environmental disaster and ecocatastrophe, and apocalyptic and post-apocalyptic visions of devastated future worlds has undoubtedly contributed to a further collapse of distinctions between literary fiction and genre fiction. Margaret Atwood's dystopian-come-apocalyptic epic about bioengineering and hyper-capitalism, the MaddAddam trilogy (*Oryx and Crake* [2003], *The Year of the Flood* [2009] and *MaddAddam* [2013]), reached a worldwide audience in the millions; and Cormac McCarthy's 2006 Pulitzer Prize-winning novel *The Road*, successfully adapted into a film in 2009, brought to immediate popular and critical attention a seismic shift in literary sensibility towards apocalyptic narratives of catastrophe and destruction.

In the British context, we can trace the increasing experimentation with genre in the works of many well-known writers whose careers have garnered literary prize nominations and awards, public recognition and scholarly attention – among them, Kazuo Ishiguro, David Mitchell, Jeanette Winterson, Sarah Hall, Rupert Thomson, Maggie Gee, Joanna Kavenna, Will Self, Jim Crace, Bernardine Evaristo, Julie Myerson and newcomer Megan Hunter.[34] As one of Britain's most-celebrated novelists, Kazuo Ishiguro's turn to science fiction is indicative of this shift. His 2005 Booker-shortlisted novel *Never Let Me Go* examines Ishiguro's signature novelistic preoccupations of repressed personal trauma and unreliable narration in a story about eugenics. Ishiguro draws on the English boarding school novel to locate his eugenicist dystopia in an alternate version of the 1990s, in which schoolgirl Kathy H. and her friends gradually piece together the chilling reality of their situation. Bred as clones to provide personalised organ donations to their 'originals', Kathy, Tommy and Ruth are trapped in an ideological war over the rights of cloned humans. While the novel conforms to the generic requirements of the literary dystopia and is premised upon scientific experimentation into genetic engineering, it remains firmly in the territory of the literary, experimental novel; and Ishiguro writes, as one reviewer puts it, if not like a realist, then 'like someone impersonating a realist'.[35]

With its miserable weather, relentless hardship and authoritarian politics, Sarah Hall's *The Carhullan Army* (2007) is a more straightforward dystopian novel. The muddy Lake District setting and frequent thunderstorms set the scene for an austere women's encampment that is training itself into a militia to mount an insurrection against the British state. Through the narrative framing device of prisoner testimony, Hall introduces her readership to a near-future world of climate change, epidemics, geopolitical instability, economic collapse and dysfunctional government. The gender politics of Hall's post-oil dystopia enact an ambiguous cautionary tale about women's equality (reproductive rights, for example, have already been lost – a common trope in feminist dystopias), inspired by a previous generation of lesbian separatist utopias such as Monique Wittig's *Les Guérilleres* (1969) and Sally Miller Gearhart's *The Wanderground* (1978). Rupert Thomson's *Divided Kingdom* (2003) is a more experimental take on the literary dystopia, departing from the generic requirement for political critique as established in the genre's foundational texts: Yevgeny Zamyatin's *We* (1924), Aldous Huxley's *Brave New World* (1932), Katharine Burdekin's *Swastika Night* (1937), George Orwell's *Nineteen Eighty-Four* and, more recently, Margaret Atwood's *The Handmaid's Tale* (1985). Thomson's vision of near-future Britain imagines a dystopia modelled on the medieval theory of the humours. The totalitarian government's 'Rearrangement' has tested and divided the population into quarters – sanguine, choleric, phlegmatic and melancholic. With its mandatory psychometric testing, splitting up of families, training camps and ubiquitous Orwellian surveillance, we might expect Thomson's novel to deliver a frightening near-future dystopia. However, rather than the constricted first-person focus of Orwell's Winston Smith or Atwood's handmaid Offred, Thomson's protagonist embarks on a picaresque travel narrative that drifts into stranger, more experimental novelistic territory as he journeys between Britain's divided quarters under a variety of guises. The phantasmagoric pull of the melancholic quarter's Bathysphere club, for instance, promises a recovery of traumatic childhood memories reminiscent of the recursive associationism of W. G. Sebald's *Austerlitz* (2001) or J. G. Ballard's New Wave science fiction. Indeed, the club's Ballardian promise of 'a journey into the depths, a probing of the latent, the forbidden, the impenetrable'[36] offers a direct echo of Kerans's Jungian descent in *The Drowned World* (1962). This kind of *writing back to genre* is also an important aesthetic ingredient of British-Nigerian author Bernardine Evaristo's 2008 novel *Blonde Roots*. Evaristo's text brings to life the horrors of slavery and racism as her enslaved white protagonist recounts the appalling experiences of surviving the Middle Passage, labouring in sugar cane fields and working as a domestic slave for a rich planter's family: in a world where slave-owners are black and slaves are white. The hybridised speculative temporalities of Evaristo's novel thus blend Europe's colonial, slave-trading past with contemporary references to plastic surgery, urban fashion and London's abandoned underground, establishing a counterfactual narrative that sits somewhere between alternate history and dystopia.

Two novels that extend this kind of generic cross-fertilisation into formal experimentation with the structure of the novel are David Mitchell's *Cloud Atlas* (2004) and Joanna Kavenna's *The Birth of Love* (2010). Both writers use pastiche to draw science fictional and genre elements (among them, the techno-dystopia and the distant post-apocalyptic future) into their multi-layered narratives. With its Matryoshka structure of nested narratives, Mitchell's multi-award-winning *Cloud Atlas* has been referred to as an exemplar of a new novelistic form that has variously been called 'translit', the 'cosmopolitan novel', the 'networked novel' and the 'hyperlink novel'.[37] The palindrome structure of *Cloud Atlas* is complemented by Mitchell's deft use of pastiche: from Herman Melville's rhythmic seafaring style in *Moby Dick* (1851), and Christopher Isherwood's ventriloquisation of the British aristocracy in the 1930s, to the clichéd blandness of generic airport thrillers, the disturbing euphemisms of dystopian neology and the societal degeneration embodied within a compressed post-apocalyptic dialect. The effect of the novel's distinctive structure is to play havoc with linear historical time and its accompanying illusion of progress (something that Jeanette

Winterson's 2007 novel *The Stone Gods* similarly attempts, although with less success). Walter Benjamin's grim reminder that '[t]here is no document of civilisation which is not at the same time a document of barbarism' in Thesis VII of the 'Theses on the Philosophy of History' (1940) is brought to vivid life in Mitchell's novel by the colonial predations of Victorian missionaries, Maori Colonisers, the twenty-second-century Korean totalitarian state of Nea So Copros and bloodthirsty Hawaiian tribes in the distant post-apocalyptic future. Joanna Kavenna's *The Birth of Love* was directly inspired by *Cloud Atlas*, as well as by Italo Calvino's metafictional experimentation in *If on a Winter's Night a Traveller* (1979). Like the modernist precursors Kavenna stylistically alludes to in the novel (notably Woolf, Eliot and Joyce), *The Birth of Love* takes place over the course of one day: pastiching nineteenth-century epistolary narrative, the Orwellian interrogation scene that Winston undergoes in *Nineteen Eighty-Four*'s Room 101, and the *künstlerroman* in sections narrated by a novelist who is hamstrung by Prufrockian inaction. Central to the novel, however, is the contemporary story of a woman who spends the entire twenty-four-hour period in labour, and whose primal struggle thematically and structurally unites the novel's different historical times and sections. Kavenna's achievement is to reorient the literary dystopia's usual exploration of subjectivity – which pits the authoritarian state against the crushed individual – into a broader consideration of the inescapably intersubjective nature of the individual as epitomised in the image of a pregnant woman.

As Andrew Tate notes in *Apocalyptic Fiction* (2017), the rapidly growing corpus of apocalyptic and post-apocalyptic novels in the twenty-first century confirms the pervasive sense that '[w]e now live in an era of apparent continual catastrophe'.[38] Maggie Gee's novelistic career neatly embodies this shift in literary sensibility since the 1980s. The effect of apocalyptic events on the lives of ordinary individuals is something that has preoccupied Gee since the publication of her second novel *The Burning Book* in 1983. The novel's formal experimentation – fractured temporalities, non-standard typography, disruptions to realist storytelling via authorial intrusion, and metafictional self-reflexivity – rework the parameters of narrative realism in a retelling of the nuclear disasters at Hiroshima and Nagasaki. Gee's 1999 novel *The Ice People* returns to this apocalyptic theme with a narrative of environmental catastrophe unfolding in the mid-twenty-first century. Damage to the biosphere has caused various viral epidemics toppling governments, while falling sperm counts have led to a demographic crisis and generational conflict sees gangs of increasingly feral children retreating to the African veld. Gee's 2004 novel *The Flood* returns to the theme of environmental disaster in an apocalyptic narrative that, as Mine Özyurt

Kiliç notes, brings the speculative imaginary home to a 'realistic, "day-after-tomorrow" setting of London'.[39] London has hosted several notable twenty-first-century post-apocalyptic retellings; including Will Self's flooded archipelagic Britain in *The Book of Dave* (2006) and Julie Myerson's brutal story of survivalism, *Then* (2011), set in an abandoned office block in Bishopsgate. After a sudden climatological event, bodies lie amid banks of snow, freezing on the capital's former streets, and collections of broken bones hint at cannibalism as London's decimated population struggles in a bitter war of survival. Filtered through the chronically unreliable account of her amnesiac narrator, Myerson's non-linear storytelling connects *Then* with the feminist Anglophone speculative tradition of Doris Lessing, Marge Piercy, Joanna Russ and Octavia Butler. Located in London's former financial district, Myerson's post-2008 novel thus imagines a truly apocalyptic conclusion to capitalist modernity at a time of ongoing austerity and economic decline in Britain.

Jim Crace's *The Pesthouse* (2007) relocates the catastrophe to North America, imagining a reversal of manifest destiny as the inhabitants of a post-civilised rural world flee the plague, driven by the dream of sailing back to Europe in hope of finding a better life. Crace's novel brings his characteristic mythopoeic texture to the genre of post-apocalypse and is notable for its distinctly optimistic, utopian tone that eschews the bleak pessimism epitomised in McCarthy's *The Road* (published in the same year as *The Pesthouse*) in favour of a scaled-down, quiet hopefulness that the American subcontinent, ravaged though its communities and social structures are, remains a place of fertile agricultural possibility and an almost pastoral landscape that welcomes Crace's characters home. Crace's novel thus reorients the English tradition of disaster narratives that dates back to Mary Shelley's *The Last Man* (1826) and Richard Jefferies's *After London: or, Wild England* (1885), was masterfully reprogrammed by H. G. Wells, and became popular again in the mid twentieth century with the 'cosy catastrophes' of John Wyndham and John Christopher. Jane Rogers's first foray into speculative fiction, *The Testament of Jessie Lamb* (2011), also writes back to this tradition in a story of viral pandemic as a modified form of HIV is triggered by pregnancy. Winner of science fiction's esteemed Arthur C. Clarke Award, Rogers's novel sidesteps the usual generic paradigms of the literary dystopia to embark upon an apocalyptic tale of ecological activism and its burgeoning youth movement in this dangerous new world, which resists the narrative exhaustion that characterised previous demodystopias such as Brian Aldiss's *Greybeard* (1964) and P. D. James's *Children of Men* (1992).[40]

Despite the dark turn of genre fiction since the 1980s and 1990s into the twenty-first century, the recent works by Gee, Crace and Rogers attest to the persistence of a kind of grim hopefulness in the face of environmental catastrophe. This is similarly expressed in Megan Hunter's debut novel *The End We Start From* (2017), the latest in a growing corpus of flood fictions that includes Maggie Gee's *The Flood*, Stephen Baxter's *Flood* (2008) and Kim Stanley Robinson's *Forty Signs of Rain* (2004) and *New York: 2140* (2017). Like Kavenna's *The Birth of Love*, Hunter's novel is preoccupied with birth and the nursing of a newborn child, which gives the novel a dreamy claustrophobic focus. Almost entirely oblivious to the catastrophe unfolding outside, the narrator feels 'like Aldous Huxley on mescaline'[41] and even as she is forced into one of Britain's many camps for climate refugees as the country is gradually deluged, her narrow world of breastfeeding and childcare filters everything beyond into the background. The surprising hopefulness that marks the end of Hunter's novel, however, reminds us of the utopian impulse that informs narratives of post-apocalypse. As Peter Boxall suggests, there is a 'kind of bleak utopianism'[42] at work in such apocalyptic and ecocatastrophic visions of futurity.

Of all the speculative and science fiction sub-genres I've considered in this chapter, post-apocalyptic literature has arguably experienced the most successful crossover into the literary mainstream. This might be attributed to the narrative and stylistic opportunities that the post-apocalypse presents to writers interested in the textures and rhythms of lyrical realism: freed from capitalism, after the end of industrial modernity and its scientific achievements, the post-apocalypse is a primordial place of mythopoeic returns as the digital world is wiped away and enduringly human values of community and narrative resurface. As Roger Bellin writes, the prevalence of generic borrowings in twenty-first-century 'literary' or 'prestige' fiction heralds 'a new marker of literariness in contemporary "literary" fiction, with a function analogous to that of the older use of modernist formal technique'.[43] The increasing visibility of genre experimentation in twenty-first-century literature thus betokens a fundamental shift in sensibility – for contemporary Britain, as well as for the literary form of the novel.

Notes

1. Z. Smith, 'Two Paths for the Novel', *New York Review of Books* (20 November 2008), n.p., www.nybooks.com/articles/2008/11/20/two-paths-for-the-novel/.
2. D. Head, *The Cambridge Introduction to Modern British Fiction, 1950–2000* (Cambridge University Press, 2002), p. 225.

3. S. Petite, 'Literary Fiction v. Genre Fiction', *The Huffington Post* (26 February 2014), n.p., www.huffingtonpost.com/steven-petite/literary-fiction-vs-genre-fiction_b_4859609.html.

4. Robinson, quoted in G. Canavan, 'New Paradigms, after 2001' in: R. Luckhurst (ed.), *Science Fiction: A Literary History* (London: British Library Press, 2017), p. 209.

5. G. K. Wolfe, *Evaporating Genres: Essays on Fantastic Literature* (Middletown, CT: Wesleyan University Press, 2011), p. 4 (emphasis in the original).

6. T. Martin, *Contemporary Drift: Genre, Historicism, and the Problem of the Present* (New York: Columbia University Press, 2017), p. 7.

7. Such as Sandman (1989–96).

8. Particularly the Anno Dracula novels (1992–8).

9. M. Featherstone and R. Burrows, 'Cultures of Technological Embodiment: An Introduction' in M. Featherstone and R. Burrows (eds), *Cyberspace/Cyberbodies/Cyberpunk: Cultures of Technological Embodiment* (London: Sage, 1995), p. 7.

10. M. Bould, 'Cyberpunk' in D. Seed (ed.), *A Companion to Science Fiction* (Oxford: Blackwell, 2005), pp. 227–8.

11. G. Jones, *Deconstructing the Starships: Science, Fiction and Reality* (Liverpool University Press, 1999), p. 91.

12. J. P. Kelly and J. Kessel, 'Introduction: Hacking Cyberpunk' in J. P. Kelly and J. Kessel (eds), *Rewired: The Post-Cyberpunk Anthology* (San Francisco, CA: Tachyon, 2007), p. x.

13. A. M. Turing, 'Computing Machinery and Intelligence' (1950) 59(236) *Mind* 433–60, 433; and J. Robson, *Silver Screen* (Amherst, NY: Pyr, 2005), p. 126.

14. Canavan, 'New Paradigms', p. 219.

15. R. Luckhurst, 'Cultural Governance, New Labour, and the British SF Boom' (2003) 30(3) *Science Fiction Studies* 417–35, 417–20, 423.

16. J. VanderMeer, 'The New Weird: It's Alive?' in A. VanderMeer and J. VanderMeer (eds), *The New Weird* (San Francisco, CA: Tachyon, 2008), p. xvi.

17. Harrison, quoted in R. Luckhurst, *Science Fiction* (Cambridge: Polity, 2005), p. 240.

18. Although Miéville's political understanding of the New Weird was not shared by all of the writers associated with the movement, I would argue that his influential position as one of the movement's most successful writers justifies a reading of his own contribution to New Weird writing as explicitly politicised post-Seattle fiction.

19. Palmer, quoted in C. Edwards and T. Venezia, 'UnIntroduction: China Miéville's Weird Universe' in C. Edwards and T. Venezia (eds), *China Miéville: Critical Essays* (Canterbury: Gylphi, 2015), pp. 8–9.

20. T. M. Wagner, 'Review of Steph Swainston, *The Year of Our War*', *SF Reviews.net* (no date), n.p., www.sfreviews.net/yearofourwar.html.

21. Rankin, quoted in P. Messent, 'The Police Novel' in C. J. Rzepka and L. Horsley (eds), *A Companion to Crime Fiction* (Oxford: Wiley-Blackwell, 2010), p. 178.

22. J. L. Cobbs, *Understanding John le Carré* (Columbia, SC: University of South Carolina Press, 1998), p. 14.

23. *Ibid.*, p. 15.

24. S. Angelini, 'Cold War Spies', *BFI Screen Online* (no date), n.p., www.screenonline.org.uk/tv/id/1008415/index.html.
25. D. Martin-Jones, *Scotland: Global Cinema, Genres, Modes and Identities* (Edinburgh University Press, 2009), pp. 153–4.
26. M. Priestman, 'Post-War British Crime Fiction' in M. Priestman (ed.), *The Cambridge Companion to Crime Fiction* (Cambridge University Press, 2003), p. 183.
27. See M. Fisher, *Capitalist Realism: Is There No Alternative?* (Winchester: O Books, 2009), pp. 1–3; C. Lam, *New Reproductive Technologies and Disembodiment: Feminist and Material Resolutions* (New York: Routledge, 2016), pp. 44–5; and F. Bigman, '"The Authority's Anti-Breeding Campaign": State-Imposed Infertility in British Reprodystopia' in: G. Davis and T. Loughran (eds), *The Palgrave Handbook of Infertility in History: Approaches, Contexts and Perspectives* (Basingstoke: Palgrave Macmillan, 2017), p. 595.
28. A. Hoberek, 'Introduction: After Postmodernism' (2007) 53(3) *Twentieth Century Literature* (Special Issue: 'After Postmodernism: Form and History in Contemporary American Fiction') 233–47, 238.
29. A. Taylor, 'An Unorthodox Detective Novel about Waitrose-Country Paedos: A Review of *The Soul of Discretion* by Susan Hill', *The Spectator* (4 October 2014), n.p., www.spectator.co.uk/2014/10/the-soul-of-discretion-by-susan-hill-review/.
30. R. Edric, 'Adding up to Zero: Review of *The Various Haunts of Men* by Susan Hill', *The Guardian* (29 May 2004), n.p., www.theguardian.com/books/2004/may/29/featuresreviews.guardianreview21.
31. L. Nilsson, D. Damrosch and T. D'haen, 'Introduction' in L. Nilsson, D. Damrosch and T. D'haen (eds), *Crime Fiction as World Literature* (New York: Bloomsbury Academic, 2017), p. 2.
32. A. Charles, '"Pictures at an Atrocity Exhibition": Modernism and Dystopian Realism in David Peace's *Red Riding Quartet*' in: K. Shaw (ed.), *Analysing David Peace* (Newcastle: Cambridge Scholars Publishing, 2011), p. 6.
33. G. Canavan and A. Hageman, 'Introduction: "Global Weirding" (Global Weirding Special Issue)' (2016) 28 *Paradoxa* 7–13.
34. A good indicator of the 'literary' or 'prestige' credentials of a writer is to consider the publishing house putting out their genre-crossover novels. Rather than SF publishing giants such as Gollancz, Orbit or Pan Macmillan (known for publishing across a range of genres, as exemplified in its poster-boy author China Miéville), the writers I will consider in this section have all published post-apocalyptic works of fiction with 'mainstream' literary publishing houses: Hamish Hamilton for Jeanette Winterson, Picador for Jim Crace and Megan Hunter, Saqi for Maggie Gee, Faber & Faber for Joanna Kavenna, Kazuo Ishiguro, Sarah Hall and Sam Taylor, Penguin for Will Self and Bernardine Evaristo, and Vintage for Julie Myerson and Rupert Thomson.
35. L. Menard, 'Something About Kathy: Review of Kazuo Ishiguro's *Never Let Me Go*', *The New Yorker* (28 March 2005), n.p., www.newyorker.com/magazine/2005/03/28/something-about-kathy.
36. R. Thomson, *Divided Kingdom* (London: Bloomsbury, 2012), p. 136.
37. See C. Edwards, 'Networked Times in the Contemporary Novel' in R. Eaglestone and D. O'Gorman (eds), *The Routledge Companion to Contemporary Fiction*

(New York: Routledge, no date), n.p.; R. Barnard, 'Fictions of the Global' (2009) 42(2) *Novel* 207–15; B. Schoene, *The Cosmopolitan Novel* (Edinburgh University Press, 2009); and D. Coupland, 'Convergences: Review of *Gods Without Men* by Hari Kunzru', *The New York Times* (8 March 2012), n.p., www.nytimes.com/2012/03/11/books/review/gods-without-men-by-hari-kunzru.html.

38. A. Tate, *Apocalyptic Fiction* (London: Bloomsbury Academic, 2017), p. 5.
39. M. Ö. Kiliç, *Maggie Gee: Writing the Condition-of-England Novel* (London: Bloomsbury Academic, 2013), p. 101.
40. N. Harrison, '*The Testament of Jessie Lamb* by Jane Rogers: A Review', *Strange Horizons* (10 October 2011), n.p., http://strangehorizons.com/non-fiction/reviews/the-testament-of-jessie-lamb-by-jane-rogers/.
41. M. Hunter, *The End We Start From* (London: Faber & Faber, 2017), p. 5.
42. P. Boxall, *Twenty-First-Century Fiction* (Cambridge University Press, 2013), p. 221.
43. R. Bellin, 'Techno-Anxiety as New Middlebrow: Science-Fictionalizing in the Fictional Mainstream of the Early Twenty-First Century' in T. Lanzendörfer (ed.), *The Poetics of Genre in the Contemporary Novel* (Lanham, MD: Lexington, 2016), p. 115.

9

JEROME DE GROOT

Transgression and Experimentation
The Historical Novel

It could be argued that the British historical novel is the most important, influential and enduring literary genre of the last thirty-five years.[1] A brief sketch of those books considered to be key since 1980 might consist solely of novels engaged in meditations upon the past and its relationship to the present: Salman Rushdie's *Midnight's Children* (1981); Angela Carter's *Nights at the Circus* (1984); Jeanette Winterson's *The Passion* (1987); Kazuo Ishiguro's *Remains of the Day* (1989); Pat Barker's *Regeneration* trilogy (1991–95); Caryl Phillips's *The Nature of Blood* (1997); Sarah Waters's *Tipping the Velvet* (1998); Ian McEwan's *Atonement* (2001); Hari Kunzru's *The Impressionist* (2002); David Peace's *GB84* (2004); Alan Hollinghurst's *The Line of Beauty* (2004); Hilary Mantel's *Wolf Hall* (2009); and Andrea Levy's *The Long Song* (2011). A number of other novels could be added as historical-esque, insofar as they have significant moments of flashback, pastiche or recollected narrative: A. S. Byatt's *Possession* (1990); Gordon Burn's *Alma Cogan* (1991); Martin Amis's *Time's Arrow* (1991); Jonathan Coe's *What a Carve Up* (1994); Jackie Kaye's *Trumpet* (1998); David Mitchell's *Cloud Atlas* (2004); Nicola Barker's *Darkmans* (2007); Doris Lessing's *The Cleft* (2007); and Ali Smith's *How to Be Both* (2014). Indeed, from a relatively marginal position in the early 1980s, the literary historical form has become increasingly 'respectable' and decidedly popular. The critical and popular importance of the form was institutionalised in 2010 with the inauguration of the Walter Scott Prize for historical fiction, one of the most valuable awards in the United Kingdom.[2] It is increasingly institutionally supported, as Creative Writing courses include modules on historical writing, societies of authors form and prizes multiply.

There is of course an international aspect to this, as British writing has not developed in a vacuum. We might mention those writers, such as W. G. Sebald, Chimamanda Ngozi Adichie, Toni Morrison, Isabel Allende, Don DeLillo, Colm Tóibín, Colson Whitehead, Peter Carey, Thomas Pynchon, Richard Flanagan, Margaret Atwood and Sebastian Barry, who have struggled with 'history' and modes of narrative in their work. Many successful, popular and prize-winning novels of the past thirty years blend types of historical narrative with an interest in migration, trauma and diaspora – one might cite the work of Michael Chabon, Amy Tan, Jeffrey Eugenides, Roberto Bolaño, Tan Twang Eng, Jonathan Lethem, Eimar McBride, Junot Díaz, Kamila Shamsie, Miguel Syjuco, J. M. G. Le Clézio, Anne Enright and Yaa Gyasi. These writers, from many different countries, often write a hybrid form – neither historical novel nor contemporary fiction – mixing precise accounts of moments in the past with historical specificity, melding past narratives to contemporary moments with little concern for 'genre' per se. They are interested in memory, but also engage in a definite 'rendering' of the past, recounting stories and outlining historical experience, often with an ironising distance. Add in the meticulous biofiction of extremely popular writers like Elena Ferrante, Patrick Modiano and Karl Ove Knausgaård, and we could suggest that the novel around the world is overwhelmingly concerned with contending temporalities, meditations upon the self and memory, and articulations of the past.

The 'classic' historical novel, as much as the bourgeois realist novel, often reflects the idea that the world can be understood, experienced, limited and described.[3] Historical fiction, for the main in the Western tradition, uses the tropes of a particular realism – contemporaneously defined – as shorthand for authenticity and therefore believability. Historical novels are often judged in this way, reviewed according to their evidentiary weight and realist purpose. Yet the historical form also, clearly, has something uncanny and strange at its heart. Presenting the past to those in the present demands a cognitive shift that is hardwired into the form. Writing pastness is itself cognitively and practically difficult, as any author that does it will attest. The different type of imaginative work that a historical novel demands of a reader is clear. The great theorist of the form, Georg Lukács, argued that the historical form might give rise to the expression of something new, of a radical potentiality.[4] The possibilities that the form presents of rendering different temporalities, different places, different genders and different forms, often militates against any possible deadening aesthetic effect of a tired 'realism' or conservative purpose.

In order to try to account for this important but immensely plural form, this present chapter will do three things. First, it will outline the development of the British historical novel since 1980, discussing some of the key moments both artistically and critically in the evolution of this mode/genre. This will build to a section outlining how 'experiment' has been the keynote of the contemporary historical novel (demonstrated through a reading of Angela Carter's *Nights at the Circus*). From being a genre often associated – wrongly or rightly – with conservatism, the historical novel instead evolved into a fundamentally experimental genre.[5] This concept of foundational experimentation will then be expanded upon in a case-study account of Zadie Smith's *Swing Time*. Carter's novel was published at the beginning of our time period, in 1984; Smith's at the end, in 2016. Both writers use history to interrogate dominant discourses (gender and race). The comparison between the novels therefore allows us to see changes in writing across the decades, but also the way that the historical mode has consistently enabled writers to posit new realities, to engage critically with contemporary politics and to discuss the nature of identity.

The 1980s and the Reinvention of 'History'

The literary historical novel seemed in a moribund state in 1980. Despite several notable exceptions, such as J. G. Farrell's *The Siege of Krishnapur* (1973), John Fowles's *The French Lieutenant's Woman* (1969), E. L. Doctorow's *Ragtime* (1975) and Doris Lessing's *The Golden Notebook* (1962), the genre post-1945 was generally considered to be conservative and stale. Indeed, the historical novel had been largely marginalised by mainstream literary critics and taste makers since the early years of the twentieth century. Historical novels did not reflect the new political realities of the time; they were nostalgic, traditional and conservative. They were associated with romance fiction, often considered too 'genre', and linked to a type of 'realist' historical practice that seemed to be conventional and straightforward.[6]

However, the examples cited above, particularly Lessing and Fowles, did show the experimental possibility of the form. Each in their various ways used narrative, language and metafictional tools to undermine the solidity of 'history'. Their formal and stylistic promptings would be taken up by a number of writers who sought to use the aesthetic tools of postmodernism to reflect upon identity, empire and gender. The postmodern challenge to central grand narratives, articulated clearly in Jean-François Lyotard's 1979 text *The Postmodern Condition*, attacked static structures of knowledge and epistemological laziness. Lyotard famously defined the postmodern as 'incredulity toward metanarratives', and inasmuch as it became aestheticised this critical stance was fundamental to the work of novelists in the early 1980s.[7] Novelists interrogated dominant discourses such as history, belief, gender and truth. The influence of two major magical realist writers, Gabriel Garcia Márquez and Günter Grass, is also central. Their key novels, respectively *One Hundred Years of Solitude* (1967) and *The Tin Drum* (1959), provided an important template for combining consideration of historical events with excessive and transgressive aesthetic experiment. The magical realist engagement with history as a means of troubling the binary of real and imaginary is central to the detaching of the British historical mode from its perceived generic shackles. Additionally, Umberto Eco's *The Name of the Rose* (1980) introduced literary theory into historical fiction through its combination of Philology, Detective genre and Structuralism. The massive success of Eco's self-consciously philosophical novel demonstrated that writing historically did not necessarily mean a closing down of aesthetic and intellectual possibility.

In the early 1980s, stimulated by these examples, Angela Carter, Jeanette Winterson and Salman Rushdie all chose to meditate upon the nature of the historical. This was noted, for instance, in the *New York Times* review of *Midnight's Children* in 1981:

> The obvious comparisons are to Günter Grass in 'The Tin Drum' and to Gabriel Garcia Márquez in 'One Hundred Years of Solitude.' I am happy to oblige the obvious. Like Grass and Garcia Márquez, Mr. Rushdie gives us history, politics, myth, food, magic, wit and dung.[8]

Their highly self-conscious novels highlight textuality, storytelling and falsehood (best articulated in Jeanette Winterson's statement of unreliability: 'I'm telling you stories. Trust me'[9]). They use the formal and stylistic innovations of magical realism to challenge traditional structures of knowledge. Yet they also, following Eco, introduce a literary theoretical aspect to the novel, staging discussions of cultural debates surrounding race, sexuality, power and political identity. This is taken to a logical extreme in Carter's dramatisation of Michel Foucault's Panopticon in *Nights at the Circus*, discussed below. Their self-consciousness has sometimes led to their work being considered a separate genre, 'historiographic metafiction', as Linda Hutcheon named it.[10] Hutcheon and other critics of the early 1980s suggested that contemporary historical fiction had a political self-awareness distinct from that which had come before. Contrarily Fredric Jameson saw this as evidence of a postmodern superficiality, a historiographical blankness:

> If there is any realism left here, it is a 'realism' which springs from the shock of grasping that confinement and of realizing that, for whatever peculiar reasons, we seem condemned to seek the historical past through our own pop images and stereotypes about the past, which itself remains forever out of reach.[11]

Jameson's concern is with the aestheticising of history into something superficial and troped, rather than jagged and 'real'. His concerns reflect theoretical worries that historical fiction might simply close down meaning and possibilities. Yet as we will see it was the historical novel's very ability to question and challenge the 'real' and 'realism' that meant it became an attractive form for writers in the early 1980s and through the 1990s.

'A Vain Sideshow': Angela Carter and the Experimental Form

To demonstrate how meditation upon history in novel form might allow such a challenge, we turn to one of the foundational texts already mentioned, Angela Carter's *Nights at the Circus* (1984). Carter's eighth novel follows the aerialist Sophie Fevvers, a circus performer and celebrity, through London and Europe in the late 1890s.[12] She visits St Petersburg and is lost in Siberia, where the novel concludes at the opening of the new century. Fevvers claims to be a bird, hatched from an egg. The picaresque, episodic novel uses the circus setting to explore bodily difference, performativity and transgression. Carter's aesthetic engagement with history here is fundamentally political, as Sonya Andermahr argues: 'Carter's use of the fantastic is never a repudiation of historical reality'.[13] Similar to Rushdie and Winterson, her use of the past is to point out the intellectual, imaginative and political consequences of conservative, patriarchal, imperial thinking, an 'ongoing project of demythologizing the male Western canon and its historical and theoretical contexts'.[14] Rather than cleave to the linear, hierarchical, linguistically exact 'HISstory' that emphasised dominion, nation, boundary and fixity, these writers looked to present a version of the past that was fluid, strange and queer. Their historiography was fundamentally transgressive, challenging and utopic, inasmuch as it sought 'non places' that might or might not exist. They were far more interested in history's strangeness and liminality than in finding origins, solutions or answers. In *Nights at the Circus*, Carter looked to find ways around normative models of time, chronology and order. She looked for female community and tradition, often found in places away from the civilised and the 'modern'.

The 'herstory' that Carter narrates consists of many elements. It is explicit in reclaiming female stories, with the novel's citation of multiple types of exemplary female political figures such as the New Woman or the Suffragette. Formally the book is episodic, essentially a number of set-pieces, and each section offers a new critique of patriarchal ordering structure, from social organisation to prison to family to government. Each episode suggests a new way of conceptualising women, and gender more generally, often pointing to a fluidity that had hitherto been unseen, or unrecognised. The circus itself is a repository of multiple transgressive identities, where the hyper-masculine strongman can be rejected for a female lover and tigers soothed by music. There are multiple invocations of imaginative feminist tropes or moments – the Maenads, Desdemona, Leda,

Scheherazade. This latter reference reminds the reader of the importance of interruption, and how aesthetics might stop time (or, rather, affect it in such a way that its seeming logic is disrupted). Often the male journalist Walser will forget where he is because of a story. Fevvers seems to be able to stretch time, to shift through force of storytelling will from one temporal universe to another:

> It took his breath away. As if the room that had, in some way, without his knowledge, been plucked out of its *everyday, temporal continuum*, had been held for a while above the spinning world and was now – dropped back into place.[15]

Storytelling might have the effect of stopping the forceful linearity of time here, disrupting or interrupting it in impressive ways that leave the audience breathless in awe. Fredric Jameson argues that 'Realism ... is a hybrid concept, in which an epistemological claim (for knowledge or truth) masquerades as an aesthetic ideal, with fatal consequences for both of those incommensurable dimensions'.[16] Through her disruption of narrative time, her introduction of strange, witty, odd aspects, and particularly through her imagining a familiar Victorian London with the addition of wondrous magical moments, Carter attacks the standard realist tradition of the historical form. She continually reinvents it as a manifesto for so much more: challenging all controlling discourses of sexual, gender, racial and anthropocentric identity. Carter's extensive use of the magical realist mode means that the 'historical' novel is constantly undermined. Her 'realism' is essentially a way of subverting that which, according to Jameson, makes an 'epistemological claim' and seeks to configure the world.

Fevvers is the key to understanding the way that the text uses the body to challenge patriarchal discourses, particularly history. She has no navel and hence has no 'history', no connection to humanness. Fevvers presents herself as unique, non-human and hence outside of the kind of history that imprisons the rest of the world: 'the grand abyss, the poignant divide, that would henceforth separate me from common humanity'.[17] She lacks the navel, that signifier (or echo) of a connection to the human, and the human body. While Walser is sceptical of her claims to be non-human and unique, she uses her bird-like qualities to challenge centuries of patriarchal definition. She is real and magical simultaneously, claiming London as her mother: 'dawn rose over London and gilded the great dome of St. Paul's until it looked like the divine pap of the city which, for want of any other, I must call my natural mother'.[18] In Fevvers's account the very built architecture becomes gendered female, the metropolitan centre of empire wrestled in the dawn light to mean something *new* and challenging to previous versions.

The novel's most profound challenge to controlling 'realist' ideologies is in its undermining of the nature of time. In this Carter contributes to an ongoing project throughout narrative prose of the 1980s and onwards to meditate upon and critique the nature of Western temporality. As Berber Bevernage and Christopher Lorenz argue:

Even though the traditional notion of (linear) time has been heavily criticised in the decades since Einstein's relativity theories, the time-concepts of historians, as well as philosophers of history, are still generally based on an absolute, homogenous and empty time. Not accidentally, this is a notion of time presupposed by the 'imagined community' of 'the nation' as Benedict Anderson famously suggested.[19]

Carter's novel is among other things a meditation on the ways that time might be challenged in order to provide political critique of other dominant 'realist' ideologies, such as gender (in this she is in a tradition of novelistic temporal experimentation reaching back to Virginia Woolf). She provides 'other' models for time perception and hence history. These include 'alternative' times – Lizzie's magical changing of time, the story-telling time already discussed, the utopic no-time of the women's prison and 'native' time in Siberia: 'nobody ever counted the heap because none of them knew *in what way the past differed from the present*'.[20] Indeed the no-place/no-time of the Siberian wilderness is presented as beyond history because of its challenge to European and American, that is, globalised (and male) temporality:

Yet, even then, even in these remote regions, in those days, those last, bewildering days before history, that is, history as we know it, that is, white history, that is, European history, that is, Yanqui history – in that final little breathing space before history as such extended its tentacles to grasp the entire globe.[21]

Reading this interest in different temporality, Valerie Henitiuk sees the manipulation of time as feminist and utopic: 'By manipulating the fourth dimension of time, she and other female characters manage to create a magical temporal space and thereby to exert a level of control over their lives'.[22]

The female community found in a Siberian prison similarly challenges the controlling discourses of modernity and of temporal order. These women challenge the disciplinary mechanism of the prison. Their challenge to power is bodily, through glance, gesture, love, hope and through the physical (blood, excrement, abject materials at the edge of identity used to communicate). They have no names, no histories and, seemingly (like Fevvers), no fathers. They communicate, plot and escape, without time and family. The prison is a Panopticon, clearly modelled on the Benthamite version of the new prison that Michel Foucault had considered 'a compact model of the disciplinary mechanism' only a few years earlier in his influential 1977 book *Discipline and Punish*.[23] The women in Siberia reject the modernist and post-Enlightenment social order that such surveillance suggests. They create a 'new', utopic society without men, without order, without modernity and without time. They step outside of history and, like Fevvers, suggest a new type of being and a unique (female) mode of living.

The stylistic innovations, formal experiments and intellectual engagements found in Carter's novel became increasingly standardised, and complex meditation upon history became to a certain extent normalised.[24] In 1989, two confidently 'historical' novels were shortlisted for the Booker Prize, and one – Kazuo Ishiguro's *The Remains of the Day* – won. The other, Rose Tremain's *Restoration*, prompted much discussion of a return to a 'classic' form of traditional literary historical fiction, in the line of Sir Walter Scott. Reviews referred to the perceived abeyance of the form, claiming that Tremain had 'restored the historical novel to its rightful place of honor after nearly two decades of degeneration into the sweet-savage imbecility of so-called historical romance'.[25] Tremain, reflecting in 2012, argued that '[w]hen I published *Restoration* in 1989, most literary novelists and critics of the literary genre were inclined to view the historical novel as a vain sideshow, an essentially unserious endeavour, unworthy of careful attention', and she cites the publication of the Australian writer Peter Carey's *Oscar and Lucinda* in 1988 as the moment this began to 'fracture'.[26] As we have seen in our discussion of Carter, 'history' allowed aesthetic consideration of a number of contemporary issues. *Restoration*, while seemingly more straightforward than *Nights at the Circus*, similarly considers rationality, time, the body, religious experience, power, sovereignty and a number of issues germane to contemporary society, particularly the perceived excessive consumerism of the post-1660 era in London which is clearly intended to echo that of the 1980s 'big-bang' City of London.

As Suzanne Keen notes, throughout the 1990s and thereafter the literary historical novel became increasingly visible and normalised. Yet the mainstreaming of the form did not mean that it lost its ability to intervene in contemporary debates about politics, identity and power. As Amy Elias has argued, the flexibility of the form through the 1990s and early 2000s reflected the developments in historical method and theory which 'to some extent repeats the contemporary debate about history in historiography'.[27] The historical novel through the 1990s continued to emphasise experiment, transgression, and the communication of new identities and possibilities. Popular literary historical novels reflected new approaches to rendering the past. The work of Sarah Waters here is illustrative. Her work opens up 'unseen' history of marginalised groups (*Affinity*, 1999), challenges the heteronormative archive (*Fingersmith*, 2002) and presents a potential socialist and queer utopia (*Tipping the Velvet*, 1998). Her most radical work, *The Night Watch* (2006), is a novel in which the narrative moves backwards, subverting chronology and temporality. Waters's work shows how the historical novel is radical and experimental, even when it is popular and widely read. Even popular historical fiction presents new temporalities, experimentally undermining narratives, and is often feminist in its revisionist, reclamatory historiography.

Over the past few years, the Man Booker prize, a useful bellwether for taking the temperature of the Anglophone novel, has been won by writers engaging with the past: Hilary Mantel (*Bring Up the Bodies*, 2012), Eleanor Catton (*The Luminaries*, 2013), Richard Flanagan *(The Narrow Road to the Deep North*, 2014), Marlon James (*A Brief History of Seven Killings*, 2015) and George Saunders (*Lincoln in the Bardo*, 2017). Each of these authors uses the tropes of contemporary historical fiction and set their stories in a recognisably *constructed* past world. They are comfortable with temporal shifts, time-slip and disrupted narratives, metafictional elements and self-referential moments, to the point that these seemingly 'postmodern' techniques for engaging with the historical have become familiar and even unremarkable.

'How Can We Know the Dancer from the Dance?': Zadie Smith

A concluding example here shows how the transgressive, experimental potential of the literary historical novel allows contemporary novelists to engage imaginatively with compelling issues relating to race, identity, temporality and post-colonial modernity. Zadie Smith reconsiders the relationship between history, identity and the body in her 2016 novel *Swing Time*. The form is multitudinous enough to encompass continuous debate, elastic enough to allow a continually evolving set of concerns to be grappled with. Representing the historical novel in the twenty-first century, *Swing Time* demonstrates the maturity of the genre, perhaps, after the formal interventions of the early 1980s and its development in the 1990s. The novel's challenges to history, to power and to hegemony, are more complicated, more nuanced and ultimately possibly less hopeful than Carter, Tremain and the novels discussed above. Like Carter, the novel is about performance – in this instance, dancing – and the strange quality of living within time and 'history'. Smith makes use of the full range of novelistic possibilities open to her when meditating upon the past. She considers history, discourse, identity, family, time; the novel is heavily influenced by post-colonial theory and models of political activism.

Smith's novel follows the teenage years of an unnamed narrator and her friend Tracey in Willesden during the late 1980s, as they learn to dance; a later narrative set in 2005–06 sees her become an adviser to the Madonna-esque singer-celebrity Aimee and travel to an unnamed African country with her in order to build a school. *Swing Time* continues Smith's career-long meditation upon race and identity, and on the contrasts and conflicts between Western modernity and non-European spaces.[28] The 'experiment' of the novel is its presentation of dancing as a way of linking the temporal and the material. Smith's engagement with dancing, and with black history, and with roots, demonstrates a keen sense of the body's material relationship with time.

The novel's title has many implications about the attitude of the text to history and temporal experience. 'Swing Time' is a type of jazz rhythm that is difficult to articulate. The basic 'feel' of swing is interpretative, implied and part of the performance of the music (rather than its notation), and is a fundamental part of swing music, the type of music that invites an audience to dance. So 'swing time' might refer to a particularly bodily, and ineffable, and definitely unnotated aspect of musical history and performance. Certainly, it challenges a notion of linear temporality – 'swing time' is that which happens simultaneously with the music's directionality, padding it out in different dimensions – not least in the response of the body to the music. The phrase refers directly to an interface between black musical practice and the ways in which it was interpreted and appropriated by white musical culture. While well-known black band leaders like Cab Calloway and Duke Ellington were developing the swing style, its wider manifestation – particularly in dance in musicals and film – was decidedly white. Wilfried Raussert argues that the 'time' of jazz is particularly culturally significant:

> ... this musical time adopts various time levels and mediates between them. Jazz negotiates between musically and culturally different conceptions of time in an innovative manner. It is characterized by a fusion of temporal continuity and discontinuity ... a unique African-American rendering of time which unfolds itself as the result of the encounter of Western and African time conceptions in the United States. This becomes most audible in jazz's swinging progression.[29]

The novel – like Carter's, and like many others cited through the chapter – aestheticises the conflict between 'temporal continuity and discontinuity', the staccato art to be made in the spaces between times. The birth of swing and jazz, and their manifestation in American popular culture, are controversial topics, and Smith's invocation of this phrase refers to a particular type of whitewash. Time is never unpolitical, and the interaction between the physically human and the politically temporal (and its representation) is something to be considered in some detail.

At the novel's opening the narrator, alone and vilified in London, visits a screening of *Swing Time* (George Stevens, 1936), a film made to capitalise on the popularity of Benny Goodman's music. Watching Fred Astaire move allows her a kind of peace and happiness, at least an escape: 'all these things felt small and petty next to this joyful sense I had watching the dance, and following its precise rhythms in my own body'.[30] The experience is not pleasurable solely because of the flatness of the screen-text, but because of the bodily imitation experienced by the viewer. She views the film, but is also 'following' it. There is simultaneity here an emotional and bodily response to the film that goes beyond reacting to the events in the movie. The viewing pleasure is empathic, enthusiastic, intellectual and bodily. Dancing is central to Smith's novel and figures various ways of knowing and understanding the self and, particularly, one's physical relation to the past. When seeking to understand dance the narrator goes to a text, but discovers a kind of affective, embodied, empathic history: 'The kind of information I was looking for, which I felt I needed to shore myself up, I dug out instead from an old, stolen library book – *The History of Dance*. I read about steps passed down over centuries, through generations. A different kind of history from my mother's, the kind that is barely written down – that is *felt*'.[31] Dance is somehow outside of time while it is similarly a measure of time, 'passed down over centuries'. It is a marker of historical movement that is unseen.

Similarly, when reflecting upon how she learns to dance, she claims 'a great dancer has no time, no generation, he moves eternally through the world, so that any dancer in any age may recognise him'.[32] This despite the fact that a dancer must have *time*, inasmuch as they move (in the Western tradition) according to musical signature, timing, their body moving in time and space. The dancer is a trained body seemingly freed within space, but simultaneously located geometrically and physiologically. Their imitation of past moves is historically queer, the body existing multi-temporally, 'where *then* and *now* punctuate each other', in Rebecca Schneider's words.[33] The dancer here presents a geometry that invokes a temporal dimension, and the roots of their movement are textual (they are taught) and bodily (they are felt and moved). Choreography and dance steps are strong motifs for historical process, inasmuch as they allow us to conceive of the body being moved according to linear promptings outside of itself, and also of moving in concord with other bodies. Dancing is circular, repetitive; in historical representation such as is found, for instance, in costume drama, it can stand for social difference, sex, collaboration, friendship, transformation, class. Dancing is something that is multi-temporal, multi-dimensional, experienced differently by the viewer and the participant, something that can generate empathy and even an affective response. It is a way of navigating space and time, kinetically reinserting the human body into the movement of time as measured by metronomic signature. The dancer generally moves according to music (itself worked around time signature). This is perhaps though a Western way of thinking, as Smith's narrator recognises when she witnesses the performance of the kankurang, something untranslateable and traditional in the African country she visits (unnamed, probably Gambia):

> I couldn't see the orange apparition any more, there was such a crowd between me and it that I could only hear it: what must have been its feet pounding the ground, and the raw clang of metal on metal, and a piercing shriek, other-worldly, to which the women replied in song, as they, too, danced. I was dancing involuntarily myself, pressed up close to so many moving bodies.[34]

Throughout the text Smith celebrates dancing as something that might be both material and imagined. It is highly meaningful, and silly. It is bodily, and temporal, and textual. Children learn to dance and enjoy themselves through expressing something. They watch film of others dancing, or appear in shows where they dance in repeat of those who have come before. They make film of themselves dancing, or watch video of performers. They learn steps, imitating and echoing each other and hundreds of others. Tracey is good at dancing, she claims, because she inherits this skill from her dad.

Particularly, dancing can seemingly connect across space and time, is physical and temporal, 'pressed up close to so many moving bodies'. The narrator sees her childhood friend in a production of *Show Boat*:

> The steps were familiar to me – they would have been to any dancer – and I wished I was up there with her. I was stuck in London, in the year 2005, but Tracey was in Chicago in 1893, and Dahomey a hundred years before that, and anywhere and any time that people have moved their feet like that. I was so jealous I cried.[35]

The body in movement in the *now* is experiencing a link with texts and material experiences, is re-inscribing something that has multi-dimensionality and multi-temporality. The type of constellation that one joins when dancing is complicated. Tracey *now* experiences bodily movement that links her somehow with different time zones, allowing her to jump across centuries and *be* simultaneously and multi-temporally. Smith's narrator feels herself involuntarily move in an attempt to join her friend: 'I felt my feet moving beneath me, trying to echo on the plush red carpet the complicated soft-shoe shuffle Tracey was performing right above me.'[36]

Smith's invocation of Chicago and Dahomey makes dance part of a Black history, giving Tracey a lineage, a genealogy, an inheritance.

Dahomey (now Benin), the famous African kingdom, is a state that lost independence to the French in 1894. Its legacy is complicated, but it has often been seen as a rallying point of resistance. Both the narrator and Tracey spend the time seeking roots and trying to tell a story about themselves, to fit and to matter. This search for roots reaches some kind of apogee when the narrator travels as a tourist to Kunta Kinteh island in the Gambia River looking for some kind of meaning in the place. Kunta Kinteh is the slave ancestor of Alex Haley whose book *Roots* led to an explosion of interest in African American genealogy when it was published in 1976 and adapted for television in 1977. The place makes very little impression ('every image had a cartoon thinness to it'[37]). Instead, she has a general, depressed epiphany:

> All paths lead back to there, my mother had always told me, but now that I was here, in this storied corner of the continent, I experienced it not as an exceptional place but as an example of a general rule. Power had preyed on weakness here: all kinds of power – local, racial, tribal, royal, national, global, economic – on all kinds of weakness, stopping at nothing, not even at the smallest girl child. But power does that everywhere. The world is saturated in blood. Every tribe has their blood-soaked legacy: here was mine. I waited for whatever cathartic feeling people hope to experience in such places, but I couldn't make myself believe the pain of my tribe was uniquely gathered here, in this place, the pain was too obviously everywhere, this just happened to be where they'd placed the monument.[38]

Smith's narrator rejects a kind of memorialisation that pinpoints meaning in a location for something more general and widespread. This clear-eyed cynicism collapses historical and geographical difference. She refuses to see literal roots that might suggest narrative closure, as the loaded word 'storied' suggests. The narrator rejects the meaning of a linear connection between then, there and now. Instead, the sense of violence she has is cross-sectional, structural, timeless and somehow transhistorical. This is reflected in the tense shift from power 'had preyed' to power 'does that everywhere'. Violence is then and now, with little sense of movement between the two temporal states. In rejecting her literal roots as having no affective meaning for her – no 'cathartic feeling' – Smith's narrator asks for a more complex sense of historical guilt related to a reading of power relations. She discards the Westernised comfort of 'catharsis' and commemorative practice itself, suggesting that this is a kind of decoy to avoid true anger. She rejects exception and uniqueness, resists her maternal instruction to see this as the other end of the road that she herself is on. This is ethically profound as much as it is historiographically bleak. It also suggests a sense of being in time that is contiguous and non-linear, which does not see a heritage as formational. Her roots are not linear and the world in which she finds herself cannot be described solely in terms of inheritance, linearity, path, tree or singularity. This refusal to see then-now as linear and a simple movement, a chronology, a temporally smooth geometric shape, situates Smith's narrator at a highly ambiguous place. She is, like Fevvers, seemingly without roots and dislocated, disrupted. This leads, though, not to a sense of celebratory uniqueness, but rather to a kind of globalised frictionlessness, a nowhereness, rather than a postmodern potentiality. Smith's shadowy, half-unseen narrator represents an identity that is unformed and flickers in and out of actuality. Rather than Fevvers's breezy confidence, Smith's narrator is depressed, guilt-stricken, indistinct. The opening scene in London situates the narrator in an apartment in which 'everything had been designed to be perfectly neutral, with all the significant corners rounded, like an iPhone'.[39] This sense of the in-between, corporate, commodified space of modernity being indistinct, smooth and without character, sees the near-contemporary world as essentially superficial and blank. The contemporary historical novel, in Smith's rendering, is freighted with melancholia, racked with shame, burdened with guilt, thoughtful about the relationship of the self to society. Smith shows how this is not necessarily celebratory, but might result in inertia, conservatism, a kind of numb post-millennial melancholia. As with Carter's experimentation, Smith's historical novel allows new spaces to be opened up and political situations to be questioned. However, it also presents a much more cynical, despondent, depressed sense of the *now* and its relationship to the past. Smith's numbed narrator reminds us that history is a place of trauma, violence and conflict, of a particular reality that must be faced, this bleak smoothness resisting the potentiality celebrated in earlier novels.

The examples of Carter and Smith, taken from near the opening and the concluding years considered by this *Companion*, shows the historical mode in good, if complicated, health. Throughout the period British novelists have sought to engage with the past, in a multitude of fashions, in order to marshal new arguments about the contemporary moment, to offer new possibilities in terms of identity, and to meditate upon the nature of aesthetics and of existence. The contending temporalities of historical fiction and its consumption point directly to an undermining of narrative authority, an implicit challenge to aesthetic conservatism. The historical novel form allows the writer to examine multiple complex issues, to meditate upon the relationship of the self to time, to think about the ethics of aesthetics, to consider the ways that we relate to family and to posit change. Its prominence and pre-eminence over the past decades illustrate an aesthetic interest in experiment, complication and innovation.

Notes

1. On definitions of the form through history, see D. Wallace, *The Woman's Historical Novel* (Basingstoke: Palgrave, 2005); J. de Groot, *The Historical Novel* (London and New York: Routledge, 2009); K. Mitchell and N. Parsons (eds), *Reading Historical Fiction* (Hampshire: Palgrave Macmillan, 2013); R. Maxwell, The Historical Novel in Europe, *1650–1950* (Cambridge University Press, 2009); and F. Moretti, *The Bourgeois: Between History and Literature* (London: Verso, 2013).
2. The prize is offered to writers from the United Kingdom, Ireland or the Commonwealth, and defines 'historical' as events taking place at least sixty years ago, the definition that Scott used in his first novel *Waverley* (1814).
3. See F. Jameson, *Antinomies of Realism* (London and New York: Verso, 2015).
4. See G. Lukács, *The Historical Novel*, trans. H. Mitchell (Lincoln, NA: University of Nebraska Press, 1983).
5. See P. Waugh, *Metafiction* (London: Routledge, 1984); L. Hutcheon, *A Poetics of Postmodernism* (London: Routledge, 1988); F. Jameson, *Postmodernism, or, the Cultural Logic of Late Capitalism* (Durham, NC: Duke University Press, 1991); and K. Mitchell, *History and Cultural Memory in Neo-Victorian Fiction* (Basingstoke: Palgrave, 2010).
6. See A. Light, '*Young Bess*: Historical Novels and Growing Up' (1989) 33(1) *Feminist Review* 57–71; and Wallace, *The Woman's Historical Novel.*
7. J.-F. Lyotard, *The Postmodern Condition*, trans. G. Bennington and B. Massumi (Manchester University Press, 1984).
8. J. Leonard, 'Books of the Times', *New York Times* (23 April 1981), www.nytimes.com/1981/04/23/books/rushdie-midnight.html.
9. J. Winterson, *The Passion* (London: Vintage, 2001), p. 5.
10. L. Hutcheon, 'Postmodern Paratextuality and History' (1986) 5–6 *Texte* 301–12.
11. F. Jameson, 'Postmodernism and Consumer Society' in H. Foster (ed.), *Postmodern Culture* (London: Pluto Press, 1985), p. 112.
12. See E. Gordon, *The Invention of Angela Carter* (Oxford University Press, 2017).
13. S. Andremahr, 'Contemporary Women's Writing: Carter's Literary Legacy' in S. Andremahr and L. Phillips (eds), *Angela Carter: New Critical Readings* (London: Bloomsbury, 2012), p. 13.
14. S. Andremahr and L. Philips, 'Introduction' in S. Andremahr and L. Phillips (eds), *Angela Carter: New Critical Readings* (London: Bloomsbury, 2012), p. 3.
15. A. Carter, *Nights at the Circus*, new edn (London: Vintage, 1994), p. 87 (emphasis added).
16. Jameson, *Antinomies of Realism*, pp. 6–7.
17. Carter, *Nights at the Circus*, p. 29.
18. *Ibid.*, p. 36.
19. B. Bevernage and C. Lorenz, 'Introduction' in C. Lorenz and B. Bevernage (eds), *Breaking Up Time* (Gottingen and Bristol, CT: Vandenhoeck & Ruprecht, 2013), p. 11.
20. Carter, *Nights at the Circus*, p. 258 (emphasis added).
21. *Ibid.*, p. 265.

22. V. Henitiuk, 'Step into My Parlour: Magical Realism and the Creation of a Feminist Space' (2003) 30(2) *Canadian Review of Contemporary Literature* 410–27, 411.

23. M. Foucault, *Discipline and Punish: The Birth of the Prison*, trans. A. Sheridan (London and New York: Vintage Books, 1977), p. 198.

24. See S. Keen, 'The Historical Turn in British Fiction' in J. E. English (ed.), *A Concise Companion to Contemporary British Fiction* (Oxford: Blackwell, 2006).

25. F. King, 'A Yuppie in King Charles's Court', *New York Times* (15 April 1990), www.nytimes.com/1990/04/15/books/a-yuppie-in-king-charles-s-court.html.

26. R. Tremain, 'Restoration', *The Guardian* (28 September 2012), www.theguardian.com/books/2012/sep/28/rose-tremain-restoration-book-club.

27. A. Elias, 'Metahistorical Romance, the Historical Sublime, and Dialogic History' (2005) 9(2/3) *Rethinking History* 159–72, 163.

28. P. Tew, *Zadie Smith* (London and New York: Palgrave Macmillan, 2010).

29. W. Raussert, 'Jazz, Time, and Narrativity' (2000) 45(4) *Amerikastudien/ American Studies* 519–34, 519.

30. Z. Smith, *Swing Time* (London: Hamish Hamilton, 2016), p. 4.

31. *Ibid.*, pp. 100–1 (emphasis added).

32. *Ibid.*, p. 38.

33. R. Schneider, *Performing Remains* (London and New York: Routledge, 2011), p. 2 (emphasis in the original).

34. Smith, *Swing Time*, p. 164.

35. *Ibid.*, pp. 361–2.

36. *Ibid.*, p. 361.

37. *Ibid.*, p. 315.

38. *Ibid.*, p. 316.

39. *Ibid.*, p. 2.

10

PETRA RAU

Fiction and Film, 1980–2018

The most common interpretation of the conjunction 'and' in the phrase 'fiction and film' is to silently convert it into a preposition; to think of adaptation of novels and short stories *into* film and TV. Given how many books have served as source texts for visual media, this is hardly surprising. The Russian director Sergei Eisenstein also noted that many of the narrative strategies of nineteenth-century popular novelists had inspired innovative directors such as D. W. Griffith or King Vidor in their development of cinematic techniques such as the close-up, the dissolve, the superimposed shot or montage.[1] In turn, modernist writers learnt from cinematography: think of the scene from *Mrs Dalloway* (1925) in which the point of view shifts back and forth between the advertising slogan being puffed into the sky by an aeroplane and different individuals on the ground: this is classic intercutting.

Equivalences in verbal and visual storytelling aside, it is worth bearing in mind that both fiction and film show us 'life as it is when we have no part in it', as Woolf put it in her 1926 essay 'The Cinema'.[2] They literally widen our scope. In the very decade that saw the invention of film cameras, Joseph Conrad suggested that writing was a multi-sensory prompt for the reader: 'My task which I am trying to achieve is, by the power of the written word, to make you hear, to make you feel – it is, before all, to make you *see*'.[3] If we take Conrad at his word we can think of the act of reading prose as facilitating a concomitant screening in our heads: fiction is the script for our imagination's cinemascope. Narratological terminology, of course, has long acknowledged fiction's technical ability 'to make [us] *see*' via point of view, focalisers, first-person or omniscient perspective.

It is no coincidence that in her essay Woolf also pondered over what many writers still consider literature's strength and cinema's limitation – the representation of inner life: 'but if so much of our thinking and feeling is connected with seeing there must be some residue of visual emotion not seized by artist or painter-poet which may await the cinema'.[4] The dialogue between fiction and film, I would argue, is particularly fruitful when it can engage each medium in its exploration of 'visual emotion' or the 'connect[ion] with seeing'. In recent decades, a number of writers have shown interest in how film works as an art form and have written treatments of their own or other novelists' fiction, or indeed entirely new screenplays. Among them are Angela Carter, Ruth Prawer Jhabvala, Hanif Kureshi, Salman Rushdie, Ian McEwan and Kazuo Ishiguro. The many literary 'connect[ions] with seeing' therefore allow us to examine the effect of film on the contemporary literary imagination, on reading and on our sense of self as refracted through fiction.

The scopic motif does not rule out discussing literary adaptations (which have often been particularly intriguing when they focused on acts or meta-phors of perception, misprision or blindness) and it usefully widens the conversational remit of the dialogue between fiction and film beyond the perennial question of fidelity – as if adhering as closely as possible to a single-authored verbal text were the prime criterion for assessing a collaborative visual-aural-kinetic form when the literary source is just one of a multitude of influences that plays into film production alongside cinematic genre expecta-tions, marketing, directorial vision, casting, editing and funding.[5]

Theorists of postmodernism, notably Jean Baudrillard in *Simulacra and Simulacrum* (1981) and Fredric Jameson in *Postmodernism or the Cultural Logic of Late Capitalism* (1984), have helped us rethink the relationship between reality and image, original and copy, present and past alongside the impact of new technologies of reproduction and changes in TV and film culture. As Peter Brooker argues, in a culture of ubiquitous simulacra, an adaptation might be a pastiche, an ironic meta-textual commentary or a Brechtian re-functioning (*Umfunktionierung*) that appropriates any text for the purpose of social critique.[6] Self-reflexivity is prevalent in both post-modern fiction and film, and also across these media: the most dangerous thing you can do in Neil Jordan's *The Company of Wolves* (1984) is read because it will give you highly erotic nightmares (courtesy of Angela Carter's screenplay, adapted from *The Bloody Chamber*). Harold Pinter's screenplay for Karel Reisz's 1984 adaptation of John Fowles's *The French Lieutenant's Woman* (1969) offers a different solution to self-reflexivity. Fowles's histor-ical novel had an intrusive contemporaneous narrator, paratextual commen-tary and multiple endings – all strategies that were meant to draw the reader's attention to the act and rules of narration. With a nudge from François Truffaut's *La nuit américaine* (1973), Pinter's ingenious solution had the same effect, within the terms of cinematic storytelling, in preventing the audience from simply consuming a story. We see a clapperboard in the very first frame: a film is being shot, set in Victorian times, and the lead actors have an affair on set that mirrors the illicit Victorian romance. Naturally, both strands have separate endings. Editing the parallel storylines nimbly dispenses with any clunky voiceover and leaves the audience to work out the parallels for themselves. To translate self-reflexive commentary into meta-cinematic framing became one of the most influential adaptive strategies. It inspired Mike Leigh's *Topsy Turvy* (1999) and Michael Winterbottom's take on *Tristram Shandy, A Cock and Bull Story* (2005).

In our increasingly screen-dominated contemporary lives, we should not assume that film and TV audiences come to a literary text first, or even know it, or that a filmic interpretation leaves the literary text quite intact: no one who has *seen* a film Ork puts up with Tolkien's more verbose version in *Lord of the Rings*; no one who has been touched by Rachel Portman's elegiac score for Mark Romanek's *Never Let Me Go* (2010) can easily (re)turn to Ishiguro's stunted narrator without retrofitting her with a richer emotional landscape. Danny Boyle's blockbuster film version of *Trainspotting* (1996), with its 'cool', upbeat soundtrack and memorable hallucinatory scenes, catapulted Irvine Welsh's novel to best-selling cult status. It is hard to imagine that this episodic, polyphonic novel about Edinburgh drug addicts, written in expletive-ridden Leith vernacular, would have found such a wide (middle-class) readership without the film's prior dilution into touristic consumability[7] – precisely the kind of commodification against which the book's critique of Thatcherite neoliberalism militates. As Linda Hutcheon argues, to some extent our imagination remains 'permanently colonised by the visual and aural world of the films'.[8] 'There's an odd way in which films can invade books', commented Ian McEwan on the effect of Joe Wright's *Atonement* (2007): in his mind, the actress Saoirse Ronan (cast as Bryony) came to replace the character he had created.[9] Note these metaphors of aggression and appropriation: filmic colonisation and invasion challenge literature's claim to priority and originality.

Contemporary fiction increasingly responds to the way in which our viewing habits on the large and small screen shape our lives, our politics and our sense of self. Mark Renton's fascination with 1980s popular culture in Welsh's *Trainspotting* (1993) includes Jean-Claude van Damme videos and soap operas. Yet the real social narcotic of the 1980s was, according to *Sight and Sound*, period drama or 'heritage cinema': 'it is this secure world of an earlier Englishness – the antithesis of the fissiparous relativism of the present – that the films recreate rather than what the novels acknowledge: that England must change, or has already changed beyond recognition'.[10] In the cinema, E. M. Forster reigned supreme thanks to David Lean's *A Passage to India* (1984), James Ivory's *Maurice* (1987), Charles Sturridge's *Where Angels Fear to Tread* (1991), Merchant-Ivory's *A Room with a View* (1985) and *Howards End* (1992). TV series such as *Brideshead Revisited* (1981) and *The Jewel in the Crown* (1984) were followed in the 1990s by mini-serialisations of classic nineteenth-century novels by Dickens, Gaskell, Eliot and Jane Austen, notably *Pride and Prejudice* (1995), which attracted

10 million viewers and made Andrew Davies the BBC's go-to screenwriter for classic adaptations. Audiences faithfully tuned in to see Helena Bonham Carter's Edwardian psyche-knots and marvel at the eloquence of Colin Firth's scowl, but critics largely dismissed period drama as offering reactionary and nostalgic versions of exportable Englishness that ignored the nuances of irony and social critique of the source texts. The artifice of the symbolic ending of *Howards End*, for instance, signals a social desideratum rather than a concrete possibility; in the film, this symbolism is subsumed into the convention of the happy ending. The effort to produce authenticity through period dialogue, sumptuous settings and wardrobe ostensibly created a surface sheen that romanticised and patinated the *haute bourgeoisie*, while largely ignoring the socio-economic conditions on which such exceptional lives depended.[11] Literary adaptations were habitually considered ideologically conservative, aesthetically staid and, in their foregrounding of romance, mainly directed at women. Films that addressed contemporary social issues were associated with a progressive social and aesthetic agenda, such as Richard Eyre's *The Ploughman's Lunch* (1983; script by Ian McEwan) and Stephen Frear's *My Beautiful Launderette* (1985; script by Hanif Kureshi).

It may be the case, however, that 1980s and 1990s period drama is not quite as anodyne a social narcotic as its critics claimed, nor that it unequivocally functions as an endorsement of a glorious imperial past one could visually retreat to.[12] If we attend closely, for instance, to what Forster's heroines look *at* in these films rather than what they look *like*, we recognise how the script has interpreted as scopic metaphors the novelist's political vision – the explosive effect of sexual desire on the social order. The same could be said for adaptations of Henry James's novels or Edith Wharton's which respond to the texts' critique of female objectification and women's desire for more scope through frequent scenes of looking out on or looking at a world that confines or excludes but expects conformity. And while the period settings may be lavishly decorated country houses, what goes on in the spacious mansions of the social and political ruling class produces stifling claustrophobia. Rather than unravel the heritage film debate here once more, though, I want to focus on how the adaptations of canonical literary classics and their reception shaped the contemporary historical novel and, in turn, its renditions for the screen.

Alan Hollinghurst's *The Line of Beauty* (2004) uses the Merchant-Ivory aesthetic and the commercial success of literary adaptation as a metaphor for his central character Nick Guest's misprision. The plot updates Evelyn Waugh's *Brideshead Revisited* for a 1980s setting, as recent Oxford graduate Nick Guest is welcomed into the Notting Hill home of Tory MP Gerald Fedden and his wife Rachel. The Feddens are every inch as horrific an establishment family as Waugh's Flytes or Dickens's Veneerings: dysfunctional, philistine, cruel, hypocritical, racist, homophobic and deeply protective of their wealth and privilege. The plot charts Guest's naive romance with the Fedden family and his relationship with closeted racial others. As the son of a provincial antiques dealer, a connoisseur of architectural elegance and literary complexity and appreciative of male physique, Nick spots beauty easily but is entirely blind to the moral failures of his chosen habitat. The novel asks, of course, whether it is possible to divorce politics from aesthetics in the 1980s; whether a gay man in the age of AIDS can innocently dance with a Prime Minister whose government would introduce Clause 28 to the Local Government Act to prohibit the so-called promotion of the acceptability of homosexuality as a regular family relationship in teaching material. The point about Nick's ideological blind spots, however, is made via film: having abandoned his PhD on Henry James, Nick's ambition is to adapt *The Spoils of Poynton*, a novel whose protagonist values material objects over people or relationships:

> He'd spent months writing a script, and it was almost as if he'd written the book it was based on: all he wanted was praise. He often imagined watching the film, in the steep circle of the Curzon cinema – absorbing the grateful unanimous sigh of the audience at the exact enactment of what he'd written; in fact he seemed to have directed the film as well. He lay awake in the bliss of Philip French's review.[13]

Note how the script all but approximates the creative effort imagined of its source, even exceeds it by letting Nick inhabit the entire collaborative effort of filmmaking by rolling author, adaptor, producer, director, actors, audience and reviewer into one as if film multiplies the achievement of authorship. This pleasurable scenario would literally be unimaginable without the success of the prevailing adaptive aesthetic for the 1980s, Merchant-Ivory productions such as *The Bostonians* (1984) and *A Room with a View* (1985), which are mentioned in the novel. In a conversation with potential US financiers for his script, Nick is told how to customise James's storyline for a modern audience by focusing on romance, happy endings and watchable passion[14] rather than depict frustrated desire and unrealised ambitions. The request for passion anticipates what Julianne Pidduck has called the 'increasingly sexual turn'[15] in classic adaptations that would eroticise (and make more accessible the verbally obfuscated relationships in) the cinematic versions of *The Portrait of a Lady* (1996), *The Wings of the Dove* (1997) and *The Golden Bowl* (2002).

Eventually, Nick imagines – scripts really – his exit from his *haut bourgeois* circle through the grammar of period drama: 'He saw a clear sequence, like a loop of film, of his friends not noticing his absence, jumping up from gilt chairs to join in the swirl of a ball. On analysis he thought it was probably a scene from a Merchant Ivory film.'[16] Where would one find gilt chairs in the 1980s other than on a hired National Trust set in a Merchant Ivory film or on *Antiques Road Show*? Where do balls still happen other than in period drama? Nick imagines himself into the political and financial establishment the way an uncritical consumer of 1980s period drama would project themselves into a plot that would most likely have socially excluded them, 'not noticing his absence'. Nick's romance with the Feddens is an extended exercise in 'not noticing' from all sides.

By the same token, we could read Kazuo Ishiguro's earlier *The Remains of the Day* (1989) as an astringent response to the patinated English past propagated throughout the Thatcherite 1980s, not least through period drama: a different way in which film invades the book. Its 1993 Merchant-Ivory adaptation tested whether this branded aesthetic could also accommodate its critique (even to the point of reprising the casting: Anthony Hopkins and Emma Thompson, who had starred in *Howards End*, also took the lead roles in *Remains*). The novel is set in 1956. Mr Stephens, the novel's first-person narrator, recalls his days as butler at Dartington Hall where he has been employed since the late 1920s and where he has remained as butler after the disgrace of Lord Dartington to serve the present owner, an American millionaire. Stephens is a consummate professional and adheres to a strict code of unquestioning servitude to his master. He regards this duty as a form of dignity. The key events in Stephens's tenure at Dartington are presented as scenes of misprision in which he sees unusual sights in the house or in the grounds, yet he cannot grasp their emotional significance or their political import if that would mean assuming agency for matters that are ostensibly outside his vocational purview: 'There are many things you or I are simply not in a position to understand', he informs Miss Kenton, the housekeeper.[17] His position, in other words, is one of strictly limited responsibility within a social hierarchy he never challenges despite signs of distress and discontent all around him. As the political climate of the 1930s invades the upstairs salon, so social discontent reaches the downstairs corridors, but Stephens remains impervious to the weather.

It is Miss Kenton, 'a silhouette against a window', who notices his father's decline. As he catches 'sight of Miss Kenton through the open doorway, signalling to me', she informs him of his father's death.[18] Repeatedly Stephen's account throws Miss Kenton into relief, as a harbinger of moral decision-making he denies. The novel achieves dramatic irony through the visual metaphors in Stephens's formal register; we can literally *see* the meaning and consequences of what Stephens merely records. The film dramatises these cognitive opportunities through its own visual metaphors or by literalising the book's: many scenes position characters before windows or frame dark silhouettes against doorways. The house's décor may be sumptuous, but it really is merely a backdrop to the stark drama of servitude and self-denial. We do not see the servants' emotions clearly because good servants do not display emotions and had better not have any. Display in such a house is only for people upstairs. When Lord Dartington gives orders to dismiss two Jewish housemaids for 'the safety and well-being of [his] guests',[19] the only thing the butler sees clearly is his duty:

> My every instinct opposed the idea of their dismissal. Nevertheless, my duty in this instance was quite clear, and as I saw it, there was nothing to be gained at all in irresponsibly displaying such personal doubts. It was a difficult task, but as such, one that demanded to be carried out with dignity.[20]

To doubt is to show personhood in an irresponsible display. 'Dignity' is not merely a mask to politely conceal opposition, but a making invisible of the self, an extinction of personhood altogether. Miss Kenton, appalled at the wrongfulness of such dismissal, threatens to resign, but fails to carry out her intention. Over a year later, Dartington regrets his decision and inquires after the maids. Only then does Stephens raise the issue directly with Miss Kenton: 'When I finally turned to look at her, she was gazing through the glass at the great expanse of fog outside.'[21] Fog is an apt metaphor for what Miss Kenton recognises as the moral turpitude in the household of a fascist collaborator and what Stephens excuses as a 'terrible misunderstanding'.[22] Time and again, Ishiguro makes his protagonist look without seeing: 'As I was leaving I glanced back towards her. She was again gazing out at the view, but it had by this point grown so dark inside the summerhouse, all I could see of her was her profile outlined against a pale and empty background.'[23] Dartington Hall is consistently pale and empty in the book – the reader gains little sense of its size or precise interior – and so is Stephen's inner life. The Merchant-Ivory adaptation offers us a much more gilded and grand house, but we spend a great deal of time downstairs understanding how much hard labour goes into polishing the silver, cleaning the rooms and cooking for a large party. Ishiguro's version of Englishness, in other words, responds to the predominant focus of the 1980s adaptations on a selective social stratum and has widened our scope. Novel and film offer us many scenes in which servants look out of windows into grounds they can tend and till, but never enjoy, and in which they are always under Mr Stephen's professionally surveilling but emotionally unseeing eyes.

The Remains of the Day is a book about what following orders and safeguarding social order do to the soul of a human being.[24] It is also a book that elides the mythologised war years in favour of the forgotten pre-war appeasement and the even less remembered nadir of the Suez crisis. Ishiguro takes a good long look at the unseen and unrecognised and at the mechanisms of wilful blindness in the name of duty and dignity. But most importantly for our discussion, the book re-visions the grandiose posturing of the Thatcher years and its selective cultural memory in the marketing of 'heritage' and Englishness in politics and in popular culture. Stephens's nostalgia for bygone days and his continued loyalty to the disgraced Dartington are not poignant; they are appalling. What precisely, the novel also asks us, makes us collude in 'not noticing [our] absence' in consuming sepia projections of the past?

If *The Remains of the Day* is a highly visual novel about a lack of perception, it also shifts the focus to those working invisibly in the basements and corridors of the establishment or hovering in the liminal spaces between upstairs and downstairs. A. S. Byatt's novella 'Morpho Eugenia' (1992) compares the Victorian social order with the organisation of insect colonies. As in Ishiguro's novel, the reader is made to see what long remains imperceptible to its male protagonist – the explorer and entomologist William Anderson. The novella contains dense descriptive passages about experiments with ant colonies set up and recorded by Anderson, who has married into the upper-class Alabaster family. His aide to scientific endeavour is sharp-eyed governess Matty Compton. The reader learns about the unfolding events from Anderson's point of view, whose powers of taxonomy and observation are more acute in relation to ants and butterflies, so it takes him a while to perceive the parallels between the drone-like existence of the Alabaster males and the royal status of the perennially reproducing females. He is similarly slow in recognising Matty's keen intellect and imagination (if she can draw insects in such detail, surely she would notice beastly behaviour), and perfectly unaware of the incestuous breeding his marriage is covering up until the servants ('*the house*') construe to make him see the siblings *in flagrante delicto*.

Byatt demonstrates the curious paradox between a society so engrossed in pinning butterflies and naming species yet unable to discern its own rather unnatural social order, in all its deviations and mutations, and the violence needed to keep the system in place. 'Morpho Eugenia' ponders where the real power lies: with the queen, the worker bees or the drones? The densely ekphrastic narrative juxtaposes the insect societies with the Alabaster household. Yet as a middle-class interloper Anderson accepts upper-class conventions just as kidnapped black ant larvae behave like the red ants among which they are raised. As Matty Comptom instructs him:

'There are people in a house, you know, who know everything that goes on – invisible people, and now and then *the house* simply decides that something must happen …

'But you know what I saw,' he said.

'Yes. There are people in houses, between the visible inhabitants and the invisible, largely invisible to both, who can know a very great deal, or nothing, as they choose. I choose to know about some things, and not to know about others. I have become interested in knowing things that concern you'.[25]

Social invisibility is a conduit to illicit knowledge, and knowing things can lend the observer some revolutionary power. But to be seen (and known) is also a means to inhabit one's role more fully, notably that of being a woman attracting a male for sex. When Matty complains 'You have *never seen me*',[26] she means that for Anderson she is neither a person nor a woman; even the servant girl Amy has greater prominence because she comes into view by dint of being raped by Alabaster junior. Matty's vigilance serves not just her own erotic aspirations but her vocational ones as well: she is an artist whose pictorial and narrative skill can earn her a living.

Philip Haas's genre-conscious adaptation *Angels and Insects* (1995) cast A-lister Kristin Scott Thomas as the governess while TV actress Patsy Kensit played Eugenia Alabaster: a knowing cinema audience will anticipate the plot to shift significance back to the star. Only because we are familiar with the conventions of period drama do we notice how the set pieces – the ball, the picnic, the stroll through the wood – are being defamiliarised. The ball at which Anderson is introduced to the Alabasters presents the ladies not in authentic period gowns but in shockingly gaudy, anachronistic frocks, driving home that these female specimens market themselves to attract suitors. The insect parallel throws into even greater relief the sexual dynamic of the social order of both microcosms: it is all about sex, labour and reproduction. Both the novella and the film direct attention to the hive-like quality of the great house, its back passages and service corridors in which tremendous amounts of labour are performed invisibly to enable the visible world to function. The film can exploit this shift more by making downstairs heave with antsy black-clad workers in a series of quietly menacing scenes that the audience only retrospectively realises prepare a kind of coup. These worker ants freeze and mutely turn to face a wall to make themselves inconspicuous the minute a drone or queen-in-waiting claps eyes on them.

It is perhaps apposite here to remind ourselves that it is not just period drama that takes a sexual turn in the 1990s; historical fiction also revisioned gender and sexual relations. Sarah Waters queered the Victorian novel and illuminated areas nineteenth-century fiction had omitted or relegated to minor episodes: psychic research, pornography, the music hall. Michel Faber's *The Crimson Petal and the White* (2002) put prostitution centre-stage. By the time these novels were adapted for TV series, more liberal post-millennial audiences were also ready to watch such retroactively historicised sex. Byatt and Haas present several sex scenes, but what we see (or read) turns out to be as implausibly pictorial as Matty Compton's enlarged illustrations. Of course, what we are shown through the frame of the bedroom door or Anderson's focalised point of view is not passion, but scheduled acts of *couverture*: planned inseminations. Where the novella encouraged the reader to transfer entomological study to the social order of humans, the film plays with cinema's scopophilic tendencies, recruiting the audience for a voyeuristic gaze that in many scenes is elevated to scientific observation through extreme close-ups. Such montage encourages us to think of the screen very much as the glass front that enables scopic access to the hive's activity: just as the audience watches humans have sex so the amateur entomologists gaze onto worker ants tending eggs.

Julianne Pidduck has observed how labour became newly visible in literary adaptations and historical films in the 1990s not least as a corrective to its cinematic invisibility in the earlier decade: these films resist simple consumption because they constantly remind us of its human cost, as do their literary sources (127–34). This culminates in Julian Fellowes's script for Robert Altman's genre-conscious *Gosford Park* (2001), in which we only see what is visible to the servants and in which the casting already signals that upstairs and downstairs have equal screen time and weight. Without rewriting the historical novel and revisioning historical film in the 1990s, *Gosford Park* would have been unthinkable.

Contemporary fiction frequently reflects on our televisual viewing habits. In Michel Faber's *Under the Skin* (2000), TV is initially the chief tool for learning English, obtaining the daily news and understanding human behaviour, but its alien protagonist soon learns that daytime cookery programmes, soap operas, cop series and game shows are of very little use in understanding the society she has to blend into. The videos and TV programmes the adolescent clones can watch in Ishiguro's *Never Let Me Go* (2004) are never tested against a reality in which they can participate, so they remain oneiric, opaque simulacra – Kathy H.'s only glimpse into a life unlived and yet, for us, as fictitious as hers. Film and clichéd pop lyrics, in *Never Let Me Go*, is as close as Kathy H. will ever get to such human affairs as love. The book asks, of course, what it is that makes us human beyond our material body and to what extent representations can produce the desire they depict. Zadie Smith's *NW* (2012) wonders what precisely visual media offer us in terms of realistic representations of race and class, returning to the issue of touristic commodification that had made Boyle's *Trainspotting* problematic. In the new millennium, audiences consumed *Shameless* or *The Wire*.

> Everyone in both Natalie's workplace and Frank's was intimately involved with the lives of a group of African-Americans, mostly male, who slung twenty-dollar vials of crack in the scrub between a concatenation of terribly designed tower blocks in a depressed and forgotten city with one of the highest murder rates in the United States. That everyone should be so intimately involved in the lives of these young men annoyed Frank, though he could not really put his finger on why, and in protest he exempted himself and his wife from what was by all accounts an ecstatic communal televisual experience.[27]

Natalie and Frank cannot consume this palatable version of racialised social exclusion on run-down urban estates because it makes their own lives as highly educated, black professionals even more exceptional and precarious. They do not recognise themselves on TV. Natalie in particular struggles with an 'image system'[28] that renders her social mobility invisible and impossible. Smith's irony suggests bourgeois audiences' viewing habits are mildly pornographic rather than genuinely interested in intimate acquaintance with a life far removed from their socio-economic stratum. As a form of smug excess, this communal ecstasy echoes the way in which we now often describe being 'hooked on' a TV series, or 'binge' on a box set.

To pull the reader away from consumption into attentive reading and reflective watching – not just to make us *see*, but to make us see *how* we are being made to see – makes contemporary fiction and its adaptation technically complex. The present tense of Hilary Mantel's Thomas Cromwell trilogy may sound more artificial than the usual narrative time of the past tense, but it reminds us that we are, as it were, zoomed into the Tudor period and see everything with Cromwell's wary eyes. Here is the opening of the trial scene in *Bring Up the Bodies* (2012) that will eventually lead to Anne Boleyn's execution:

> When the prisoners are brought in, the three gentlemen draw away from Mark; they want to show him their scorn, and how they are better than he. But this brings them into proximity with each other, more than they will allow; they will not look at each other, he notices, they shuffle to create as much space as they can, so they seem to be shrinking from each other, twitching at coats and sleeves.[29]

We move with our focaliser Cromwell, seeing only what he notices, although the book's scenes can feel both oddly static and familiar, as if we were perambulating through an exhibition of Hans Holbein's work in a well-restored Tudor mansion. Having to make sense of the power play at Henry VIII's court, Cromwell's task is twofold if he wants to prosper and survive: to observe acutely and to render himself entirely opaque and inscrutable to others. 'His expression is as carefully blank as a freshly painted wall'[30] might as well be a stage direction for any Renaissance politician. Many of Mantel's dialogues read like mises-en-scène in which the editor has cut between over-the-shoulder shots (what does he see?) and close-ups of Cromwell's face (what is he thinking?) – a strategy that made the TV adaptation's audience work hard to figure out what is going on and arranged the actor Mark Rylance's face into a permanently melancholic, guarded mien.

The reader's alertness also pays off in Ian McEwan's *Atonement* (2001), which intermittently signals the constructedness of what we are reading, through ventriloquised styles and genres, reflections on writing, and re-played set pieces seen from an alternative point of view. Precocious Bryony ostensibly contemplates writing a 'scene three times over, from three different points of view'.[31] And indeed the novel repeatedly offers the reader this so-called *Rashomon* effect, borrowed from Akira Kurosawa's eponymous 1950 film in which the same events are shown from four different points of view to underline the subjectivity of both experience and truth. Joe Wright's adaptation used McEwan's already filmic technique[32] by replaying hinge scenes and using rewind. Perhaps the most interesting correspondences between film and fiction are, as in Mantel's novels, moments of 'visual emotion' in which our attention is drawn to what characters *think* they see and in which the difficulty of understanding what is before them is real cognitive labour for character and reader:

> At first ... she saw nothing at all. The only light was from a single green-glass desk lamp which illuminated little more than the tooled leather surface on which it stood. When she took another few steps she saw them, dark shapes in the furthest corner. Though they were immobile, her immediate understanding was that she had interrupted an attack, a hand-to-hand fight. The scene was so entirely a realisation of her worst fears that she sensed that her over-anxious imagination had projected the figures onto the packed spines of books. The illusion, or hope of one, was dispelled as her eyes adjusted to the gloom.[33]

Bryony's optical and cognitive challenge in this novel is to distinguish between violence and desire. In this mise-en-scène we can observe filmic editing and intercutting between Bryony and what she peers at (the lamp, the leather surface, 'them', an attack, the figures, shelves, the gloom). The film adaptation renders this exactly through intercutting and again makes us wonder, progressively, what Bryony sees and what she is thinking as a thin beam of light from the desk lamp falls across her face and torso in a tightly edited chiaroscuro scene that alternates between her and the 'dark shapes'. In the novel, we should be alert to the quasi-voiceover full of Freudian and cinematic vocabulary (scene, realisation, imagination, projection): this cannot come from young Bryony's mind, but is from the retrospective script of a much older, knowing narrator, who also notices a 'tooled' leather surface. Such hints change the lenses in McEwan's narrative, drawing attention to the constructedness of its vision; the direction and cinematography of the story. Let us return here once more to Virginia Woolf's early insight about the cinema: – 'if so much of our thinking and feeling is connected with seeing there must be some residue of visual emotion not seized by artist or painter-poet which may await the cinema'. What we can certainly observe about contemporary fiction is that this connection with seeing and this opportunity for 'visual emotion' or visualised thought has indeed been seized in a variety of ways. Film has made fiction see more; in turn, filmic fiction has made us see more when we read.

Notes

1. S. Eisenstein, 'Dickens, Griffith, and the Film Today (1944)' in J. Leyda (ed.), *Eisenstein. Film Form: Essays in Film Theory* (New York: Meridian, 1949), pp. 198, 200, 202.
2. V. Woolf, 'The Cinema (1926)' in D. Bradshaw (ed.), *Virginia Woolf: Selected Essays* (Oxford University Press, 2009), p. 173.
3. J. Conrad, *The Nigger of the Narcissus*, ed. R. Kimbrough (New York: Norton, 1979), p. 147 (emphasis in the original).
4. Woolf, 'The Cinema', p. 174.
5. R. Stam, and A. Raengo, 'Introduction' in *Literature through Film* (Oxford: Blackwell, 2004), p. 45; C. Geraghty, *Now a Major Motion Picture: Film Adaptations of Literature and Drama* (Plymouth: Rowman & Littlefield, 2008), p. 5. For the turn away from fidelity, translation or transposition in adaptation studies, see, for instance, D. Cartmell and I. Whelehan (eds), *The Cambridge Companion to Literature on Screen* (Cambridge University Press, 2007); T. Leitch, *Film Adaptation and Its Discontents* (Baltimore, MD: Johns Hopkins, 2007); and J. M. Welsh and P. Lev (eds), *The Literature/Film Reader: Issues of Adaptation* (Plymouth: Scarecrow, 2007).
6. P. Brooker, 'Postmodern Adaptation: Pastiche, Intertextuality and Re-Functioning' in Cartmell and Whelehan (eds), *The Cambridge Companion to Literature on Screen*, pp. 109–10.
7. D. Petrie, 'Trainspotting the Film' in B. Schoene (ed.), *The Edinburgh Companion to Irvine Welsh* (Edinburgh University Press, 2010), p. 43.
8. L. Hutcheon, *A Theory of Adaptation* (London: Routledge, 2006), p. 122.
9. *The Film Programme* (2017).
10. C. Craig, 'Rooms without a View' (1991) 1(2) *Sight and Sound* 10–14, 11.

11. A. Higson, *English Heritage, English Cinema: Costume Drama since 1980* (Oxford University Press, 2003); and L. Cooke, *British Television Drama: A History*, 2nd edn (London: BFI/Palgrave, 2015), p. 177–80.
12. C. Monk, 'The British Heritage-Film Debate Revisited' in C. Monk and A. Sargeant (eds), *British Historical Cinema: The History, Heritage and Costume Film* (London: Routledge, 2002), pp. 189–90.
13. A. Hollinghurst, *The Line of Beauty* (London: Picador, 2004), p. 434.
14. *Ibid.*, p. 435.
15. *Ibid.*, p. 90.
16. *Ibid.*, p. 486.
17. K. Ishiguro, *The Remains of the Day* (London: Faber & Faber, 1993), p. 149.
18. *Ibid.*, pp. 66, 105.
19. *Ibid.*, p. 147.
20. *Ibid.*, p. 148.
21. *Ibid.*, p. 152.
22. *Ibid.*, p. 153.
23. *Ibid.*, p. 154.
24. G. Rose, 'Beginnings of the Day: Fascism and Representation' in B. Cheyette and L. Marcus (eds), *Modernity, Culture and 'the Jew'* (Cambridge: Polity, 1998), p. 250.
25. A. S. Byatt, 'Morpho Eugenia' in *Angels and Insects* (London: Vintage, 1995), p. 155 (emphasis in the original).
26. *Ibid.*, p. 156 (emphasis in the original).
27. Z. Smith, *NW* (London: Penguin, 2013), p. 279.
28. *Ibid.*, p. 269.
29. H. Mantel, *Bring Up the Bodies* (London: Fourth Estate, 2013), p. 434.
30. *Ibid.*, p. 13.
31. I. McEwan, *Atonement* (London: Jonathan Cape, 2001), p. 40.
32. Y. Griggs, 'Writing for the Movies: Writing and Screening *Atonement*' in D. Cartmell (ed.), *A Companion to Literature, Film and Adaptation* (Oxford: Blackwell, 2012), pp. 345–58.
33. McEwan, *Atonement*, p. 123.

PART IV

Contexts

11

BEN MASTERS

The Mid-Atlantics

'I Pitched My Voice Somewhere in the Mid-Atlantic'

In a eulogising essay following the death of John Updike in 2009, Ian McEwan wrote: 'American letters, deprived in recent years of its giants, Bellow and Mailer [and now Updike], is a levelled plain, with one solitary peak guarded by Roth.'[1] Philip Roth would go on to announce his retirement from writing in 2012 and passed away in 2018, thus eradicating the final face from McEwan's literary Mount Rushmore. McEwan's friends and peers, Martin Amis and Julian Barnes, similarly wrote eulogies for Updike; just as McEwan and Christopher Hitchens (another member of their literary set) had done for Saul Bellow in 2005 ('What other American novelist', asked Hitchens, 'has had such a direct and startling influence on non-Americans young enough to be his children?'[2]), while Amis and McEwan both spoke at Bellow's memorial in New York. Amis also wrote an account of Roth's oeuvre the year after his retirement,[3] and followed this with an appreciation after his death, while McEwan remembered Roth on BBC Radio.[4]

Thus, in the early years of the twenty-first century, three of Britain's most acclaimed and criticised novelists – Amis, Barnes and McEwan – found themselves reflecting on the enormous influence of a senior generation of American writers now passed, and were perhaps left wondering where this placed their own generation on the altered literary landscape. Certainly, Zadie Smith, one of the major-voices-to-be of a new twenty-first-century literary generation, regarded Amis, Barnes and McEwan as a collective in its own right: 'Better to cultivate a cipher-like persona, be a featureless squib called Mart, Jules, Ian', writes Smith in her debut novel, *White Teeth* (2000), suggesting her indebtedness in perhaps the way they would most appreciate – ironically.[5] Smith was not the first to identify these writers as a group or gang. Since at least the 1980s the media has imagined them as an exclusive all-male group of cronies and sometimes rivals, also including Salman Rushdie and Hitchens among their ranks (both of whom became American citizens), as well as the poets Craig Raine and James Fenton, and more senior figures like Clive James and Ian Hamilton. Many of these writers were first corralled under the stewardship of Hamilton at the *New Review* in the 1970s, attending 'boozy' lunches that have become the stuff of literary legend,[6] and worked together in various combinations on publications like the *New Statesman* and the *Times Literary Supplement* through the 1970s and 1980s; some shared agents, editors and publishers (McEwan, Amis, Barnes and Rushdie have all been published by Jonathan Cape for the majority of their careers); and have gone to bat for one another in the media on numerous occasions. Ever since Amis, Barnes, McEwan and Rushdie became four of the headline figures on Granta's influential first Best of Young British Novelists list in 1983, this group has cast an inordinate shadow over the British literary world, often to the irritation of other writers and reviewers. But although journalists have been quick to view them as a peer group (to be gossiped about almost as much as critiqued), Amis, Barnes, McEwan *et al.* have never been formally evaluated as a substantive literary coterie. (In fact, very little critical work has been done on late-twentieth-century and twenty-first-century literary sets at all.) This needs correcting, for Amis *et al.* have fundamentally shaped one another's careers as well as the wider literary landscape. There are, of course, differences in their writing styles, but they do share many intellectual preoccupations, philosophical and political views, and attitudes about aesthetics, and have helped to evolve the novel form in particular directions.

One of the most significant characteristics that binds their work together is the extent to which it has been influenced by American literature. It was a commonplace of literary criticism of the 1970s, when these writers were first establishing themselves, to play the British novel against the US novel. Bernard Bergonzi in his influential *The Situation of the Novel* (1970) contrasted 'the prevalent English non-style' with American 'panache';[7] while Tony Tanner's *City of Words* (1971) implicitly found greater ambition and vitality in the American post-war novel. Certainly, younger British writers coming up in the 1970s recognised a fundamental difference between the home-grown novel and the exports arriving from across the Atlantic. McEwan has recalled how encountering American writers like Roth, Updike, Bellow, Norman Mailer and William Burroughs as a student at UEA had a profound effect on him. 'The American novel seemed so vibrant compared to its English counterpart at the time. Such ambition, and power, and barely concealed craziness. I tried to respond to this crazed quality in my own small way, and write against what I saw as the prevailing grayness of English style and subject matter.'[8] Updike and Roth, McEwan has said, have 'loomed over my writing life'.[9] Likewise, Amis recalls how at the start of his career, 'the English novel was very depressed: it was 225 pages on the ups and downs of the middle classes. The American novel was huge, like a Victorian novel';[10] and Barnes, when asked to distinguish American fiction from

British, says that 'American fiction displays scope, audacity, and linguistic vigor'.[11] Barnes identifies as a European writer and talks far more of the grand European tradition than American literature; but for all his bowing to the great French and Russian novelists of the nineteenth and early twentieth centuries, Updike and Roth seem more tangible presences in his work. He is perhaps throwing us off the scent a little when he says: 'American novelists are so different from English novelists. They really are. No point trying to write like them.'[12] Amis, in contrast, has proclaimed that: 'The project is to become an American novelist.'[13]

In the post-war decades, then, American writers seemed to represent verve and gusto as opposed to plainness and restraint; they suggested ambitious ways forward from modernism (for McEwan they 'were free of the shadows of modernism, though they had learned all its lessons'[14]); they were unabashed about grappling with the zeitgeist and what it means to be contemporary; and they exuded the intoxicating gravitas of writing from the centre of power. 'That imperial confidence has now shifted to America', says Amis, 'and you think quite coldbloodedly, quite selfishly, I want some of that. I want the amplitude that is no longer appropriate to England.'[15]

Accurate or inaccurate – certainly crude – these generalisations about American and British literature appeared to hold sway for the younger British novelist of the 1970s and 1980s. Rather than falling into the trap of a dubious American versus British essentialism (which Paul Giles's nuanced transatlantic criticism has so persuasively deconstructed), it is worth noting that when Amis, Barnes and McEwan talk of their reverence for the American novel, they are really talking about a very limited pantheon of white male writers – namely Bellow, Updike and Roth[16] – who could not be said to stand for the American novel in general. In fact, they are too individualistic to ever be flag-bearers for anything much at all. Nevertheless, I would suggest that they represent what American influence came to mean for Amis, Barnes and McEwan.

That's not to say that Amis *et al.* are doting acolytes. Indeed, Amis has written many a critical piece on Roth and Updike. But these particular Americans suggested alternative paths for the novel, which had a strong pull for Amis, Barnes and McEwan at the start of their careers and shaped them into the writers they are today. Most importantly, for Amis *et al.*, they had style. Ann Massa and Alistair Stead have noted that Richard Poirier's seminal 1966 study of American literature, *A World Elsewhere*, is subtitled 'The Place of Style in American Literature', and that for such critics 'it is the attention to language and the foregrounding of style that are so frequently perceived as characteristically American'.[17] As we shall see, it is the pure artistry of prose style that Amis, Barnes and McEwan return to again and again in their essays and reviews of their American heroes. Writing about novels like Bellow's *The Adventures of Augie March* (1953) and *Herzog* (1964), Roth's *The Counterlife* (1986), and Updike's Rabbit books seems to turn them into old-fashioned aesthetes. It is as though American writers provide the model for what it means to be a *stylist* – that most lofty and vague of statuses, which brings with it another vaunted role: that of the moralist.

It is the question of style above all that enables us to trace an important lineage (albeit faint and circuitous in places) from Bellow, Updike and Roth to Amis, McEwan and Barnes. Not only does the latter group's readings of the senior American generation offer indirect routes into understanding their own aesthetic development, as well as revealing deflected self-criticisms and insecurities (as critics like James Diedrick, Gavin Keulks, Isabelle Zahar, Victoria N. Alexander and Brian Finney have recognised in Amis's work in particular); but their absorption of American models also points to one of their own greatest legacies – a quasi-Americanisation of the British novel. Indeed, they are of that first generation of British writers to have come of age during the perceived Americanisation of post-war British culture. Perhaps unsurprisingly, transatlanticism is a recurring theme in their work. They have all gone to America in their novels and Amis has even published an entire essay collection on American themes. But in this chapter I am interested in how America gets into the prose. I'm interested in sentence-level transatlanticism and Malcolm Bradbury's notion that 'Amis's own fictional voice and vital style is itself a midatlantic one, filled with street-talk, wise-crack, American easy speaking, mixed in with the elegances and mannerisms of British literary style'.[18] A central claim of this chapter, then, is not only that we need to think of Amis, Barnes and McEwan as part of a definite literary set, but that the development of a mid-Atlantic style is one of their hallmarks.

Towards the High Style

In 1971, Tony Tanner observed that the 'ambiguous relationship of the self to patterns of all kinds – social, psychological, linguistic'[19] was a dominant trope and structural principle in contemporary US fiction, highlighting the work of Thomas Pynchon, John Barth, William Burroughs and other postmodernists as exemplary. Although Bellow and Updike could not be described as postmodern in any conventional sense, a similar concern about the relationship between the individual and larger governing patterns presents itself in their work – especially the encroachments of 'organised power', global politics, rampant capitalism, scientific innovation and cultural revolution on the local self; while in Roth's more postmodern vein the self's vulnerability (in a fairly ambivalent sense) to organising powers of narrative and artifice forms a central theme. In Amis, Barnes and McEwan's work, the tension between individual freedom and governing patterns appears to be simultaneously regretted and relished, creating the prevailing ironies of their work. Much of the regret appears to be for the seeming unviability of humanist values and self-possession in a fragmented late-capitalist world that is haunted by the atrocities of twentieth-century history; while much of the relish comes from the opportunities for authorial expressiveness generated, somewhat paradoxically, by the very diminution of the individual's autonomy, as if contemporary threats to possessed selfhood and personality justify an assertion of rampant authorial personality.

Bellow was instructive for Amis in this regard. 'From Bellow', writes James Wood (another British writer who had a close relationship with Bellow), 'Amis gets his streaming syntax and parenthetical interruptions, his boisterous plurals and compounds'.[20] In Bellow we also find forerunners to Amis's sprung rhythms, jazzy repetitions, poetic excess, and that galvanising movement between the universal and the local, between grand statement and complicating detail, which mobilises his prose. For Amis, these kinds of effect taken in sum are uniquely American: '*Augie March* isn't written in English; its job is to make you feel how beautiful *American* is ... *Augie March*, finally, is the Great American Novel because of its fantastic inclusiveness, its pluralism, its qualmless promiscuity.'[21] But it is Amis's discovery of what he calls the High Style in Bellow's writing that truly liberates his own style:

> [Bellow's] heroes are well tricked out with faults, neuroses, spots of commonness: but not a jot of Bellow's intellectuality is withheld from their mediations. They represent the author at the full pitch of cerebral endeavour ... This careful positioning allows Bellow to write in a style fit for heroes: the High Style.[22]

From Bellow Amis gleans a way to justify authorial presence (i.e. the kinds of poetic expressiveness and ingenuity that break the characterological frame), for Bellow gives his characters 'a shove upwards, hierarchically, towards the grand style'.[23] Something similar has been identified in Amis's writing, particularly in *Money* (1984), by critics like Jon Begley and James Diedrick who explore the political and ethical connotations of the novel's ironic interplay between Amis's fecund rhetorical talents and the narrator's (John Self's) limited perspective.[24] In *Novel Style*, I call this a reversed free indirect style that purposefully shifts the angle of vision by ironising point of view.[25] Something similar to Amis's reversed free indirect style takes place in Barnes's first-person narrators too. Take, for example, *Love, etc* (2000), a novel with a transatlantic theme. Narrated by multiple first-person narrators (one of whom has just returned from several years living in America), there are numerous bursts of that jazzy improvisation of high and low, of the literary and the street-smart, and of the cynically knowing, that we get in Amis, which feels in itself curiously mid-Atlantic. So Barnes's narrators say things like: 'The death of my father, that was a real corners-up day. Some toilsome cyclopaedists of the psyche, earnest calibrators of angst, have apparently estimated that the stress resulting from the death of the father is right up there with the pain of moving house'; 'As I swooped down the sliproad to mingle with the credulous on the motorway, I decided to idle away the dull furlongs with literary genre'.[26] These aren't far in tone and rhythm from Amis's own mid-Atlantic voice. In Amis's adaptation of the Bellovian High Style, and Barnes's comparable first-person overrides, we get the limited point of view of character souped up by the expressive, knowing and often ironising authorial self. This arguably plays out a postmodern take on the illusion of free will, although I will suggest that something more fundamental is going on.

Roth and Updike are equally instructive to Amis, although his relationship to their work is more complex than his assenting devotion to Bellow's. Amis has named their particular kind of writing the Higher Autobiography (an umbrella under which he gathers Bellow too), such that:

> The present phase of Western literature is inescapably one of 'higher autobiography', intensely self-inspecting. The phase began with the spittle of Confessionalism but has steadied and persisted. No more stories: the author is increasingly committed to the private being.[27]

But Amis is suspicious of the writer's life getting into the narrative when it isn't sufficiently transformed from raw experience into some kind of larger artistic form and shape. Through a series of reviews of Roth in the 1970s and 1980s, Amis criticises Roth for being too self-involved.[28] In Amis's estimation, Roth's self-obsession leads to 'compulsive self-circlings'[29] and an inability to sift, select and transform the details that he includes in his prose: 'My Life as a Man', Amis writes, 'sags with the minutiae that belong to life and not to art; it displays a wooden fidelity to the inconsequential, a scrupulousness about detail which isn't significant, merely true.'[30] Similarly in Updike Amis complains of an 'undifferentiated love of detail'.[31] But Updike and Roth push Amis towards defining his own aesthetic principle. For Amis, style is a writer's essence, so that rather than the Higher Autobiography existing at the level of plot or theme, we get a *higher style*; a personal style.

> [Style is] all [the writer's] got. It's not the flashy twist, the abrupt climax, or the seamless sequence of events that characterizes a writer and makes him unique. It's a tone, it's a way of looking at things. It's a rhythm.[32]

According to Amis, it is the style that carries the moral sensibility of the author: 'When I read someone's prose I reckon to get a sense of their moral life.'[33] And Bellow was instrumental in shaping this philosophy. It's when writing on Bellow's *The Adventures of Augie March* that he arrives at the conclusion that style 'is intrinsic to perception ... And style is morality. Style judges. No other writer and no other novel makes you feel surer about this'.[34] This leads Amis to an aesthetic theory that posits style as intensely personal, but also social in its affective reach. Perhaps this is what he means when he says that Updike's finest writing 'wins one's deepest assent; it seems to enlarge the human community'.[35] The personal style is the transformative element, the *art*, because it offers new perceptions and angles of vision, and it both carries and nurtures sensibility, such that authorial individuality might individualise the reader too.

In many ways, Amis's is an old-fashioned humanistic notion of literary morality and value. It embraces the concept of a moral education that is facilitated by the fine attentiveness and rich expression of an elevated author figure – in this sense not dissimilar from the Jamesian model defended by neo-humanist ethical critics like Wayne C. Booth and Martha Nussbaum. Yet Amis's style, which is so volubly expressive of authorial individuality and autonomy, almost spurns character and the very possibility (or even illusion) of characterological autonomy. This creates ethical and aesthetic tensions that differentiate Amis's writing from Updike's and Bellow's. Indeed, Updike said of Amis that he 'writes out of a sensibility on the edge of the post-human. His characters strikingly lack the soulful, willful warmth that he admires in Saul Bellow; they seem quick-moving automata'; while *Night Train* and its characters are 'pure diagram, on a blackboard as flat as it is black'.[36] For Updike this is a cop out – a 'convenient category of the less-than-human',[37] leaving him hungering for the more challenging demands of human understanding. After reading *Time's Arrow*, Updike says: 'One wishes for more empathy.'[38] Updike levelled similar criticisms at Barnes too: 'The effect', Updike writes, having grappled with the knowing implied-authorial point of view of *Flaubert's Parrot* (1984), 'is ingenious but not, quite, moving.' In the same review Updike says: 'Whatever we want from novels, we want more than conversation with the author, however engagingly tricksome.'[39] Bellow's fascinatingly knotty and obscure letter to Amis upon reading his *The Information* (1995) echoes Updike's sentiments: 'Page by page the writing gave me pleasure ... The words bowl me over. But I find myself resisting your novel and in the end I back away from it.'[40]

But there is a guardedness to the writing of Amis, Barnes and McEwan (more on whom below) that we rarely find in Bellow, Updike and Roth – what one senses Updike might deem a peculiarly English quality – as if the writer must take pride in being sceptical, knowing, common-sensical, so as not to be taken in by the idealism of the mystical or transcendental. Often, this means protecting oneself with irony. The illusion of control can never quite be given up. Updike remarks on Barnes's recourse to clever literary language in *Flaubert's Parrot* as if it is a defence mechanism against the risks of true feeling: 'The effect is ingenious but not, quite, moving ... By the time the narrator comes clean, we are tired of his voice, by turns arch, quarrelsome, curt, cute, and implausibly literary.'[41] And David Malcolm notes how McEwan adds 'formal vocabulary' into an otherwise looser, more plentiful style in his story 'Homemade'[42] (a story that McEwan has called 'a *very* conscious homage to Roth'[43]). Perhaps this is what James Wood means when he describes 'the old English balance between composure and collapse' in Amis's work.[44]

But the 1980s and 1990s fiction of Amis, Barnes and McEwan intentionally exposes what Dominic Head calls 'the absence of foundational beliefs' in late-twentieth-century society;[45] an absence which undermines the moral, humanist values that justifies the lyrical realism and sentiment of writers like Bellow and Updike. Nevertheless, for all their postmodernist credentials (including the rejection of so-called grand narratives), one senses in Amis *et al.* a yearning for the grandness of their American heroes' visions; a grandness that is fortified precisely by the kinds of fundamental guiding principles that postmodern thinking is so sceptical of – whether it be Bellow's humanistic mysticism, Updike's spiritual metaphysics or even Roth's (albeit conflicted) self-reliance. As Amis says of Bellow's High Style: 'The High Style is not a high style just for the hell of it: there are responsibilities involved. The High Style attempts to speak for the whole of mankind, with suasion, to remind us of what we once knew and have since forgotten or stopped trying to regrasp.'[46] It is the ability of writers like Bellow, Updike and Roth to speak in supposedly large universal terms, to craft wisdom (Barnes called Updike's *In the Beauty of the Lilies* (1996) 'a novel of accumulated wisdom'[47]) at the same time as cultivating an idiosyncratic personal style, which seems to have especial resonance for these younger English writers. This illuminates one of the great animating struggles of their own work: a thwarted desire to speak for humankind, to be moralists in postmodern times when the viability of these positions has been cast in doubt, so that such an aspiration can only ever be a posturing of authority, a pose of universality. As Updike says of Amis's *Time's Arrow*: 'With its cloudy and flirtatious metaphysics, the novel longs for the cleansing old absolutes.'[47]

From Irony to Sincerity

But the longing seems to be half of the point. Rather than being celebratory postmodernists, Amis, Barnes and McEwan are conflicted humanists.

As their careers progress, it is as though their earlier postmodern directions of thought become tempered by a greater faith in the authenticity (though often a conflicted and problematic authenticity) of individual experience; a faith which is partnered by a growing receptiveness to non-ironic modes of sincerity and so-called 'human interest' – what we might call quiddity. This is reflected in their readings of Updike and Bellow, in whose work all three are struck by the flexibility and richness of the free indirect style. 'How masterfully Updike deploys free indirect style', writes Barnes, 'switching us in and out of the main characters' consciousness';[49] 'Like Bellow', says McEwan, 'his only equal in this, Updike is a master of effortless motion – between third and first person, from the metaphorical density of literary prose to the demotic, from specific detail to wide generalization.'[50] It is significant that they are so admiring of this capacity of Updike's and Bellow's prose to render otherness while maintaining its own authorial self-possession (its own authorial high style), especially when this doesn't trigger an ironic interplay between author and character of the kind found in Amis and Barnes's reversed free indirect styles. Updike and Bellow's free indirect style pertains to something more collaborative than combative, such that the attentive depiction of the material world in all its peculiar detail, texture and quiddity can speak to a grander metaphysics without collapsing into a weightless relativism or the despair of isolated subjectivity. And the key to this is how the free indirect style, in Sianne Ngai's compelling paraphrasing of Amanda Anderson, epitomises '[t]he novel's investment in the tension between life and theory'.[51]

The tension between life and theory is characteristic of Barnes's writing of the twenty-first century. In novels like *Arthur & George* (2005) and *The Sense of an Ending* (2011), there is a movement away from the wryness and trickiness of his previous work towards a quasi-humanistic vision of the world, which relies less on satire and irony (though traces remain) and more on feeling and sentiment. The latter novel tells the story of Tony Webster, a retiree whose life is up-ended when he learns of the suicide of an old school friend. Like many of Barnes's narrators and characters, Tony is an inveterate theoriser: 'Eventually, I came up with a theory'; 'I could only reply that I think – I theorise – that something – something else – happens to the memory over time'.[52] Tony's longing for wisdom cues many familiar Barnesian traits: the perpetual arrivals at aphorism, the barbs of sardonic observation and the rhetorical addresses to an imagined reader or listener. Certainly, Tony is obsessed with logic and knowledge, driven by a dry – sometimes morose – skepticism that feels oddly English, and accordingly he pursues classic Barnesian themes. But it all seems finessed by an Updikean texture and tone that allows for greater doubt, surprise and wonder than in

Barnes's earlier work. Even the list of remembered sense impressions that are detailed at the start of the novel and braid the narrative throughout has a lucid particularity that feels redolent of Updike's way of looking at the world:

> I remember in no particular order: ... gouts of sperm circling a plughole, before being sluiced down the full length of a tall house ...[53]

> Lying spent and adrift he listens again to the rain's sound, which now and then quickens to a metallic rhythm on the window glass, quicker than the throbbing in the iron gutter, where ropes of water twist.[54]

Indeed, Barnes was re-reading Updike in the years preceding the publication of *The Sense of an Ending*, as he tells us in the two essays he wrote upon Updike's death in 2009, which feel like cribs for his own novel, especially in their focus on Updike's themes of transience and disillusionment.

There is also something of Updike's tone of spiritual yearning in Tony's search for clarity and meaning, not least in the pathos of his attempts to understand so much unknowability. This gives the novel a different kind of sincerity from the quasi-satirical comedy and gamesmanship of novels like *Flaubert's Parrot*, *A History of the World in 10½ Chapters* (1989), *Talking it Over* (1991), *England, England* (1998) and *Love, etc.* It is as though Barnes allows for greater sentiment (though his narrator resists it) than in his earlier work – something that Bellow, Updike and Roth seem far more comfortable in expressing in their own work. What we get in *The Sense of an Ending*, then, is a realisation that empathy requires more than intellectual manipulations of point of view. This is a dawning lesson for Tony: 'I sat on the train home not thinking at all, really, just feeling. And not even thinking about what I was feeling. Only that evening did I begin to address what had happened.'[55] Tony's journey is one towards depth and the knowledge that experience will always exceed one's attempts to contain it. But rather than resulting in wry postmodern despair or ironic knowingness, this is something that the novel (and eventually Tony) embraces. As Tony admits towards the novel's end: 'I don't know if there's a scientific explanation for this – to do with new affective states reopening blocked-off neural pathways. All I can say is that it happened, and that it astonished me.'[56] At last, life is allowed to get one over on theory.

There is a subtle shift in style and emphasis in the twenty-first-century work of McEwan too. McEwan himself has contrasted the early and later periods of his career. In the 1970s and early 1980s he 'looked for extreme situations, deranged narrators, obscenity and shock – and to set these elements within a careful or disciplined prose'.[57] In this we sense Roth's influence; indeed, McEwan has called his story 'Homemade' 'a genuflection in the direction of Roth's Portnoy'.[58] (Roth's *Portnoy's Complaint*, with its linguistic licence and shock value feels like something of a ur-text for all three authors' earliest books.) But like Roth in his later work, McEwan becomes increasingly preoccupied with the interplay between public and private, between the individual and larger historical forces. This is true of McEwan's writing from at least the late 1980s, but it is accompanied by a denser lyrical realism that reaches its pinnacle in his twenty-first-century work. 'Now I take a completely opposite view', he has said, reflecting on the existential minimalism of his early work: 'I think that the lifeblood of the novel is, in fact, much to do with the specific, the local, the actual, the naming of things.'[59] The change is prominent in 2001's *Atonement* (of which Updike wrote a praising review) and continues in McEwan's most self-consciously Bellovian and Updikean novels, *Saturday* (2005) and *Solar* (2010), which take their tone-setting epigraphs from Bellow and Updike respectively.

The Updike epigraph to *Solar* reads: 'It gives him great pleasure, makes Rabbit feel rich, to contemplate the world's wasting, to know the earth is mortal too.' McEwan has acknowledged the extent to which his antiheroic protagonist, Beard, is a descendent of Updike's Rabbit. Rabbit 'was the example at my side', he says, and refers to Updike's 'heightened realism', which 'gives Rabbit [Updike's] ... thoughts, and yet somehow ... makes them plausibly Rabbit's'[60] – again reflecting these authors' preoccupation with reconciling elaborate authorial rhetoric with limited characterological points of view. But more than sharing Rabbit's appetites and imperfections – and therefore his raw humanity – Beard shares Rabbit's symbolic power, embodying the fraught relationship between the personal and global. Beard's wasting body and failed resolutions (in love and in life) become allegories for large-scale issues (particularly climate change) and our inability to solve them.

As the Updike epigraph intimates, in *Solar* McEwan finds the personal within the universal and vice versa. Bellow's example offers something similar to *Saturday* which takes its epigraph from *Herzog*:

> For instance? Well, for instance, what it means to be a man. In a city. In a century. In transition. In a mass. Transformed by science. Under organised power. Subject to tremendous controls. In a condition caused by mechanization. After the late failure of radical hopes. In a society that was no community and devalued the person. Owing to the multiplied power of numbers which made the self negligible ...

Although the prose here is unusually clipped for Bellow, its inclusion in *Saturday* alerts us to the dawning of a wider perspective in McEwan's work – a scoping of the grand stage, letting the global and the cosmic into the living room. This is the novel's neuroscientist protagonist, Henry Perowne, looking out of the window from his Fitzrovia home:

> Standing here, as immune to the cold as a marble statue, gazing towards Charlotte Street, towards a foreshortened jumble of facades, scaffolding and pitched roofs, Henry thinks the city is a success, a brilliant invention, a biological masterpiece – millions teeming around the accumulated and layered achievements of the centuries, as though around a coral reef, sleeping, working, entertaining themselves, harmonious for the most part, nearly everyone wanting it to work. And the Perownes' own corner, a triumph of congruent proportion ... an eighteenth-century dream bathed and embraced by modernity, by street light from above, and from below by fibre-optic cables, and cool fresh water coursing down pipes, and sewage borne away in an instant of forgetting.[61]

As well as an enlarging of perspective, *Saturday* reveals McEwan honing an even finer capacity for close-up, for the minute and forensic, as though the novelist can do what scientists cannot: marry the widescreen of general relativity with the extreme zoom of quantum mechanics. And so Perowne – who forms the central consciousness of the novel (a novel that pays fidelity to modernist modes of interiority to a degree that Amis and Barnes's fiction never really has) – watches a burning object lighting up the night sky. This triggers a narrowing of focus: 'In the first moment, in his eagerness and curiosity, he assumes proportions on a planetary scale: it's a meteor burning out in the London sky ...'; 'In an instant, he revises his perspective outward to the scale of the solar system ... It's a comet'. Then comes a contraction: 'he revises the scale again, zooming inwards this time, from solar dust and ice back to the local'.[62] And it is with this final revision that he realises he is watching a burning airplane crashing towards earth: 'It's directly south of him now, barely a mile away, soon to pass into the topmost lattice of the bare plane trees, and then behind the Post Office Tower, at the level of the lowest microwave dishes.'[63] In *Saturday*, McEwan relishes the metaphysical possibilities of manipulated magnitudes and proportions. (Amis too, following Bellow's lead, obsesses over the cosmic perspective in novels like *London Fields* (1989), *The Information* and *Night Train* (1997).) These novels assume the grandeur of cosmic and historic scale against which Updikean and Bellovian characters so often bristle. And as McEwan learnt from Bellow: 'These elements are not dealt with in abstract, but sifted through the vagaries of character.'[64] All of this is enabled by the license of a more lyrical and busy prose style than we find in McEwan's earlier work, indulging in the 'heightened realism' of the kind he associates with the great American writers. Most of McEwan's twenty-first-century writing, in fact, is packed with carefully patterned repetitions (double takes, tricolon, hesitations and feints) and compulsive listing, as well as qualifying interruptions, parentheses and interpolations – some of Amis's favourite techniques – so that the prose takes on a far more improvisatory feel than the hard, cool prose of his first stories and novels. Indeed, the writing feels more Updikean and Bellovian. It feels mid-Atlantic.

Stylists

The evolution of a prose style for these writers is a momentous thing. Reading their literary criticism, one could be forgiven for thinking that everything takes place in style. Again and again they circle back to form, to the sentence, to prose. Barnes calls Roth's *The Counterlife* 'fizzing and formally audacious'[65] and talks about 'the hushed Joyceanism' of Updike's *Rabbit Run*;[66] Amis calls *The Counterlife* 'a work of such luminous formal perfection that it more or less retired post-modern fiction', and proclaims that 'Roth's sentences are dapper and sonorous'.[67] Bellow's 'sentences simply weigh more than anybody else's'; and Updike is 'perhaps the greatest virtuoso stylist since Nabokov'.[68] McEwan enthuses about 'the miraculous lacquer of [Updike's] prose',[69] the 'pulse of [Bellow's] prose'[70] and praises Updike's 'routinely brilliant adjective-noun couplings, and sentence rhythms fine tuned to a poet's ear'.[71] It's as though style is the vehicle for all meaning. In this sense, Amis, Barnes and McEwan are aesthetes. And it is noticeable that their criticism hardly ever reflects (at least not explicitly) on the politics of style; nor does it seriously question where style might come from (i.e. how it might stand for inherited modes of thinking or other unexamined dynamics). For these writers style relates back to the author's vision. They have little time for deconstructive complications like the death of the author.

It is as though in the absence of 'foundational beliefs' the self retreats into individual style. Perhaps such a dynamic has always characterised the novel form. It is fundamental to the novel's ethical secularism. Fredric Jameson recognises something similar in modernist writing (although he would probably deny Amis *et al.* the status of individual style, being writers of the postmodern period), while Geoffrey Hill takes a similar line of thought all the way back to the humanist prose writers of the sixteenth century:

> It is as if the effort 'to translate wisdom into political action' which baffled humanists like Elyot and Starkey translates itself, in the prose of Nashe and Burton, into the praxis of an individual style. The energy has to go somewhere; since it cannot realize itself as a legislative act, it turns back into the authority and eccentricity of style itself.[72]

Like Hill's great humanists of the early modern period, one senses in Amis *et al.*'s fiction – as well as in their extra-literary commentary – the desire to 'speak for the whole of mankind'; to have a kind of authority that is at the very least unfashionable in our current times. And so the energy 'turns back into the authority and eccentricity of style itself'. But it is a question of degree rather than of kind that marks Amis, Barnes and McEwan out. If they are frustrated humanists in search of a greater, universal meaning at a time when such a notion has been radically destabilised, then in place of 'the old cleansing absolutes' we get the near (and not unproblematic) elevation of style to something like an absolute value. As Amis says, '[Style is] all [the writer's] got'.

This kind of principled stylism has been extended in different directions by a younger generation of British writers influenced by American literature, as well as by Amis, Barnes and McEwan themselves. Amis in particular (mostly 1980s Amis) towers over the contemporary British novel. Zadie Smith has described (somewhat facetiously) how she was 'busy plagiarising' Amis as a young writer,[73] and her early novels certainly suggest a degree of influence;[74] and Nicola Barker has called Amis her literary 'Daddy'.[75] Adam Thirlwell, whose early literary mentor, Craig Raine, is another member of the Amis, Barnes, McEwan literary set, has often been compared to Amis, while his personal blend of European and American influences is reminiscent of Barnes's cosmopolitan style. David Mitchell (whose Amisian tendencies I have adumbrated elsewhere[76]) even appears to model one character on Amis in his 2014 novel *The Bone Clocks*, and the compilation technique of several of his books blurs the lines between story collection and novel in a way that recalls Barnes's approach in *A History of the World in 10½ Chapters*, just as his multi-voiced narratives could draw useful comparison to Barnes's *Talking it Over* and *Love, etc.*

Rushdie also needs mentioning in this context of influence. Rushdie was a later member of the Amis, Barnes, McEwan set and is a writer so tangibly influenced by a larger body of world literature that he exceeds this mid-Atlantic frame of reference, such that I haven't discussed him here. Nevertheless, he too has drawn upon a similar pantheon of US writers (especially Bellow and Roth, but also Pynchon) and, like with Amis, this has contributed to an elaborate style of excess. Rushdie's international style has been a considerable influence on later writers like Smith, Mitchell and Hari Kunzru (the latter of whom has expressed more sceptical views on Amis *et al.*, although Carol Ann Duffy described his 2004 novel, *Transmission*, as 'like the young Martin Amis, only nicer'[77]) – all writers with their own mid-Atlantic credentials. It is also important and refreshing that this broadly conceived generation of younger British writers takes a more diverse and inclusive position on US literature, calling upon writers like Zora Neale Hurston, Toni Morrison, James Baldwin, Ursula Le Guin and Ralph Elison, in addition to Roth, Bellow and Updike. And whereas Amis *et al.* look upwards to American elders rather than across to US writers that we might think of as their direct contemporaries, many of the younger writers I have mentioned sit comfortably in their own contemporary mid-Atlantic context with American peers like Dave Eggers, Jonathan Safran Foer and David Foster Wallace – often writing alongside one another in the same publications[78] so that twenty-first-century mid-Atlanticism feels more like a two-way, contemporaneous dynamic.

Nevertheless, Amis *et al.*'s limited group of literary heroes remains influential. For example, Smith and Thirlwell have both written and spoken about Bellow and Nabokov, whose impacts still reverberate today. And more generally there is a prevailing interest in the substance and centrality of style, which feels like a continuation of Amis *et al.*'s aesthete sensibility. Smith has called style 'a writer's way of telling the truth' and has argued that '[a] writer's personality is his manner of being in the world: his writing style is the unavoidable trace of that manner',[79] exploring the morality and politics of style in her essays, as well as in novels like *On Beauty* (2005) and *NW* (2012). Thirlwell's *Miss Herbert* (in which he calls style 'a quality of vision; a soul'[80]) is in some respects a five-hundred-page meditation on style, with full chapters on Bellow and Nabokov. In many ways, then, they are extending the discussions and preoccupations of Amis *et al.* before them, although I would argue that this younger generation of writers is more attuned to the political implications of style, particularly as it relates to questions of identity.

Returning to Amis, Barnes and McEwan, what is striking about their work is the fact that they have developed comparable directions of thought while belonging to a distinctive literary set – something which begs more socio-historic interrogation than I can manage here. For all the explanatory systems of science and politics that McEwan's novels explore, or the weighty themes that Amis is drawn to (the Holocaust, Stalinist Russia, nuclear weapons, environmental crises, the sexual revolution), or Barnes's philosophising over memory, time and death, there is a basic, shared assumption in their work that it is in fact the style that carries the true value; because it is the style that registers the material and embodies an individual's fallible though sincere truth (an assumption expanded upon by the younger generation of stylists in this century). It is also the style that, while being openly expressive of its own conditionality, can make connection with an imagined other. Which is something, I would suggest, they derive from their appreciation of the American writers of the generation before them (remember, Updike's prose 'seems to enlarge the human community'). All of this could be taken for obsessive formalism. But within Amis, McEwan and Barnes's writerly admiration for Bellow, Updike and Roth's craft – indeed, bound up with it – is a deep respect for their ethical richness and singular authority. Because, for Amis, Barnes and McEwan, the style *is* the authority, the morality, the meaning – or the closest thing possible.

Notes

1. I. McEwan, 'On John Updike', *New York Review of Books* (2009), p. 4, www.nybooks.com/articles/2009/03/12/on-john-updike/. Note that the quote in the heading above is taken from M. Amis, *Money* (London: Jonathan Cape, 1984), p. 196.
2. C. Hitchens, 'Giant Steps', *The Guardian* (2005), www.theguardian.com/books/2005/apr/10/fiction.saulbellow1.
3. M. Amis, 'Martin Amis on Philip Roth', *Guardian*, 26 May (2018), https://www.theguardian.com/books/2018/may/26/martin-amis-on-philip-roth-the-kind-of-satirical-genius-that-comes-along-once-in-a-generation.
4. M. Amis, 'His Subject, Himself', *New York Times* (2012), www.nytimes.com/2013/10/20/books/review/claudia-roth-pierponts-roth-unbound.html.
5. Z. Smith, *White Teeth* (London: Hamish Hamilton, 2000), p. 251.
6. See J. Barnes, *Nothing to Be Frightened of* (London: Vintage, 2009), p. 79; C. Hitchens, *Hitch-22* (London: Atlantic, 2010), pp. 168–73; and C. James, *North Face of Soho* (London: Vintage, 2007), pp. 138, 187.
7. B. Bergonzi, *The Situation of the Novel* (London: Macmillan, 1970), p. 69.
8. R. Roberts (ed.), *Conversations with Ian McEwan* (Jackson, MS: University Press of Mississippi, 2010), p. 91.
9. *Ibid.*, p. 119.
10. M. Amis, 'Martin Amis: I Wasn't Trying to Impress My Father', *Salon* (2013), www.salon.com/2013/07/23/martin_amis_partner/.
11. V. Guignery and R. Roberts (eds), *Conversations with Julian Barnes* (Jackson, MS: University Press of Mississippi, 2009), p. 76.
12. *Ibid.*
13. Z. Leader (ed.), *On Modern British Fiction* (Oxford University Press, 2002), p. 3.
14. Roberts, *Conversations with Ian McEwan*, p. 160.
15. M. Bradbury and J. Cooke (eds), *New Writing* (London: Minerva, 1992), vol. 1, p. 182.
16. A. S. Byatt has observed how this obsession with the glamour of American prose seems to be a strangely male impulse (Leader, *On Modern British Fiction*, p. 3).
17. A. Massa and A. Stead (eds), *Forked Tongues* (London: Longman, 1994), p. 3.
18. M. Bradbury, *Dangerous Pilgrimages: Trans-Atlantic Mythologies and the Novel* (London: Penguin, 1996), p. 481.
19. T. Tanner, *City of Words* (London: Jonathan Cape, 1971), p. 15.
20. J. Wood, *The Broken Estate: Essays on Literature and Belief* (London: Jonathan Cape, 1999), p. 187.
21. M. Amis, *The War against Cliché* (London: Jonathan Cape, 2001), pp. 468–9.

22. M. Amis, *The Moronic Inferno* (London: Jonathan Cape, 1986), p. 5.
23. Amis, *The War against Cliché*, p. 454.
24. J. Begley, 'Satirizing the Carnival of Postmodern Capitalism: The Transatlantic and Dialogic Structure of Martin Amis's Money' (2004) 45(1) *Contemporary Literature* 79–105; and J. Diedrick, *Understanding Martin Amis*, 2nd edn (Columbia, SC: University of South Carolina Press, 2004), pp. 24–7.
25. B. Masters, *Novel Style: Ethics and Excess in English Fiction since the 1960s* (Oxford University Press, 2017), p. 111.
26. J. Barnes, *Love, etc* (London: Jonathan Cape, 2000), pp. 28, 156.
27. Amis, *The Moronic Inferno*, p. 200.
28. 'Will the vision re-expand, as it seems to yearn to do, or will it squirm deeper in to the tunnel of the self?' (*ibid.*, p. 45).
29. M. Amis, *Experience* (London: Jonathan Cape, 2000), p. 176.
30. Amis, *The War against Cliché*, p. 286.
31. *Ibid.*, p. 374.
32. Gourevitch 2008: 347.
33. M. Amis, *Koba the Dread* (London: Jonathan Cape, 2002), p. 90.
34. Amis, *The War against Cliché*, pp. 466–67.
35. *Ibid.*, p. 378.
36. J. Updike, *More Matter* (London: Hamish Hamilton, 1999), pp. 364–5.
37. *Ibid.*, p. 358.
38. *Ibid.*, p. 359.
39. J. Updike, *Odd Jobs* (London: Andre Deutsch, 1992), pp. 631–2.
40. B. Taylor (ed.), *Saul Bellow: Letters* (London: Viking, 2010), p. 523.
41. Updike, *Odd Jobs*, p. 631.
42. D. Malcolm, *Understanding Ian McEwan* (Columbia, SC: University of South Carolina Press, 2002), p. 25.
43. Roberts, *Conversations with Ian McEwan*, p. 161.
44. Wood, *The Broken Estate*, p. 193.
45. D. Head, *Ian McEwan* (Manchester University Press, 2007), p. 15.
46. Amis, *The Moronic Inferno*, p. 5.
47. J. Barnes, 'Grand Illusion', *The New York Times Book Review* (1996), www .nytimes.com/1996/01/28/books/grand-illusion.html.
48. Updike, *More Matter*, p. 362.
49. J. Barnes, *Through the Window* (London: Vintage, 2012), p. 211.
50. McEwan, 'On John Updike'.
51. S. Ngai, *Our Aesthetic Categories* (Cambridge, MA: Harvard University Press, 2012), p. 7.
52. J. Barnes, *The Sense of an Ending* (London: Jonathan Cape, 2011), pp. 94, 120.
53. *Ibid.*, p. 3.
54. J. Updike, *Rabbit Is Rich* (London: Penguin, 1981), p. 111.
55. Barnes, *The Sense of an Ending*, p. 129.
56. *Ibid.*, p. 120.
57. Roberts, *Conversations with Ian McEwan*, p. 91.
58. *Ibid.*, p. 92.
59. *Ibid.*, p. 160.
60. 'Ian McEwan on the Books that Shaped His Novels', http://fivebooks.com/inter view/ian-mcewan-on-books-that-have-helped-shape-his-novels/.

61. I. McEwan, *Saturday* (London: Jonathan Cape, 2005), p. 5.
62. *Ibid.*, pp. 13–14.
63. *Ibid.*, pp. 14–15.
64. I. McEwan, 'The Master', *The Guardian* (2005), www.theguardian.com/books/2005/apr/07/fiction.saulbellow.
65. J. Barnes, 'Philip Roth in Israel', *London Review of Books* (1987), www.lrb.co.uk/v09/no5/julian-barnes/philip-roth-in-israel.
66. Barnes, *Through the Window*, p. 214.
67. Amis, *The War against Cliché*, pp. 296, 285.
68. M. Amis, *The Rub of Time* (London: Jonathan Cape, 2017), pp. 21, 291.
69. I. McEwan, 'Updike's Intimations of Mortality', *Financial Times* (4 February 1995), p. 13.
70. McEwan, 'The Master'.
71. McEwan, 'Updike's Intimations of Mortality', p. 13.
72. G. Hill, *Style and Faith* (New York: Counterpoint, 2003), pp. 54–5.
73. Z. Smith, *On Beauty* (London: Hamish Hamilton, 2005).
74. See Masters 2012: 142.
75. N. Barker, 'A Glorious Confusion', www.powells.com/fromtheauthor/barker.html.
76. B. Masters, 'From the Family', Times Literary Supplement (26 September 2014), p. 19.
77. C. A. Duffy, 'Our Planet, Speeded Up', *Telegraph* (2004), www.telegraph.co.uk/culture/books/3618420/Our-planet-speeded-up.html.
78. See *The Book of Other People* (2007) edited by Smith, and magazines like *McSweeney's* and *The New Yorker*.
79. Z. Smith, 'Fail Better', *The Guardian* (13 January 2007).
80. A. Thirlwell, *Miss Herbert* (London: Vintage, 2009), p. 308.

12

REBECCA POHL

Sexual Dissidence and British Writing

In *Sexual Dissidence* (1991), Jonathan Dollimore traces the history of the word and the concept of perversion to show how what has become a predominantly sexual term started out as a term signifying deviance more broadly, literally 'straying from the path'. Perversion is, in Dollimore's words, 'a concept bound up with insurrection',[1] it is about the challenging of authority, and hence political. He argues that 'perversion is a concept that takes us to the heart of a fierce dialectic between domination and deviation, law and desire, transgression and conformity'.[2] Perversion, while sexualised in modernity, has its roots in political dissidence. It is this politics that Dollimore is interested in recuperating from what he sees as the dominant narrative of perversion as pathology, predicated on Freud's theories. For Freud, perversion in the broadest sense is 'the abandonment of the reproductive function'.[3] This refusal of reproduction renders perversion in its more limited, sexual understanding interesting for cultural materialist approaches, which want to critique social reproduction. Here, the sexual is clearly political.

In the United Kingdom today the term 'dissidence' may sound outdated. We have, after all, witnessed the progressive liberalisation of society over the past decades, in which we have moved steadily towards a more just social order. One of the measures of this progress has been sexual politics, starting with the Sexual Offences Act of 1967, which decriminalised sex between men – so long as this sex happened in private and between men aged at least 21. In 2017, this milestone's fiftieth anniversary was celebrated across the United Kingdom as the marker of a continuously progressive society, where major cultural institutions could package a history of dissent for mass consumption, for instance in the shape of an art exhibition (Tate Modern) or a radio programme (BBC's Gay Britannia). But as David Alderson reminds us, while sexual liberation has – in certain parts of the world – demonstrably taken place, the recent past 'can only reductively be treated as a period of straightforward progress'. Rather, any such progress must be conceived of as 'reconfigurations of power that have accompanied, and even facilitated, that liberalisation'.[4] The critique here is twofold: not only has progress not been 'straightforward' – we might think of Section 28 passed in 1988[5] – in many places dissent, conceived as the struggle leading to 'progress', has been, to use Raymond Williams's terms, incorporated into the dominant social order.

A retrospective on queer art, which suggests that the struggle for queer recognition has concluded, that not only relegates sexual dissidence to the past, but also enfolds it in a national historical narrative to be proud of, is one such example. It illustrates what Herbert Marcuse calls repressive desublimation. For Marcuse, modernity is characterised by the absence of the politically charged tension between cultural production and social reality, a tension he deems crucial for change. He laments '[t]he absorbent power of society' that 'depletes the artistic dimension by assimilating its antagonistic contents' which leads to 'a harmonizing pluralism, where the most contradictory truths peacefully coexist in indifference' to the extent that '[t]hey are no longer images of another way of life but rather freaks or types of the same life, serving as an affirmation rather than negation of the established order'.[6] These 'contradictory truths' can then be displayed to and reproduced for a mass audience and market whose members feel comforted. The protest of the existing order that Marcuse sees as constitutive of art – he calls it 'the Great Refusal'[7] – which resists social reproduction, is incorporated and loses its political charge. Attending the Queer British Art exhibition allows us to feel good about the fact that the subjectivities it puts on display are no longer repressed while evacuating the works of art of their politics of resistance as they are transformed into agents of the reproduction of the established social order, with just a bit more variation. Equal rights are an indicator of this. Meanwhile, struggles over sexuality and citizenship continue (the Northern Irish bakery who refused to supply a cake for a same-sex marriage or the Cornish B&B owners who turned away a gay couple are only two examples) even as certain kinds of sexualities and perversions have been 'absorbed'.

What constitutes 'dissident sexuality' is context-specific. For much of recent history, homosexuality has dominated discourses of dissident sexuality, and it is important to account for the histories and presences of injury and loss tied to queer positionality vis-à-vis a heteronormative social order. As Sarah Brophy and Kasim Husain point out, 'queer belonging is still unresolved, still precarious, with multiple political edges'.[8] It is equally important to acknowledge the fact that sexual dissidence has always encompassed a range of 'perversions'. These might include the spinster, for example, who in her apparent asexuality, refusal of reproductive sexuality and insistence on female autonomy also disrupts the conventional model of sexuality. Following Marcuse's argument of repressive desublimation, the relationship between the dominant and the dissident is prone to shifting. 'Perversions' or queer sexuality are hence not in and of themselves dissident, but can be seen as one among a range of practices in radical anti-patriarchal politics. British fiction of the period under consideration here has explored homosexuality in all kinds of ways, and critics have written widely on the subject. This includes the tension between hedonistic individualism and collective political responsibility that Alan Hollinghurst writes about in *The Swimming-Pool Library* (1988) and *The Line of Beauty* (2004), cross-cultural gay desire and normativity in Hanif Kureishi's *My Beautiful Laundrette* (1986) and troubled masculinity in Pat Barker's *Regeneration* trilogy (1991–95). The subject of much scholarly attention, Jackie Kay's novel *Trumpet* (1998) traces the struggles of non-normative kinship formation across race, sex, sexuality and gender that challenges the dominant social order.[9]

Sexuality and Reproduction

The issue of reproduction has also been central to queer theory. Robyn Wiegman describes the so-called antisocial thesis as 'queer theory's most enduring debate'.[10] The antisocial thesis is a response to the affirmative culture that characterised the pride movement in the late twentieth century, arguing instead for the political value of negativity. Its critique of reproduction is also a helpful way of thinking about 'sexual dissidence' on display in contemporary British fiction. One of its most influential post-millennial renditions is Lee Edelman's polemic *No Future: Queer Theory and the Death Drive* (2004). In it, Edelman argues that queer dissidence can manifest only in the refusal of the figure of the Child which symbolises what he terms 'reproductive futurism', the privileging of heteronormativity as the 'organizing principle of communal relations'.[11] The figure of the queer, by contrast, symbolises 'the bar to every realization of futurity, the resistance, internal to the social, to every social structure or form'.[12] According to his logic, queerness constitutively endangers the central 'presupposition that the body politic must survive'.[13] It is, so to speak, anti-reproductive. José Esteban Muñoz, in his own polemic, also asks, 'Can the future stop being a fantasy of heterosexual reproduction?',[14] but his discussion is oriented towards that future. Like Marcuse, Muñoz sees sexual dissidence as crucial to political change, and artistic production as a key vehicle because 'queer aesthetics map future social relations' and 'the aesthetic fuels the imagination'.[15] To Muñoz, queerness is utopian because it rejects the present and speculates about a concrete alternative future. This means, like Marcuse, and even like Edelman, Muñoz is agitating against the 'reproductive function' and its manifestation as social reproduction. Utopian imaginings, and queerness is utopian thinking and living, work towards this in his reading of the contemporary.

Utopias have a long tradition in British writing, and the literary history of the twentieth century is punctuated by imaginings of the future. One recent example of dystopian British fiction is Sarah Hall's *The Carhullan Army* (2007). Set in an unspecified near-distant future following a global energy crisis that has led to the so-called Civil Reorganisation managed by a sinister Authority, the novel is narrated retrospectively by Sister, a prisoner of the regime. Sister attempts to escape the Authority's totalitarian rule by abandoning her fraught marriage, overcrowded accommodation and alienating work to search for the legendary farm of Carhullan. Carhullan, a self-sufficient, all-female commune of sorts, was already a place of dissent before the current regime came to power, distanced in space and sociality from the dominant order. The women, who are friendly to other women and diffident with men, wear uniform yellow tunics, sell organic produce and are the subject of fierce town gossip, which conflates political and sexual perversions: the women are derided as 'dykes' and 'cunt-lickers' as well as 'communists'.[16] Carhullan itself is described as by turns 'utopian' or 'monastic'.[17] Now, under the Authority, it is even more a symbol of dissent. Located outside of the so-called habitable or safety zone, which spatially marks the boundary of citizenship, the women are Unofficials, a residual resistance in the Cumbrian wilderness. But the logic of othering has not changed, despite the enormous shifts in the dominant. The driver who gives Sister a lift during her escape is aghast when he learns of her destination, likening the women to 'a gang of bloody terrorists' and exclaiming, 'It's sick if you ask me.'[18] It is the threat of sexual dissent, a pathology, that seems more upsetting to him than political resistance, but he frames the former through the latter, binding them together.

One of the key modes of control exerted by the Authority is the disciplining of women's bodies through the forced insertion of contraceptive devices. The novel speaks here to other texts that explore the connection between women's reproductive rights, female sexuality, authoritarian regimes and dissidence, such as Margaret Atwood's *The Handmaid's Tale* (1985), Doris Lessing's *The Cleft* (2007) or Hillary Jordan's *When She Woke* (2011). The contemporary resonance of Atwood's novel is reflected in the recent highly successful television adaptation of the text by Hulu (2017). For Sister, the process of forced contraception is degrading and dehumanising, intensely gendered and highly politicised. When her number comes up, Sister reports to the hospital where she will be 'fitted'.[19] While the hospital staff involved appear nonchalant, the procedure is physically and emotionally painful.

Having been fingerprinted upon arrival, Sister is subsequently haunted by the image of the doctor 'inserting the speculum and attaching the device as efficiently as a farmer clipping the ear of one of his herd'.[20] In fact, the device opens up a temporality of disciplining, as women are subjected to spot checks where monitors force them to 'display themselves' in order to ensure their device is still in place. For Sister, the degradation of the 'fitting' is the final straw rather than the beginning of her political dissidence; for her, too, the two are tightly wound up in each other. She marries Andrew because they share anger and frustration in the face of the governmental crisis and its authoritarian response. One night, after Andrew is beaten up at a demonstration, they have unprotected sex, despite a strict population control policy ('we knew what would happen if I conceived'[21]). However, 'it was the only protest left for us'.[22] In this scenario, it is precisely reproductive futurism that represents one avenue of protest, or dissidence, that threatens the established order, and hence is not reproductive of the social, but disruptive.

Although there are other, explicitly homosexual forms of dissidence in the novel as well, it is female sexuality as forcibly non-reproductive that ultimately serves as the trigger for Carhullan to be transformed from a peaceful, rural community into a women's resistance army. Sister, who like all newcomers to the farmstead tells the women her story, is encouraged by Carhullan's founder, Jackie, to talk about the contraceptive coil and its humiliations. The state exerts its control through women's bodies. The device is turned into a kind of totem, and, passed around during Sister's talk, it ultimately goes missing. That evening marks the beginning of Jackie's explicit, systematic campaign of preparing the women for battle with the aim of besieging and holding the Northern regions via the capital, Rith, in an attempt to overthrow the Authority. And it is the disciplining of women's bodies through their sexuality that motivates the army, even if its leader's motivations remain more oblique. When the device is returned to Sister on the eve of the attack on Rith, the woman who had taken it says, 'I needed something to remind me of why I came here'.[23] The women are decreed 'category-one insurgents' and Sister declares 'we had a duty to liberate society, to recreate it'.[24] The novel does not suggest that sexuality in itself is dissident, but it does show how political dissidence – the imaginary construction of a resistance movement – is bound up with these kinds of sexuality.

The Carhullan Army shows that queer sexuality isn't in and of itself dissident, or socially non-reproductive – it is so in a social order predicated on reproduction. In a non-reproductive social order, reproductive sexuality becomes a possible vehicle for dissidence. This reading is, of course, susceptible to conservative anxieties about reproduction being under threat. Alfonso Cuarón's film *Children of Men* (2006) (loosely adapted from P. D. James's 1992 novel) is one such instance. Here, female infertility has caused the breakdown of civilised society and the emergence of a pregnant refugee is imbued with the aura of a religious miracle that warrants the sacrifice of lives, including those of other women. Although here the pregnant woman's body is protected to the point of death, it is also, in a roundabout way, disciplined, protected only so long as it is the vehicle for new life. The film *Children of Men* proposes that any future is indeed predicated on reproduction which is neither empowering nor liberating nor tied to sexual desire.

In *The Carhullan Army*, anti-reproduction is only one of the ways in which women's bodies are disciplined: the members of Jackie's patrol are subjected to brutal military training regimes that discipline both their bodies and their minds – and their femininity. Political dissidence is here given the form of military discipline. The narrative, then, is not critiquing the disciplining of women's bodies per se so much as the particular form that discipline takes in the hands of the Authority. This ambivalence is carried through to the end of the novel, where Jackie's insurgent army is defeated by the Authority. Nevertheless, despite the defeat, the insurrection and the disciplining that preceded it are worthwhile in the context of the narrative. The book imagines a collectivism outside of capitalist social relations and technological complacency. It does this in part through the idea of wildness. Carhullan is situated in the wilderness which links its dissidence, a form of collectivity, with the uncivilised. Throughout the book, there is an ambivalence about the relation between discipline and indiscipline, or wildness, as elements of dissidence. As Sister first approaches Carhullan, the Cumbrian landscape 'verging on wildness' triggers thoughts of Jackie lamenting the 'disunity' encouraged by the current social order and exclaiming: 'It's time for a new society.'[25] There appears to be something radically disruptive about the wilderness, something with social potential.

The notion of wildness has recently gained traction in discourses surrounding sexual dissidence, especially in the work of Jack Halberstam, who builds on conversations with Muñoz and Tavia N'yongo. For Halberstam, wildness as a concept, reclaimed from its colonial history of epistemological and ontological violence, signifies 'queer vitality' – queer life figured as anarchy, or 'what lies beyond current logics of rule': 'a utopian space of play and pleasure'.[26] The term's potential lies in the existential threat it poses to 'the system as a whole',[27] to the social order. Understood in these terms, wildness is a stage, borne out of practice, en route to Muñoz's queer utopia. Hall's women are all engaged in modes of wildness, in sexual dissidence that ruptures the social fabric. Halberstam emphasises two important aspects of this wildness. With Muñoz, wildness offers an anti-colonial critique. Essential to the project is the acknowledgement that not all bodies are marked in the same way. As Halberstam puts it: 'Queerness without wildness is just white homosexual desire out of the closet and in sync with the new normal.'[28] Like Marcuse, Williams, Muñoz and Edelman, Halberstam points to the potential 'appropriative mechanism of neoliberalism' of sexual and political dissidence.[29] His response is to reposition failure as possibility rather than as an endpoint. Wildness then becomes the 'name for the faltering efforts of incorporation, as a name for all that quietly and in insignificant acts picks away at the fabric of hegemony'.[30] In this logic, failure is creative, and one of the crucial arenas for working through the tension between discipline and wildness is art.

Hall revisits this tension in her short story collection *Madame Zero* (2017), again tying it to an ambivalent perspective on pregnancy, birth and abortion. In 'Theatre 6', the second-person narrator, an anaesthetist called out to an obstetric emergency, makes a calculated choice to save the maternal rather than the foetal life. This goes against the law, predicated on the phrase 'God's Jurisdiction'. Where abortion is outlawed, her decision represents an act of political dissidence in another system that has disciplined women's bodies through an insistence on reproductive sexuality. But in the same collection Hall explores the possibility of reproductive sexuality itself constituting a form of dissidence through wildness and indiscipline. In the award-winning story 'Mrs Fox', the narrator's wife metamorphoses into a fox once she is pregnant. Through this metamorphosis social reproduction is disrupted. As the wife, seen as an enticingly unknowable but masterable possession, shifts into a wild creature – pregnancy renders her wild, other – who must ultimately be released into the wilderness, the social system is ruptured. *The Carhullan Army*'s ending suggests a similar logic. The women take and hold Rith, bombing the clinic and executing medical staff, but they ultimately fail inasmuch as they are militarily defeated by an all-too-familiar military-technological complex deployed in support of the Authority. The social order remains in place, but it does not remain intact. Jackie's final order to Sister is to surrender herself to ensure that their story is told: 'Tell them everything about us, Sister. Make them understand what we did and who we were.'[31] The novel is then a performance of this telling, ensuring that the story is kept alive, in circulation.

Retelling Stories

Stories and their telling are, as Alan Sinfield has shown, intensely political: 'Social conflict manifests itself as competition between stories.'[32] He contends that 'the prevailing stories are believed to be the most plausible ones'.[33] This is why cultural production is crucial to any discussion of political resistance, one form of which is sexual dissidence. In Sinfield's understanding, literature is one of the key ways through which belief systems are naturalised, through which individuals and societies arrive at their self-understanding and then organise the social order. The rewriting of familiar stories, literary and historical, has also been one important literary mode of sexual dissidence since the 1980s. One potential starting point for a discussion of this development is the publication in English of the first volume of Michel Foucault's *History of Sexuality* (1978). Another is the publication of two of Angela Carter's seminal texts, *The Bloody Chamber* and *The Sadeian Woman*, shortly afterwards in 1979. All three texts are concerned with the stories Western society tells about sexuality as much as the stories it doesn't tell. Foucault critiques what he sees as the modern mode of confession that constructs the position of the liberated individual in opposition to an earlier historical subject characterised by repression, the purported 'injunction to silence'.[34] He terms this the repressive hypothesis, and instead argues that the period from the seventeenth century onwards witnessed a 'discursive explosion': sexuality was narrativised as never before across medical, social and legal discourses that 'transform ... desire ... into discourse' such that 'Western man has become a confessing animal'.[35] The contemporary mode, claiming a liberated vantage point arrived at through transgressing the taboos surrounding (talk of) sexuality, is shown by Foucault to be a continuation of rather than a rupture with a regime of power predicated on controlling sexuality by systematising it in order better to regulate it. Like the critics already discussed here, Foucault saw this process as the 'incorporation of perversions' and it is in this context that he makes his famous remark: 'The sodomite had been a temporary aberration; the homosexual was now a species.'[36]

Where Foucault critiques the historical narrative surrounding sexuality, Carter approaches the problem of historical narrative and transgressive sexuality through creative practice, by rewriting those narratives. Simultaneously, she acknowledges that her 'fiction is very often a kind of literary criticism'.[37] While frequently invoked to represent a high postmodern aesthetic of apolitical parody, fanciful bricolage and superficiality at odds with both cultural materialism and identity politics, Carter's writing has more recently been recognised for its political commitment. Her own articulation of this bears a striking resemblance to Sinfield's notion of competing stories and the power of stories to normalise certain lives over others. Having read Adorno and Marcuse, Carter articulates her project as a feminist 'investigation of the social fictions that regulate our lives' and declares: 'I believe that all myths are products of the human mind and reflect only aspects of material human practice. I'm in the demythologising business.'[38]

These commitments are very much borne out in her writing. Sexuality is a key component of her feminism, as made evident in her polemic *The Sadeian Woman*. Carter is interested in Sade's writing because 'of his refusal to see female sexuality in relation to its reproductive function'.[39] Her self-titled 'Cultural History' with its 'Polemical Preface' remains a controversial work in Carter's oeuvre. Published during the heyday of the so-called porn wars, *The Sadeian Woman* was criticised for being insufficiently feminist because of its theorisation of women's complicity in the conventional Madonna-whore binary:

> All the mythic versions of women, from the myth of the redeeming purity of the virgin to that of the healing, reconciling mother, are consolatory nonsenses; and consolatory nonsense seems to me a fair definition of myth, anyway. Mother goddesses are just as silly a notion as father gods. If a revival of the myths of these cults gives women emotional satisfaction, it does so at the price of obscuring the real conditions of life. This is why they were invented in the first place. Myth deals in false universals, to dull the pain of particular circumstances.[40]

Carter's dissidence here is double: she deviates from patriarchal conceptualisations of female sexuality as well as refusing to conform to the mode of second-wave feminism dominant at the time. Following the Marxist theorists she reads, this dissidence is grounded in a materialist critique: 'Sexuality, in short, is never expressed in a vacuum.'[41] Hence, its political import.

It is in *The Bloody Chamber* that Carter's intertextual and metafictional narrative strategies come together with her queer and feminist politics as she rewrites conventional narratives of sexual desire and agency. Although the collection has been criticised for simply re-inscribing phallogocentric patriarchy, including male sexual domination and unequal power relations, and has been described as a missed opportunity for queering the form,[42] Carter's retellings do explore perversion – in the sense that Dollimore proposes, of 'a fierce dialectic between domination and deviation'[43] – and wildness, understood as unruly desire. This is especially the case in the stories that investigate what we might call trans-species sexuality, taking the queerness of 'Mrs Fox', where sexual desire is interrupted by metamorphosis, further. 'Wolf-Alice', a retelling of Little Red Riding Hood, culminates with the girl asleep 'between the paws of the tender wolf' after she has not only undressed him on her own initiative, but 'laughed at him full in the face' when he threatens to eat her as the well-worn dialogue between the two characters reaches its climax.[44] This laughter in the face of cliché disrupts the conventional arc of patriarchal sexual agency and desire by which the virginal female body becomes sacrificial. It opens up the possibility for female sexual agency as well as queer forms of desire, but also for narrative control. Little Red Riding Hood is wresting control from the familiar telling of her tale, symbolised by the chorus punctuating the story: 'The wolf is carnivore incarnate.'[45] While the story may end in sexual domination, it is unclear who is dominating who, and it is clear that the girl's desire has been fulfilled as she resists the familiar script.

The narrator of 'The Tiger's Bride', a reimagining of Beauty and the Beast, similarly defies the conventional fairy-tale script of Beauty's plight, who takes control of her story through first-person narration. Beauty is fully aware of her gendered position in society, the 'white meat of contract'.[46] But the figure of Beauty is carefully unstitched from her conventional portrayal. She was 'a wild wee thing' whose nurse 'could not tame [her] into submission', and whose laugh is remonstrated as unladylike.[47] It is this laugh, 'a raucous guffaw'[48] reminiscent of Little Red Riding Hood's outburst, that signals Beauty's resistance to the position of sacrificial virgin in the face of the voracious beast who requests to behold her immaculate flesh. She will not submit passively to the patriarchal gaze. But this Beast is himself an inversion of the script, not a man trapped in a monstrous body, but a ferocious tiger masquerading as a man. When the Beast bares himself to Beauty in the snowy wilderness, 'Nothing about him reminded [her] of humanity'[49] and '[t]herefore' she, too, strips bare. She controls the gaze here, she gains agency, and it is this inhumanity, the fact that he is not a participant in the patriarchal economy that barters women's bodies, that stirs her desire.[50] The story ends with Beauty walking into the Beast's lair and being transformed, through the licks of his tongue, into a beast herself while the walls of the palazzo, symbols of the classic tale, 'disintegrate' around her reminding us of the valet's earlier remark that '[n]othing human lives here'.[51]

Patricia Duncker's suggestion that Carter 'could never imagine Cinderella in bed with the Fairy Godmother'[52] may here seem accurate – and Emma Donoghue will remedy this apparent failure of imagination in her rewritings *Kissing the Witch: Old Tales in New Skins* (1993). Duncker's own short stories, *Seven Tales of Sex and Death* (2003), as well as her 2002 novel *The Deadly Space Between*, explore the intersection of female sexual agency, queer desire and complicity. Both Donoghue and Duncker represent a more explicitly homosexual dissidence. But Carter's stories are consistent with her artistic and political project of 'demythologising' because they don't shy away from exploring female complicity in systems of heteronormative sexual regulation. As Rebecca Munford has argued, pleasure is the key problematic in Carter's reception. She is an improper feminist in the context of second-wave Anglo-American feminism, who finds 'dual pleasure in profanation and cultural reappraisal'.[53] It is in this context, too, that Carter's engagement with Sade can be seen as 'a serious feminist investigation of [his] contribution as a theorist of sexuality and power – one that does not rest upon a separation of aesthetics and politics, or material reality and representation'.[54] This reading emphasises the politics, and specifically the sexual politics, of Carter's rewritings, whose commitment is to a materialist critique through the form of exuberant textuality that remains concerned with narrative – it matters, the stories we tell.

Retelling stories is one kind of political dissidence. The US-American poet and critic Adrienne Rich famously argued: 'Re-vision – the act of looking back, of seeing with fresh eyes, of entering an old text from a new critical direction – is for us ... an act of survival' because literature is 'a clue to how we live, how we have been living, how we have been led to imagine ourselves, how our language has trapped as well as liberated us; and how we can begin to see – and therefore live – afresh'.[55] Carter similarly speaks of 'putting new wine in old bottles, especially if the pressure of the new wine makes the old bottles explode'.[56] The fairy tale is a form especially suited to Rich's proposition, designed as it is to ensure social reproduction. But there is also an element of joy to resistance, of the anarchic as 'pleasure and play', and this runs through other writing on sexual dissidence.

Jeanette Winterson, who has written about dissident sexualities since the early 1980s and influenced the formation of the field, is another writer who has rewritten narratives of sexuality through fairy tales and tropes, binding together pleasure and dissent, exuberance and critique. Winterson made her debut with *Oranges Are Not the Only Fruit* in 1985, a coming-out narrative that deploys biblical tropes, fairy-tale conventions and a child narrator to chart the pain and absurdity of 'the assumptions in which we are drenched'.[57] Her 1989 novel *Sexing the Cherry* is a postmodern *bildungsroman* of sorts that traces the travels of the ingénu Jordan from gritty seventeenth-century London across a fantastically imagined globe in pursuit of love. One of Jordan's encounters is with the twelve princesses from the Grimms' fairy tale. In the Grimms' version, the unruly princesses, who mysteriously dance the nights away despite being securely locked into their chamber by the king each evening, must be corralled into the heteronormative order by the patriarchy. The fairy tale ends with the eldest princess being married off to the soldier who eventually finds out their secret (which is to enjoy themselves with members of the opposite sex and of their class, so not that rebellious, really, but nevertheless insisting on autonomous female desire and sexual agency). Winterson picks up the strand where the Grimms abandon it. In her retelling, the singular narrative is unwound into multifarious narratives of desires, lives lived 'according to our tastes',[58] and together forming a chorus of dissident sexuality. There is the princess who abandons her prince for a mermaid, another one who laments her prince's love of young boys, the princess who is vilified for cohabiting with her young girl lover Rapunzel, and the one whose prince, to her own great delight, turns out to be a woman.

Sexing the Cherry goes beyond the retelling of discrete tales, though. It rewrites the received historical narratives of empire and exploration as stories of sexual and political repression and dissidence. Winterson's earlier novel The Passion (1987) similarly rewrites the conventional historical narrative of the Napoleonic wars from marginalised perspectives, re-inscribing sexuality into history. One of these perspectives is that of the fantastical Villanelle, a Venetian boatman's daughter whose webbed feet – the mark of a boatman's son – trouble the sex binary, whose cross-dressing troubles gender performance and perception, and whose desire for the Queen of Spades troubles heteronormative futurity. Returning to Halberstam's thinking on wildness and the queer, Villanelle's body and desire can be seen 'to challenge the unity of the symbol and to fracture meanings that have coalesced around marked bodies'.[59] This is an explicit challenge marked by the character's resistance to a stable narrative, which in a chorus reminiscent of the cliché deployed by Carter in 'The Company of Wolves' insists: 'I'm telling you stories. Trust me.'[60] The text is making explicit its textuality, in this case a narrative of fantastic bodies and spaces that seems entirely implausible. To use Alderson's words, the novel proposes 'questions of history and narrative as a means of grasping these reconfigurations and evaluating the potential for continuing dissident challenge'.[61]

Sarah Waters's historical novels also stage such an evaluation. Her six novels to date are all concerned with that elusive historical figure Terry Castle has called 'the apparitional lesbian'.[62] Waters writes her into a queer desiring subject across various periods in British history. As Jerome de Groot argues: 'Historical novels critique the hegemonic structure of a totalizing, explaining past.'[63] They trouble the plausible stories that have become culturally habituated. It is, then, unsurprising that Waters has articulated her interest in the form on account of 'the historical novel's capacity for *interference* with literary and cultural models'.[64] This interference is conducted most formally explicitly in The Night Watch (2006), a novel that moves back in time tracing the lives of an ensemble of characters whose dissident desires – lesbian, gay male, adulterous – don't progress towards a queer horizon, a promise of happiness. The novel begins in

1947, when the social order has been restored after its wartime suspension, to find its characters isolated and constrained, unable to live their lives 'according to their tastes'. The novel ends where the stories begin, in 1941, when dissident sexual lives seem possible in the context of a social order whose existence is threatened from outside.

More recently, Joanna Walsh has taken on the genre of the fairy tale in her collection *Grow a Pair: 9 ½ Fairytales about Sex* (2015). Walsh is a writer of experimental fiction, fiction editor at *3:AM Magazine*, and founder of the critical Twitter account @Readwomen (2014–18). Her interlinked fairy tales are absurdly matter-of-fact retellings of undisciplined, wild sexuality that rely on word play and cliché. A girl steals a 'ripe dick' from a 'penis-bush' simply 'because she couldn't resist it'. Said dick 'came off easily in her hand' and swiftly attached to her crotch, though she soon forgets about it – life is busy.[65] In another story, instead of three little pigs living in the forest, 'there lived three big dicks' of varying shapes and sizes who 'were always looking for pussy'.[66] Determined to solve their supply problems, the dicks set about creating pussies first from matchsticks then from Jell-O, both of which fail. When one of them meets a 'cunt' in the wild, however, 'he failed to recognise [her], never having encountered one before'.[67] Elsewhere, the princess is not herself tested by a pea, but tests the country's cocks for 'one that could make itself felt, whatever the circumstances'.[68] When she finally encounters a satisfactory specimen, it will not vacate her vagina and begins to cause trouble by shouting 'prickish' remarks in public.[69] She has to recall its previous owner, himself relieved to be rid of his cock and having caught himself a vagina, they 'still bred in the wild', as well as 'diving for tits'.[70] It is sex between the princess and the transsexual that ultimately resolves the problem, making the dick disappear in the moment of a double female orgasm. This is an instance of what Libe García Zarranz, building on Sara Ahmed's concept of the feminist killjoy, has called 'pleasurable dissent'.[71] Zarranz argues for the importance of 'formulating positive passions, not only as a mode of survival, but also as an act of disobedience'.[72] Walsh's stories relish in their own linguistic, narrative and political waywardness, offering a mode of dissent predicated on pleasure.

Such a recuperation of 'positive passions' might allow us to reframe the work of another queer writer, Ali Smith, in relation to the idea of sexual dissidence. Smith's texts take pleasure in language even while they interrogate its dominant modes, and despite their faith in forging connections – linguistic and personal – they don't offer up an easy promise of happiness. Smith's novels and short stories are populated by non-normative desire, and yet they are rarely read as 'dissident' texts (apart from her queer rewriting of Ovid's Iphis and Ianthe myth, *Girl Meets Boy* (2007)). This is perhaps because of the matter-of-factness with which dissident desire is narrated in her writing. Privileging child narrators and ungendered speakers, her texts rarely narrate a struggle – implicit in the idea of dissidence – or of desire having some meaning or symbolic resonance as resistant to a dominant order. Her texts don't stage the dominant in the same way that Hall's work does, for instance. With their humanist bent, Smith's novels and stories risk tipping over into a notion of universal love, but they are in fact primarily concerned with the politics of recognition and misrecognition. In many of her texts, adolescence is a staging ground for the transition between non-recognition and recognition of desire. 14-year-old George, in *How to Be Both* (2014), for instance, commits to an ethical project of re-watching a particular porn film on her iPad every day in an attempt to acknowledge the young actress's existence, 'in witness'.[73] What is misrecognised by her father as her awkward 'sexual awakening' is in fact a form of solidarity with the actress. It is also a moment in which the absence of desire and hence what might constitute desire and sexuality is recognised by George, who finds herself insistently at odds with the dominant social order.

Conclusion

Many of the texts discussed in this chapter have been nearly seamlessly incorporated into the dominant political regime. Most of them are published by large-scale conglomerate publishing houses primarily concerned with financial returns; Carter and Winterson figure on the A-Level syllabus, recently dedicated to transmitting 'British values'; Smith and Winterson have been the recipients of numerous awards and are regularly invited to speak publicly on arts and politics, performing their cultural authority and absorption into the mainstream. More radical writing takes place elsewhere, in small presses (e.g. Readux, Peepal Tree) or modes other than the literary novel. Walsh's 'experimental digital novella' *Seed*, for instance, is designed for the smartphone. Most queer Black and Asian British writing takes shape as poetry, drama or writing for screen (e.g. the work of Ricki Beadle-Blair, Suniti Namjoshi, Jaqueline Rudet).[74] Narratives of transgender and transsexual experience predominantly find their way in life writing (e.g. Juliet Jacques) or YA fiction.

There has been, across the period under consideration here, a significant shift in the cultural dominant afforded by its incorporation of, among many other things, particular forms of sexual dissidence. Alan Hollinghurst recently remarked in an interview that when he started writing in the 1980s he had 'that sense that I was very fortunate in a way, coming along just as gay lit as a genre was really coming into its own', but that now '[t]he distinctive purpose of gay writing, its political purpose or its novelty or its urgency have gone'.[75] If we take dissident sexuality to signify resistance or threat to dominant forms of social relations, however, it has hardly lost its urgency. We might think here of recent threats to reproductive rights in the United Kingdom and the United States as the political mainstream reorients itself towards the authoritarian. Angela Carter warns against 'consolatory nonsense' which gets in the way of political insurrection. Sarah Hall describes the short story as non-consolatory and an important 'reminder that you ... might end up staring over a precipice'.[76] Her fiction enacts this lack of comfort, making a case for the importance of resistance in the face of and through failure. This is less a move of reducing sexual dissidence to a straight-gay binary, than it is of accounting for sexuality as manifold. Sexuality in itself is not what transforms social relations. However, it is a significant aspect of radical politics. Writing on sexual dissidence since 1980, with its exuberances and its failures to console, actively intervenes in the struggle towards a queer horizon, while reminding us that the stories we tell ourselves are not yet done.

Notes

1. J. Dollimore, *Sexual Dissidence: Augustine to Wilde, Freud to Foucault* (Oxford: Clarendon Press, 1991), p. 103.
2. *Ibid.*
3. S. Freud, *Introductory Lectures on Psychoanalysis*, trans. J. Strachey (Harmondsworth: Penguin, 1973), p. 358.
4. D. Alderson, 'Introduction: Queerwords: Sexuality and the Politics of Culture' (2015) 13 *Key Words: A Journal of Cultural Materialism* 11–16, 11.
5. Section 28 of the Local Government Act 1988 declared that:
   A local authority shall not –
   (a) intentionally promote homosexuality or publish material with the intention of promoting homosexuality; (b) promote the teaching in any maintained school of the acceptability of homosexuality as a pretended family relationship.
   It was only finally repealed across the United Kingdom in 2003.
6. H. Marcuse, *One-Dimensional Man: Studies in the Ideology of Advanced Industrial Society*, 2nd edn (London: Routledge, 2002), pp. 64, 62.
7. *Ibid.*, p. 66.
8. S. Brophy and K. Husain, 'Innovations in Queer Writing' in D. James (ed.), *The Cambridge Companion to British Fiction since 1945* (Cambridge University Press, 2015), p. 96.
9. For examples of these analyses, cf. J. Medd, 'Queer Fiction in Contemporary Britain' in R. DeMaria, H. Chan and S. Zacher (eds), *A Companion to British Literature* (Chichester: Wiley-Blackwell, 2014), pp. 424–39; Brophy and Husain, 'Innovations in Queer Writing'; and M. Richardson, '"My Father Didn't Have a Dick": Social Death and Jackie Kay's *Trumpet*' (2012) 18(2–3) *GLQ* 361–79.

10. R. Wiegman, 'Sex and Negativity; or, What Queer Theory Has for You' (2017) 95 *Cultural Critique* 219–43, 222.
11. L. Edelman, *No Future: Queer Theory and the Death Drive* (Durham, NC: Duke University Press, 2004), p. 2.
12. *Ibid.*, p. 4.
13. *Ibid.*, p. 3.
14. J. E. Muñoz, *Cruising Utopia: The Then and There of Queer Futurity* (New York University Press, 2009), p. 49.
15. *Ibid.*, pp. 1, 106.
16. S. Hall, *The Carhullan Army* (London: Faber & Faber, 2007), p. 48.
17. *Ibid.*, pp. 48, 49.
18. *Ibid.*, p. 18.
19. *Ibid.*, p. 27.
20. *Ibid.*, p. 28.
21. *Ibid.*, p. 26.
22. *Ibid.*
23. *Ibid.*, p. 205.
24. *Ibid.*, pp. 161, 196.
25. *Ibid.*, pp. 50, 51.
26. J. Halberstam, 'Wildness, Loss, Death' (2014) 32(4) *Social Text* 137–48, 138, 138 and 143, respectively.
27. *Ibid.*, p. 139.
28. *Ibid.*, p. 140.
29. *Ibid.*, p. 145.
30. *Ibid.*, p. 147.
31. Hall, *The Carhullan Army*, p. 207.
32. A. Sinfield, *Literature, Politics and Culture in Postwar Britain*, 2nd edn (London: Continuum, 2004), p. 29.
33. *Ibid.*
34. M. Foucault, *The History of Sexuality*, vol. I: *The Will to Knowledge*, trans. R. Hurley (London: Penguin, 1978), p. 4.
35. *Ibid.*, pp. 17, 21, 59.
36. *Ibid.*, p. 43.
37. J. Haffenden, 'Angela Carter' in J. Haffenden (ed.), *Novelists in Interview* (London: Methuen, 1985), p. 71.
38. A. Carter, 'Notes from the Front Line' in M. Wandor (ed.), *On Gender and Writing* (London: Pandora, 1983), pp. 70, 71.
39. A. Carter, *The Sadeian Woman: An Exercise in Cultural History* (London: Virago: 1979), p. 1.
40. *Ibid.*, pp. 5–6.
41. *Ibid.*, p. 12.
42. P. Duncker, 'Re-Imagining the Fairy Tales: Angela Carter's Bloody Chambers' (1984) 10(1) *Literature and History* 3–14.
43. Dollimore, *Sexual Dissidence*, p. 103.
44. A. Carter, *The Bloody Chamber* (London: Vintage, 2006), pp. 139, 138.
45. *Ibid.*, pp. 129, 136, 138.
46. *Ibid.*, p. 73.
47. *Ibid.*, pp. 61, 65.

48. *Ibid.*
49. *Ibid.*, p. 71.
50. *Ibid.*, p. 72.
51. *Ibid.*, p. 66.
52. Duncker, 'Re-Imagining the Fairy Tales', p. 8.
53. R. Munford, 'Angela Carter and the Politics of Intertextuality' in R. Munford (ed.), *Re-visiting Angela Carter: Texts, Contexts, Intertexts* (London: Palgrave, 2006), p. 7.
54. R. Munford, *Decadent Daughters and Monstrous Mothers: Angela Carter and European Gothic* (Manchester University Press, 2013), p. 29.
55. A. Rich, 'When We Dead Awaken: Writing as Re-vision' (1972) 34(1) *College English* 18–30, 18.
56. Carter, 'Notes from the Front Line', p. 69.
57. Rich, 'When We Dead Awaken', p. 18.
58. J. Winterson, *Sexing the Cherry* (London: Vintage, 1989), p. 48.
59. Halberstam, 'Wildness, Loss, Death', p. 144.
60. J. Winterson, *The Passion* (London: Vintage, 1987), pp. 5, 13, 69, 160.
61. Alderson, 'Introduction: Queerwords', p. 11.
62. T. Castle, *The Apparitional Lesbian: Female Homosexuality and Modern Culture* (New York,: Columbia University Press, 1993).
63. J. de Groot, '"Something New and a Bit Startling": Sarah Waters and the Historical Novel' in K. Mitchell (ed.), *Sarah Waters: Critical Perspectives* (London: Bloomsbury, 2013), p. 57.
64. S. Waters, 'Wolfskins and Togas: Lesbian and Gay Historical Fictions, 1870 to the Present', unpublished PhD thesis (University College London, 1995), p. 145 (emphasis in the original).
65. J. Walsh, *Grow a Pair: 9 ½ Fairytales about Sex* (Berlin: Readux, 2015), p. 1.
66. *Ibid.*, p. 10.
67. *Ibid.*, p. 12.
68. *Ibid.*, p. 23.
69. *Ibid.*, p. 25.
70. *Ibid.*, pp. 23, 27.
71. L. G. Zarranz, 'Joyful Insurrection as Feminist Methodology; or the Joys of Being a Feminist Killjoy' (2016) 14 *452°F* 16–25, 18.
72. *Ibid.*, p. 24.
73. A. Smith, *How to Be Both* (London: Penguin, 2014), p. 37.
74. For analyses of this work, see, e.g., K. Batra, 'British Black and Asian LGBTQ Writing' in D. Osborne (ed.), *The Cambridge Companion to British Black and Asian Literature 1945–2010* (Cambridge University Press, 2016), pp. 159–76; and J. S. Allen, 'Black/Queer/Diaspora at the Current Conjuncture' (2012) 18 (2–3) *GLQ* 211–48.
75. A. Hollinghurst, 'I Was Fortunate to Come Along Just as Gay Lit Was Coming into Its Own', interview in *The Guardian* (22 September 2017), n.p., www .theguardian.com/culture/2017/sep/22/alan-hollinghurst-gay-lit-interview.
76. S. Hall, 'I Don't Want Only Female Readers or Young Readers', interview in *The Telegraph* (12 June 2015), n.p., www.telegraph.co.uk/culture/books/author interviews/11660349/Sarah-Hall-I-dont-want-only-female-readers-or-young-readers.html.

13

STEPHEN MORTON

Fiction, Religion and Freedom of Speech, from 'The Rushdie Affair' to 7/7

The controversy surrounding the publication of Salman Rushdie's novel *The Satanic Verses* (1988) brought the public function of the contemporary British novel as a form of mass communication and the cultural values it represented into sharp focus. Champions of *The Satanic Verses* typically defended the publication of the novel as a sign of British democratic values, particularly the author's right to free speech, even if that speech was felt to be offensive or blasphemous. Critics of the novel typically pointed to the ways in which it denigrates Islam by rehearsing Orientalist stereotypes of the Prophet and the Qur'an. The public burning of copies of Rushdie's novel and the injunction issued by the religious leader of Iran, Ayotollah Khomeini, on 14 February 1989 called on Muslims around the world to kill the author of *The Satanic Verses* and his associates. Such an injunction clearly exemplifies the strength of feeling which the novel generated. This response may seem surprising when one considers that *The Satanic Verses* seemed to exemplify the postmodern turn in contemporary fiction, a move which celebrated the crisis of representation, the so-called waning of affect or feeling, and made a virtue out of blurring the boundaries between fiction and the real. Yet the Rushdie affair clearly demonstrates how the printed form of the contemporary novel and its mass circulation in the global public sphere produces strong and powerful feelings among different reception cultures.

In *The Satanic Verses*, Rushdie re-frames the history of Islam through the deluded consciousness of a Bollywood film star called Gibreel Farishta, who imagines himself to be a religious figure in a Bombay movie genre known as a theological at the precise moment that he arrives in 1980s Britain after falling out of an aeroplane. The fantastical conventions of textual details such as this may prompt readers to wonder why the novel facilitated the controversial response that it did. The difficulty is that the novel assumes that all historical events can be framed as the subject of postmodern satire, without regard for the historical events that are being represented.

Rushdie, *The Satanic Verses* and the Global Literary Marketplace

To better understand the politically charged response to *The Satanic Verses*, it is worth considering the context of the novel's production. At the time of the novel's publication, Rushdie was already something of a literary celebrity. His second novel, *Midnight's Children*, had won him major recognition in the global literary marketplace, following the award of the Booker Prize in 1981. His third novel, *Shame*, had also been well received by critics and literary reviewers. Rushdie's literary agent, Andrew Wylie, was well connected to mass market multinational publishing houses. Had Rushdie not been as well-regarded a writer of contemporary fiction in the British-based multinational publishing industry at the time, the novel may not have received the wide global circulation and publicity that it did. In this respect, the technology of the printing press and the transnational networks of book distribution and sales played a significant role in disseminating this controversial fictional representation of Islamic history, its reflections on communal tensions in modern India, and its account of the demonisation and hostility expressed towards postcolonial migrants in 1980s Britain. The debate over *The Satanic Verses* was expressed as a debate over representation and ideas. But it was also a debate over who has control and access to modern technologies of representation. It is important to remember that the cultural form of the novel was made possible by the technologies of global print capitalism. As a major author of contemporary fiction, Rushdie had access to a global technology of representation; many readers, non-readers or partial readers, who were particularly offended by the novel's representation of Islamic history, felt that they did not have access to such a technology of representation. To understand why the novel was understood as Islamophobic, one needs to understand that the novel used injurious words to misrepresent the values and beliefs of some British Muslims who felt that they did not have a voice in the British public sphere. But one also needs to understand that the wider transmission and reception of the novel in the non-Anglophone world questions and complicates the assumption that European liberal ideas of textual interpretation and literary value are universally held.

The world press, radio, and television played a significant role in the controversy over the *Satanic Verses*. As Joel Kuortti has argued in his *Salman Rushdie Bibliography*, the *Satanic Verses* affair received such wide coverage in the press that it would be impossible to document all of this material.[1] If the magnitude of this press coverage exemplifies the role that both print media and broadcast media played in transmitting a certain impression of *The Satanic Verses* and its author, contemporary literary reviews of the novel identify how the novel's experiments with the conventions of aesthetic representation also mediate its critique of religious thought. Madhu Jain in a review of the novel published in *India Today* praised the 'kaleidoscopic' quality of the novel, and links its radical shifts in time and space to the aesthetics of Bombay cinema; yet she also adds that the novel is 'an uncompromising, unequivocal attack on religious fanaticism and fundamentalism, which is largely Islamic'[2] and which is 'bound to trigger an avalanche of protests from the ramparts'.[3] In a similar vein, the literary critic Hermione Lee, in a review that was originally published in the London *Observer* on 25 September 1988, notes the cinematic quality of the novel and describes Rushdie's fictional reinvention of Islamic history as 'the Koran rewritten as science fiction by Burroughs or Ballard'.[4] Yet at the same time, Lee argues that there is 'about this massive, wilful undertaking a *folie de grandeur* which sends its brilliant comic energy, its fierce satiric powers, and its unmatchable, demonic inventiveness plunging down, on melting wings, towards unreadability'.[5] Patrick Parrinder's review of *The Satanic Verses*, originally published in *The London Review of Books*, situates the novel in relation to historical accounts of the apocryphal Satanic Verses episode, and Western translations of the Islamic scriptures which 'argue that the Koran as a whole is a forgery'.[6] Rather than elaborating on the broader significance of this history, and speculating on the possible repercussions of Rushdie's allusions to this history in his novel, however, Parrinder concludes that the novel is 'damnably entertaining, and fiendishly ingenious'.[7] Such comments clearly work to frame the novel in the terms of a Romantic idea of aesthetic creativity or genius, and assume that literary fiction has an inherent right to be fiendish if it is also ingenious. In a review that is perhaps more alert to the cultural nuances and wider implications of Rushdie's fiendish novel, Robert Irwin notes the connections between Rushdie's 'story of the Imam, a grim religious bigot in exile in London (who is and is not the Ayatollah Khomeini in exile in Paris)' and the distorted echo of the historical origins of Islam in Rushdie's story of Jahilia.[8] What many contemporary reviews of the novel indicate, in other words, is an awareness of the novel's aesthetic achievements on the one hand and of its participation in an Orientalist representation of Islam, on the other.

In response to the novel's proscription in India, the riots it prompted in Pakistan and the burning of *The Satanic Verses* in Bradford, England, Rushdie expressed his sadness about 'Labour councillors in Bradford, and Labour MPs in Westminster joining forces with the mullahs';[9] and argued that *The Satanic Verses* is not 'an anti-religious novel', but 'an attempt to write about migration, its stresses and transformations, from the point of view of migrants from the Indian subcontinent to Britain'.[10] In a similar vein,

Michiko Kakutani argued that the novel 'deals only incidentally with Islam', and is more concerned with 'the broader questions of good and evil, identity and metamorphosis, race and culture'.[11] Jonathon Yardley echoes this view in his claim that *The Satanic Verses* is a 'relatively non-political book' in comparison to *Shame* and *Midnight's Children*, and is more of a 'philosophical novel about the tangled relationship between good and evil, the angelic and the satanic'.[12]

What many of the literary reviews of *The Satanic Verses* in the British and American press assume, however, is a global readership that is both familiar with the codes and conventions of contemporary fiction and shares its secular values. Some of the critical responses to the novel certainly reject the secular values upon which the novel's representation of Islamic history is based. As one commentator puts it:

> Rushdie not only reviles the Prophet in the most vulgar ways, but also portrays the Prophet's wives in the most shameful and indecent manner. The Prophet's wives, according to Qur'anic parlance, are the 'mothers of the Faithful' and are respected by Muslims in the same way that the Prophet is revered. By calling the brothel a 'curtain' and locating it in the Ka'ba, Rushdie on the one hand, ridicules the Islamic tradition of *Hijab* (Muslim women's dress) and on the other, defiles the sanctity of the Ka'ba, the House of God, the symbol of Muslim unity, towards which Muslims the world over face in their five daily prayers.[13]

In this quoted passage, the use of verbs such as 'reviles', 'defiles' and 'ridicules' clearly suggests that *The Satanic Verses* was regarded as an obscene representation of the life of the Prophet rather than raising epistemological questions about the structure of belief and revelation (as Rushdie argued in his defence of the novel). Such a response is echoed in Shabbir Akhtar's observation that 'There is nothing in *The Satanic Verses* which helps to bring Islam into a fruitful confrontation with modernity, nothing that brings it into thoughtful contact with contemporary secularity and ideological pluralism'.[14] What is implicit in such responses to *The Satanic Verses* is that the postmodern form of the novel and its superficial treatment of Islamic history betrays a failure to imagine the nuances of the Islamic past, and the ways in which that past is understood in the late twentieth century.

The Satanic Verses and the Islamic Public Sphere

The Satanic Verses affair became part of a global political debate in what Aamir Mufti calls the Islamic public sphere, especially after Ayatollah Khomeini declared that it was the responsibility of Muslims around the world to kill Rushdie.[15] Yet to attribute all expressions of Muslim outrage to the novel to 'fundamentalists and the mullahs' is, as Tariq Modood has suggested, a form of racism, which treats all Muslims as the same, and forecloses rational critical debate.[16] The so-called Muslim response to *The Satanic Verses* is complicated by an edited collection of essays entitled *For Rushdie*, which offers a series of responses from leading Muslim intellectuals and writers to *The Satanic Verses* in defence of Rushdie. Many of these responses criticise Khomeini's political tyranny, and suggest that Rushdie's 'condemnation to death … is contrary to the spirit of Islam'.[17] Others question the legitimacy of Ayatollah Khomeini's *fatwa*,[18] and his charge that Rushdie is an 'apostate';[19] instead, they argue that 'the critical position taken by Rushdie is actually essential to the modern historical development of the Arab and Muslim worlds'.[20]

It is worth noting too that many commentaries on *The Satanic Verses* affair do not actually engage with the novel itself. This may be a consequence of the way in which Rushdie and his novel were transformed into a symbol of the cultural values of the secular British nation-state. As Jean Kane argues: 'Whether depicted as a person, a book, or as the nation-state itself, the metonymic structure of the individual in these binaries is structured as a fetish'.[21] The framing of Rushdie's proper name as a metonym for British secular values may overlook his more complex position as a secular diasporic Indian Muslim writer, whose satirical reflections on migration and Islamic history in *The Satanic Verses* are partly informed by the cultural practices of both Bombay cinema and Urdu poetry. Yet arguments in favour of Rushdie's cosmopolitanism also downplay the ways in which the hybrid cultural form of the Anglophone postmodern novel translates linguistic, cultural and historical differences in order to reproduce the secular values of liberalism. Certainly, the novel's subordination of the history of Islam to a story of postcolonial migrant life in 1980s Britain can be seen to assume a sophisticated cosmopolitan and secular reader who is prepared to imagine the possibility that the act of revelation could be explained away as a cinematic conceit or the delusions of a schizophrenic. The difficulty with such a postmodern mode of historical writing about the history of Islam is that it might also be taken to be Islamophobic. Indeed, this risk was further accentuated in the context of a changing geopolitical order, which saw the decline of the Soviet Union and the attempt to extend American influence across the Muslim world. If the publication of *The Satanic Verses* and the 'Rushdie affair' coincided with the clash of civilisations between 'the West' and 'the Islamic world', it is worth considering how Rushdie has tried to make sense of this concatenation of his events in his own writing.

Joseph Anton and the Rushdie Affair

The publication of Rushdie's memoir of the *fatwa* years, *Joseph Anton*, in 2012 offers some insight into the ways in which the autobiographical self denoted by the authorial signature, Salman Rushdie, understood and experienced the reception of the novel. Indeed, a critical assessment of this memoir can help to shed light on the afterlife of *The Satanic Verses* and the ways in which the Rushdie affair has shaped and inflected debates about the politics of the contemporary novel, particularly in the aftermath of the terrorist attacks on America of 11 September 2001, and the subsequent wars on terror in Afghanistan and Iraq.

In the early chapters of *Joseph Anton*, Rushdie offers a suggestive account of his childhood and intellectual formation in India and the United Kingdom. Specifically, the third-person narrator of Rushdie's memoir explains how it was Rushdie's father, Anis, who had invented the proper name Rushdie. As the narrator proceeds to explain, 'Muhammad Din Khaliqi died young, leaving his son the fortune which he would squander and a name that was too heavy to carry around in the modern world'.[22] It was for this reason that 'Anis renamed himself "Rushdie" because of his admiration for Ibn Rushd, "Averroës" to the West, the twelfth-century Spanish-Arab philosopher of Cordoba who rose to become the *qadi*, or judge, of Seville, the translator of and acclaimed commentator upon the works of Aristotle'.[23]

This detailed account of the history of Rushdie's proper name contributes to Rushdie's own self-fashioning as a secular Muslim writer who is concerned to explore the experience of revelation as an event that takes place within history. As the narrator puts it, 'his father, a true scholar of Islam who was also entirely lacking in religious belief, had chosen [this name] because he appreciated Ibn Rushd for being at the forefront of the rationalist argument against Islamic literalism in his time'.[24] The parallels do not end here. Writing in the late twelfth century, Averroës had not only been tried and exiled by the caliph Yaqub Al-Mansur for his rationalist belief that truth can only be attained through philosophical reason; his works had also been banned and burned.[25] If such ideas were once seen as 'dangerously heretical', they also 'constituted a crucial antecedent of modern secular arguments for the separation of church and state, religion and philosophy, [and] faith and reason', as Cesare Casarino and Antonio Negri have argued.[26]

By invoking the legacy of Averroës, then, the narrator of *Joseph Anton* presents the life of Salman Rushdie as the heroic struggle of a secular intellectual against the violent forces of Islamic fundamentalism. By framing his defence of *The Satanic Verses* as a rational inquiry into the history of Islam through the metaphor of conflict or war, Rushdie's narrator recalls some of the criticisms of the novel, which focused on the use of tropes from medieval Christian Europe to discredit the claim of the Prophet to be the true messenger of Allah. That 'Rushdie' seems insensitive to the implications of such an analogy should not perhaps strike us as surprising, given his apparent unwillingness to consider how the cultural form of the novel is itself bound up with a liberal, secular tradition – a tradition which is itself imbricated in the history of European Orientalism. Instead, Rushdie's self-fashioning as part of a rational, intellectual tradition works to reassert his authority over the meaning of *The Satanic Verses*. And that he does so via the history of the proper name 'Rushdie' tells us something about how Rushdie's narrator misreads the *Satanic Verses* controversy in this autobiographical text, which is subtitled 'a memoir'.

The distance between the third-person narrator of *Joseph Anton* and its main protagonist may appear to dramatise how Salman Rushdie understood and experienced the Rushdie affair. Indeed, during the height of the Rushdie affair, the narrator remarks how the 'gulf between the private "Salman" he believed himself to be and the public "Rushdie" he barely recognized was growing by the day';[27] and in a later episode he speaks of how 'his name had been stolen from him, or half his name anyway, when *Rushdie* detached itself from *Salman* and went spiralling off into the headlines, into newsprint, into the video-heavy ether, becoming a slogan, a rallying cry, a term of abuse, or anything else that other people wanted it to be'.[28]

By documenting the way in which the body of the author 'Salman Rushdie' lived on in the protective custody of the British police, *Joseph Anton* seeks to reclaim the subjectivity and authority of the author of *The Satanic Verses*. A powerful instance of this can be found in the narrator's account of Salman Rushdie's research into Islamic history as a final year undergraduate at King's College, Cambridge, during the academic year of 1967–68. Here, Rushdie's narrator tries to evoke a sense of the social world of Mecca and Medina in the seventh century in a historical mode of writing that seems straightforwardly realist. Both Mecca and Medina, the narrator explains, were new cities inhabited by 'nomads who had just begun to settle down ... Mecca was only a few generations old. Yathrib, later re-named Medina, was a group of encampments around an oasis without so much as a serious city wall'.[29] This descriptive historical narrative may seem fairly innocuous. Yet it is revealing how the narrator proceeds to read the pre-Islamic world of Mecca and Medina in the terms and categories of post-Enlightenment thought:

> A nomadic society was conservative, full of rules, valuing the well-being of the group more highly than individual liberty, but it was also inclusive.

The nomadic world had been a matriarchy. Under the umbrella of its extended families even orphaned children could find protection, and a sense of identity and belonging. The city was a patriarchy and its preferred family unit was nuclear. The crowd of the disenfranchised grew larger and more restive each day. But, Mecca was prosperous, and its ruling elders liked it that way. Inheritance now followed the male line. This, too, the governing families preferred.[30]

Here, the narrator's description of pre-Islamic history may seem to echo Rushdie's repeated insistence that the Mahound sections of *The Satanic Verses* should be understood as an attempt to make sense of the life of the Prophet and the birth of Islam as events that took place *within* history. Yet the terms in which that history is represented raise questions about Rushdie's cultural and ideological standpoint as a literary historiographer of Islam. The narrator of *Joseph Anton* explains that Rushdie tried to heed the words of his Cambridge tutor, the medieval historian Arthur Hibbert: 'You must never write history … until you can hear the people speak.'[31] Yet Rushdie's use of phrases such as 'individual liberty' and 'nuclear family unit' strongly imply a reading of pre-Islamic history through the lens of a post-Enlightenment, secular understanding of history and society. The narrator's subsequent description of the Prophet's experience of divine revelation on Mount Hira as one of madness further privileges a secular, post-Enlightenment understanding of Islamic history over an explanation that situates events in Islamic history within the values and world view of the time. Moreover, the narrator's recollection of reading about the 'satanic verses' episode in 'the collections of Hadith … compiled by Ibn Ishaq, Waqidi, Ibn Sa'd, Bukhari and Tabari'[32] rests on a 'politically motivated reading' of the history of Islam that the narrator loosely attributes to the historians, William Montgomery Watt and Maxime Rodinson. The 'satanic verses' episode is, of course, often linked to an apocryphal verse, which follows a passage in sura 53 in which the Prophet sought to convert the people of Mecca to the Islamic faith. In this passage, Muhammad seems to accept three winged pagan goddesses of Mecca into the Muslim faith. Yet as the ninth-century commentator, al Tabari, argues, these verses were subsequently discovered to be the words of a demon rather than the divine words of Allah. Once these verses were discovered to be a mistake by the angel Gabriel, al-Tabari reports that God annulled 'what Satan had put upon the prophet's tongue'.[33] In the 'politically motivated reading' of this episode presented in *Joseph Anton*, Muhammad's acceptance into the Muslim faith of three pagan goddesses can be understood as a strategic decision (rather than a divine revelation) that would put a stop to the persecution of Muslims by the people of Mecca and 'Muhammad himself would be granted a seat on the city's ruling council'.[34] Furthermore, Rushdie's post-*fatwa* reflection on his first reading of these apocryphal verses during his undergraduate years seems to challenge the patriarchal basis of Islam: 'The "true" verses, angelic or divine, were clear: it was the femaleness of the winged goddesses – the "exalted birds" – that rendered them inferior and fraudulent and proved they could not be the children of God, as the angels were ... At the birth of this particular idea, femaleness was seen as a disqualification from exaltation.'[35] Here, the narrator's reflections on the patriarchal foundations of Islam may align him with Muslim women writers such as Assia Djebar and Fatima Mernissi, who have sought to articulate the position of women in Islam (as Sara Suleri has argued[36]). Yet in foregrounding this aspect of the 'satanic verses' episode, the narrator downplays the way in which Rushdie drew on Orientalist stereotypes of Islam to suggest that the Qur'an is an invented text rather than a Holy Book. For it was after all the early twentieth-century Orientalist scholar William Muir who first described these verses as the 'satanic verses' in chapter 5 of his *Life of Mohammad* (1912). By adopting the description of this episode as the title of his novel, Rushdie clearly aligns his imaginative representation of this apocryphal story with western Orientalist accounts of Islamic history.

It is worth noting too that the narrator's concluding reflections on Rushdie's reading of Islamic history at Cambridge are immediately followed by a brief reference to the *évènements* of 1968 in Paris. Such a juxtaposition of these events would seem to reinforce Timothy Brennan's observation that Rushdie's provocative representation of the 'satanic verses' episode in *The Satanic Verses* can be read as a sign of the '"soixante-huitard" sensibility of a uniquely situated cosmopolitan'.[37] Yet if Rushdie's encounter with the 'satanic verses' episode in Islamic historiography in the late 1960s at Cambridge and his subsequent fictionalisation of this history in *The Satanic Verses* twenty years later are to be understood in the terms of a challenge to cultural and political authority (in the spirit of 1968), it is curious that this challenge to the authority of a religious text ends up re-inscribing the authority of the individual author.

In a certain sense, Rushdie's attempt to understand the experience of revelation and the foundation of Islam as events within history also entails a tacit investment in, rather than a decentring of, the Romantic idea of the author as a secular God. Rushdie's self-fashioning as a literary hero is certainly evident in his choice of alias during the '*fatwa* years': Joseph Anton is, of course, an invented name borrowed from Conrad and Chekhov. Furthermore, it is the comparison Rushdie's narrator draws between the role of the contemporary writer in 1986 and Shelley's often-quoted statement that poets are 'the unacknowledged legislators of the world'[38] that seems to reinforce Rushdie's belief in the Romantic idea of the author. By invoking Shelley's essay, Rushdie may invite readers to draw parallels between Shelley's secular appropriation of Prophetic motifs from Christian scripture as metaphors for the Romantic imagination and Rushdie's literary representation of Islamic history in the form of the contemporary novel. Bryan Shelley has noted how for Shelley in *A Defence of Poetry* 'the biblical idea of God as Creator becomes the supreme metaphor of poetic creation'.[39] In *The Satanic Verses*, the figure of the author is similarly presented as a subversive and secular figure that appropriates the creative power of God. Such investment in a rather belated idea of the author may seem antithetical to the anti-foundational idea of literary representation with which much of Rushdie's fiction has been associated. And yet the authority with which Rushdie's third-person narrator speaks of the 'satanic verses' episode as both a historical event and a 'good story' in *Joseph Anton* also confers a significant degree of knowledge and authority onto the authorial figure of Rushdie. In this respect, the account of Islamic history presented in *Joseph Anton* lends support to Timothy Brennan's argument that the novel 'projects itself as a rival *Quran* with Rushdie as its prophet and the devil as its supernatural voice'.[40]

In an illuminating reading of Rushdie's fictional reworking of Islamic history in *The Satanic Verses*, Anshuman Mondal highlights many of the difficulties with Rushdie's self-consciously presentist interpretation of Islamic history, and how this reading generated further misreadings in some of the responses from self-identified Muslim readers. Specifically, he points to Rushdie's conflation of Islamic history and Islamism, and his suggestion that one can trace an unbroken historical line between the foundation of Islam in the seventh century and the authoritarian interpretation of Shariah law associated with Muslim fundamentalists such as Ayatollah Khomeini; Mondal also offers some subtle reflections on Rushdie's rather glib treatment of Islamic history, and his conflation of different cultural and historical understandings of the satanic.[41] It might, of course, be argued that to challenge Rushdie's imaginative rewriting of the 'satanic verses' episode on historical grounds is to ignore the postmodern terms in which Rushdie re-presents Islamic history in the novel. To be sure, Rushdie's account of revelation in chapter 2 of *The Satanic Verses* involves a complex layering of narrative frames in which the narrator puts words into the mouth of the film star, Gibreel Farishta, who in turn puts words into the mouth of the Prophet. The following passage exemplifies this point well:

> It happens: revelation. Like this: Mahound, still in his notsleep, becomes rigid, veins bulge in his neck, he clutches at his centre ... The dragging again, the dragging and now the miracle starts in his my our guts, he is straining with all

his might at something, forcing something, and Gibreel begins to feel that strength that force, here it is *at my own jaw* working it, opening, shutting; and the power, starting within Mahound, reaching up to *my vocal cords* and the voice comes.

Not my voice I'd never known such words I'm no classy speaker never was never will be but this isn't my voice it's a Voice.

... My lips moving, being moved by. What, whom? Don't know, can't say. Nevertheless, here they are, coming out of my mouth, up my throat, past my teeth: the Words.

Being God's postman is no fun, yaar.

Butbutbut: God isn't in the picture.

God knows whose postman I've been.[42]

The slippage between pronouns and registers here foregrounds a complex scene of narrative ventriloquism in which it is not quite clear who is speaking for whom. While this chapter is supposedly set in seventh-century Jahilia, it is also reported from Gibreel's point of view as a migrant and a former film star in late twentieth-century London. Roger Clark has claimed that the voice that possesses Gibreel is that of Rushdie's satanic narrator.[43] This satanic narrator's mode of operation, Clark argues, is a diabolical form of indeterminacy, which 'moves in and out of the text in order to insinuate that there is no such thing as a single, transcendental Meaning and Unity'.[44] By suggesting that the historical event of revelation can be understood through the analogy of an embedded series of narrative frames, this quoted extract can certainly be seen to highlight the way in which the rhetorical organisation of the text draws attention to the necessity of misunderstanding *The Satanic Verses*. By embedding the revelation of this fictionalised prophet in the dreams of an Indian film star, who is in turn possessed by the third voice of a satanic narrator, Rushdie prevents readers from deciding with any certainty whether a satanic narrator has possessed Gibreel, whether Gibreel is a prophet or whether he is suffering from mental illness.[45] Such a narrative technique may serve to reinforce Rushdie's stated aim in *The Satanic Verses*: to expose the invention and interpretation of Islam through (a secular idea of) history. Yet to read the novel in this way is to confuse the stated intentions of its implied author in 'In Good Faith' and *Joseph Anton*, and the radical indeterminacy that Clark attributes to the rhetorical function of the satanic narrator. The novel certainly encourages such a contemporary reading in its suggestion that Satan is a post-Romantic hero who challenges religious authority in the manner of a postmodern Prometheus. But this would be to valorise a certain ethos of secular misreading that ignores the way in which Rushdie's postmodern representation of Islamic history assumes a secular reading public that is broadly sympathetic to the post-Christian, secular ideology of the novel. In doing so, we run the risk of foreclosing the value and significance of some of the more polemical readings of the novel that led to the emergence of what Aamir Mufti has called the Islamic public sphere.[46]

In an attempt to think through and beyond the implications of the many and varied responses of self-identified Muslim readers to *The Satanic Verses*, as well as Rushdie's own defence of the novel, Anshuman Mondal has raised some important questions about Rushdie's use of historical sources, and his equivocation between anti-foundational claims about revelation on the one hand and more straightforwardly empirical claims about Islamic history on the other.[47] The realist account of Islamic history and the apocryphal story of the 'satanic verses' episode presented in *Joseph Anton* can be seen to further exemplify this empirical approach to history, as I have already suggested. This empirical account of seventh-century Mecca as it is understood through the mind of a young Cambridge history undergraduate in the late 1960s is, of course, subordinated to an account of the narrative of Rushdie's subsequent development as a novelist. And in this move from superficial historical description to the novelisation of Islamic history, Rushdie elides what Mondal has called the distinction between the specific ethical and political reasons for the Prophet's acceptance of pagan goddesses into Islam on the one hand and contemporary, epistemological questions of belief on the other.[48] In other words, by presenting the moral parable of the Prophet's ethical commitment to the survival of his community as a sign of the Prophet's unreliability, Rushdie seems to ignore the lessons of his history professor, Arthur Hibbert. Rather than listening to the way in which the people speak and understand their cultural and historical circumstances, Rushdie seems to foreclose their voices.

In defence of *The Satanic Verses*, Rushdie has argued 'that millions upon millions of people ... have been willing to judge *The Satanic Verses* and its author, without reading it'.[49] One of the difficulties with such a claim, however, is that it assumes that the meaning of 'reading' is self-evident, and one that is universally shared. It may be true, as Gayatri Spivak claims, that the media representations of book burnings 'wrenched [*The Satanic Verses*] into rumor, criticism by hearsay, a text taken as evidence, talked about rather than read'.[50] This is not to suggest, however, that the transformation of the text into a source of rumour that circulates in an emergent Islamic public sphere is without value or significance. Indeed, what Bethan Benwell, James Procter and Gemma Robinson call 'not reading' can also be understood as a meaningful response to controversial books such as *The Satanic Verses*: a response that challenges the elite and secular assumptions underpinning Rushdie's sense of an appropriate form of reading.

In a discussion of religion, race and hate speech, the anthropologist Saba Mahmood claims that the framing of the Danish cartoon controversy 'in terms of blasphemy and freedom of speech'[51] has rendered unintelligible a specific concept of moral injury that derives from an intimate ethical relationship 'between a devout Muslim and the exemplary figure of Muhammad'.[52] Mahmood is primarily concerned with the ways in which Europe's hate speech laws function 'as instruments of secular power [that] demarcate and performatively produce normative notions of religion and religious subjectivity'.[53] Yet her argument about how the dominant discourse of liberal secularism produces 'normative notions of religion and religious subjectivity' can shed light on the (secular) meaning of reading after the Rushdie affair.

In the aftermath of the terrorist attacks on London of 7 July 2005, the framing of *Joseph Anton* and the Rushdie affair in relation to the global 'war on terror' exemplifies how the life writing of a 'uniquely situated cosmopolitan' author such as Rushdie can also contribute to the cultural narratives that frame the so-called clash of civilisations. Indeed, it is significant that Rushdie concludes his memoir with a discussion of the attacks on New York of 11 September 2001. By retrospectively framing the experience of a life lived in protective custody as a 'little battle' that was the 'prologue' to 'the main event' of the war on terror,[54] the narrator not only implies that there is a causal relationship between the Rushdie affair and the war on terror; he also mobilises the quasi-military rhetoric of the clash of civilisations to shore up his writerly self. In so doing, he continues to ignore the injurious power of print culture. If the so-called Rushdie affair prefigured the clash of civilisations that defined global politics in the first decade of the twenty-first century, it also prefigured an affective turn in criticism of the contemporary novel. Sara Ahmad has suggested that the 'figure of the melancholic migrant is the one who refuses to participate in the national game' and 'holds on to the unhappiness of difference as an historical itinerary'.[55] Ahmad's account of the melancholy migrant is apposite to describe the affect of injurious speech which the mediatised transmission of *The Satanic Verses* came to symbolise. By attending to the ways in which the novel framed Islamic history using the neo-Orientalist conventions of postmodern pastiche, and how the global media, in turn, framed the reception of this postmodern literary representation, we can begin to understand the different ways in which the generic and narrative codes of the novel form aid and abet and at some points contest the injurious discourse of Islamophobia, and the asymmetrical relations of economic, political and military power that underpin it.

Acknowledgement

Earlier versions of this essay were published in *The Journal of Commonwealth Literature* (2018) and *Salman Rushdie: Fictions of Postcolonial Modernity* (Palgrave Macmillan 2008).

Notes

1. J. Kuortti, *The Salman Rushdie Bibliography: A Bibliography of Salman Rushdie's Work and Rushdie Criticism* (Frankfurt am Main: Peter Lang, 1997), p. 7.
2. M. Jain, 'An Irreverent Journey' in *Contemporary Literary Criticism* 55 (Detroit, MI: Gale Research Inc., 1988), p. 215.
3. *Ibid.*, p. 216.
4. H. Lee, 'Falling towards England' in *Contemporary Literary Criticism* 55, p. 217.
5. *Ibid.*
6. P. Parrinder, 'Let's Get the Hell Out of Here' in *Contemporary Literary Criticism* 55, p. 218.
7. *Ibid.*, pp. 218–19.
8. R. Irwin, 'Original Parables' in *Contemporary Literary Criticism* 55, p. 220.
9. S. Rushdie, *The Satanic Verses* (London: Penguin, 1988), p. 223.
10. *Ibid.*
11. M. Kakutani, 'Review of The Satanic Verses' in *Contemporary Literary Criticism* 55, p. 223.
12. J. Yardley, 'Wrestling with the Angel' in *Contemporary Literary Criticism* 55, p. 224.
13. M. M. Ahsan and A. R. Kidwai (eds), *Sacrilege versus Civility: The Muslim Perspective on the Satanic Verses Affair* (Markfield: Islamic Foundation, 1993), p. 33.
14. S. Akhtar, 'Be Careful with Muhammad' in D. Bowen (ed.), *The Satanic Verses: Bradford Responds* (Bradford and Ilkley Community College, 1994), p. 29.
15. See A. Mufti, 'Reading the Rushdie Affair: "Islam," Cultural Politics, Form' in M. K. Booker (ed.), *Critical Essays on Salman Rushdie* (New York: G. K. Hall, 1999), pp. 51–77.
16. T. Modood, 'British Asian Muslims and the Rushdie Affair' (1990) 61(2) *Political Quarterly* 143–60, 155.
17. E. Adnan, 'On the Subject of Rushdie' in *For Rushdie: A Collection of Essays by 100 Arabic and Muslim Writers* (New York: George Braziller, 1994), p. 16.
18. S. J. Al-Azm, 'Is the Fatwa a Fatwa?' in *For Rushdie*, p. 22.
19. A. D. Gandjeih, 'For Rushdie' in *For Rushdie*, p. 153.
20. A. Al-Azmeh, 'Rushdie the Traitor' in *For Rushdie*, p. 26.
21. J. M. Kane, 'Embodied Panic: Revisiting Modernist "Religion" in the Controversies over *Ulysses* and The Satanic Verses' (2006) 20(3) *Textual Practice* 419–40, 432.
22. S. Rushdie, *Joseph Anton* (London, Jonathan Cape, 2012), p. 22.
23. *Ibid.*

24. *Ibid.*, pp. 22–3.
25. C. Casarino and A. Negri, *In Praise of the Common: A Conversation on Philosophy and Politics* (Minneapolis, MN: University of Minnesota Press, 2008), p. 249 n. 21.
26. *Ibid.*
27. Rusdhie, *Joseph Anton*, p. 131.
28. *Ibid.*, p. 164 (emphases in the original).
29. *Ibid.*, p. 41.
30. *Ibid.*
31. *Ibid.*, p. 40.
32. *Ibid.*, p. 43.
33. Quoted in *ibid.*, p. 44.
34. *Ibid.*, p. 44.
35. *Ibid.*, p. 45.
36. S. Suleri, 'Contraband Histories: Salman Rushdie and the Embodiment of Blasphemy' in M. D. Fletcher (ed.), *Reading Rushdie: Perspectives on the Fiction of Salman Rushdie* (Amsterdam: Rodopi, 1994), pp. 221–36.
37. T. Brennan, *Wars of Position: The Cultural Politics of Left and Right* (Chicago, Ill.: University of Chicago Press, 2006), p. 24.
38. Quoted in Rushdie, *Joseph Anton*, p. 78.
39. B. Shelley, *Shelley and Scripture* (Oxford: Oxford University Press, 1994), p. 123.
40. T. Brennan, *Salman Rushdie and the Third World: Myths of the Nation* (London: Macmillan, 1989), p. 139.
41. A. Mondal, *Islam and Controversy* (Basingstoke: Macmillan, 2014), pp. 97–146.
42. Rushdie, *The Satanic Verses*, p. 112 (emphases in the original).
43. R. Clark, *Stranger Gods: Salman Rushdie's Other Worlds* (Montreal: McGill Queens University Press, 2001).
44. *Ibid.*, p. 75.
45. *Ibid.*, p. 76.
46. A. Mufti, 'Reading the Rushdie Affair: An Essay on Islam and Politics' (1991) 29 *Social Text* 95–116.
47. Mondal, *Islam and Controversy*.
48. *Ibid.*, p. 105.
49. S. Rushdie, 'In Good Faith' in *Imaginary Homelands: Essays and Criticism* (London: Granta, 1991), p. 397.
50. G. C. Spivak, *Outside in the Teaching Machine* (London: Routledge, 1993), p. 228.
51. Mahmood in T. Asad, S. Mahmood and J. Butler, *Is Critique Secular? Blasphemy, Injury, and Free Speech* (Berkeley, CA: Townsend Center for the Humanities, 2012), p. 79.
52. *Ibid.*, p. 76.
53. *Ibid.*, p. 150.
54. Rushdie, *Joseph Anton*, p. 626.
55. S. Ahmad, *The Promise of Happiness* (London: Routledge, 2010), p. 143.

14

PATRICK DEER

British Cosmopolitanism after 1980

In the wake of the Brexit referendum on Britain's membership of the European Union of June 2016 the idea of a specifically British cosmopolitanism has come to the fore. Yet for much of the post-Second World War period it was a less familiar term than more typically British values of 'tolerance' or 'respect' towards immigrants, refugees or citizens of other countries. The term's original meaning, derived from Greek κοσμοπολίτης or 'citizen of the world', combines the Greek word κόσμος for 'world' and πολίτης for 'citizen' to suggest a political ethos that moved beyond ties to the city-state or 'polis' to embrace commonalities with the wider world. Its English definitions pull in contradictory directions: on the one hand, describing people or species that transcend nationality, 'Belonging to all parts of the world; not restricted to any one country or its inhabitants';[1] on the other hand, describing places often viewed with suspicion, 'Composed of people from many different countries'.[2] In an interview in 2006, Stuart Hall captured the ambivalence surrounding the term even for its advocates. Critiquing the impact of globalisation, he argues: 'If we don't move towards the more open horizon of cosmopolitanism-from-below, we will find ourselves driven either to homogenization from above or to the barrier of, the war of all against all.'[3] Yet when his interviewer, Prina Werbner, asks him, 'Do you feel yourself to be a cosmopolitan?' Hall pauses uncomfortably, 'You know you hear me hesitate every time I use the word.' Hall's hesitation has to do with the idea's origins in Enlightenment philosophy and ties with colonialism which excluded non-Western subjects. But his hesitation to invoke the term is typical in a British context, to do with its rarified or elitist connotations. Yet this ambivalence and global reach, this double quality of belonging out there in the world and bringing the whole world home to challenge local loyalties or identities, has made cosmopolitanism a rich source of fictional exploration. I will argue here that despite its utopian aspirations, cosmopolitanism is frequently a disruptive force in British fiction, producing disturbing scenes, narrative doubling and conflict, as often as it represents hospitable people and spaces or imaginary alternatives to provincialism, nationalism and xenophobia.

Since the Brexit crisis, cosmopolitanism has become much more visible in public discourse. Yet its meanings seem to have splintered and contracted, fracturing the sense of doubleness that animates it as a political ideal. On the one hand, those committed to an internationalist, pro-European vision of British national identity have found themselves retreating into the *polis*, looking askance at the rest of the country from the city-state of London and other more diverse English metropolitan areas, which voted alongside majorities in Scotland and Northern Ireland to Remain in the European Union. London in particular has been both celebrated and attacked as a bastion of cosmopolitanism placed at odds with the 'communitarianism' of rural and marginal post-industrial communities who voted Leave. On the other hand, 'cosmopolitanism' has been coded by its opponents as severed from the nation-state, representing the preserve of unaccountable transnational elites following finance capital, leisure and privilege across the globe. Both cosmopolitan elites, immigrants and refugees are coded as a threat to British 'sovereignty'. Here, 'communitarian' and 'sovereignty' seem to function as floating signifiers that provide cover for anti-immigrant anxieties, resurgent nationalism and outright racism. This seems to be the charge behind Prime Minister Theresa May's gnomic utterance at the Conservative Party Conference in October 2016, 'if you believe you are a citizen of the world, you are a citizen of nowhere'. Delivered without irony from a podium decorated with an all-blue union jack and the slogan 'A Country that Works for Everyone', her declaration sparked a Twitter backlash for its apparent nationalism and xenophobia.[4]

This simplification of cosmopolitanism's complexity suggests that as a political tradition or cultural disposition it is inevitably opposed to British nationalism or the localisms of Englishness. But its representations in British fiction since 1980 reveal a different story. These suggest that the intense anxiety and disruptive energy around representations of cosmopolitanism derive not from its distance or difference from, but its close proximity to and rivalry with, both nationalism and globalisation. In the British context, post-imperial traditions of cosmopolitanism coexist often uneasily with the external threats of resurgent nationalism, war and neo-liberal globalisation which they aspire to transcend. As Jackie Stacey has argued: 'The ease promised by cosmopolitanism is one characterized by the absence of fear and antipathy. Cosmopolitanism is thus necessarily something of an aspirational project, haunted by that which it seeks to overcome: prejudice, intolerance, aversion, hatred, antagonism and violence.'[5] This tension and antagonism around cosmopolitan figures and scenes is a reminder of the ongoing struggle to define British society as tolerant, hospitable and open.

'How Come I've Never Seen You People Before?':
Cosmopolitan Scenes

These conflicts provoked by the internationalisation of British culture are often made visible in what can be called cosmopolitan scenes. I use the term 'cosmopolitan scene' here in both the literary sense of a discrete fictional unit, the performative and affective sense of 'making a scene', and the creative and collaborative 'scenes' of music or popular culture. Such a collision between good and bad cosmopolitanisms is powerfully represented in Stephen Frears's film *Dirty Pretty Things* (2002), where the protagonist, Okwe, an undocumented Nigerian doctor in political exile, struggles to save himself and Senay, a young woman Kurdish refugee, from the machinations of an international crime syndicate operating out of a shady London hotel. The film is a profoundly dystopian retelling of the vision of multicultural London transformed by Thatcherite enterprise culture offered in Hanif Kureishi's screenplay for *My Beautiful Laundrette*, which Frears directed in 1985.

In *My Beautiful Laundrette*, the film's protagonist, Omar, finds himself in a tug of war between his alcoholic father, a journalist in political exile, his lover Johnny, a former neo-fascist skinhead and punk Bohemian, and the patronage of his prosperous South Asian uncle and family. Each of them demands that Omar show his true colours, yet Kureishi shows him pursuing a fluid identity as a gay, 'Paki' entrepreneur in Thatcherite multicultural London. His gangster cousin's wife Cherry has little time for this hybrid experimentation:

CHERRY: I know all your gorgeous family in Karachi.

OMAR: (*This is a faux pas*) You've been there?

CHERRY: You stupid, what a stupid, it's my home. How could anyone in their right mind . . . call this silly little island off Europe their home? Every day in Karachi, every day your other uncles and cousins come to our house for bridge, booze and VCR.

BILQUIS: Cherry, my little nephew knows nothing of that life there.

CHERRY: Oh god, I'm sick of hearing about these in-betweens. People should make up their minds where they are.[6]

Omar's irrepressible openness, partly informed by his father's socialist internationalism, to the foreign elements of contemporary Britishness allows him to pass across boundaries and elude the ever-present threat of violence.

But in *Dirty Pretty Things*, the film's protagonists have their cosmopolitan solidarity forced on them by their political and economic vulnerability as they work the night shift at the Baltic Hotel. To be 'in-between' is far more dangerous. By contrast, the debonair and terrifying Spanish night manager known only as Señor Juan wields near total power to bully and sexually abuse the undocumented, offering EU passports and new identities to desperate undocumented people of colour in return for organs illegally harvested in hotel bedrooms, sexual favours and rape. His power derives from his mastery of both neo-liberal governmentality, personified by the thuggish agents of Immigration Enforcement Executive, and the criminal networks of cosmopolitan globalisation. In a final cosmopolitan scene, a doctor arrives in the hotel's underground garage to collect an illegally harvested human kidney. The first white English character encountered in the film, as Frears ironically casts even the immigration agents as people of colour, the doctor is surprised to encounter Okwe and Senay, along with Juliet, a Black British prostitute, instead of the night manager whom they have tricked, drugged and operated on upstairs in the hotel. Handing over the cash unwittingly in return for Señor Juan's kidney, he asks:

DOCTOR: How come I've never seen you people before?
OKWE: Because we are the people you do not see. We are the ones who drive your cabs. We clean your rooms, and suck your cocks.[7]

Here, the enforced cosmopolitanism of the underclass of immigrants and refugees empowers their rebellious turning of the tables on Señor Juan.[8] The plot twist is at once comic, violent and unsatisfactory, freeing Okwe to return from the alienated global city exile to his African homeland and family away from the young Turkish refugee he loves. It also reveals London to be a frightening and exploitative zone. Like Omar, Okwe discovers both solidarity and agency. But now he has to leave.

Similar tensions disturb the narrative structure of Zadie Smith's novel, *NW* (2012). Once again, we can see a much bleaker rewriting of a more utopian multicultural vision, of Smith's breakthrough first novel, *White Teeth* (2000). Now her characters struggle with the burden of representing cosmopolitan values while enmeshed in the corporate rewards of globalisation. In a section entitled, '135. *Contempt*', Natalie, one of Smith's two protagonists from a North London working-class neighbourhood, meets for brunch with her husband and friends, like her people of colour and affluent professionals. They are against an unnamed war, perhaps the war in Iraq:

They were all agreed that the war should not be happening. They were against war. In the mid-nineties, when Natalie Blake was still sleeping with Imran, the two of them had planned a trip to Bosnia in a convoy of ambulances...[9]

Smith anatomises uncomfortably their distracted gaze, the narration filtered through Natalie's ambivalence and discomfort: 'Only the private realm existed now ... Was it possible to feel oneself on a war footing, even at brunch?' They consume tabloid scandals in the Sunday newspapers, performing for the rest of the café. They mean well. Yet the world is out of focus.

> Global consciousness. Local consciousness. Consciousness. And lo they saw their nakedness and were not ashamed ... Wouldn't it be cruel to leave, now, when they'd come this far? They were all four of them providing a service for the other people in the café, simply by being here. They were the 'local vibrancy' to which the estate agents referred. For this reason, too, they needn't concern themselves too much with politics. They simply *were* political facts, in their very persons. 'You're fooling yourself,' said Frank. 'You can't get anything on the park for less than a million.'[10]

Left out of this fashionable brunch is Natalie's childhood friend, Leah Hanwell, who the novel suggests ironically may be more open to the world and its painful differences than her upwardly mobile friend. Like previous generations of British cosmopolitans, their moral ambiguity troubles ethical codes and political loyalties, and their mobility through space and time often has violent consequences.

As these cosmopolitan scenes reveal, British writers of all stripes find themselves intervening – in practice if not in theory – in the vibrant, often messy debate about traditions of cosmopolitanism. Its currency in political theory, anthropology, international relations, or literary and cultural studies involves a remarkable struggle to modify and salvage the term from its relations with globalisation, militarism and neo-liberalism. Notable examples include 'discrepant', 'vernacular', 'critical', 'from-below', 'rooted' and even 'negative' cosmopolitanisms, each of which can find their fictional echoes in British writing and media representations.[11]

In the last decade the debate around cosmopolitanism has involved four main traditions.[12] The first is a philosophical approach emphasising detachment from the nation and 'allegiance to ... the worldwide community of human beings', drawing on a genealogy stretching from ancient philosophy through Kant to moral philosophy.[13] The second is a social sciences approach which, as David Harvey notes, is 'mainly concerned with the question of rights and institutional arrangements, including how these might work in relation to a globalising capitalism, and which asks if institutional arrangements can work in a more egalitarian, more humanitarian way'.[14] Thirdly, there is the more anthropological approach often referred to as the 'new cosmopolitanism' that explores, as Bruce Robbins puts it, 'instead of an ideal of detachment', real-world instances of '(re-)attachment, multiple attachment, or attachment at a distance'.[15] Finally, a cultural studies approach which emphasises 'vernacular or popular tradition that values the risks of social deviance and the resources of consumer culture and urban mobility'.[16] Each of these traditions has contributed to the proliferation of adjectival forms of the term, which, as Robbins has observed, 'try to reconcile cosmopolitanism, seen as an abstract standard of planetary justice, with a need for belonging and acting at levels smaller than the species as a whole'.[17]

The imperial legacy of British cosmopolitanism also complicates its claims to be the antidote to British nationalism. In the nineteenth century, as Edward Said noted in *Orientalism*, British politicians like Balfour and Lord Cromer themselves espoused a universalising Orientalist vision of 'enlarged cosmopolitanism' to counter anti-colonial nationalism in the Middle East and to bolster the imperial mission.[18] The very expansionist energies which advocated world citizenship as a utopian antidote to abuses of the sovereignty of the nation-state or of rapacious transnational actors emerged in parallel to imperial expansion in the eighteenth and nineteenth centuries, as did modern cosmopolitanisms alongside neo-colonialism after the Second World War, or globalisation and neo-liberalism in the late twentieth and early twenty-first centuries. As Jason Hill has noted: 'One of the reasons for the current upsurge in interest in cosmopolitanism, it goes without saying, is our own relation to empire.'[19]

In the post-Second World War era of decolonisation and relative geopolitical decline, British cosmopolitanism has been caught up in the powerful triangulation of British national identity between the Special Relationship with the United States, its ambivalent relations with the European Union, and ongoing loyalties and obligations to citizens of the Commonwealth and former colonies. This has produced an often agonistic relationship between cosmopolitanism and national identity in the British context.

Post-War Cosmopolitanisms: Anger and Experimentation

Periodising contemporary British fiction since 1980 through the lens of cosmopolitanism we can see two major shifts in the ways in which British writers participated in what Bruce King has called 'the internationalization of English literature'.[20] One, profoundly concerned with the status of international elements, people of colour and otherness within British culture, was triggered by the advent of Thatcherism in 1979; the second, more outward-looking transformation, with the end of the Cold War in 1989–91.

These decisively challenged the often insular mood of post-war British culture. The Angry provincial neo-realism of the 1950s generation of Kingsley Amis, John Wain and John Osborne launched a full-blown attack on literary Modernism and its 'myth kitty', which was personified for this hypermasculine literary insurgency by a decadent cultural establishment supposedly overshadowed by Virginia Woolf, Forster and Bloomsbury. For the Angry Generation, the cosmopolitanism and internationalism of literary Modernism represented a decadent and 'queer' elite leisure class whose hold on the institutions of culture they were determined to break.[21] This provincialising neo-realist turn of the 1950s was in part a reaction against the often camouflaged aesthetic experimentation of the British wartime literary boom.[22]

During the Second World War, the official war culture incorporated an inclusive high culture cosmopolitanism mobilised against fascist ultranationalism. This highbrow tendency rubbed shoulders both with the more demotic and regional cultural forms of the People's War, and a powerful resurgence of popular imperialism as millions of Empire, Commonwealth and Dominion troops joined the war against fascism. Thus, Cyril Connolly famously recounted receiving letters from RAF pilots praising *Horizon* magazine for representing all that they were fighting for. This wartime tradition of crossing race and class lines was kept alive in part by the post-1948 Windrush generation of immigrants from the Caribbean which was celebrated in the work of Samuel Selvon, George Lamming, V. S. Naipaul and Calypso music. The Angry Generation thus participated in the insular ethnographic turn away, as Jed Esty has persuasively argued, from the ironic alienated vision of cosmopolitan and metropolitan high modernism to late modernist and neo-realist representations of English national culture.[23] These redemptive visions of Englishness were a powerful response to retrenchment and imperial contraction. Yet, for all the polemics and pyrotechnics of the Angry Generation, these powerful and often antagonistic cultural strains continued to coexist into the post-war era.

During the Cold War, this cosmopolitan vision of an internationalist Anglo-American high culture persisted on the pages of *Encounter* magazine, which was later revealed to have been covertly subsidised by the CIA as an instrument of anti-Soviet cultural policy by the front organisation the Congress for Cultural Freedom. Cold War cultural politics promoted a depoliticising universalist mode of Anglo-American modernism and cosmopolitanism that saw itself as the culture of a transnational elite above the provincialism of local identity, whose anti-Communist universalism resisted both postcolonial nationalism and the Soviet socialist realism.

This anti-cosmopolitan ethos and disavowal of aesthetic experimentation persisted into the 1960s, putting British literary culture firmly out of synch with the emergent experimentalism of Beat Generation writers, African American jazz and early postmodernism in the United States and the Nouveau Roman and other forms of experimentation in Europe. It was buttressed by the racist backlash against the 'Open Door' policy on immigration in the late 1950s and early 1960s, which saw Enoch Powell deploy his cosmopolitan classical education in his 'Rivers of Blood' speech in 1968.

Pitched against both Cold War cosmopolitanism and Angry neo-realist provincialism, however, was the progressive internationalism of anti-nuclear peace movements like CND and anti-colonial movements, as well as the cosmopolitan sympathies of much popular culture, often energised by traditions of British anti-Americanism. During the social liberalisation of the 1960s and 1970s, cosmopolitans could offer a seductive, yet dangerous, bridge between the dominant culture and the counter culture.

The ascendancy of Thatcherism in the 1980s hardly seemed conducive to cosmopolitanism in theory or practice. Resurgent cultural nationalism that viewed Europe and the European Union with suspicion merged with a neo-imperial nostalgia at home that was reinforced by the British victory in the Falklands-Malvinas war and the escalation of the undeclared war in Northern Ireland. British foreign policy was dominated by the 'New Cold War' revival of the Anglo-American Special Relationship which followed the Soviet invasion of Afghanistan and escalation of the nuclear arms race. Militarised policing and covert surveillance used in Northern Ireland were deployed against domestic enemies within, like the inner-city youth who rioted in the summer of 1981 and the National Union of Miners during the Miners' Strike. Yet, despite the convulsive effects of Thatcherism on British society and culture, the 1980s nevertheless inherited a fairly stable Cold War antagonism between an official anti-Communist cosmopolitanism of Anglo-American elites that promoted universal Western values, and a liberal/Left internationalism sympathetic to decolonisation, anti-colonial nationalism and the Peace Movement, both of which had to contend with a dominant British national culture that remained resilient in the face of the United Kingdom's relative economic and geo-political decline. During the 1980s, these competing visions of Britain's relations with the world were framed by the familiar post-Second World War triangulation between the Special Relationship with the United States, the ambivalent relations with Europe, and commitments to citizens of the former colonies and the British Commonwealth.

Despite Thatcherism's nationalist revival and imperial nostalgia, the period nevertheless saw, as historian Brian Harrison has observed, a remarkable increase in international influences on British life.

Between 1970 and 1990 Britain experienced waves of overseas influence in every area of national life: from Italy and France on approaches to planning and on the film industry; from Japan on manufacturing methods; from Singapore on social discipline; from European clubs on football; from Scandinavia on welfare issues and public administration; from Denmark and the Netherlands on sexual liberation; from the USA on free-market economics, civil liberties, and feminism. British opinion could not be insulated from over-seas influence.[24]

Nevertheless, Harrison observes, 'institutionally, political internationalism lagged behind', with the Conservative government increasingly suspicious of a European super-state and tending to reserve its commitments to immi-grants and refugees from former colonies of its overseas Empire:

> ... economic internationalism was far outrunning political. The political foun-dations of the new international world order therefore seemed likely to grow only out of regional political mergers; until then, political internationalism could rest securely only upon internationalism of the cultural and economic variety.[25]

In the 1980s, literature and culture took on an outsize importance.

Remapping Thatcher's Britain

Looking at the 1980s from the vantage point of cosmopolitanism yields a different picture from the conventional literary account of the decade. Typically, the 1980s are seen as dominated by a postmodern and postcolonial literary turn pushing back against an emergent and rapidly dominant Thatcherite enterprise culture. But even in retrospect the rapidly canonised fiction of Kazuo Ishiguro, Martin Amis, Salman Rushdie and Graham Swift offers strikingly indirect representations of the social and economic impact of neo-Conservative 'authoritarian populism'. Novelistic responses to Thatcherism seemed to lag drastically behind the often gritty social realism of other genres, whether in feature films like *The Long Good Friday* (John Mackenzie, 1980), *Meantime* (Mike Leigh, 1981, TV), *Boys from the Blackstuff* (Alan Bleasdale, 1982, TV), *Local Hero* (Bill Forsyth, 1983) and *The Ploughman's Lunch* (dir. Richard Eyre and screenplay Ian McEwan, 1983), or in drama like Caryl Churchill's *Top Girls* (1982) and *Serious Money* (1987), Howard Brenton's *The Romans in Britain* (1980), David Edgar's *Maydays* (1983), or David Hare and Howard Brenton's *Pravda* (1985).

Framed in terms of the representational struggle between cosmopolitan themes, resurgent nationalism and the neo-Conservative economic agenda, however, British fiction of the period can be read as much more responsive to the decade's radical social upheavals. It would be tempting to confine British cosmopolitanism since 1980 to an exemplary tradition of predominantly metropolitan writers of colour. Yet this would be to radically simplify the discrepant nature of cosmopolitan by mapping it onto an older tradition of elite metropolitan literature. This also risks simply reversing the polarity of the attacks on fiction with an international bias that have resonated powerfully since the 1950s. We need instead to preserve the contradictory nature of British cosmopolitanism as an extensive, differential mode of cultural affiliation defined as much by its relationship to violence and negation as by its more inclusive utopian and global impulses. Rather than locating the cosmopolitan impulse in specific genres, literary traditions or counter-canons, we can track its persistence across the work of writers who seek to represent — in cosmopolitan scenes — the collision of specifically English or national subjects with the claims of the rest of the world.

The 1980s inherited a post-war fictional internationalism which self-consciously positioned itself as a belated, late modernist offshore experimentalism. Anthony Burgess's sprawling magnum opus *Earthly Powers* (1980) is perhaps the most notable example, kicking off the decade with an exuberant exploration of a twentieth-century British literary émigré's engagement with the wider world. The novel's playfully unreliable narrator, Kenneth Toomey, is based loosely on Somerset Maugham, whose globe-trotting tendencies and queerness he shares, as he narrates his own ironic *bildungsroman* through modern history and literature. Toomey's story shadows that of his brother-in-law Carlo Campanati, who ascends to the Papacy and is being considered for Sainthood despite his worldliness and immersion in earthly powers, rather than spiritual. Like the alternative canon Burgess conjured in a fit of pique at being left off a list of 100 Best Novelists, his novel both celebrates cosmopolitan erotics and divided loyalties, representing England as both hostile to outsiders – as well as tax exile authors – and an inevitable point of return. *Earthly Powers* also defiantly capped Burgess's career of decidedly un-English productivity and experimentation. Such an alternative tradition might include the work of Angela Carter, Geoff Dyer, Gilbert Adair and Christine Brooke-Rose. From his suburban stronghold in Shepperton, J. G. Ballard also pursued a transgressive internationalism in the genres of science fiction and speculative fiction, memorably excavating his own childhood experiences of internment in Shanghai during the Second World War in *Empire of the Sun*.

Alasdair Gray's late modernist novel, *Lanark: A Life in Four Books* (1981), was similarly encyclopaedic in ambition, combining social realist descriptions of working-class urban life in Glasgow with Kafkaesque fantasy tracing the path of its protagonist, Duncan Thaw, through the Orwellian precincts of a city-state called Unthank. Gray's novel showed off its cosmopolitan sympathies by including a 'Dictionary of Plagiarisms' in its margins. The novel's critical success helped draw attention to the remarkable literary productivity of Scotland during the contemporary period, by writers like James Kelman, Janice Galloway, Irvine Welsh, A. L. Kennedy, Ian Rankin, Iain Banks (also writing sci-fi as Iain M. Banks), Alan Warner and Ali Smith.

Angela Carter explored a feminist internationalist vision in both the essay and experimental fiction, informed by her experiences in Japan and as a visiting writer in the United States. Like Rushdie, her work showed the influence of Latin American 'Boom' writers like Garcia Marquez, but also drew on European traditions of fantasy and romance. Carter's short stories in *The Bloody Chamber* evoked a powerful and playful feminist appropriation of gothic fantasy, fairy tales and folk tales, often set in a deterritorialised trans-European past. Her screenplay adaptation of her story, 'The Company of Wolves', was vividly realised for the screen by director Neil Jordan in 1984. Her novel, *Nights at the Circus*, followed the literally carnivalesque adventures of a winged trapeze artist 'Fevvers' and her fellow circus members from London to St Petersburg and Siberia. Although her writing career was cut short by her untimely death in 1992, Carter blazed a trail along with other British writers in the 1980s.

Straddling the divide between postcolonial critique and metropolitan worldliness, Salman Rushdie's seminal fictions of the 1980s also showed a commitment to cosmopolitan style at the level of both form and content. The fabulist playfulness that echoed the magical realism of Latin American 'Boom' writers like Gabriel Garcia Marquez, Borges and Alejo Carpentier allowed Rushdie's narratives to propel his protagonists across national borders. In his Booker-Prize-winning novel *Midnight's Children*, Rushdie's narrative celebrated the mobility and hybrid identities of his characters in ways that powerfully resonated with postcolonial theory. Drawing on traditions of international fiction, which included Desani's *All About H. Haterr*, Rushdie's narrative voice brilliantly projected a sprawling, dialogic formal solution to the damage and losses wrought by displacement and exile. Lurking behind the exuberant playfulness, Rushdie made clear in his nonfiction prose both a postcolonial melancholy and a universalising ambition that claimed to be the heir to Western traditions of cosmopolitanism.

> ... the writer who is out-of-country and even out-of-language may experience this loss in an intensified form. It is made more concrete for him by the physical fact of discontinuity, of his present being in a different place from his past, of his being 'elsewhere'. This may enable him to speak properly and concretely on a subject of universal significance and appeal.[26]

This was for many a far more appealing and liberal vision than that of a conservative postcolonial writer like V. S. Naipaul. Defending *Midnight's Children* against condemnations by Indian critics of the despair of its protagonist, Saleem, Rushdie argued:

> What I tried to do was to set up a tension in the text, a paradoxical opposition between the form and content of the narrative. The story of Saleem does indeed

lead him to despair. But the story is told in a manner designed to echo, as closely as my abilities allowed, the Indian talent for non-stop self-regeneration. This is why the narrative constantly throws up new stories, why it 'teems'. The form – multitudinous, hinting at the infinite possibilities of the country – is the optimistic counterweight to Saleem's personal tragedy. I do not think that a book written in such a manner can really be called a despairing work.[27]

Yet, as Rushdie made clear in his remarkable and more self-restrained novel *Shame* (1983), the pull of borders and the political conflicts of Pakistan as postcolonial nation-state acted as a powerful reality check to cosmopolitan fantasy. Despite its ironic critique of Western metropolitan culture, Rushdie's novel *The Satanic Verses* (1988) became, whether its author liked it or not while under protection of the British state, a standard bearer for Western liberal values against the fundamentalist censorship of the *fatwa*. Here, the cosmopolitan will to imagine fictional worlds detached from national borders collided with the realpolitik of the end of the Cold War. In his essays collected in *Imaginary Homelands*, Rushdie powerfully criticised the imperial nostalgia and 'Orwellmania' of the mid-1980s as representing a dangerous confluence of resurgent nationalism and political quietism that characterised the cultural response to Thatcherism. He proclaimed both his commitment to the imaginative reconstruction of 'imaginary homelands' as a response to the pain and privations of exile and sectarian violence, and to a politicised role for literature 'Outside the whale'.

As Burgess, Ballard, Carter and Rushdie's fiction vibrantly demonstrates, British cosmopolitanism's ambivalence and instability is often rendered visible in fictional representations of doubles and doubling, of violent incursions into hospitable spaces and of the excavation of foreign presences from within the heart of national culture. Cosmopolitanism is shadowed by its doubles. This can produce violence, as in René Girard's account of mimetic desire, 'the combat of doubles results in the expulsion of one of the pair, and this is identified directly with the return to peace and order'.[28] This proliferation of doubles can also produce a sense of the uncanny, as Nicholas Royle has noted of Freud's essay on the subject, whether in the simple form of the figure of actual doubles or in 'a more complex conception, in which it is no longer possible to know which come first or indeed whether there is a "first"'.[29] And the ironic doubling provoked by cosmopolitanism can also produce comedy, often of a very dark nature.

Vernacular Elements and Alternative Histories

The literary 1980s saw the British novel finally catch up with postmodern experimentation displaying a common interest in excavating alternative histories that Linda Hutcheon described in her *A Poetics of Postmodernism* (1988) as 'historiographical metafiction'. But much of its vibrancy was also informed by an ethnographic attention to working-class and immigrant culture that drew on traditions of the documentary and neo-realism. This attention to the vernacular also helped defamiliarise that most deeply English of genres – the comedy of manners. Strikingly, many of their narratives were energised and disturbed by plots involving the revelation of foreign secrets, cosmopolitan genealogies and inheritances. Here, cosmopolitanism is clearly mobilised against nationalist parochialism, and the excavation of alternative histories that was identified as one of the characteristic tendencies in the postmodern British novel, of what Hutcheon influentially termed 'historiographic metafiction', often involved the discovery of the repression or destruction of foreign elements within Deep England.

For Martin Amis, the United States represented both the apotheosis of Thatcherite enterprise culture and a fictional alternative to the gravitational force of London's class hierarchies and cultural capital. Martin Amis's novelistic satire of the American film business, *Money: A Suicide Note* (1984), for example, follows the hedonistic and self-excoriating transatlantic travails of its half-American protagonist, John Self.[30] Amis both participated in and critiqued the resurgence of Anti-Americanism during the decade provoked by Margaret Thatcher's embrace of the Special Relationship with Reagan's America during the military escalation of the New Cold War. The novel also maintains his appalled fascination with London's hypermasculine Cockney culture. Amis also took a transatlantic approach in his book of short stories about the Cold War threat of nuclear annihilation, *Einstein's Monsters*, provoked in part by his engagement with the work of American environmentalist and peace activist Jonathan Schell and in the literary journalism collected in *The Moronic Inferno: And Other Visits to America* (1986).

The excavation of alternative histories also motivates the revelations in Kazuo Ishiguro's *The Remains of the Day* (1989), for example, as Stevens the butler looks back from the vantage point of 1956 Britain of the Suez Crisis at a life devoted to serving a morally bankrupt aristocrat. At the core of his self-incriminating and meandering first-person narration is his failure to defend two Jewish housemaids from being fired by the antisemitic Lord Darlington in the 1930s, which will likely result in their deportation back to the Holocaust. This refusal of cosmopolitan sympathies is compounded by Stevens's wilful blindness to and complicity with the unpatriotic actions of his employer, Lord Darlington, who moves from defending Germany from punitive reparations after the Versailles Conference to actively conspiring to appease Nazi Germany. These themes of complicity and wilful blindness also resonate in Ishiguro's extraordinary previous novel, *The Artist of the Floating World*, set in post-war Nagasaki, narrated by a renowned artist who simply cannot comprehend his family and neighbour's moral outrage at his collaboration with the fascist imperial regime. The transgressive force of cosmopolitan sympathies also disturbs the tropes of dominant Englishness in *When We Were Orphans* (2000), in the hallucinatory quest of Ishiguro's ponderous yet sympathetic detective for his long-dead parents in Shanghai during the Japanese bombing of the city in 1932.

The deeply English genre of the comedy of manners was also disturbed by cosmopolitan energies during the ascendancy of Thatcherism. This is strikingly visible in the work of Penelope Fitzgerald, for example, a latecomer to British fiction who published a series of remarkable and critically acclaimed novels in the 1980s. Having co-edited with her husband a short-lived journal of world literature, *World Review*, in the 1950s and only turning to fiction after she retired from teaching in her 60s, Fitzgerald seems strongly attuned to the disruptive power of foreign influences. The fictional crisis of her Booker-Prize-nominated second novel, *The Bookshop* (1978), for example, is unleashed by her protagonist's decision to stock Nabokov's *Lolita* in a village bookshop in East Anglia. Her next novel, *Offshore* (1979), the surprise winner of that year's Booker Prize, explores the subtly destabilising influence of its Canadian single-parent mother and her children on an eccentric community of boat dwellers on the River Thames in the 1960s. Fitzgerald's succeeding novels, slim but incandescent, left autobiographical material behind in favour of historical fictions, often with foreign settings like her imaginative reconstruction of family dynasty in Italy in *Innocence* (1986). In *The Beginning of Spring* (1988), the tolerant liberalism of a British expatriate printer and his feisty children in Moscow leads them to unwittingly give refuge to a young revolutionary internationalist, Lisa Ivanova, who departs for Berlin leaving everything changed. Fitzgerald explores the genteel interplay in pre-First World War Cambridge of the rival international scientific traditions that will produce quantum physics in *The Gate of Angels* (1990), showing her characters collide like particles across the boundaries of class and gender. This imaginative openness to foreign elements disrupting fictional microcosms produced a *tour-de-force* representation of European Romanticism colliding with German bourgeois families and Enlightenment university life in her prize-winning novel about the poet Novalis, *The Blue Flower* (1995).

A more demotic fictional engagement with what would be called cosmopolitanism-from-below or vernacular cosmopolitanism involved writers with stronger ties to realist representation of everyday life and popular culture. This is visible across Hanif Kureishi's work in *My Beautiful*

Laundrette, The Buddha of Suburbia and *My Son the Fanatic*. Jeanette Winterson's queer fiction explores the tolerance displayed towards her young lesbian heroine among evangelical Christians in Northern England in *Oranges Are Not the Only Fruit*. Scottish writer James Kelman has produced perhaps the most remarkable sustained project of internationalist social realism originating in the 1980s in both short fiction collections like *Greyhound for Breakfast* (1987), *Not Not While the Giro* (1983) and *The Burn* (1991), and novels like *How Late It Was, How Late* (1994). Kelman expands the scope of his interrogation of narratives fractured by violence and neo-liberal governmentality to unnamed nations scorched by the extreme violence of genocide, torture and civil war in *Translated Accounts* (2001) and to immigrant life in the United States in *You Have to Be Careful in the Land of the Free* (2004). In these fictions, cosmopolitanism-from-below is empowered by the ferocious auto-didacticism and tolerant internationalism of their protagonists.

Vernacular cosmopolitanism also powerfully informed 1980s popular fiction, which was more frequently adapted for film and television than literary fiction. Here, the typically masculine, melancholy and isolated figure of the detective or the spy with cosmopolitan sympathies exploring the darker reaches of British culture proved a persistent presence, often confronting the corruptions of the dominant culture or political establishment. John Le Carré's Cold War spy fiction memorably pitted humane liberal openness of George Smiley against the murderous internationalism of the KGB spymaster, Karla, in his trilogy *Tinker, Tailor, Soldier, Spy* (1974), *The Honourable Schoolboy* (1977) and *Smiley's People* (1979), the first and last of which were adapted for British television. With the end of the Cold War, Le Carré continued to write about the depredations of transnational capitalism, the global arms trade, big pharma and intelligence agencies on the Global South in novels like *A Perfect Spy* (1986), *The Night Manager* (1993), *The Constant Gardener* (2001) and *The Mission Song* (2006).

Turning Outward: Optimism and Melancholy

All this took a darker and more ambivalent turn towards the global following the end of the Cold War in 1989–91. The break-up of the Cold War order and the ensuing dominance of the United States was greeted as ushering in a Pax Americana and a harmonious era of economic and cultural globalisation and transitions to democracy. Yet this era of the reunification of Germany, end of apartheid and Truth and Reconciliation in South Africa, and a peace process in Northern Ireland also saw genocides in Bosnia and Rwanda, and an emerging Western consensus about the use of military force in the name of humanitarian interventionism in the face of resurgent neo-nationalism, genocide and civil wars in the former Eastern Bloc and the Global South. This led to an intense post-Cold War debate about often-conflicting definitions of a 'new cosmopolitanism' in relation to war, nationalism and the institutionalisation of international human rights through the United Nations, international tribunals and NGOs. The terms of this debate have intensified and escalated, but not profoundly changed, after the 11 September 2001 terrorist attacks and the wars in Afghanistan, Iraq and the ongoing US Global War on Terror.

Along with the optimism of confronting and working through historical trauma through fictional narrative, the post-Cold War decade seemed to imbue literary representations of the figure of the cosmopolitan with a more damaged and melancholy vision, perhaps because the tension between nationalism and cosmopolitanism was relaxed and confused in the era of globalisation and neo-liberal governmentality. This scepticism challenged the post-Cold War mood of optimism in international relations where the international legal order associated with cosmopolitan human rights seemed to have yielded such remarkable achievements as the end of Apartheid in South Africa, and the apparatus of Truth Commissions aided in transitions to democracy in other former authoritarian regimes in the Global South. Nevertheless, the civil war in the former Yugoslavia that led to a Bosnian genocide as well as the Western failure to confront the genocide in Rwanda dealt a blow to visions of a peaceful era of international human rights to accompany the seemingly irresistible economic logic of globalisation and Americanisation. Cosmopolitanism was also mobilised in the name of humanitarian military intervention, reviving critiques of its relationship to cultural imperialism and militarism.

The post-Cold War era opened up the utopian prospect of a cosmopolitanism-from-below in which writers of multiple ethnicities could celebrate an openness to diversity. Zadie Smith's remarkable debut novel, *White Teeth* (2000), seemed to encapsulate the decade's optimism. Coinciding with the end of the Thatcherite Conservative rule from 1979–97, the New Labour election victory and the cultural rebranding of the nation in the wake of Britpop as 'Cool Britannia', Smith's novel seemed to signal a new multicultural optimism in the self-image of many Britons. Spanning three generations of English and immigrant life, the novel exuberantly represents the enduring friendships, travails and adventures of two London families, one Anglo-Caribbean the other South Asian, while somehow bringing in retrospective episodes in colonial Jamaica, North Africa in the Second World War and speculations about the future of genetic engineering and animal rights.

Unlike Samuel Selvon's masculine, marginalised cast of West Indian immigrants of the Windrush generation in *The Lonely Londoners*, Smith's characters were anything but lonely, and claimed a defiantly metropolitan sociality and centrality. In retrospect, this vision of an inclusive Britishness may have leaned heavily on London as *polis*. As I suggested above, Smith's novel *NW* explores a considerably darker, more violent and formally disjunctive vision of the city. Her short story, 'The Embassy of Cambodia' (2013), about Fatou, a woman struggling to escape wage slavery in suburban London, retains Smith's more typical optimism of the intellect Smith, as does her influential reflection on the EU Referendum, 'Fences: A Brexit Diary' (2016). Smith's success as both a literary novelist in the tradition of British social comedy and a highly visible public intellectual of colour was made possible by generations of British writers with international engagements, many of whom were writing from outside the London literary world. This was strikingly visible in the alternative genealogies reconstructed by Caryl Phillips or James Procter at the end of a decade that saw the fiftieth anniversary of the arrival of Caribbean immigrants on the SS Empire Windrush.[31]

The other remarkable fictional debut in the late 1990s, this time representing the more melancholy sense of British cosmopolitanism, was that of W. G. Sebald. An expatriate academic whose literary writing career began late and was cut short by a car crash in 2001, Sebald explored the damaged lives and circuitous, often retrograde journeys of his eponymous narrator and his protagonists in a remarkable trilogy, *The Rings of Saturn*, *The Emigrants* and *Vertigo*. Like his final novel, *Austerlitz*, their meandering, layered late modernist, often baroque prose narratives were written in German and carefully translated, exploring with melancholy irony and obsessive care the human and environmental consequences of the Holocaust and the Second World War for European refugees and exiles in England. Sebald also intervened decisively in the revisionist historical and political debate about the Allied area bombing of Germany in the Second World War in his 1999 lectures, which were translated as *A Natural History of Destruction* (2003). Sebald remained intensely sceptical about the travel genre that he decisively transformed and quietly disrupted.

> That is what is so awful about modern life – we never return. One year we go to India and the next year to Peru and the next to Greenland. Because now you can go everywhere. I would much rather have half a dozen places that meant something to me than to say, at the end of my life, 'I have been to practically everywhere.' The first visit doesn't reveal very much at all.[32]

His characteristic tropes deal with the constant doubling back and obsessive returns required if his narrators are to confront actively and courageously the damage of the European past.

Melancholy as an activist emotion also pervades William Boyd's novel, *Armadillo* (1998), whose protagonist, Lorimer Black, camouflages his Transnistrian gypsy family origins to get ahead as an insurance risk adjuster in London's corporate financial sector, only to collide with the machinations of an aristocratic elite intent on pulling off a multinational real estate and insurance fraud. Observing another character of undefined ethnicity, Lorimer Black wonders, 'Cypriot? Lebanese? Spanish? Egyptian? Syrian? Greek? Like himself, Lorimer knew, there were many types of Englishmen.'[33] The narrative steadily strips him of his protective shell and forces him back on the vernacular cosmopolitanism of his trans-European origins, and a comic subplot crosses his path with the faux internationalism of a rock megastar, David Watts, he accidentally introduces to Afro-pop. Here, the rendering visible of the foreign elements within Englishness takes a more comic and redemptive turn, although cultural outsiders like Lorimer Black have to armour themselves against the dominant culture and construct their own escape routes.

The exuberant energies of international travel and expatriate life also took on a darker side in the face of greater popular awareness of the environmental damage, social alienation and economic exploitation that accompanied globalisation as traced in Scottish novelist Alan Warner's *Morvern Callar* (1995) and English writer and director Alex Garland's best-selling fiction, *The Beach* (1996), both successfully adapted for the screen. Nowhere was this more brilliantly represented than in director Jonathan Glazer's satire of the British crime film *Sexy Beast* (2000), in which 'Gal', played by Ray Winstone, has his sun-soaked Spanish retirement on the 'Costa del Crime' rudely interrupted by Don Logan, Ben Kingsley's relentless anti-Gandhian Cockney gangster. Once again, the antagonism between cosmopolitan sympathies and Deep England provokes a rewriting of such classic British crime film narratives as *Get Carter* (1971) or *The Long Good Friday* (1979).

British writers responded powerfully to the post-Cold War engagement with historical trauma and historical justice in public discourse in historical fictions about the national experience of total warfare in the two world wars. Pat Barker's First World War trilogy, beginning with her Booker-Prize-winning novel, *Regeneration* (1991), placed the real-life cosmopolitan characters of the Great War poet Siegfried Sassoon and the colonial anthropologist and English Freudian W. H. Rivers at the heart of its fictional exploration of the ethical dilemma of military psychiatrists treating shell-shocked soldiers at Craiglockhart Hospital in Scotland during the First World War. The Second World War and the Holocaust are at the unstable fissile fictional core of

Martin Amis's Swiftian narrative, *Time's Arrow: or The Nature of the Offence* (1991). Narrated in reverse chronology by a parasite within an expatriate Nazi doctor who escaped to the Mid-West after the fall of the Reich, *Time's Arrow* shows the ways in which Todt has cosmopolitanism forced upon him by America and by the reverse passage of time which undoes both his work as an ER physician and his murderous role in a Nazi death camp. Amis's novel displays a profound scepticism about the declarations of the 'end of history' by intellectuals like Francis Fukuyama and the ushering in of an era of harmonious economic globalisation and Pax Americana that greeted the end of the Cold War and the fall of the Soviet Union in 1989–91.

Michael Ondaatje's Second World War fiction and imperial romance, *The English Patient* (1992), also won the Booker Prize, counterpointing the Italian Campaign of 1943–44 with the adventures of archaeological explorers in the North African desert. The 1996 Oscar-winning film adaptation directed by Anthony Minghella, whose depoliticised cosmopolitanism defused much of Ondaatje's critical treatment of imperialism in the novel, provided a triumphant boost to the British film industry's international prestige in the era of globalisation. Ondaatje's next novel, *Anil's Ghost*, departed decisively from the subject matter of British 'Heritage Cinema'. Set during the Sri Lankan Civil War and written in a similarly fragmented style, the novel offers a superbly literary and haunting exploration of the ethical and political compromises facing Anil Tissera, a US-trained forensic anthropologist working for international human rights NGOs as she returns home to confront the violence of state terror and the pressures of economic globalisation.

These darker fictional representations warned of the dangers of cosmopolitan globalisation and military interventionism. The period after 11 September 2001 saw Britain join the United States in its invasion and occupation of Iraq in 2003, whose disastrous consequences were widely protested, and a long-standing military commitment in Afghanistan from 2002 to 2014. While British fiction writers have not yet engaged with these recent wars to the same degree as dramatists or documentarians or the growing body of recent US war writing, some notable examples include Ian McEwan's novel *Saturday* (2005), and British veteran Harry Parker's remarkable autobiographical novel, *Anatomy of a Soldier* (2016), narrated from the point of view of the objects surrounding a British soldier who loses his legs in an IED attack in Afghanistan.

During this more violent and uncertain period of war, anxieties about terrorism and a global refugee crisis, British writers have continued to engage powerfully with the transnational and vernacular dimensions of British life in fictions like Hari Kunzu's *The Impressionist* (2002) and *Transmission*

(2005), Monica Ali's *Brick Lane* (2003), Andrea Levy's *A Small Island* (2004), Guatam Malkani's *Londonstani* (2006), Helen Oyeyemi's *The Opposite House* (2007), Zadie Smith's *NW* and Sunjeev Sahota's *The Year of the Runaways* (2015). At its most benign, cosmopolitanism reminds us of loyalties to other people that go far beyond the limits of the nation or locality, and reveals in Julia Kristeva's terms how we are 'strangers to ourselves'. In its more violent representations, it confronts Edward Said's vision of cosmopolitanism as a 'troubling, disabling, destabilizing secular wound'.[34] As Jacqueline Rose asks in response to Said: 'Can we envisage a wounded cosmopolitanism that takes up into its own vision – rather than repudiating or claiming to resolve – the most damaging elements of both history and who we are?'[35] These two strands of British cosmopolitanism, the damaged melancholy consciousness of the lonely cosmopolitan subject under attack and the celebration of a vibrantly populated space for cosmopolitanism coexist uneasily into the post-Brexit future. They make clear the importance of avoiding a simple binary choice between good (or bad depending on your view of the European Union) 'cosmopolitan' London and bad/racist (or good patriotic) 'communitarian' locales full of Brexiteers. Better to try and find some more inclusive and complicated ongoing vision of national identity that incorporates diverse forms of Englishness and otherness. The Brexit vote in June 2016, like the anti-immigrant backlash against the unprecedented global Refugee Crisis, the rise of neo-fascist parties in Europe and the United States, or the neo-nationalist populism of the Trump administration, can be seen as bringing this longer crisis home to British shores. This makes a complex understanding of the conflicting traditions of cosmopolitanism, as a vocabulary for understanding Britain's obligations and responsibilities to others within its borders and the world outside, all the more relevant and urgent to British writers and citizens.

Notes

1. *Oxford English Dictionary*, dating back to the mid-nineteenth century.
2. *Ibid.*, early twentieth century.
3. S. Hall, 'Cosmopolitanism: Stuart Hall in Conversation with Prina Werbner' (2006), my transcription, n.p., www.youtube.com/watch?v=zcaGhyYvMlo.
4. T. May, 'Theresa May's Conference Speech in Full', The Telegraph (5 October 2016), n.p.
5. J. Stacey, 'The Uneasy Cosmopolitans of Code Unknown' in N. Glick Schiller and A. Irving (eds), *Whose Cosmopolitanism?: Critical Perspectives, Relationalities and Discontents* (New York: Berghahn Books, 2014), p. 163.
6. H. Kureishi, *My Beautiful Laundrette and The Rainbow Sign* (Boston: Faber & Faber, 1986), p. 60.

7. S. Knight, *Dirty Pretty Things: Screenplay* (New York: Miramax, 2002), n.p.
8. On the darker side of cosmopolitanism, see K. Eddy, 'Introduction' in *Negative Cosmopolitanism: Cultures and Politics of World Citizenship after Globalization* (Montreal: McGill-Queen's University Press, 2017), pp. 3–26.
9. Smith 2012, p. 299.
10. Ibid., p. 300. Emphasis in the original.
11. For invaluable surveys, see P. Cheah and B. Robbins, 'Introductions' *Cosmopolitics: Thinking and Feeling beyond the Nation* (Minneapolis, MN: University of Minnesota Press, 1998); A. Appiah, *Cosmopolitanism: Ethics in a World of Strangers* (New York: W. W. Norton, 2007); B. Robbins, *Perpetual War: Cosmopolitanism from the Viewpoint of Violence* (Durham, NC: Duke University Press, 2012), p. 194 n25; and Glick Schiller and Irving (eds), *Whose Cosmopolitanism?*.
12. This overview draws on the invaluable surveys of Robbins, 'Introduction Part I' in *Cosmopolitics*; D. Harvey, 'What Do We Do with Cosmopolitanism?' in Glick Schiller and Irving (eds), *Whose Cosmopolitanism?*; and R. Walkowitz, *Cosmopolitan Style: Modernism beyond the Nation* (New York: Columbia University Press, 2006).
13. Nussbaum, cited in Robbins, 'Introduction Part I', p. 2.
14. Harvey, 'What Do We Do with Cosmopolitanism?', p. 51.
15. Robbins, 'Introduction Part I', p. 3.
16. Walkowitz 2006, p. 17.
17. B. Robbins, *Perpetual War: Cosmopolitanism from the Viewpoint of Violence* (Durham, NC: Duke University Press, 2012), p. 194 n25.
18. E. Said, *Orientalism* (London: Penguin Classics, 2003), p. 37.
19. J. Hill, 'Cosmopolitanism' in J. Protevi (ed.), *The Edinburgh Dictionary of Continental Philosophy* (Edinburgh University Press, 2005), p. 108. Jason Hill argues that Stoic philosophy in the Hellenistic era emerged 'as a reaction to the gradual disappearance of the small city-state in an age of empire'.
20. B. King, *The Internationalization of English Literature* (New York: Oxford University Press, 2004).
21. See A. Sinfield, *Literature, Politics and Culture in Postwar Britain* (London: Bloomsbury, 2004), pp. 81–102.
22. P. Deer, *Culture in Camouflage: War, Empire, and Modern British Literature* (Oxford University Press, 2009), pp. 235–42.
23. J. Esty, *A Shrinking Island: Modernism and National Culture in England* (Princeton University Press, 2004).
24. B. Harrison, *Finding a Role? The United Kingdom, 1970–1990* (Oxford: Clarendon, 2011), p. 6.
25. Ibid.
26. S. Rushdie, 'Imaginary Homelands' in *Imaginary Homelands: Essays and Criticism, 1981–1991* (New York: Penguin, 1992), p. 12.
27. Ibid., p. 16.
28. R. Girard, 'Things Hidden' in J. G. Williams (ed.), *The Girard Reader* (New York: Crossroad Publishing Company, 2000), p. 146.
29. N. Royle, 'Freud's Double' in L. Marcus and A. Mukherjee (eds), *Concise Companion to Psychoanalysis, Literature, and Culture* (Oxford: Wiley, 2014), p. 132.

30. In interview, Amis observes of his protagonist: 'I think Money makes a break from the English tradition of sending a foreigner abroad in that (a) John Self is half American, and (b) as a consequence cannot be scandalised by America. You know the usual Pooterish Englishman who goes abroad in English novels and is taken aback by everything. Well, not a bit of that in John Self. He completely accepts America on its own terms and is perfectly at home with it' (M. Amis, 'Martin Amis by Patrick McGrath', *Bomb Magazine* (1 January 1987), n.p.).

31. See C. Phillips, *Extravagant Strangers: A Literature of Belonging* (London: Faber & Faber, 1997); and J. Procter, *Writing Black Britain, 1948–98: An Interdisciplinary Anthology* (Manchester University Press, 2000).

32. A. Lubow, 'Crossing Boundaries' in L. S. Schwartz (ed.), *The Emergence of Memory: Conversations with W. G. Sebald* (New York: Seven Stories Press, 2007), p. 167.

33. W. Boyd, *Armadillo* (New York: Vintage, 1998), p. 111.

34. Said, *Orientalism*, p. 54.

35. J. Rose, 'Wounded Cosmopolitanism' in Glick Schiller and Irving (eds), *Whose Cosmopolitanism?*, p. 48.

PETER BOXALL

Conclusion
Imagining the Future

'And now we are looking only to the future.'
Donald Trump, Inauguration Speech, 20 January, 2017

'I will live in the Past, the Present, and the Future. The Spirits of all Three shall strive within me.'
Charles Dickens, *A Christmas Carol*

To bring this *Companion* to a close is necessarily to reflect on the future, on the ways in which the historical formations that we have traced in the preceding chapters allow us to conceive, at this brief and troubled threshold of our shared present, of the time to come.

This is perhaps the case with any historical study which ends with the present moment, wherever and whenever that present happens to be. But the task of imagining a future for and in the British novel is particularly pressing for us now, as I write, at the end of the second decade of the twenty-first century. As the contributions to this volume have demonstrated, the period 1980–2018 is one in which the cultural and political forms that allow us to conceive of a national literature have been particularly unstable and volatile. Mutations in the novel form over the last forty years have been deeply entangled in shifts in the ways in which we imagine our communities, as the question of how the novel shapes consciousness has been bound up with successive transformations in the nature of the democratic public sphere. The story of the British novel that we have told here is concerned, to a large degree, with this relation between history and form; but the balance of this relationship is currently skewed, as the political and literary forms with which we have imagined our democratic communities are entering into a state of transition – a transition that makes it unusually difficult to conceive of the future, either at a national or a global scale.

To address the nature of this transition – and of the current disorientation in our relationship with the future – I want to begin by considering four interventions made by world leaders at key moments in the historical span covered by this *Companion*.

The first of these is perhaps the most famous, and reflects the national tone in Britain in the 1980s, under Margaret Thatcher. 'And you know', Thatcher says in an interview with *Woman's Own* in 1987, 'there's no such thing as society. There are individual men and women and there are families.'[1] Thatcherism, the iron lady herself suggests here, requires the dismantling of collective forms of community, as the model of free trade upon which monetarism relies sees each person as a single entity, an individual man or woman, competing with others for advantage and for capital. As David Harvey argues, it 'proposes that human well-being can best be advanced by liberating individual entrepreneurial freedoms and skills within an institutional framework characterized by strong private property rights, free markets, and free trade'.[2] It is the role of government not to build communities, but to oversee unfettered competition between free individuals, who should be encumbered as little as possible by the state, or any other collective institutions. 'No government', Thatcher says in that same interview, 'can do anything except through people, and people must look after themselves first'.[3]

Fast forward fourteen years, to Brighton in October 2001, and to Tony Blair's speech to the Labour Party Conference, less than a month after the terrorist attacks that took place in New York on 11 September. Blair, for many political commentators, is Margaret Thatcher's heir, his 'third way' a means of adapting a centre-left commitment to social justice to the orthodoxies and demands of free trade.[4] But here, as Blair quickly (slickly, perhaps) adapts his conception of benign globalisation to the seismic shifts in the world order caused by 9/11, his account of 'society' could not diverge more widely from Thatcher's. Thatcher says there is no such thing as society; Blair insists that the only way of overcoming the evils of terrorism – or the dissent of any group who violently opposes 'our way of life' – is to imagine that there is no outside to society, that globalisation sees the production of an all-encompassing world community. It was immediately clear to Blair that the atrocities of 9/11 posed a significant threat to the consensus that history was moving towards the ever-more complete hegemony of the global market place. The attacks seemed to offer evidence, even to neo-conservative ideologues such as Francis Fukuyama, that there was a real and effective resistance to the very concept of Western democracy – but for Blair in 2001, the response to such resistance was not to lose faith in the concept of the global community, but to see it as the only solution to the experience of deprivation and alienation that led to the attacks in the first place.[5] It is the power of community – the very possibility of people and governments working together to create inclusive societies that Thatcher decried in 1984 – that Blair offers as the palliative to the unrest manifest in the 9/11 attacks. Blair acknowledges that there are 'critics' who doubt that 'the world' can be a 'community'. 'Nations act in their own interest', he admits, 'of course they do', just as individuals act in their own interests, apart from the claims of 'society'. But the 'lessons' of globalisation, he insists, are that 'our self-interest and our mutual interest are today inextricably woven together'.[6] We must not kick against such forms of connection, out of some fear that in doing so we expose ourselves to hostile forces outside the family or outside the nation; rather, we must accelerate the historical movement towards co-dependence. The 'problem' that comes to light on 11 September, he argues, is 'not that there is too much [globalization]; on the contrary there's too little of it'.[7] The way to overcome the violence of global terrorism is not to defend Western nations against hostile opponents, but to recognise a global common cause (an argument made recently, from a rather different perspective, by Judith Butler).[8] 'The starving, the wretched, the dispossessed', he says, as he winds up to his emotional peroration, 'the ignorant, those living in want and squalor from the deserts of Northern Africa to the slums of Gaza, to the mountain ranges of Afghanistan: they too are our cause'.[9]

Fast forward, again, to 2016, the annus horribilis for what we have become used to calling the 'liberal elite'. Blair's showy investment in the power of global community gave way quickly to military aggression – to US and allied wars fought in Iraq and Afghanistan, on spurious grounds, to defend the interests of the West against the ill-defined threat of Islamic terrorism.[10] The combination of military action in the aftermath of 9/11 with the economic crisis of 2008 derailed the forms of consensus that underwrote late-twentieth-century globalisation – the forms of global community that Blair sought to endorse in 2001. In North America, this denunciation of globalisation takes the form of a misanthropic (not to say misogynistic and racist) nationalism and protectionism, manifest in the figure of Donald Trump. Where Blair declared, in 2001, that 'our self-interest and our mutual interest are today inextricably woven together', Trump insists, throughout his 2016 election campaign, and in the 2017 speech he gave on his inauguration as President of the United States, that national self-interest must be opposed, directly, to any wider global concerns, economic, political or ecological. 'We assembled here today', Trump declares on 20 January 2017,

are issuing a new decree to be heard in every city, in every foreign capital and in every hall of power – from this day forward a new vision will govern our land – from this day forward it is going to be only America first – America first.[11]

Where, for Blair, it is necessary to recognise that the people of Afghanistan are not our enemies, but 'our cause', for Trump, reaping the dubious benefits of failed military operations in Afghanistan and Iraq, it has become clear that we must denounce the claims of all countries other than our own. 'We must protect our borders', he says, 'from the ravages of other countries, making our products, stealing our companies and destroying our jobs'.[12]

Globalisation gives way, in North America, to nationalism and protectionism; and in the United Kingdom we see the ugly twin of Trumpism in the form of UK nationalism, a version of the nationalism now spreading across the continent of Europe, and threatening the forms of consensus that were forged in the wake of the Second World War. The phenomenon of 'Brexit', still underway as I write, offers arguably the biggest challenge to the possibility of global integration, and the most dangerous assertion of European nationalism, since 1945. As the UK Prime Minister Theresa May puts it, in a speech given in October 2016, Brexit marks the end of the idea that communities can extend across national boundaries, the idea that self-interest and mutual interest might be woven together. In 'Brexit Britain', May declares, in an echo of Trump's 'America First' doctrine, it will no longer be possible for 'employers' to prioritise international concerns over the concerns of the nation – over 'the people down the road, the people they pass in the street'. In Brexit Britain, she declares in a caustic phrase that Patrick Deer discusses in this volume, 'if you believe you're a citizen of the world, you're a citizen of nowhere. You don't understand what the very word "citizenship" means'.[13]

The shifts in the idea of community that these interventions represent can be felt throughout the British cultural life of the period, its structure of feeling. The British novel, as we have pictured it in this volume, is shaped by the movement from Thatcher's dismantling of the post-war welfare state, to the forms of globalism represented by Blair's hollow utopianism, to the uncertain challenge to such globalism represented by 9/11, economic crisis and the waning of US power. One can see that many of the energies that animate the fictional imagination in the period – that determine the evolution of postcolonial and postmodern forms, as well as the tension in the British novel between cosmopolitanism and localism – are shaped by this trajectory. The novel of the late twentieth century – from the postmodern inventiveness of Rushdie, Amis and Carter, to the nationalism of Irivine Welsh, Janice Galloway and the earlier James Kelman, to the watchful British realism of a novel such as Ian McEwan's *Atonement* – is determined to a significant degree by the movement that one can discern from Thatcherism to Blairism, from the forms of consensus that were developed in the post-war decades, to the neoliberal globalisation of the model of Western democracy that both Thatcher and Blair sought to endorse and extend. Both Zadie Smith's *White Teeth* and Ian McEwan's *Atonement*, in their different ways, are the products of that consensus, of that balance that is struck, at the close of the century, between the national and the international – the world view that is determined by the proposition, still self-evident to Blair in the immediate aftermath of 9/11, that 'our self-interest and our mutual interest' are 'inextricably woven together'. But, even as Blair makes that speech in Brighton in 2001, this balance was already changing, and the relation between national and global, the quality and texture of democratic sovereignty, was being redrawn. As Blair put it, rather hauntingly, in his 2001 speech, the 'kaleidoscope has been shaken, the pieces are in flux'. 'Soon', Blair says in 2001, 'the pieces will fall'.[14] It seems likely that the phenomena of Trump and Brexit are one way that the pieces have fallen, one of the new patterns that has formed from that shake of the kaleidoscope. A political legacy of 9/11 is a resurgent, right-wing nationalism. But if this is the political response to that upheaval, the literary response, both in the British novel and more broadly, has been to seek new models for the production of national identities, and new ways of thinking about how historical forms of commitment and belonging relate to the strange new world to come, a world that seems no longer to accord with the paradigms and orthodoxies that stretched from the post-war to the turn of the century. British fiction's uncertain strain of postmodernism, as traced here by Ben Masters and Martin Paul Eve, is one of the formal means by which the novel reflected the passage towards late century globalisation – a cosmopolitan postmodernism that finds an exemplary model in Smith's *White Teeth*. But 9/11 was a trigger for a widespread waning of postmodernism as a cultural dominant, and with it the emergence of a generation of writers who were seeking to produce new narrative models of community, and of democracy.[15] The hermeneutic of suspicion adopted by late century postmodernism gives way to the perception that the novel has a responsibility to fashion new forms in which we might bring our shared histories into contact with a differently constituted public sphere, one which does not correspond to the models of political sovereignty bequeathed to us by the last century.

One of the ways in which this responsibility makes itself felt in the British post-millennial novel is in the perception, shared across a wide range of writers, that the novel has the capacity, and possibly the duty, to gestate images of the future, pictures of a world to come that might escape the narrow horizons thrown up by regressive twenty-first-century nationalisms. It is the case, of course, that these nationalisms themselves are also committed to the production of the future. As Trump puts it, in a chilling passage in his 2017 inauguration speech, 'now we are looking only to the future'.[16] Like all radical political projects, the task of 'making America great again', or of freeing Britain from the cold clutch of the European Union, involves the adoption of a year zero, a revolutionary calendar, which projects us into a time which begins anew on 20 January 2017, or on a 'Brexit day' currently envisaged to take place in March 2019. But the rise of twenty-first-century Western nationalism, while it might gesture towards a future, towards a new beginning that rejects the legacies of Obama, or of Blair, is also an avowedly reactionary movement, a movement that is anchored firmly in the past, in the version of the United States enshrined in the constitution, or in the fantasy of Britain as an imperial power, splendid in its isolation. It is against this version of the future, a future that is shaped by exclusive conceptions of a narrowly shared national past, that the post-millennial novel offers to produce pictures of futurity which are unstructured, which might open a space in which to envisage forms of imagined community that are not hemmed in by existing national boundaries and discriminations.

Across the range of British fiction written in the wake of 9/11, one can see these images of the future recurring – images which require the reinvention of the forms in which we have conceived of prose realism, and which suggest a new set of terms with which to represent and imagine our environments. We might think, for example, of David Mitchell's *Cloud Atlas*, a novel which is, in the words of the novel's narrator, 'gravid with the ancient future'[17] – a novel whose elaborate Russian doll structure, story within story within story, is designed to reach towards a world of distant futurity which lies at its heart, a distant futurity which stretches and dismantles the nested forms in which we encounter the time to come. Or we might think of Zadie Smith's *NW*, a novel that turns around the passing from one generation to the next, and that tries to imagine how we form a bridge between these generations, how we fashion a form of prose that brings a past generation into delicate contact with the generations to come. The novel's title suggests its regionalism, its interest in a specific corner of Northwest London, and its belonging to a long history of realism that has sought to capture the history and atmosphere of a specific place. But, in a chance echo of Theresa May's brutal refusal of cosmopolitanism ('if you're a citizen of the world, you are a citizen of nowhere'), Smith's title refers also to the designation 'nowhere' – a fascination with empty space, with unmade time, which grows throughout the novel, and comes to signify the space of the future itself, the utopian 'no place' in which we meet the generation to come. Encountering the naked future, shorn of its connections with the past, Smith's novel discovers, involves 'going nowhere', a peculiar negation of the postcode which declares the novel's allegiance to place, to nationhood.[18] Or we might think of Julian Barnes's 2011 novel *The Sense of an Ending*, which imagines the future as an encounter with the next generation, a generation whose relation to us we struggle to understand or narrativise, and to whom we remain, in Barnes's bleak vision, deaf and blind. Or we might think of two of James Kelman's novels of the twenty-first century, *Kieron Smith, Boy* and *Translated*

Accounts. The latter novel gives perhaps the most vivid and inventive account we have of the violence of twenty-first-century translation – of the extraordinary damage that is done to the integrity both of mind and of body when we are forced into discursive conditions that are not our own, by the pressures of globalisation that Blair speaks of with such enthusiasm in 2001. *Translated Accounts* stands as a devastating refusal of the political forms in which we envisage global community; but *Kieron Smith, Boy*, in depicting, with stunning precision and immediacy, the experience of growing up in a Glasgow housing project, refuses to offer community, or attachment to place, as a simple corrective to the deprivations of translation, of stateless-ness. Kelman does not offer localism as an antidote to globalism, as May sets 'Brexit Britain' against the 'nowhere' of Blair's cosmopolitanism. Rather, *Kieron Smith, Boy* is a beautiful hymn to the delicate futurity of childhood itself, to the sense that the child thinks and imagines with a mind that has not yet been fully formed, that belongs still to the time to come. Take, for example, the breathtaking opening of *Kieron Smith, Boy*, in which Kieron describes trying to catch a fish with his bare hands:

> If a fish came by ye saw it and just waited till it came in close. If it just stayed there over yer hands, that was how ye were waiting. It was just looking about. What was it going to do? Oh be careful if ye do it too fast, if yer fingers just move and even it is just the totiest wee bit, its tail whished and it was away or else it did not and it stayed there, so if ye grabbed it and ye got it and it did not get away. So that was you, ye caught one.[19]

Kelman here invents a distinctive tense with which to capture something of the open temporality of childhood, something of the sense that the child's mind moves in a medium that is different from the adult's, as the fish moves in a medium that is different from the human's. The passage opens in an imperfect past tense – catching a fish in this way was something that Kieron used to do periodically as a child. But the beauty of this passage, its mesmerising, mercurial fluidity, arises from the fact that the tense will not stay static, but shifts, as Kieron thinks, into a peculiar kind of present tense that is also tipping continually into a futural mode. As we are presented with the compelling picture of the fish 'just looking about', we shift from a general fish – the kind of fish that Kieron used to catch – to a specific fish, here in front of us; and then in the following line, 'What was it going to do?', from a past fish to a future fish, a fish who belongs to such a slippery temporal medium that it is almost impossible to catch. There is something spellbinding about the child's warning to himself – 'Oh be careful' – something that sets the temporal tone for the rest of the novel, bringing us to the disappearing threshold, at which a present that is too big for a childish mind to grasp tips into a future that has not yet been made. Kieron is not speaking to us in a retrospective narrative voice here, but speaking to himself, as the fish glides over his hands, immersing himself, and us, in the kinetic intricacies of a moment in the throes of passing, a moment that relies for all its tension and texture upon the intense proximity between the present time and the time to come, a future time which shimmers just out of the reach of the sentence, but which nevertheless pervades it, as the child himself is pervaded by the unlived time that defines him.

This preoccupation with an immanent futurity – the sense that we are surrounded by a latent, untensed time that we cannot quite grasp, waiting for an instrument to arrive that might measure it, a language that might articulate it – is a structuring feature of post-millennial narrative life. And in responding to this prospect of a strangely unreadable future, in adapting formal structures with which to capture it, one can see that the contemporary novel is involved in a refashioning of the legacies not only of realism, but also of modernism, and the postmodernism that we associate with the late twentieth century. If our present predicament requires us to construct new ways of imagining community – a fresh means of understanding how shared life is embedded in collective pictures of a national past, while also entering into international, diasporic conjunctions that belong to an unforeseen future – then the means by which the novel reaches for such images is in large part through a critical engagement with a history of form.

One might glimpse the nature of this critical engagement, and see too its deployment across the range of British contemporary fiction, by attending to a perhaps surprising symmetry that is discernible between the postmillennial work of Ian McEwan and Ali Smith, a symmetry that arises from a relationship with the commingled spirits of Dickens and of Joyce that both writers share, despite McEwan's and Smith's manifold differences from each other both in form and in temperament. It is in his 2014 work *The Children Act* that McEwan most fully extends this dialogue with Dickensian realism and Joycean modernism, as a means of imagining the future – the future as manifest, in this novel, in the figure of the child. The opening of McEwan's novel announces a debt to Dickens:

> London. Trinity term one week old. Implacable June weather. Fiona Maye,
> a High Court judge, at home on Sunday evening, supine on a chaise longue.[20]

This opening ventriloquises the first lines of Dickens's 1853 novel *Bleak House*:

> London. Michaelmas Term lately over, and the Lord Chancellor sitting in
> Lincoln's Inn Hall. Implacable November weather.[21]

In sharing its opening with *Bleak House* in this way, *The Children Act* announces a kinship with the earlier novel, a kinship which deepens as the novel progresses. Dickens's great novel stands in part as a rebuke to the law, which becomes barbarous when it is ensnared in its own laborious processes and vested interests rather than serving the interests of the citizens it is designed to protect. But it is also a rich meditation on the relationship between the law and literary fiction, as both discursive forms work at the junction between naked being in the world, and that being as it is given spatial and temporal extension, as it is brought forth into the sovereignty of subjecthood, as opposed to bare life.[22] The famous figure of Jo the crossing sweeper, in *Bleak House*, is the closest Dickens comes to a representation of bare life – of a being that does not have the sovereignty granted either by law or by narrative. Jo, as he puts it himself, 'don't know nothink',[23] and is entirely dead to the call of written language, to the discursive signs in which we encode our being. His, the narrator writes, is a 'wonderfully strange' being, one which appears human, but which, without language, cannot partake of human time, or human space. How strange, the narrator thinks, 'to be like Jo', to

> shuffle through the streets, unfamiliar with the shapes, and in utter darkness as to the meaning, of those symbols, so abundant over the shops, and at the corners of the streets, and on the doors, and in the windows! To see people read, and to see people write, and to see the postmen deliver letters, and not to have the least idea of all that language – to be, to every scrap of it, stone blind and dumb.[24]

Dickens's project in *Bleak House* is to imagine a literary means of granting discursive power to the kind of naked being that he discovers in the figure of Jo, without that power becoming corrupted by legal and political institutions which serve their own interests rather than the common good. Standing as a blank opposite to Jo is the despicable lawyer Vholes, a man so versed in the cruel and empty letter of the law that he has almost no body, and certainly no literary soul; he has a surplus of legal language, to counterbalance Jo's utter lack. And between these opposites is Esther Summerson, whose gentle narrative becoming is an experiment in the process by which a well-balanced and crafted realism can found being in language, without such foundation becoming a servitude or a fixity: this is language as the gift of self-determination, rather than language as the imposing of a tyrannical law.

The Children Act opens with its obeisance to Dickens in part because it too is interested in the relationship between law and fiction (which, as McEwan has recently suggested, are 'rooted in the same ground'), and in particular in the question of how legal or literary forms might grant us the freedom to enter into a future that is at once legally or discursively controlled, and open to our own creative capacities and caprices.[25] The Children Act of 1989, after which McEwan's novel is named, decrees that 'when a court determines any question with respect to … the upbringing of a child … the child's welfare shall be the court's paramount consideration',[26] and *The Children Act* turns around the difficulties and contradictions that this legislation sets in train. As the judge Fiona Maye puts it, 'the duty of the court was to enable the children to come to adulthood and make their own decisions about the sort of life they wanted to lead'.[27] The law protects the child, and looks after his or her interests, in a way that maximises his or her capacity to reach an age when they can think for themselves. But the cases that McEwan's novel is interested in are those in which the rights of the child to self-determination are in conflict with their own well-being, in which the law has to set one freedom against another, in order to *shape* the future that the child will enter. This takes the form, early in the novel, of a case of conjoined twins named Matthew and Mark. Mark is healthy and autonomous, but Matthew cannot live independently, as he has a body that does not function – a damaged brain and a heart that barely squeezes. Here, the law does not simply protect a child's life, but has to create it, to step in and determine how the narrative of a life is linked to, and written upon, the child's body. The judge has to decide whether the just course is to separate the twins, or to leave them conjoined. 'Separating the twins', Fiona recognises, 'would be to kill Matthew. Not separating them would, by omission, kill both'.[28] The simple calculus, and the hospital's wish, is to perform the surgery that separates the twins – as one life spared is better than both lives lost. But the legal case is more demanding. How does the law legitimise the decision to withdraw life from one being, in order to confer it on another; what power is it granting itself when it decides that the experience of sovereignty denied to Dickens's Jo, the narrative of discrete selfhood, should be granted to one biopolitical assemblage, and not another?

In this early case – and then in the case that forms the central plot of the novel, concerning a young Jehovah's Witness with leukaemia – Fiona's judgement is that the law should step in, and shape the child's future in accordance with its own definition of well-being, even if that means prioritising a stronger, more viable subject over a weaker one, or prioritising the decision-making power of the adult over that of the child. In the case of the Jehovah's Witness, named Adam, this involves the legal instruction that Adam's leukaemia should be treated by blood transfusion, despite the fact that it is against his religious principles to allow 'blood products' to 'enter his body'.[29] As Adam's father puts it, Adam's decision to refuse the transfusion is driven by his sense that his biological being is a discrete and sacred gift from God. 'You have to understand', the father says, 'that blood is the essence of what's human. It's the soul, it's life itself.'[30] Adam is nearly old enough to act as an adult, so the law, in requiring him to accept treatment, is imposing its own view of the boundaries of the sovereign being (it is porous, and thus can accept blood from another body without losing its uniqueness) over those held by the Adam himself, a subject nearing his majority. Even though Fiona can see that Adam is lucid and able to think for himself, she cannot accept that his interests are served by allowing him to take a sovereign decision that will end his life. His 'welfare', Fiona decrees, invoking the Children Act of 1989, 'is better served by his love of poetry, by his newly found passion for the violin, by the exercise of his lively intelligence and the expressions of a playful, affectional nature, and by all of life and love that lie ahead of him'.[31]

In making this judgement, Fiona acts both as an agent of the law, and as a kind of author, a narrator of the life that 'lies ahead' for Adam. As *Bleak House* offers a narrative framework within which characters can come to self-determined being (in which Esther ends up living out the life and love ahead of her in a perfect [but miniature!] duplicate of the Bleak House in which she was brought up by her guardian[32]), Fiona's judgement offers Adam a benign narrative of life, love and poetry. This granting of a narrative shape to being in time is the gift of realism. But what is most striking about *The Children Act*, and what makes it such a compelling reflection on the history of form, is that the narrative implicit in Fiona's judgement – the narrative that has its genesis in the Dickensian opening of the novel – is slowly dismantled as the novel moves through its exquisitely controlled phases. The judgement, coming at the end of act three of this five-act drama, marks the climax of a certain realist logic, in which a past generation is able to set the terms in which a future generation comes to language and to being. But from this point on, another logic starts to insinuate itself in the narrative, and with it a completely different model of futurity; and as this other logic begins to surface, so the influence of Dickens begins to give way to the influence of Joyce, and the legacies of realism give way to the legacies of modernism. Fiona's judgement grants Adam a new lease of life and of health. His body starts to regenerate itself (Fiona admires the 'whorls of his healthy young dark brown hair') and, as Adam writes to Fiona, he recovers his vitality, 'getting stronger all the time'.[33] Fiona has granted him this strength, this health; but the legal and fictional processes by which one generation makes the space in which the next might flourish are disturbed, in McEwan's novel, by a certain refusal of narrative sequence. Adam, armed with his new strength, does not want to look forwards for life and love, but rather looks backwards, to Fiona, with whom he has fallen in love; and Fiona, suffering from childlessness and lovelessness, feels herself drawn to the child, not as a member of a future generation which she has set free, but as the extension of her own present, as someone who can give her the love that she half unconsciously craves.

At a critical moment in the second half of the novel, as one temporal logic begins to give way to another, this meeting between generations takes the form of a kiss, nearly a chaste kiss, but also 'more than a mother might give her grown up son':

> Over in two seconds, perhaps three. Time enough to feel in the softness of his lips that overlay their suppleness, all the years, all the life, that separated her from him.[34]

From this point on, the question that drives McEwan's novel is how we might capture the years, and the life, that separate one generation from the next, years and life that don't obey the narrative trajectory of a realist plot, but that lie in the interstices, a kind of lived time that resists our narrative powers; that defies our models of responsibility, of prudence, of sequence; that does not have a language with which to express itself. And as this question comes to the fore, the model upon which it rests is no longer *Bleak House*, but 'The Dead', a text which begins to make itself felt in *The Children Act* with a vibrant, lyrical intensity. 'The Dead' is itself concerned, above all, with the turning of the generations – with the ways in which the dead impose themselves on the living, through the perpetuation of models of community sustained by national myth. Gabriel Conroy's after-dinner speech, at his aunt's Christmas party in Dublin, sets a nostalgic lament for a passing Dublin community against an acknowledgement that there is a coming international generation, which disrupts such forms of belonging. His aunts are the last bastions, he says, of a 'tradition of genuine warm-hearted courteous Irish hospitality', a tradition which is threatened by a 'new generation' which is 'growing up in our midst, a generation actuated by new ideas and new principles'.[35] The Irish tradition, which lends the story a rich, festive warmth, is sustained by the folk music that runs through the story, by the strains of the 'Lass of Aughrim' that Gabriel finds his wife listening to, with a strange, rapt intensity, at the turn of a staircase. The new generation takes its cue from what Gabriel calls the 'thought-tormented music' of Robert Browning's difficult verse – the prosodic accompaniment to a 'sceptical and ... a thought-tormented age'.[36] But these oppositions – Ireland versus Europe, tradition versus modernity – are radically upset at the close of the story, as Gabriel misreads the intense, distracted mood that the 'Lass of Aughrim' has kindled in his wife, Gretta. He sees that 'there was colour on her cheeks and that her eyes were shining', and a 'sudden tide of joy went leaping out of his heart',[37] as the memory of their shared life together, captured in the strains of distant music, is mingled with a surge of present desire for her. He thinks to himself that perhaps 'her thoughts had been running with his', that 'she had felt the impetuous desire that was in him, and then the yielding mood had come on her'.[38] The music, he thinks, has produced in them both a moment of shared belonging, nourished by a collective national mythology. But, as the story comes to a softly crushing end, Gretta reveals that she is moved by the music to recall not the life she shares with Gabriel, but the life that she has *not* lived, with a delicate boy named Michael Furey, a figure from her past who died for his love of her. The 'Lass of Aughrim' has conjured not community, but a great distance between Gretta and Gabriel, between the dead and the living, the past and the future, a distance that yields the story's closing image, an image which has come to mark the threshold between realism and modernism.[39] Gabriel stands at the window, reflecting on the snow falling 'all over Ireland', falling 'on every part of the dark central plain, on the treeless hills, falling softly on the Bog of Allen and, farther westward, softly falling into the dark mutinous Shannon waves'.[40] The imagined prospect of such cold community leads him to a gesture of national belonging, a commitment to that Irish tradition that he (insincerely) celebrated at his aunts' party. 'The time had come', he thinks, 'to set out on his journey westward'.[41] But whatever evocation of a shared time and space this homeward, backward journey is, it is of a piece, too, with the difficult futurism of a thought-tormented age. In the very moment that he travels westward, he heads, too, towards an ecstatic dismantling of being that he finds in the broken distance that opens between himself and his wife, a distance which no music can cross, no myth can overcome: 'His soul swooned slowly as he heard the snow falling faintly through the universe and faintly falling, like the descent of their last end, upon all the living and the dead.'[42]

To understand the modernism that Joyce invents after *Dubliners* – to understand how *Ulysses* produces forms which sustain a mythological and historical past, while opening themselves also to a form of dismantled being, a being that belongs to a future that has not already been made – it is necessary to approach this moment at the end of 'The Dead', a moment when a lyrical epiphany brings a commitment to a shared past into contact with a swooning surrender to the groundlessness of being. And it is this moment, this turning to that is a turning away, that animates McEwan's novel, as he approaches the space that opens between Fiona and Adam, a space between generations that cannot come under the jurisdiction of the law. As McEwan's novel draws to a close, the elements of 'The Dead', which have been gathering under the skin of the narrative throughout its second half, rise to the surface, producing a strangely intense moment of double-voicing. Fiona learns, during a public recital of Bach, and of a Yeats ballad that she had earlier sung with Adam, that Adam's leukaemia had returned, that having reached his majority he was able to refuse treatment, and that as a result he has died. As Gretta says of her young lover that 'I think he died for me',[43] so Fiona discovers that Adam chooses death over the future that she had made for him, the future to which she had propelled him. On her return to the flat that she shares with her estranged husband Jack, Fiona enters into the same unstructured distance that opens between Gabriel and Gretta. As Gabriel feels a closeness to his wife on their return to their room at the end of the evening – as he is overcome, as he puts it, by his 'clownish lust'[44] for her – so Jack expects a reconciliation with Fiona after her triumphant recital. He is in an 'elevated state, excited by her performance, and by what he thought lay ahead'.[45] But rather than sex, which might 'make everything easy between them once more', the evening ends in what Fiona thinks of as a 'great distance', filled by the spectre of Adam, the 'very strange and beautiful young man' who had died for love of her.[46] The novel closes in semi-darkness, with rain rather than snow outside the window, as the 'great rain-cleansed city beyond the room settled to its softer nocturnal rhythms',[47] and Fiona and Jack look upon the future of a marriage which will have to accommodate the ghost of a boy who chose, through love, to renounce 'all of love and life that lay ahead'.

The effect of this Joycean presence at the close of the novel is magical, endowing the prose with an epiphanal grace that McEwan's style rarely reaches – taking the prose beyond itself, as McEwan himself suggests music can sometimes take us beyond ourselves, in 'those rare moments when musicians together touch something sweeter than they've ever found before in rehearsals or performance, when their expression becomes as easy and graceful as friendship or love'.[48] But, of course, this magical presence, this peculiar collaboration, is bound up with the contradiction, explored both in 'The Dead' and *The Children Act*, between presence and distance, between the communal and the estranged. In summoning 'The Dead' with such intensity, McEwan's novel calls to a moment in the history of the novel at which the very possibility of community – and the very possibility that realist fiction can access and sustain such community – yields to the perception that communal experience is shadowed by an estrangement, a statelessness that it cannot overcome; when national identity meets what Stephen Dedalus famously called the 'uncreated conscience of my race'.[49] The end of 'The Dead' produces a new, tormented affinity between community and estrangement, and suggests the first stirrings of a Joycean modernism that can give expression to such affinity, and in doing so produce a model of becoming in time that slips by the nets of narrative sequence. As it is reanimated in *The Children Act*, it offers a means of reflecting on the questions that drive McEwan's novel – how legal institutions and literary fiction bring the future into contact with the present and the past, how we can enable the future without predetermining it. *The Children Act* imagines a relationship between Fiona and Adam that does not quite belong to any of the conventions or the forms that structure it. Adam is not the child that Fiona longs for, nor the lover, and she is neither his mother nor his god. Their contact, caught in the short seconds of their kiss, does not have a temporal, theological or juridical form in which to ground itself. But it does suggest an encounter between the past and the future – loving, open, undecided – that cannot quite take place in a realist mode, and that resides in the strange semantic shifting that happens, in *The Children Act*, when Dickensian narrative sequence gives way to Joycean hauntology, to a dialogue with the past that happens outside of the sequential protocols of storytelling, and that summons a different mode of futurity.

McEwan's prose summons a modernist forebear, in order to gesture towards a future that is beyond the sequential power of realism to conjure. But his own formal range remains peculiarly narrow – there is a soft dissolution, as the novel moves from its Dickensian opening to its Joycean conclusion, that is delicious to the same extent that it is denied by the well-made realism of the narrative. It is in the work of Ali Smith, and particularly in her seasonal cycle beginning with the novels *Autumn* and *Winter*, that one can see an address to the future which is conducted through formal experiment as well as through historical critique, a future which, she has recently argued, is made 'negotiable' by the power of fiction.[50] In these novels, written at speed under the pressure of the passing moment, as if in 'real time', Smith seeks to respond to the seismic political upheavals of 2016 and 2017 – the Brexit campaign, Trump's election, the murder of Jo Cox, the Grenfell fire – producing an almost overwhelmingly vivid picture of the zeitgeist, of a year in which the socio-economic consensus that has held since the Thatcher-Reagan era has been suddenly dismantled. The novels offer the first developed fictional depiction of the fever that has gripped the United Kingdom since the referendum of June 2016 – in which, as Smith's narrator puts it, 'All across the country, there was misery and rejoicing' ('All across the country, people looked up Google: *what is EU?* All across the country, people looked up Google: *move to Scotland*').[51] But, despite this deep investment in the present, both *Winter* and *Autumn* suggest that, to understand our current predicament – the peculiar season in which we are living – we need to see it as part of a logic that has been unfolding in the United Kingdom since the election of Thatcher in 1979 – that is, over the period covered by this

Companion. The intense focus on 2016–17 loops back repeatedly to absorb the longer history of our present – the historical presence of the past that I discuss in the introduction to this volume. Theresa May's denial of the possibility of world citizenship in 2016 is cast as an echo of Thatcher's own manifesto; we've been refusing the larger possibility of community, a character in *Autumn* says, 'since Thatcher taught us to be selfish and not just to think but to believe that there's no such thing as society'.[52] And the timeline of *Winter* begins, in a sense, with its beautifully evocative depiction of the establishment of the Greenham Common women's peace camp in the early 1980s ('Come with me now back to an early sunny Saturday morning in September 1981, to a piece of English common land fenced off by the American military in agreement with the British military'[53]).

Smith's novels depict a turbulent present, by producing a looping set of histories that locate it, that help us to focus it. But what connects Smith's cycle, with an almost uncanny insistence, to McEwan's dramatisation of the contemporary in *The Children Act*, is that both seek to capture the experience of passing time through an act of ventriloquism, which merges the voice of Dickens with that of Joyce. *The Children Act* begins by quoting the opening of *Bleak House*; the beginning of *Autumn* ('It was the worst of times, it was the worst of times'[54]) echoes the famous opening of *A Tale of Two Cities* ('It was the best of times, it was the worst of times'[55]); and the beginning of *Winter* ('God was dead: to begin with'[56]) echoes the opening of *A Christmas Carol* ('Marley was dead, to begin with'[57]). These opening homages to Dickens then resonate through Smith's novels, as *Bleak House* resonates through *The Children Act*, so one can feel a Dickensian presence in every line, acting as a foundation to the narratives, to the turning of Smith's seasons. The exploration of revolutionary time in *Autumn* is impelled by Dickens's response to the French Revolution in *A Tale of Two Cities* – the revolutionary experience that both Dickens and Smith think of as being 'recalled to life';[58] and *Winter* is, at its heart, a story of Christmas redemption that works as a retelling of *A Christmas Carol*. As in *The Children Act*, however, the legacy of Dickens is interwoven with an equally powerful Joycean bequest. The dazzling opening sequence of *Autumn* depicts Daniel Gluck, the ancient guru figure who presides over the novel, being reborn on a strip of beach, and as Gluck experiences this Dickensian recall to life, it is impossible not to feel the presence of *Ulysses*, stirring within the language. With Gluck's first return to consciousness, as an 'old man [who] washes up on a shore',[59] he is inhabited by the figure of the drowned man who floats off the shore throughout Joyce's novel, the 'bag of corpsegas sopping in foul brine',[60] the 'corpse rising saltwhite from the undertow';[61] and as he rejuvenates, as his youthful body grows around him and he finds himself standing on a 'sandy stony strand, the wind distinctly harsh',[62] he becomes the young Dedalus, 'walking into eternity along Sandymount strand' (who is himself composed of 'dead dust', of the 'dead breaths I living breathe',[63] and who is himself clothed in the 'strandentwining cable of all flesh'[64]). *Ulysses* attends Daniel Gluck's narrative birth, and then, later in the novel as Gluck finds himself unrequitedly in love with Pauline Boty – the 1960s British pop artist who is another of the novel's guiding figures – it is 'The Dead' which offers the framework to Smith's narrative, that allows the dead to speak. Gluck stands outside Boty's house, 'in the rain in the back yard', as Michael Furey stands outside Gretta's house in 'The Dead', as Adam stands outside Fiona's hotel in the rain in *The Children Act*. As he does so, Gluck thinks to himself that

> there is a famous short story, The Dead, by James Joyce, in which a young man stands at the back of a house and sings a song on a freezing night to a woman he loves. Then this young man, pining for the woman, dies. He catches a chill in the snow, he dies young. Height of Romanticism! That woman in that story for the rest of her life, has that young man's song always riddling through her like woodworm.[65]

Smith, like McEwan, draws both on a realist and on a modernist tradition, to capture the presence of the past, which is riddled through us like woodworm. But where McEwan stages a gradual move from the former to the latter, allowing a realist conception of duration to dissolve into the Joycean epiphany with which *The Children Act* ends, Smith's novel cycle refuses any such linear history of form, offering instead a dizzying blend of ages and styles, crunching Dickens together with Joyce, as well as with a vast range of other influences, voices and images, from Barbara Hepworth, to Pauline Boty, to Elvis, to Paddington Bear. Just as the chronological passage from 2016 to 2017, from autumn to winter, is repeatedly disrupted by the appearance of jumbled images and sequences from the past – from Greenham in 1981, or from Christmases past that continually interfere with the unfolding of Christmas present in *Winter* – so the shifting influences that shape Smith's narrative are never clearly distinguished from one another, but can be felt jostling against one other in every line. It is as if, for Smith, the experience of this present season, the temporal quality of our own passing moment, does not have a form in which it might be given shape. The past mingles with the present, one voice mingles with another, in a way that defies the protocols of narrative sequence. As Smith's narrator says – of Daniel Gluck's regeneration, but also of the writing of *Autumn* itself – 'here's an old story so new that it's still in the middle of happening, writing itself right now with no knowledge of where or how it will end'.[66]

Now, this shapeless mix of the old and the new, the high and the low, the realist and the modernist, might sound quite familiar, another restaging of the hybridity of formal styles that we associate with postmodernism.[67] As the character Art says, in *Winter*, this is a familiarity which could become rather wearisome. 'It is the dregs, really', he says, 'to be living in a time' when it is mandatory to be 'post-postmodern consciouser-than-thou'.[68] The perennial return of postmodern bricolage might resemble what another character thinks of as the reassuring reappearance of the same Christmas songs every midwinter, which mark 'the rhythm of passing time, yes, but also, and more so, the return of time in its endless and comforting cycle'.[69] If, as the Dickensian opening of *Winter* has it, we are surrounded by the signs of cultural as well as ecological death ('the earth', we hear, is 'also dead'[70]), then this is perhaps because the literary and visual forms with which we have narrated the passing of time – even those postmodern forms which seemed, late last century, to be so revolutionary – have lost their freshness, have become recycled commodities as tinny as the horribly familiar strains of George Michael's *Last Christmas*. 'God was dead: to begin with', the narrator of *Winter* says,

> And romance was dead. Chivalry was dead. Poetry, the novel, painting, they were all dead, and art was dead. Theatre and cinema were both dead. Literature was dead. The book was dead. Modernism, postmodernism, realism and surrealism were all dead.[71]

But if Smith's cycle is concerned with recycling, with the deathly return of the old, the shining of every morning's sun on Samuel Beckett's 'nothing new', then it is equally invested in the future, in the imperative that we imagine a time to come that has not already been seen, that does not belong to cyclical time, but that glimmers on the other side of a seasonal, temporal threshold, unclothed by any hand-me-down narrative form.[72] Even as her restless investment in the chopped-up histories of narrative form produce a feeling of déjà vu, a reanimation of the ghosts of modernism and of postmodernism, of Dickens and of Joyce, she brings such histories into contact with a futurity, an open narrative horizon, that remakes them, as old stories are always made new just as they are in the middle of happening. What marks Smith's aesthetic above all, not only in *Autumn* and *Winter*, but in earlier works, such as *How to Be Both* and *The Accidental*, is its singular, characteristic attention to the ways in which time inhabits material, the forms which allow a temporal consciousness to act within, to cleave to, the bodies and environments in which it recognises itself. In *Autumn*, the narrative explores the process by which Gluck's mind is given rejuvenated form, encased in flesh, or, in one of the novel's recurring fantasies, in a body of green wood, a flowering pine (echoed in his 'pining' for Paul Boty). In *Winter*, the fascination with the sculpture of Barbara Hepworth leads to a repeated figuring of body as stone, and the dwelling inside the body as a dwelling inside stone. There is no other contemporary novelist who works with such idiosyncratic precision at the boundary where art meets with its materials (with stone or wood or canvas), or where mind meets with body. When a character in *Winter*, reflecting on 'mind, matter, the structure of reality', thinks that 'mind and matter are mysterious and, when they come together, bounteous',[73] he is stating a credo of Smith's work – her recurrent fascination with 'meeting' that runs through her work at least since her 2007 novel *Girl Meets Boy*. Smith seeks to reveal that junction at which mind meets with matter, at which one person meets with another, and this junction is the place, too, peculiarly fugitive and groundless, where the past meets with the future. The seasons may make this meeting point cyclical, may give a rhythm and a familiarity to the passing of time; indeed, Smith is deeply attuned to this rhythm, and to the gathered mythologies that give a history to the transformative contact of old and new. But even as the turning of the seasons accords to such a rhythm, it also thrusts us into a strange flaw in the 'structure of reality', a suspended space between the gathered past and the empty future, a space that is 'like two weatherfronts meeting, like the coming season getting ready midway through the old one to make itself heard'.[74]

It is this temporal and material junction, this suspended ground between weather fronts, that Smith seeks to bring to thought and to form in her novel cycle, and that marks the far limit of the British novel now in its striving to imagine the future. In reaching to the future, *Autumn* and *Winter* are guided in part by the spirit of Dickens, and particularly by the spirits that speak in Dickens's *A Christmas Carol*. It is one of the great gifts of the realist novel, as it is brought to a particular form of perfection by Dickens, that it grants a shape to passing time, and allows us to bring the future into contact with the past. This is the gift that is given to Scrooge by the spirits that visit him on Christmas Eve. 'I will honour Christmas in my heart', Scrooge promises at the end of the novel, as he is confronted with the bankruptcy of his own stunted refusal of passing time. 'I will live in the Past, the Present and the Future. The Spirits of all three shall strive within me.'[75] It is this capacity, to extend oneself in time, that Smith is searching for in her novel cycle, as we look to bridge the gap between the future and the past opened by the revolutions of Trumpism, and of Brexit. Trump declares, in January 2017, that 'we are looking now only to the future', that his own revolution requires us to reject the past. Smith's novels offer a direct rebuke to this address to the future. We need now, like Scrooge, to feel both the future and the past striving within us.

Only by working with both imperatives can we see past the current crisis in the passage of world history. But if this is so, what Smith's cycle suggests – what the British novel now suggests, as it experiments with formal means of imagining the future – is that we need a new mechanism with which to address the turning of the seasons, the passage from shared past to unknown future, from adult to child. Smith takes Theresa May's declaration, that 'if you believe you're a citizen of the world, you're a citizen of nowhere', as an epigraph to *Winter*, and it is difficult to resist the feeling that all the novel's energies are directed against this sentiment; there must be, Smith's novel cycle suggests, ways of extending citizenship across the globe, ways of imagining shared worlds, that are not reducible to the hegemony of the west offered by Blair, at the turn of the current century, as a phoney cure to the experience of dispossession. But if Smith's aesthetics are directed by this urge towards citizenry, towards shared worlds, she also counterintuitively shares something of May's sentiment here. It may be that, to be a citizen of the world now, we need also to be a citizen of nowhere, the no place that has haunted the novel's utopian imagination since Thomas More's 1516 work *Utopia*. Scrooge feels past, present and future striving within him, and Dickens crafts a literary form that resolves such striving into sequence. Smith, however, suggests that it is necessary now for us to give expression not only to accommodations between the past and the future, but also to gulfs between them, gulfs that can only be experienced as a kind of nowhere, a wasteland between a shared past and a future that may grow out of our collective past, but which does not belong to it, or follow from it.

It is this attention – to a communal nowhere that, like Zadie Smith's *NW*, lies between generations, between the past and the future – that makes Smith's novel cycle so timely, so attuned to the state of the British novel now. 'The book was dead', Smith's narrator thinks at the opening of *Winter*, 'Modernism, postmodernism, realism and surrealism were all dead.'[76] This may be so – it may be the case that the passage from realism to modernism to postmodernism that is reanimated in McEwan and in Smith has led to a postmillennial wasteland, a stony ground in which no roots clutch and no branches grow, and to which we can offer only a heap of broken images. But for Smith and McEwan, and for a generation of British novelists working now, at a transitional moment in the passage of world history, it is only by clearing such a passage, by imagining what it would be to be a citizen of nowhere, that we can craft the forms in which we can look to the future, while feeling our shared past strive within us.

The book is dead; long live the book.

Notes

1. M. Thatcher, 'Interview for Woman's Own', *Woman's Own* (31 October 1987), n.p., transcript available at www.margaretthatcher.org/document/106689.
2. D. Harvey, *A Brief History of Neoliberalism* (Oxford University Press, 2005), p. 2.
3. Thatcher, 'Interview for Woman's Own', n.p.
4. For a theoretical account of Blair's third way, see A. Giddens, *The Third Way: The Renewal of Social Democracy* (London: Polity Press, 1998).
5. For Fukuyama's famous account of the hegemony of the West, see F. Fukuyama, *The End of History and the Last Man* (London: Hamish Hamilton, 1992). For Fukuyama's immediate, and defensive, response to 9/11, see his essay in *The Guardian*, 'The West Has Won'. For a more trenchant response to US hegemony, see N. Chomsky, *Hegemony or Survival* (New York: Henry Holt, 2003).
6. T. Blair, 'Speech to the Labour Party Conference', *The Guardian* (2 October 2001), n.p., www.theguardian.com/politics/2001/oct/02/labour conference.labour6.
7. Ibid.
8. See Judith Butler, *Precarious Life*, where Butler argues that we need to pit 'long range prospects for global co-operation' against 'the binarism that Bush proposes, in which only two positions are possible – "Either you're with us or you're with the terrorists"' (J. Butler, *Precarious Life: The Powers of Mourning and Violence* (London: Verso, 2004), pp. 3, 2).
9. Blair, 'Speech to the Labour Party Conference'.
10. For an account of the relation between 9/11 and the wars in Afghanistan and Iraq, see J. Burke, *The 9/11 Wars* (London: Penguin, 2011).
11. D. Trump, 'Inauguration Speech', *The Guardian* (20 January 2017), n.p., www.theguardian.com/world/2017/jan/20/donald-trump-inauguration-speech-full-text.
12. Ibid.
13. T. May, 'Conference Speech', *The Telegraph* (5 October 2016), n.p., www.tele graph.co.uk/news/2016/10/05/theresa-mays-conference-speech-in-full/.
14. Blair, 'Speech to the Labour Party Conference', n.p.
15. For two accounts of the passing of postmodernism in the current century, see: J. Nealon, *Post-Postmodernism, or the Cultural Logic of Just-in-Time Capitalism* (Stanford University Press, 2012); and J. Toth, *The Passing of Postmodernism: A Spectroanalysis of the Contemporary* (Albany, NY: State University of New York Press, 2010).
16. Trump, 'Inauguration Speech', n.p.
17. D. Mitchell, *Cloud Atlas* (London: Hodder & Stoughton, 2004), p. 510.
18. Z. Smith, *NW* (London: Penguin, 2012), p. 318. For a fuller reading of the status of 'nowhere' in Smith's novel, see P. Boxall and B. Cheyette, *The Oxford History of the Novel*, vol. 7: *British and Irish Fiction since 1940* (Oxford University Press, 2016), pp. 580–6.
19. J. Kelman, *Kieron Smith, Boy* (London: Hamish Hamilton, 2008), p. 1.
20. I. McEwan, *The Children Act* (London: Vintage, 2014), p. 1.
21. C. Dickens, *Bleak House* (Oxford: Oxford University Press, 1996), p. 1.

22. For his most influential account of bare life, see G. Agamben, *Homo Sacer: Sovereign Power and Bare Life*, trans. D. Heller-Roazen (Stanford University Press, 1998).
23. Dickens, *Bleak House*, p. 235.
24. *Ibid.*, p. 236.
25. I. McEwan, 'The Law versus Religious Belief', *The Guardian* (5 September 2014), n.p., www.theguardian.com/books/2014/sep/05/ian-mcewan-law-versus-religious-belief.
26. McEwan, *The Children Act*, n.p.
27. *Ibid.*, p. 38.
28. *Ibid.*, p. 27.
29. *Ibid.*, p. 65.
30. *Ibid.*, p. 75.
31. *Ibid.*, p. 123.
32. *Ibid.*, p. 891.
33. *Ibid.*, pp. 167, 140.
34. *Ibid.*, p. 169.
35. J. Joyce, *Dubliners* (London: Secker & Warburg, 1994), p. 183.
36. *Ibid.*, p. 183.
37. *Ibid.*, p. 191.
38. *Ibid.*, p. 197.
39. There is a wealth of critical literature devoted to this closing image of 'The Dead'. For a helpful summary of positions, and for a powerful reading in its own right, see E. Nolan, *James Joyce and Nationalism* (London: Routledge, 1995), pp. 24–36.
40. Joyce, *Dubliners*, p. 202.
41. Ibid.
42. *Ibid.*, p. 203.
43. *Ibid.*, p. 199.
44. Ibid.
45. McEwan, 'The Law versus Religious Belief', p. 206.
46. *Ibid.*, pp. 207, 208 and 208, respectively.
47. *Ibid.*, p. 213.
48. I. McEwan, *Saturday* (London: Jonathan Cape, 2005), p. 171.
49. J. Joyce, *A Portrait of the Artist as a Young Man* (London: Penguin, 1992), p. 276.
50. A. Smith, '"Vital, Witty, Formidably Blithe": Ali Smith on Muriel Spark at 100', *The Guardian* (29 January 2018), n.p., www.theguardian.com/books/2018/jan/29/ali-smith-on-muriel-spark-at-100.
51. A. Smith, *Winter* (London: Hamish Hamilton, 2017), p. 59.
52. A. Smith, *Autumn* (London: Hamish Hamilton, 2016), p. 112.
53. Smith, *Winter*, p. 143.
54. Smith, *Autumn*, p. 3.
55. C. Dickens, *A Tale of Two Cities* (Oxford University Press, 1998), p. 7.
56. Smith, *Winter*, p. 3.
57. C. Dickens, *A Christmas Carol and Other Christmas Books* (Oxford University Press, 2006), p. 9.
58. Smith, *Autumn*, p. 213; Dickens, *A Christmas Carol*, p. 14.

59. Smith, *Winter*, p. 3.
60. J. Joyce, *Ulysses* (London: Penguin, 1986), p. 41.
61. *Ibid.*
62. Smith, *Winter*, p. 4.
63. Joyce, *Ulysses*, p. 42.
64. *Ibid.*, p. 32.
65. Smith, *Autumn*, p. 97.
66. *Ibid.*, p. 181.
67. For an influential early account of postmodern bricolage, see J. Derrida, 'Structure, Sign and Play in the Discourse of the Human Sciences', reprinted in J. Natoli and L. Hutcheon (eds), *A Postmodern Reader* (State University of New York Press, 1993), pp. 223–42.
68. Smith, *Winter*, p. 158.
69. *Ibid.*, p. 39.
70. *Ibid.*, p. 5.
71. *Ibid.*, p. 3.
72. S. Beckett, *Murphy* (London: Picador, 1973), p. 5.
73. Smith, *Winter*, p. 303.
74. *Ibid.*, p. 268.
75. Dickens, *A Christmas Carol*, p. 77.
76. Smith, *Winter*, p. 3.

FURTHER READING

A number of authors cited in this volume have been the subject of single-author studies. Readers should consult Bloomsbury's *Contemporary Critical Perspectives* series and the *Glyphi Contemporary Writers: Critical Essays* series.

General

Acheson, J. and Ross, S. C. E. (2005). *The Contemporary British Novel*. Edinburgh University Press.

Adiseshiah, S. and Hildyard, R. (2013). *Twenty-First-Century Fiction: What Happens Now?* Basingstoke: Palgrave.

Bentley, N. (2008). *Contemporary British Fiction*. Edinburgh University Press.

Bentley, N., Hubble, N. and Wilson, L. (2015). *The 2000s: A Decade of Contemporary British Fiction*. London: Bloomsbury.

Boxall, P. (2013). *Twenty-First Century Fiction: A Critical Introduction*. Cambridge University Press.

Boxall, P. and Cheyette, B. (2016). *The Oxford History of the Novel in English: British and Irish Fiction since 1940*. Oxford University Press.

Bradford, R. (2007). *The Novel Now: Contemporary British Fiction*. Malden, MA: Blackwell.

Brooker, J. (2010). *Literature of the 1980s: After the Watershed*. Edinburgh University Press.

Connor, S. (2006). *The English Novel in History: 1950–1995*. London: Routledge.

Davies, A. and Sinfield, A. (2000). *British Culture of the Postwar: An Introduction to Literature and Society 1945–1999*. London: Routledge.

Head, D. (2002). *Cambridge Introduction to Modern British Fiction: 1950–2000*. Cambridge University Press.

Horton, E., Tew, P. and Wilson, L. (2014). *The 1980s: A Decade of Contemporary British Fiction*. London: Bloomsbury.

Hubble, N., Tew, P. and Wilson, L. (2015). *The 1990s: A Decade of Contemporary British Fiction*. London: Bloomsbury.

James, D. (2015). *The Cambridge Companion to British Fiction since 1945*. Cambridge University Press.

Marks, P. (2018). *Literature of the 1990s: Endings and Beginnings*. Edinburgh University Press.

Morrison, J. (2003). *Contemporary Fiction*. London: Routledge.

Nasta, S. (2001). *Home Truths: Fiction about the South Asian Diaspora in Britain*. Basingstoke: Palgrave.

Osborne, D. (2016). *British Black and Asian Literature, 1945–2010*. Cambridge University Press.

Stein, M. (2004). *Black British Literature: Novels of Transformation*. Columbus, OH: Ohio State University Press.

Tew, P. (2007). *The Contemporary British Novel*, 2nd edn. New York: Continuum.

'Theory' and the Novel / Modernism to Postmodernism and After

Attridge, D. (2004). *The Singularity of Literature*. London: Routledge.

Brouillette, S. (2007). *Postcolonial Writers in the Global Literary Marketplace*. Basingstoke: Palgrave.

Carroll, R. (2012). *Rereading Heterosexuality: Feminism, Queer Theory and Contemporary Fiction*. Edinburgh University Press.

Cooke, J. (2013). *Scenes of Intimacy: Reading, Writing and Theorizing Contemporary Literature*. London: Bloomsbury.

Currie, M. (1995). *Metafiction*. London: Longman.

    (2010). *Postmodern Narrative Theory*, 2nd edn. Basingstoke: Palgrave.

Dawson, P. (2013). *The Return of the Omniscient Narrator: Authorship and Authority in Twenty-First Century Fiction*. Columbus, OH: Ohio State University Press.

Eagleton, T. (2004). *After Theory*. London: Penguin.

Elias, A. J. (2001). *Sublime Desire: History and Post-1960s Fiction*. London: Johns Hopkins University Press.

Elliott, J. and Attridge, D. (2011). *Theory after 'Theory'*. London: Routledge.

Hale, D. J. (2005). *The Novel: An Anthology of Criticism and Theory*. Oxford: Blackwell.

Hutcheon, L. (1988). *A Poetics of Postmodernism: History, Theory, Fiction*. London: Routledge.

James, D. (2012). *The Legacies of Modernism: Historicising Postwar and Contemporary Fiction*. Cambridge University Press.

    (2012). *Modernist Futures: Innovation and Inheritance in the Contemporary Novel*. Cambridge University Press.

McCulloch, F. (2012). *Cosmopolitanism in Contemporary British Fiction*. Basingstoke: Palgrave.

McNally, L. (2013). *Reading Theories in Contemporary Fiction*. London: Bloomsbury.

Mulhern, F. (2016). *Figures of Catastrophe: The Condition of Culture Novel*. London: Verso.

Peacock, J. and Lustig, T. (2013). *Diseases and Disorders in Contemporary Fiction: The Syndrome Syndrome*. London: Routledge.

Shields, D. (2010) *Reality Hunger: A Manifesto*. London: Hamish Hamilton.

Vermeulen, P. (2015). *Contemporary Literature and the End of the Novel*. London: Palgrave.

Waugh, P. (1984). *Metafiction: The Theory and Practice of Self-Conscious Fiction*. London: Methuen.

International Intellectual Contexts

Butler, J. (1990). *Gender Trouble: Feminism and the Subversion of Identity*. London: Routledge.

Derrida, J. (1992). *Acts of Literature*. London: Routledge.

(2003). *Specters of Marx: The State of the Debt, the Work of Mourning and New International*, trans. P. Kamuf. London: Routledge.

Gilroy, P. (2013 [1987]). *There Ain't No Black in the Union Jack*. London: Routledge.

(1993) *Small Acts: Thoughts on the Politics of Black Culture*. London: Serpent's Tail.

Hall, S. (2017). *Selected Political Writings: The Great Moving Right Show and Other Essays*. London: Duke University Press.

Haraway, D. (1991). *Simians, Cyborgs, and Women: The Reinvention of Nature*. London: Free Association Books.

Jameson, F. (1981). *Political Unconscious: Narrative as a Socially Symbolic Act*. London: Cornell University Press.

(1991). *Postmodernism, or, the Cultural Logic of Late Capitalism*. London: Duke University Press.

Mulvey, L. (1989). *Visual and Other Pleasures*. Basingstoke: Palgrave.

Rose, J. (1986). *Sexuality in the Field of Vision*. London: Verso.

Said, E. (2006). *On Late Style*. London: Bloomsbury.

Sedgwick, E. (1990). *Epistemology of the Closet*. London: University of California Press.

Selected Non-Fiction by Novelists

Carter, A. (2013). *Shaking a Leg: Collected Journalism and Writing*. London: Vintage.

McCarthy, T. (2017). *Typewriters, Bombs, Jellyfish: Essays*. New York Review of Books.

Naipaul, V. S. (2002). *The Writer and the World*. London: Alfred Knopf.

Phillips, C. (2001). *A New World Order: Selected Essays*. London: Secker & Warburg.

Rushdie, S. (1991). *Imaginary Homelands*. London: Granta.

Smith, A. (2015). *Public Library and Other Stories*. London: Hamish Hamilton.

Smith, Z. (2011). *Changing My Mind: Occasional Essays*. London: Penguin.

(2018). *Feel Free: Essays*. London: Hamish Hamilton.

Winterson, J. (1995). *Art Objects: Essays on Ecstasy and Effrontery*. London: Jonathan Cape.

INDEX

INDEX

Cambridge Companions to ...

AUTHORS